Emile de Antonio

Emile de Antonio

Radical Filmmaker in
Cold War America

◄O►

RANDOLPH LEWIS

[signature: Randolph Lewis]

THE UNIVERSITY OF WISCONSIN PRESS

The University of Wisconsin Press
2537 Daniels Street
Madison, Wisconsin 53718

3 Henrietta Street
London WC2E 8LU, England

5   4   3   2   1

Printed in the United States of America

Library of Congress Cataloging-in-Publication Data

Lewis, Randolph, 1966–
    Emile de Antonio : radical filmmaker in Cold War America /
    Randolph Lewis.
        pp.   cm.
    Includes bibliographical references and index.
    ISBN 0-299-16910-3 (alk. paper)
    ISBN 0-299-16914-6 (pbk. : alk. paper)
    1. De Antonio, Emile.   2. Motion picture producers and directors—
United States—Biography.   I. Title.
PN1998.3.D3846 L48   2000
791.43'0233'092—dc21   00-009309

Other historians relate facts to inform us of facts.
You relate them to excite in our hearts and minds
an intense hatred of lying, ignorance, hypocrisy,
superstition, tyranny; and the anger remains even
after the memory of facts has disappeared.

–Diderot on Voltaire

Contents

Illustrations

ix

Acknowledgments

Writing this book has been a long process, and I have incurred many debts of gratitude, beginning with the professors with whom I worked in the American Studies Department at the University of Texas at Austin. Doug Kellner encouraged this project when it was little more than an idea. Now the first holder of the George F. Kneller Chair in Philosophy of Education at the University of California at Los Angeles, Doug graciously made available his own collection of papers on Emile de Antonio, read through several versions of this manuscript with seemingly unfeigned enthusiasm, and offered a productive blend of encouragement and criticism. Mark Smith humanized the combine known as graduate school with his candor and good cheer. Bill Stott offered good advice on all sorts of matters and patiently explained the difference between well-crafted prose and nonsense. Ira Abrams, now chair of film studies at Columbia College in Chicago, guided me through the intricacies of documentary filmmaking and, like any good film director, told me to never lose sight of the story. Finally, Robert M. Crunden was an invaluable intellectual resource and good friend until his death in March 1999, just a few days before I completed the final manuscript. Bob was a demanding teacher, a prolific cultural historian, and a wise mentor, and he will be missed greatly.

The support of the University of Texas, which generously provided a 1993–1994 University Fellowship, allowed for more than a year of uninterrupted research, including a productive venture into the extensive de Antonio archive at the Wisconsin Center for Film and Theater Research at the State Historical

Society of Wisconsin on the Madison campus of the University of Wisconsin. For unrestricted access to this archive, I would like to thank Nancy de Antonio, who has been unflaggingly gracious in offering her assistance. For answering numerous questions about Emile de Antonio, I would like to thank especially Dr. William Ayers, Bernardine Dohrn, Kathy Boudin, Robert Rauschenberg, Jasper Johns, and the late Leo Castelli.

I would like to express my gratitude to my friends in the American Studies Department at the University of Texas and elsewhere, especially those brave souls who offered their services as proofreaders and whose suggestions saved me time and effort—Todd Basch, Robert Byington, Ted Hamm, John Logan, Jonathan Silverman, Christopher Shipman, Norman Stolzoff, Richard Watson, and Drew Wood. I must single out Todd, Norman, and especially Jon for special praise. Each labored far beyond the call of friendly duty. Their early support was as essential to the completion of this book as that of friends and colleagues in Oklahoma, my new home, where Ben Alpers, John Bruce, Joan Cuccio, Julia Ehrhardt, John Feaver, Ann Frankland, Morris Foster, Julie Gozan, Sandy Huguenin, Stephanie Jung, Tom Keck, Ari Kelman, Leslie Kelman, Josh Piker, Karl Rambo, Francesca Sawaya, Karen Schutjer, and others are creating an intellectual milieu that defies stereotypes about the windswept heartland.

Publishing this book with the University of Wisconsin Press has been a delight. Associate Director Steve Salemson and his colleagues are keeping alive an older model of publishing, one that includes professionalism, courtesy, and intellectualism at all levels of the institutional hierarchy. In particular, I must mention Polly Kummel, who provided copyediting that was both thorough and insightful. I am a fortunate author to be in such hands.

Finally, on a more personal note, I would like to thank my parents, Thomas and Joyce Lewis, who have long supported my unaccountable forays into the not-so-distant past. Without their encouragement much of this would not have been feasible. And most of all I would like to thank an extraordinary friend and partner: Circe Sturm, an anthropologist with a poet's sense of language, who read each chapter meticulously and offered invaluable advice and support of both an intellectual and emotional nature. For her loving interest in this project and its author, no words of thanks could suffice. I dedicate this book to her.

Emile de Antonio

Introduction

From McCarthyism to modern art, Vietnam to the checkered career of Richard Nixon, Emile de Antonio (1919–1989) brought his passion and intelligence to bear on some of the most difficult issues in postwar America. During the last three decades of his life, he earned a reputation as "America's foremost radical documentary filmmaker" for his willingness to take on tough political controversies, even in the face of FBI harassment and other forms of intimidation.[1] This book traces the turbulent development of his film career from its beginnings among the New York avant-garde of the late fifties through the ten documentaries that followed: *Point of Order* (1963), *That's Where the Action Is* (1965), *Rush to Judgment* (1967), *In the Year of the Pig* (1969), *America Is Hard to See* (1970), *Millhouse: A White Comedy* (1971), *Painters Painting* (1973), *Underground* (1976), *In the King of Prussia* (1983), and *Mr. Hoover and I* (1989).[2]

These unusual films are the product of a second-generation Italian American who blended profound idealism and bitter disillusionment in his angry view of the world. De Antonio fixed a critical gaze on the institutions he believed were crushing human beings and their cultures and sought to illuminate where things had gone wrong, to redeem the failure of American democracy, to regain what he believed to be the promise of its origins. In his films he attacked the hypocrisy of American power as he discerned it in the careers of Joseph McCarthy, Richard Nixon, J. Edgar Hoover, and Lyndon Baines Johnson. At the same time he sought heroic dissenters and found them in an eclectic assortment of artists, activists, philosophers, and politicians.

3

More than any other filmmaker, de Antonio changed the face of American documentary in both style and content, bringing radical politics back into the medium for the first time since the depression. In his hands "the documentary became a genuine instrument of historiography, a medium for diachronic social analysis with its own validity and authority, relying on visual documents in the same way that the traditional writing of history relied on written documents," as the film critic Thomas Waugh has claimed.[3] To achieve this level of complexity de Antonio developed an uncommon method of filmmaking, based in part on his understanding of collage, which he picked up from his friends Robert Rauschenberg and Jasper Johns. The result was a technique known as "compilation documentary," a blend of archival footage and contemporary interviews that set the past and the present into a dialectical tension only the audience could resolve. Viewed by tens of thousands of urban intellectuals and college students in the United States and hundreds of thousands of Europeans on television, de Antonio's rough-looking films exhibited the merits as well as the limitations of American political filmmaking and presented a vision of U.S. history that remains challenging and polemical.

This cinematic vision penetrated the haze of denials, misinformation, and public relations tricks that had become, in de Antonio's mind, a central part of the American political landscape. "America is hard to see," de Antonio complained, borrowing the title of a 1962 poem by one of his favorite poets, Robert Frost.[4] In this verse Frost depicts Christopher Columbus as a pathetic figure unable to make sense of the continent he stumbled upon in 1492—and the implication is that we have done little better in the five hundred years since. I believe this sentiment inspired de Antonio because in many ways he too was a reckless explorer of Italian descent, though his aspirations were far more noble than those of his controversial predecessor. Fascinated with the complex and elusive nature of "Americanness" as a result of the deracinated sensibility he claimed for himself, de Antonio was always looking for America in a metaphorical sense. With an independence of mind, an active conscience, a sense of humor, and a love of art, he demonstrated how one can see the contours of this landscape in a way that was far beyond the powers of Frost's lost navigator.

To make sense of de Antonio's films, I have analyzed them in terms of four elements: production, reception, text, and context. Production traces the hectic conditions of independent filmmaking in the various stages between the idea for the film and its appearance on screen and includes research, financing, shooting, editing, distribution, and promotion, all of which can present special challenges for independent nonfiction filmmaking. Reception is a more troublesome issue because knowing what audiences make of the movies they watch is always difficult.[5] Rather than engage in speculation about how viewers have interpreted de Antonio's films, I have asked how and where these films were screened—and often harassed and censored—and examined reviews as a window into the delicate politics of cinematic reputation and as a counterbalance to the interpretations I offer for each film.

The final two categories need some clarification because this book exists somewhere between the domain of film theory and the traditional turf of the cultural historian, in other words, between those who examine "texts" and those who examine "contexts." One recent school of thought attempts to bridge this dichotomy between theorists and historians. The historian John E. O'Connor calls this new focus "the expanded text," which requires film scholars "to locate their subjects in the wider realm of society and culture" and to explore the *practice* of filmmaking, rather than simply the filmmaker or the film.[6]

With this in mind, I have made several questions central to this investigation of the difficult art of political filmmaking: What did it mean to be an independent filmmaker with radical politics during the cold war? How was de Antonio able to finance and coordinate the production of his films? What was his vision of U.S. politics and how successfully did he express it on film? To answer these questions I have sought the various contexts—biographical, intellectual, creative—in which the elusive meaning of his films becomes clearer, richer, and more relevant. Few filmmakers of any political stripe have shared his wide-ranging intellectual proclivities; his interests in literature, politics, and modern art shaped his films far more than his limited knowledge of film history and production. The literary theorist Julia Kristeva has observed that "every text is the absorption and transformation of other texts," and for de Antonio, film was simply where his diverse interests came together with a crash of dissonance, where competing perspectives could coexist uneasily in an intellectual montage of the sort Bertolt Brecht had called for in the 1930s.[7] The technique is powerful; as Bill Nichols puts it, "Insight replaces recognition, new possibilities suggest themselves, alternatives come to light." De Antonio was the first U.S. filmmaker to create such films.[8]

The structure of this book is primarily chronological, though each chapter emphasizes a different theme. Chapter 1 looks for the roots of de Antonio's political and cinematic sensibilities in the forty years of his life before film, a period of equal parts privilege and alienation. Chapter 2 describes the production of his first film, *Point of Order* (1963), a groundbreaking distillation of the Army-McCarthy hearings.

With his next film, *Rush to Judgment* (1967), de Antonio took his crew to Dallas, Texas, to make the first film skeptical of the Warren Commission's report on the assassination of John F. Kennedy. In chapter 3, I trace de Antonio's stormy relationship with Lee Harvey Oswald's defender, the lawyer and writer Mark Lane, showing how *Rush to Judgment*, a thought-provoking investigation of the Warren Commission's report, emerged from their partnership. Chapter 4 examines de Antonio's visual history of the war in Vietnam, *In the Year of the Pig* (1969), and its domestic counterpart about the presidential campaign of Senator Eugene McCarthy, *America Is Hard to See* (1970), in order to reveal de Antonio's vision of American history. Chapter 5 explores the details of producing *Millhouse: A White Comedy* (1971)—the misspelling of Nixon's middle name was a deliberate effrontery and an apt title for a film that brought together documentary and satire to attack a sitting president. This chapter is based in part on White House memoranda and concludes with a reconstruction of the small panic the film caused in the Nixon White House.

Chapter 6 follows an apparent change of direction for de Antonio. In this chapter I discuss his interest in the New York art world, one that led to the making of *Painters Painting* (1973), and I highlight the conflicts between art and politics in the late sixties and early seventies. De Antonio returned to overtly political subjects in his next film, *Underground* (1976), which focuses on the flamboyant young revolutionaries known as the Weather Underground Organization. In chapter 7, I describe the cloak-and-dagger melodrama surrounding the production of this film, which the Federal Bureau of Investigation attempted to stop.

The final chapter explores de Antonio's films of the eighties, both of which were unlike any others he made. In 1983 he made a "docudrama" entitled *In the King of Prussia* (1983), starring Martin Sheen and Daniel Berrigan in a dramatic reenactment of the trial of the Plowshares Eight, a group of peace activists who had broken into a nuclear weapons plant and vandalized nose cones for Mark 12A missiles with vials of their own blood. De Antonio's final film, *Mr. Hoover and I* (1989), is a beautiful summing up of a life of dissent that traces his forty-year surveillance by the FBI. Finally, the epilogue surveys his accomplishments as well as the state of political documentary since his death, looking for heirs to his legacy of passionate intellectual filmmaking and finding it in some unlikely places, such as the Internet, where some exciting new "documentaries" are just beginning to emerge. In the epilogue I describe why de Antonio is considered the most significant documentary filmmaker in the postwar United States and a pioneer of cultural criticism in the age of television. The lessons we can learn from de Antonio are more important than ever as we enter a new century in which the influence of video (broadly defined to include film, television, and other forms of moving pictures) will continue to expand in unprecedented directions. Showing us how to subvert the commercialization of media culture, if not the commercialization of American culture itself, may be de Antonio's most lasting legacy.

De Antonio's reputation was enormous among those who knew his work—Thomas Waugh described him in 1976 as "one of the major American filmmakers of our time," Richard Barsam called him a "master," and Jack C. Ellis wrote in 1989 that, along with Frederick Wiseman, de Antonio was the "sturdiest and most influential" American documentarian of the previous twenty years. Yet he is little known today outside film circles, in part because no book-length study and few scholarly articles have been written about him, despite the existence of hundreds of secondary sources and a considerable archive.[9] The most important exception to this dearth of scholarship on de Antonio is Waugh's article, "Beyond Vérité: Emile de Antonio and the New Documentary of the Seventies," which appeared in *Jump Cut* in the summer of 1976.[10] Now a classic of film studies, this article situates de Antonio in film history, establishing his "democratic didacticism" as an extension of John Grierson and Sergei Eisenstein and giving de Antonio credit for inspiring an entire wave of contemporary filmmaking.[11] Waugh paints de Antonio as an exemplar of a third way in documentary—a sophisticated filmmaker working somewhere between the network films whose independence he could not trust and radical collectives like Newsreel whose films were too confrontational to reach a broad audience. Given his influence on other filmmakers, as well as "the rich creative energy, the obstinate commitment to rationality and to change, and the clearsighted historical consciousness" that he brought to his own films, de Antonio seemed ripe for further analysis. But few scholars have followed Waugh's lead in examining the significance of de Antonio's work.[12]

That a filmmaker of this stature would remain unexamined for so long is due in part to the general neglect of independent nonfiction filmmaking by film scholars and historians, which the film scholar Ray Carney calls "one of the continuing disgraces of film studies."[13] Documentary filmmakers as disparate as de Antonio, George Stoney, Richard Leacock, D. A. Pennebaker, and David and Albert Maysles warrant more than the scant attention they have received. Scholars have paid even less attention to contemporary documentary filmmakers who focus on political issues, as the editors of *Jump Cut* complained almost two decades ago:

"Sometimes they have been completely ignored or misrepresented by the critical establishment." The situation has been improving in recent years, and I have had the benefit of several excellent models for writing about documentary filmmakers, if not overtly political ones: Barry Keith Grant's *Voyages of Discovery: The Cinema of Frederick Wiseman* and Richard Barsam's *The Vision of Robert Flaherty: The Artist as Myth and Filmmaker*. Still, much work remains to be done, and I hope that extensive criticism of de Antonio's life and films, making use of documents that became available only after his death, will be a small step toward rectifying what remains, as Carney says, a largely "unwritten chapter in American film history."[14]

In addition to drawing on hundreds of interviews, articles, and reviews published in both mainstream and obscure periodicals, I have relied heavily on de Antonio's unpublished journals, correspondence, business records for his production companies, research notes and manuscripts for books and films, and assorted other material from the extensive de Antonio archive at the Wisconsin Center for Film and Theater Research of the State Historical Society of Wisconsin on the Madison campus of the University of Wisconsin.[15] This archive includes declassified memoranda on de Antonio from the FBI, the Nixon White House, and other documents that de Antonio obtained in the late 1970s as part of his requests through the Freedom of Information Act. All unpublished sources were drawn from this archive unless otherwise noted. I was able to obtain unusual access to many rare documents in the archive through the generosity of not only Nancy de Antonio, the filmmaker's widow, but also the literary executor of the de Antonio estate, Professor Douglas Kellner of the University of California, Los Angeles. Finally, whenever possible I have attempted to interview or correspond with people who participated in the making of his films.

1

◄◦►

Life Before Film

Déraciné

"All Americans are underground men because we dig for roots," Emile de Antonio said in the late seventies. "There are none of course. They were severed in transit." De Antonio could trace his own roots to the soil of northern Italy, where his grandfather had lived a century before.[1] Tall and handsome with "an angelic smile revealing the candor of his affections," Francesco de Antonio (1821–1881) was a distinguished pediatrician and a progressive politician in the small city of Alessandria. In the midst of two flourishing careers he found time to translate Lucretius's *De Rerum Natura* with such beauty that the residents of Alessandria voted to bear the cost of its first printing.[2]

The sons of Francesco de Antonio upheld the good name of the family. They included a professor of literature, a general in the Italian army during the First World War, a lawyer in Turin, and a physician, the father and namesake of the filmmaker. The physician, Emilio de Antonio, was born in Alessandria in 1870 and educated at the Royal University of Turin and Pavia University where he received a medical degree in 1894. With a blossoming medical practice and election to the Alessandria city council, he seemed poised to follow the path of his father. But in 1903 he suddenly left his hometown under mysterious circumstances that he never explained to his son and moved to Scranton, Pennsylvania. Good fortune returned, and once again

10

he became a prosperous and respected member of the community. Then in early middle age he married a young nurse from the hospital where he was an administrator. A native of Pennsylvania, Anna Conapinch gave birth to the first of seven children in 1919: Emile Francesco de Antonio.[3]

From his earliest years the boy was torn between the wistful Old World stories of his intellectual father and what he saw as the simple patriotism and conventional views of his mother. Though he would acquire a version of his mother's patriotism, for the most part the sensibility of his father prevailed, and the young de Antonio learned to think of himself and his family as "the distanced, the deraciné, the alienated."[4] Listening to his father's stories of Mediterranean heroes from Odysseus to Garibaldi, whose grandson once dined at their table in white tie with medals on his jacket, Emile began to perceive his hometown in the Lackawanna Valley of Pennsylvania as hopelessly provincial.[5] In his journal he remembered being "surrounded by the hyphenated Celts, Anglo-Saxons, Teutons, smug in the superiority of their hollow middle class manner." He wrote that he sometimes felt stranded in an alien country, and once said in a published interview that he remained "deeply conscious of my foreign origins" throughout his life.[6]

Even the wealth of his family was little comfort, because it separated him from less fortunate Italian Americans. On some days a chauffeur drove him to school on a route that wound through the poor sections of Scranton. "I hated the difference between those who had nothing but false hope and those of us who had the world," he remembered in Dickensian cadences. The discrepancy between those bleak lives and his own pushed him to question the opulence of his family's lifestyle, and like many young Americans in the thirties, he began to wonder about alternatives, some of which he may have found in the "progressive, liberal agnostic's library" his father maintained.[7] Despite the discomfort it caused his mother, he began to voice his curiosity about socialism and the Soviet Union during his adolescence, when he also began to lose interest in religion.[8] Loss of faith "may make you an artist or a political animal or a crook or something of all three," he wrote to a friend in 1973, intimating that he had fallen into the final category.[9] In the confines of the posh preparatory school to which he was sent at the age of fourteen, his rebellion began in earnest. Close enough to home for weekend visits under the watchful eyes of his parents, the Wyoming Seminary in Kingston, Pennsylvania, was "a cruel, Methodist, cramped kind of school," where a fence topped with broken glass surrounded the playgrounds to keep out trespassers.[10] Young de Antonio refused to put his head down during prayers and began to get in trouble, along with the only other Italian American boy in the school, prompting his teachers to complain about de Antonio's inability to accept "moral or spiritual restrictions."[11]

Despite his unhappiness in the dour atmosphere of the Wyoming Seminary, he did well enough in his classes to gain entrance to Harvard at the age of sixteen in 1936. All his parents wanted for their first born was a smooth transition to adulthood, but this proved too much for the "sensitive, proud, uneasy boy who entered Harvard, lost, without a friend."[12] The freedom of college life presented new opportunities for overcoming loneliness, boredom, and angst in the form of sports cars, wild parties, and a never-ending stream of gin rickeys, the beginning of the heavy consumption of alcohol that plagued him for the rest of his life. Education was a minor detail of his Harvard experience, almost a nuisance, but somehow he managed a respectable academic record during his freshman year despite a surprising failure in Italian.[13] He enjoyed only one class, an English class taught by a young Daniel Aaron—an "elf-like liberal who pushed me into radicalism over a martini and a ritz cracker"—though by this point de Antonio needed very little encouragement.[14] The interest in Marxism that worried his mother had begun to blossom.

Although the level of his knowledge of Marxism is difficult to determine, the reason he was drawn to it is not. Marxism appealed to him simply "because I didn't fit. . . . I was uneasy. . . . I remembered Scranton and saw boys in Cambridge with convertible sedan Pierce Arrows with coats of arms gracefully crowning the doors." Despite his burgeoning idealism and interest in radical politics, he continued to emulate those well-bred boys who made him so uncomfortable. He was a walking contradiction in his "black tie and beautiful pumps," sporting a monocle and looking for friends in left-wing organizations such as the John Reed Club, the Young Communist League, and the American Student Union. He joined all these groups, though he confessed that "I was never a true believer" and certainly not the sort who would lead a Communist parade down Fifth Avenue in New York City in May 1938, as someone erroneously reported to the FBI.[15] "I was never good at discipline," he said late in his life, though he had more serious objections to the shape of American Marxism: "I disliked the Soviet domination of the American Communist Party."[16] More in keeping with his conflicted personality was his decision to resign from the Young Communist League over the question of T. S. Eliot's poetry, which his comrades had condemned as reactionary. De Antonio excused the strange politics of the poet with the assertion that "the first duty of an artist is to be honest with himself. And then if you're lucky you can hope to express the aspirations and truth of your time."[17]

Throughout his life de Antonio struggled with this paradoxical blend of cultural elitism and radical politics, which was typified among anti-Stalinist leftists by the writer Dwight Macdonald. Though he was more than a decade younger and did not know the critic, de Antonio shared many of Macdonald's attitudes. Both were radicals who scorned the Soviet Union as much as the capitalist consumer culture of their own country. Both were political democrats and cultural conservatives, at least in their defense of artistic standards and tradition, which in de Antonio's case included concepts and heroes that were hardly in fashion among American Marxists. He was fixated upon honor, quality, and taste almost to the point of chivalry, and it carried over into his choice of literary icons—Eliot, Santayana, Dostoevsky—men whose conservatism and interest in religion were at odds with de Antonio's self-described Marxism and atheism.[18]

Aware of the paradoxes of his personality, he called himself a "Marxist of sensibility," someone who would oppose all forms of authority and orthodoxy with the bonhomie of a gentleman. About Senator Joseph McCarthy, the subject of his first film, he once said, "The most glaring flaw I saw in him was his impoliteness and his disrespect."[19] Indeed, de Antonio's revulsion toward capitalism was as much aesthetic as economic, and his notion of radicalism was based not just on Marx but also on a line he attributed to Sartre and memorized: "It is our task as writers to cast light on the eternal values which are involved in these social and political disputes."[20] Yet in the years before he tried his hand at writing, and long before he discovered film, de Antonio's attempts at political criticism were limited to small outbursts of good-natured dissent, such as the occasion he wore a sandwich board that read "Scalp the scalpers" and picketed the illegal sale of tickets to the Harvard-Yale football game. A photograph of the picketing de Antonio ran in a variety of newspapers across the country. Looking like a self-confident young dandy—not quite the "enormous, powerfully built man with a Rabelaisian taste for life," as the *Harvard Crimson* later described him—he wore a mischievous grin on his face.[21] Despite these antics, he might have graduated from Harvard as member of the class of 1940 and used his experiences as a springboard to the ranks of the American aristocracy, a station to which he halfheartedly aspired. Instead he set fire to an elevator in Claverly Hall during a drunken spree and then doused a university official with a fire hose. In its decision to expel him from Harvard, the administration remarked that "he was fundamentally of good character, but had behaved in a very irresponsible manner, and had shown very little interest in college work."[22]

Chastened and embarrassed, de Antonio went back to Scranton with "the grubbiest of ambitions": he enrolled at the University of Scranton, then called St. Thomas's College, a fact he later dropped from his résumé. He found himself in a place where his fellow students were preparing to become dentists and undertakers. Yet among these more socially diverse students, for the first time he began to meet working-class intellectuals, including a clique of young radicals who held secret meetings near the black panther cage at the local zoo where one of their friends worked as a night watchman.[23]

During this period in Scranton he married Ruth Baumann, the first of his six wives. They had one child before their marriage dissolved, and de Antonio left Scranton forever in 1940, returning only for his mother's funeral in 1949.[24] Finding work as a longshoreman and other physical labors (which would have pleased his political friends from the panther cage), he moved for a short period to Baltimore to be close to his younger brother at Johns Hopkins.

Then in 1942, six months after Pearl Harbor, he enlisted in the Marine Corps with the goal of receiving an officer's commission. Unfortunately, his patriotic gesture was short-lived—unable to complete his courses in a satisfactory manner, he was discharged from the corps within three months. Several weeks later he tried again, enlisting in the U.S. Army Air Corps as a prospective aviation cadet. The army sent him to "the most inferno-like place I've ever seen"—San Marcos, Texas—where he scored the highest IQ among fifteen hundred cadets.[25] However, poor eyesight forced the army to release him, and he ended up in the Office of Production Management in Washington, D.C., as a clerk charged with rationing raw materials to private companies. Though he saw enough corporate lobbying to confirm any suspicions about the nature of the relationship between government and big business, he kept quiet about his radical ideas during the war. Nevertheless, reports of his past communist affiliation soon led to a security check, and in 1943 the FBI compiled a report that listed aspects of his personality: "Intelligent; has leadership ability; good speaker; talkative; well read; phenomenal memory; argumentative; impulsive." He was twenty-four. He had one child, one ex-wife, and the first pages of what would become a voluminous FBI file.[26]

"Praxis fell away" during the war de Antonio said, recalling how he moved into a period of questioning his political commitment. He retained a distaste for free enterprise and the American

Emile de Antonio in his U.S. Army uniform, 1944. Courtesy Wisconsin Center for Film and Theater Research.

bourgeoisie, but this did not prevent him from "hugely and self-indulgently savor[ing] the contradictions of cold war capitalism" in a variety of unlikely settings.[27]

During the late forties he studied philosophy and English at Columbia University, received a master's degree, and taught for a year at the College of William and Mary in Virginia. As a lecturer in introductory English, he led his students through classic readings from Chaucer to Eliot, whom he still praised as "the poet of our time."[28] But he was probably better known for the wild living that was ruining his marriage—his second, this time to the heiress Mimi Vanderbilt, who bore him a daughter he did not meet until her adolescence. He wore sneakers to class, sat cross-legged on his desk like an Italian Buddha, conducted affairs with his female students, and drove a flashy car. Needless to say, he was a controversial figure among the southern gentry with whom he socialized. At one academic party a professor offered him a glass of sherry, and de Antonio refused with a belligerent demand for an entire bottle of whiskey. He later said it was as if he could hear his teaching career going "into the garbage with the wretched middle class doilies." An arrest for drunken driving ended any hopes for redeeming his academic future—"it was the end of my teaching and of my marriage."[29]

He returned to Columbia in 1948 and found what some might consider the ideal job for a graduate student in English literature: barge captain. With few responsibilities he was able to sit and read all afternoon, while the barge was towed up and down the river. One day he arrived at the dock where he had left the barge the day before, but it was nowhere to be found. In a mild panic he cabled the owners of the vessel: "SIRS. RESIGNING POSITION BARGE CAPTAIN. TAKING POSITION INSTRUCTOR PHILOSOPHY."[30]

Continuing his academic work with some reluctance, and apparently supported by a sizable inheritance from his father (who had died at home in Pennsylvania on D-Day in 1944), de Antonio fashioned himself into an extraordinary thing—a playboy graduate student who occasionally commuted to school from a suite at the Plaza Hotel. Yet graduate school itself held little appeal for him. Realizing that academics are "bloodless and spiteful," as he put it, he found himself unwilling to write what he sarcastically described as another unwanted and unreadable dissertation about the comma in *Finnegans Wake*.[31]

From then on de Antonio held few steady jobs. Living by his wits in New York, he worked as a freelance editor, going over textbooks for firms such as Alfred A. Knopf. He worked briefly as an economist with the U.S. Department of Labor, though he had to pretend to have advanced degrees in the subject.[32] He even toyed with the idea of going to Europe but feared he would never come home, a reluctance he never explained.[33] So like many intelligent young people with nothing better to do, he attempted to write a novel. He claimed to have thrown the manuscript, entitled *Save Honor*, from the window of an airplane—his only "perfect act of criticism."[34] Perhaps he did: no trace of it remains. Awkward short stories intended for the *New Yorker* never saw the light of day, either, though presumably they escaped the plight of his novel and were simply placed in the garbage.[35]

Writing always bedeviled him, and his prose rarely reflected the eloquence of his speech, which served him so well in both conversations and lectures. With the jealousy of the failed novelist toward the graceful and successful writer, he had no use for American writers who were coming to prominence in the fifties. He dismissed James Jones and William Styron as "pot boilers and totally unserious"; Norman Mailer, whom he sometimes came across at parties, received the grudging compliment of being "a squinty outrageous beetle who has turned into a sometime good journalist."[36] Putting aside his aspirations to become a writer before the age of thirty, de Antonio looked for creative expression in the work of others, which he began to support and encourage in ways that were often useful and sometimes crucial.

Art

Because he had never dabbled in painting, de Antonio had no sense of rivalry with the young painters he began to meet in the late 1940s in New York. In taverns such as the Cedar Room and the San Remo, he could drink all night and listen to the passionate conversations between abstract expressionists and poets such as Dylan Thomas. His real connection to the art scene began in the mid-1950s with the group he called the "homintern," a pun on Comintern (Communist International). The jibe had first been used by the writer and critic Cyril Connolly to describe a clique of gay writers at Oxford in the thirties.[37] In much the same fashion de Antonio used it to describe up-and-coming artists in a variety of media, several of whom would become internationally celebrated. "I moved among the smirks, talents, shyness and nastiness of the homintern," he remembered, "like a spy from Venus, an ambassador to narcissism and anxiety."[38] For someone whose notorious womanizing had established him as resolutely heterosexual, he was an unlikely presence in what he called "the gay underground," where he played an important role as friend, adviser, and business associate to major artists at critical points in their careers. For his earnest labors and forthright opinions, he gained lifelong friends, the gift of paintings that would multiply in value, and the connections to many future investors in his films. And the painters gained someone who was, as the dealer Leo Castelli remembered, "immensely lively, involved, and incredibly interesting."[39]

"I've just started a new business—artist's agent," he wrote his sister-in-law in 1956.[40] He was beginning to demonstrate a remarkable facility for being in the right place at the right time, and his friends included several artists on the verge of serious critical and public recognition. But when they first met de Antonio, they sometimes still needed work to pay the rent, so he arranged jobs for "Matson Jones," which was the name Jasper Johns and Robert Rauschenberg used for commercial jobs, such as window displays in stores like Tiffany's.[41] He did the same and more for Andy Warhol.

His friendship and four-year love affair with Tina Fredericks, the young editor at *Vogue* who had given Warhol his first commercial illustration work in New York, led to his meeting the artist in

the late fifties.[42] His relationship with Warhol was professional at
first and began when de Antonio brought the artist to the owner
of a Puerto Rican theater who wanted advice on decorating. Pink
and gaudy was what Warhol suggested, and he received a fee from
which de Antonio subtracted his own. Making money this way
struck him as ludicrous, but he did his best to help the friends
who were his only clients. Because he generally did not receive
a commission, he was loathe to think of himself as an agent and
preferred the term *catalyst*.[43] "De connected artists with everything from neighborhood movie houses to huge corporations,"
remembered Warhol, who had reason to be grateful to him.[44]

"The person I got my real art training from was Emile de
Antonio," Warhol recalled in his memoir of the period, echoing
the sentiment he expressed to de Antonio's cameras in *Painters
Painting* (1972). In the late fifties, when his commercial illustrations brought him a comfortable income, Warhol was beginning to experiment in the pop art style that he soon epitomized.
Warhol was insecure about these canvases, which looked more
like advertisements than serious art, and turned to de Antonio for
advice and support, something he usually offered with generosity.
Because their offices were in the same neighborhood, de Antonio
could stop by for glasses of whiskey with the young painter, who
would listen to him speak "beautifully, in a deep, easy voice with
every comma and period falling into place."[45]

On one such evening in early 1960 Warhol brought out two
paintings for his friend's opinion. Both were of Coke bottles.
One was covered with wild brush strokes in a blend of pop and
abstract expressionism. The other was stark, empty, black and
white. The first painting was garbage, decreed de Antonio, but
the second was genius—"It's our society, it's who we are, it's
absolutely beautiful and naked, and you ought to destroy the
first one and show the other." Warhol took his advice to heart
and remembered the evening as a turning point for him. His
appreciation only increased when de Antonio convinced Eleanor
Ward—with whom de Antonio had recently ended a short love
affair—to give Warhol his first New York show at the prestigious

Stable Gallery.[46] De Antonio justified his efforts on Warhol's behalf with an unswerving faith in his importance: "Like Richard Nixon," de Antonio wrote, "Warhol is the American dream."[47]

Although de Antonio remained friends with the painter, he spent less time in his old haunts once he became involved in his own film career. Warhol was also making movies in the mid-1960s while his studio, the Factory, developed into an avant-garde circus where de Antonio never felt comfortable. Still, Warhol seemed to miss their evenings together. When he spotted his old friend at the Russian Tea Room in 1965, Warhol proposed a cinematic collaboration.

"I make serious, boring political films," de Antonio responded, "and you make boring frou-frous; there's nowhere to meet." When Warhol's normally impassive face showed a flash of disappointment, de Antonio relented—"We'll make a film on Thursday," he decided suddenly. "I'll do something for you that I'm sure nobody's ever offered to do for you and you can film it: I'll drink an entire quart of Scotch whisky in twenty minutes."[48]

De Antonio arrived at the appointed time, bottle in hand. Without a word he faced Warhol's camera and downed the scotch in twenty minutes. In the half hour it took Warhol to figure out how to load the second roll of film, de Antonio had sunk to the floor, singing and cursing and unable to stand. When the film was returned from the lab several weeks later, Warhol invited his star to a private screening. Privacy, however, was difficult to preserve at the Factory, and the poet Gerard Malanga and several dozen others were soon present, curious to see de Antonio's performance. What they saw was an unedited seventy-minute film entitled *Drink*, part of Warhol's trilogy that included *Eat* and *Sleep* in which people did just what the title said and nothing more. What de Antonio saw, however, was "the degradation of a human being totally wiped out. It's disgusting." As a result of his opinion, and the lawsuit that he half-seriously threatened if the film were shown in public again, the movie has remained out of sight.

De Antonio was useful to other major artists as well. After he met Frank Stella at Princeton in 1958, de Antonio lobbied strenuously to find a gallery for the young painter and eventually encouraged the prestigious Leo Castelli Gallery to take on the twenty-four-year-old artist. For several decades de Antonio would remain friends with the painter—both were Italian American, both the sons of doctors—and like many of the artists de Antonio met, Stella would support de Antonio's film career in various ways, including a financial investment and on-screen appearance in the film *Painters Painting* (1972).[49]

De Antonio also befriended the photographer Diane Arbus. He met her in 1959 through his friend Tina Fredericks, who had switched from *Vogue* to *Glamour* and then to *Ladies' Home Journal*. "De knows everybody in the art world," Fredericks said as she introduced him to Arbus. De Antonio took Arbus to the New Yorker Theater on the Upper West Side to watch a revival of Tod Browning's *Freaks* (1932), in which a cruel, beautiful circus performer marries a goodhearted midget for his money. This film turned out to have a significant influence on the photographer's increasingly baroque style and cemented a bond between de Antonio and Arbus, who often dropped by his offices to talk.[50]

In addition to being the sort of adviser Arbus, Warhol, and Stella needed, de Antonio was serving as an impresario, someone who knew how to promote an event. He acted in this capacity twice for John Cage, whom he considered "*the* seminal character in American arts in post—World-War-II America." Living for a time in the early 1950s near the composer in rural Pound Ridge, New York, de Antonio and his third wife, the designer Lois Long, spent many evenings with their unusual neighbor. "We had a house, a piano, books, booze and time," de Antonio remembered. "John was lonely [and] bored." With bottles of Irish whiskey on the table, Cage contrasted his Zen philosophy with de Antonio's leftist rationality. De Antonio began to realize how the masterpieces of art and literature were hanging over his head like "a boulder on a string." Meanwhile, he had tried to write a novel that could never measure up to the Homer, Dante, and Balzac he knew almost by heart. "So, I drank and drank and read and read and remained silent before marble greatness," overawed and creatively immobilized by the grandeur of the canon his father and his schooling had erected, one that "made me feel it was impossible to become an artist."[51] Cage's Zen philosophy provided de Antonio with a new way of seeing and subverting the authority of tradition. Although he never abandoned rationality for the philosophy of chance that Cage espoused, or followed his friend's philosophy to what he considered its nihilistic extreme, de Antonio called the composer "the greatest influence in my life as an artist."[52]

In appreciation de Antonio wanted to help his friend however he could. In addition to finding buyers for Cage's hand-picked wild mushrooms, one of the composer's few sources of income at a time when his music royalties came to less than $15 a year, de Antonio promoted two concerts of Cage's experimental music. On October 15, 1955, he arranged a concert of Cage's *Music for Piano* at Clarkstown High School in upstate New York. Despite the furious storm raging outside, the hall was filled with local music lovers who quickly decided that the performance was neither musical nor lovable. However, more favorable responses came from the luminaries of the New York art scene who were present: Franz Kline, Robert Motherwell, and Willem de Kooning.[53]

Then, on May 15, 1958, de Antonio put together a similar event in collaboration with his friends Robert Rauschenberg and Jasper Johns. Describing de Antonio as "a volatile entrepreneur," Calvin Tompkins reported how the various parties worked with de Antonio and "pooled their talents and their funds to sponsor a major New York concert of Cage's music at Town Hall" in New York City. A twenty-five-year retrospective of Cage's work, the historic concert was recorded and released as a boxed set of records.[54] Merce Cunningham took part in the performance as well, which de Antonio recalled as the dancer's "first in a theater of that size and done professionally with ads."[55] De Antonio made a bold claim for the significance of the occasion, which he said bore the same relationship to "postwar art, music, and *weltanschauung* in America" as the premiere of Stravinsky's *The Rite of Spring* to French society in 1913, an opinion seconded by an unnamed elderly painter who de Antonio claimed had been present at both events.[56]

De Antonio rarely made money on such occasions. He claimed that his compensation was simply the pleasure he derived from being at the center of things, from seeing important works before anyone else. Consider his relationship with Jasper Johns, who invited him to his apartment on many occasions in the 1950s for drinks and conversation. One evening stood out in de Antonio's memory because Johns had made the invitation with a rare note of formality, as if something unusual were planned. When de Antonio arrived, he noticed that the artist's loft was empty except for several remarkable paintings hung on the walls—the flags and targets and numbers that were to make Johns's reputation. "I was knocked out," de Antonio said. "You feel something like that with your insides, the words for it come later—'dryness,' 'austerity.' "[57]

De Antonio also appreciated the company of the artist, whom among his friends he viewed as "the most elusive, the least sane, the wittiest . . . [most] disputatious, precise in his thinking, neat as in his painting and closer to the artist as thief and charlatan than most." One night they went to the movies to see Ingmar Bergman's *The Seventh Seal* (1957). Much to the annoyance of the solemn moviegoers in the audience, the appearance of the figure of death in gray robes brought peals of laughter from both of them.[58] Johns offered this sort of camaraderie, whereas Rauschenberg provided something deeper: "I talk better with Jap but Bob is finally more real and more rooted in life," de Antonio said. As tokens of their friendship during the fifties, both painters gave him presents of their early work—in Rauschenberg's case nearly thirty of his blueprint drawings.[59]

Despite such presents, which de Antonio would later sell for large sums, his work in the arts did not support his high standard of living. Sometimes, however, his social relationships with prominent artists paid off in a more immediate and tangible form. For example, through his wide acquaintance with creative people in New York he came to know the architect Philip Johnson. When the Bronfman family wanted to decorate their austere Seagram Building for Christmas in 1959, Johnson contacted de Antonio to recommend a creative consultant. De Antonio brought in the designer Gene Moore, who had used the work of Matson Jones in the windows of Tiffany's in New York. "We charged them [$]10,000 for the idea of using Xmas trees," de Antonio recalled with some amusement, and each year thereafter, when the Seagram Co. put up a conventional Christmas display, he received a sizable check.[60]

Because he was engaged with such eclectic activities during the late fifties, his friends often complained "how difficult it is to define exactly what it is that 'You Do,'" as the fashion photographer Richard Routledge observed.[61] One thing de Antonio did was play the stock market, usually with tips from friends who were well placed in corporate America. "If you have capital and information," he later said in the 1970s during a lapse of political conscience, "there is no excuse for poverty."[62] With his two children living with their mothers, he was able to continue the playboy lifestyle he had begun as a Harvard undergraduate.[63] His philosophy was to make as much money as possible in a short period, even in just a few days, so that he could live comfortably for the rest of the year. "All artists have some of the criminal in them," de Antonio explained to his daughter, Adrienne, a point he often made with allusions to Thomas Mann's *The Confessions of Felix Krull*. Some of his money-making schemes, if not criminal, relied on the sort of financial chicanery that later served him well in funding his films.[64] He founded a company called Conservative Enterprises, Inc., whose name reflected the satirical nature of the endeavor. With a letterhead filled with impressive-sounding but utterly fictitious names ("Elton Marsh III"), the company even had a facetious motto: *Quis facit per alium facit per se* (What a man does through an agent, he does himself). De Antonio's satirical business ventures even made money on occasion, such as the time a few phone calls enabled him to sell some military-surplus steel cables for a profit of $100,000.[65] At other times he found himself deeply in debt, musing with aristocratic self-assurance that he might be thrown in jail by his creditors.[66]

De Antonio had the aura of someone who was worth knowing, someone with a reputation for speaking his mind with intelligence and bluntness, even if the latter quality sometimes was most striking. People knew he was the sort of person who would throw a party and tell his friend Frances FitzGerald, not yet a well-known writer, that she could not bring Adlai Stevenson with her—"because I don't like his politics."[67] This sort of directness, which made his judgments so valuable to the painters he knew, would also make him a welcome addition to New York's avant-garde film scene in 1959.

Film

"Film brought me to seriousness again and I love film."[68] De Antonio's sudden passion was a reversal of his earlier point of view; like his father, he had long seen movies as a technological opiate of the masses, something to be avoided lest it stamp its crude imprint upon a consciousness reserved for loftier things.[69] He conceded only a few exceptions to his sweeping generalization: anything by Charlie Chaplin, Jean Renoir's *Rules of the Game* (1939), Roberto Rossellini's *Open City* (1945), the Marx brothers' *A Night at the Opera* (1935), and W. C. Fields's *It's a Gift* (1934), a satirical rags-to-riches story that de Antonio interpreted as "a devastating attack on the impersonal and inhuman aspects of capitalism."[70]

His first tentative step toward film was as distributor of the Beat classic, *Pull My Daisy* (1959). Codirected by the painter Alfred Leslie and the photographer Robert Frank, whose book *The Americans* was about to be published to great acclaim, *Pull My Daisy* was based on Jack Kerouac's unproduced play about various adventures and began in Neal Cassady's home. In the half-hour film version Kerouac reads a lyrical voice-over while the camera follows the exploits of bohemian characters played by well-known painters (Larry Rivers, Alice Neal, Alfred Leslie) and poets (Allen Ginsberg, Peter Orlovsky, Gregory Corso). With a gritty sort of low-budget realism the film greatly influenced and inspired the development of American underground cinema in the sixties.[71] De Antonio became involved in the project when Robert Frank decided to dub the film into French. Kerouac volunteered to translate his narration, but his accent was so appalling—"Ju swee Jacques Ker-ou-ac"—that Frank thought de Antonio might be useful.

"I hate articulate people, but I happen to like you and we need help. . . . Can you come over?" Frank said on the telephone. De Antonio agreed and was soon listening to Kerouac's narration of *Pull My Daisy*, which he found more eloquent than any of the novels by the writer. De Antonio did what he could to improve the translation and afterward sat on a curb with Kerouac in front of the Seagram Building in New York, drinking from a gallon of Californian red wine and discussing the nature of film in general.[72] De Antonio was soon serving as distributor for the film, looking for theaters willing to book it, as well as working out business details such as a contract with the singer Anita Ellis, who contributed the film's opening song, "The Crazy Daisy."[73]

Fascinated by his experience with *Pull My Daisy*, de Antonio found his way into a new and experimental filmmaking organization, the New American Cinema Group, which came together on September 28, 1960.[74] As a member of the temporary executive board, he joined filmmakers, critics, and assorted artists, including Robert Frank, Alfred Leslie, Lionel Rogosin, Peter Bogdanovich, Jonas and Adolfas Mekas, Shirley Clarke, and Daniel Talbot. Inspired by films such as *Pull My Daisy* and John Cassavetes' *Shadows* (1959), the group wanted to help one another make daring low-budget films that might even turn a profit.[75] For de Antonio the group was the ideal place to learn how "film could be made with an economy of means," as he put it. But unlike other members of the group, or so he thought, de Antonio wanted his films distributed to audiences—"not to *archives*!"[76] Combined with his general inability to work in collective situations, this difference of opinion caused him to drop out of the group within a year to become involved in projects of his own.[77]

His next step was to produce Dan Drasin's *Sunday* (1961) on a $500 budget. Drasin, a Harvard undergraduate, had made the short documentary about the "folk music riot" that occurred in Washington Square when the police banned folk singers and other undesirables from the park in April 1960.[78] De Antonio was also meeting with the television journalist Mike Wallace to turn his television interviews with various luminaries into short films. Wallace was excited about the idea, but only one short conversation between the architect Frank Lloyd Wright and Wallace made the leap to the wide screen at the New Yorker Theater, which was owned by two of de Antonio's acquaintances, Dan Talbot and Henry Rosenberg.[79] De Antonio and Talbot also became interested in showing Josef von Sternberg's *The Blue Angel* (1930), which had made Marlene Dietrich an international star. With a few hours of research they were shocked to learn that Paramount had not renewed the option on the film's copyright. Their response was to draw up bogus corporate documents, complete with an official-looking red seal, that made them appear to own the rights to the film. De Antonio then used the documents to obtain the original prints of the film from its warehouse, and he and Talbot remained the distributor of the film for the next decade, with the New Yorker Theater alone making $15,000 from the film.[80]

Talbot's importance to de Antonio would soon become evident, but as the sixties began, de Antonio was forty years old and desperate, "living well, bored, not too much to do, drunk," as he remembered it.[81] Film seemed to offer a way out of this malaise, a way to explore his uncomfortable relationship with the country his father had chosen for his son. "I am an American," he conceded somewhat reluctantly. "I may also be a Marxist, a lush, [a] neurotic, a bad husband, [and] faithless but I am an American." His films would confront this simple fact.[82]

2

◄◦►

Point of Order!

Entrepreneur

In the spring of 1954 the American public was witness to a bizarre political spectacle. At the height of his communist-hunting activities, Senator Joseph R. McCarthy had accused Secretary of the Army Robert T. Stevens of harboring officers with subversive tendencies. The army responded with an accusation of its own, claiming that McCarthy's chief counsel, Roy Cohn, had lobbied for preferential treatment on behalf of a rich young friend who had just been drafted—a former aide to McCarthy named G. David Schine. To settle the matter hearings were held in the Senate Caucus Room, with an audience of more than twenty million watching the first great confluence of politics and entertainment that television offered. Somewhere in the course of the hearings viewers' support for McCarthy began to unravel. The scrutiny of the cameras was too much for the senator to bear, even though he had welcomed the public's attention with confidence. "I'm glad we're on television," he claimed before berating a fellow senator toward the end of the hearings: "I think the viewing people can see how low that a man can sink." To many people these words seemed better applied to McCarthy himself.

At the time de Antonio did little to protest McCarthy's influence, but over the next decade he held McCarthy responsible for the wave of political intolerance that "introduced witchcraft, terror, falsehood, a debasement of language, manners, and mind;

29

and created for the first time in our history an atmosphere that was truly totalitarian."[1] By early 1961, several years after the death of McCarthy and a shift in the political climate, de Antonio and Dan Talbot began to think these qualities would make an extraordinary film that could be profitably screened at Talbot and Henry Rosenberg's New Yorker Theater. Despite their uncertainty about the kind of film that would emerge from the hearings—no one, after all, had ever made a film from television footage for theatrical release—the three entrepreneurs plunged ahead and formed a corporation in 1961 under the name of Point Films, a reference to McCarthy's repeated cry of "point of order!" during the hearings.[2]

Their first problem was finding the footage. Always blessed with an abundance of personal connections, de Antonio called upon a friend named Richard Ellison, who worked at CBS (and later produced *Vietnam: A Television History* for the Public Broadcasting System). When the network claimed to have lost its record of the hearings, Ellison prowled among the files and found a 16mm kinescope negative stored in a warehouse in Fort Lee, New Jersey.[3] Armed with this information, de Antonio began to pressure the network for a copy of the negative, a process he regarded with his customary irreverence. During the negotiations he made a point of showing up at serious meetings in khakis and tennis shoes. In astonishment Rosenberg watched him sprawl on the floor, using his "intellectual arrogance as a kind of hustle," as Rosenberg called it. On one occasion de Antonio even suggested flipping a coin to set a price for the footage—heads, he paid $50,000; tails, he paid nothing—though the network executives quickly declined.

Several months of such brash tactics began to soften the network's position, though its price remained stiff by the standards of Point Films. To improve the fiscal situation of their underfunded corporation, de Antonio paid a visit to a friend named Elliot Pratt, a liberal heir to the Standard Oil fortune. Over hamburgers and drinks at a Manhattan diner that ended with the millionaire leaving a ten-cent tip (an irony that stuck in the filmmaker's memory), de Antonio persuaded Pratt to contribute $100,000, which formed the bulk of the film's budget and allowed de Antonio to sign a contract with CBS on April 6, 1961.[4] In exchange for the use of footage it had either forgotten or purposefully neglected in a warehouse across the Hudson, CBS received the considerable sum of $50,000, half the profits, and assurance that the filmmakers would purchase a $1 million indemnity policy to cover CBS in the event of litigation. The network also made it clear that any mention of CBS in connection with the film at any time would result in the cancellation of the contract and forfeiture of the $50,000.

The details of producing the film fell to Talbot and de Antonio. Emboldened by his experience with *Pull My Daisy*, de Antonio thought he could make the film. But Talbot, wanting someone with experience and a reputation, cabled Orson Welles. "What could I say to that?" de Antonio recalled. However, Welles was unavailable, as was the second choice, Irving Lerner, who had worked on films such as *Spartacus* and once had been a cameraman for the great documentarian Robert Flaherty. As the partners continued looking for a professional filmmaker, de Antonio expressed his frustration during a chance encounter with his old friend John Cage. "Be Zen . . . just let it ride," the composer encouraged him. "You will be doing the film within months."

De Antonio had little reason to believe what Cage said, because Talbot had now hired a well-known film editor, Paul Falkenberg. The new editor had asked Richard Rovere, a writer at the *New Yorker* who had published an elegantly condemnatory book about McCarthy, to write narration for the voice of Mike Wallace, the television journalist.[5] Falkenberg put all these elements together over several months, then presented a rough cut of the film to the producers in a private screening. This marked the turning point for the film, as Talbot, Rosenberg, Pratt, and de Antonio stared with astonishment as the screen filled with images of starving African children, American flags flapping in the wind, Soviet tanks rumbling through Moscow, the wedding of Senator McCarthy, and scenes of Vermont churches.

"It was a disaster," de Antonio said with a hint of satisfaction. But neither he nor his partners had reason to gloat over the dire financial situation into which Point Films had descended. Someone within the corporation—which meant either Talbot or de Antonio—would have to start over with more modest aspirations, because they had no more money to spend on professional editors or writers from the *New Yorker*. Talbot had worked for three years as a story editor for Warner Brothers and had edited an important book on film but had no more practical experience in filmmaking than de Antonio.[6] So when de Antonio announced his willingness to work without pay, he was given free rein to make his first film at the age of forty-two. Point Films had nothing more to lose.

Filmmaker

"I'd never seen a piece of film. I'd never seen an editing machine. I started from scratch," de Antonio recalled.[7] All he possessed was a vision of what he wanted to do and an abundance of raw material—more than 188 hours of footage.

He spent several months in 1961 simply watching the hearings before hiring a young, inexperienced, nonunion editor, Robert Duncan, to make the cuts where he directed. Then de Antonio made a critical decision: he scrapped the narration Rovere had written, cut the irrelevant footage of rustic churches and starving children, and vowed to use only the grainy black-and-white shots from the vantage of the two stationary cameras in the Senate Caucus Room—no commentary, no music, no extraneous shots.

Instead he would create a political drama from the words of others, extracting a concise, coherent story from the mass of visual history on the kinescopes. The idea evoked earlier attempts to create a narrative from a collage of images, such as John Dos Passos's news montages in the three novels of the *U.S.A.* trilogy.[8] De Antonio's plans for the film also reflected and foreshadowed the new "documentary theater" of the 1960s, which relied upon the transcripts of historical events. A few years later de Antonio would become well acquainted with several examples of this sort of theater, including Peter Weiss's *The Investigation*, Heinar Kipphardt's *In the Matter of J. Robert Oppenheimer*, and Daniel Berrigan's *The Catonsville Verdict*.[9] Clearly, de Antonio knew as well as the German philosopher Walter Benjamin, Dos Passos, or Weiss that the process of selection was a form of writing that would give him a clear authorial voice in the resulting text. He also knew that the technique posed its own set of creative dilemmas, such as limiting him to what appeared on the kinescopes, because he could not return to the field to shoot additional footage, as other documentarians might. And distilling the essence of 188 hours could easily have overwhelmed his limited understanding of film editing, had he not balanced this inexperience with an intimate and relevant knowledge of the work of John Cage, Robert Rauschenberg, Jasper Johns, and other artists who set the climate of creativity in which he had found himself for more than a decade.[10]

Cage's influence was the most practical for getting the film completed, for whenever de Antonio reached a creative impasse, he would recall what the composer had told him during their long drunken conversations on summer evenings in the mid-1950s. He looked upon Cage's Zen-influenced philosophy as a therapeutic ethos that allowed him to pare down the footage with the reassurance that his editorial decisions, if not perfect, would work out in the end, that his inexperience was not an insurmountable handicap.[11] "Without John, I would never have been able to make *Point of Order*," he confessed in appreciation, but his praise obscures another source of inspiration in the New York art scene, one he rarely mentioned.

In its 1961 exhibition called "The Art of Assemblage," the Museum of Modern Art presented works that were "predominantly *assembled* rather than painted, drawn, modeled, or carved" from "preformed natural or manufactured materials, objects, or fragments not intended as art materials."[12] This goes to the heart of de Antonio's technique. Consider his material, the kinescopes of the hearings, as another form of industrial debris languishing in a New Jersey warehouse, the same sort of detritus that had found its way into the "combines" of Robert Rauschenberg, the sculpture of Jasper Johns, or the crushed car sculptures of John Chamberlain—all of whom de Antonio knew (and persuaded to appear in *Painters Painting* [1972]). From Rauschenberg to de Antonio, from the scraps of industrial America to the scraps of the entertainment industry, from the welding equipment of John Chamberlain to the editing machine of de Antonio is but a short cognitive leap, one that resulted in a motion picture, or, in some metaphoric sense, a motion sculpture. Had de Antonio finished it earlier, his temporal form of junk sculpture could even have been placed alongside Rauschenberg's work in the "The Art of Assemblage" exhibition, perhaps as an ironic commentary on the nature of television. Yet even at this early stage in his career, de Antonio was showing signs of a reluctance to indulge in formal experimentation that might obscure the political impact of his films. He would never, for example, extend his idea of film collage into something as surreal as Bruce Baillie's *Quixote* (1968) in which shots were superimposed on one another. Unlike other independent filmmakers with avant-garde tendencies, some of whom he had known in the New American Cinema Group, de Antonio wanted to balance cinematic complexity with accessibility to a wide audience.[13]

The Film

Point of Order begins with fifty-nine seconds of black leader during which de Antonio sets the stage with the basic facts of the hearings. His voice then exits the film and de Antonio the editor takes over, providing thumbnail sketches of the ten central members of the cast. Joseph Welch, the wizened attorney for the army, appears on screen in a still photograph as we hear his voice: "I came down from Boston in the guise of a simple trial lawyer. I

Joseph Welch in a still from *Point of Order* (Point Films, 1964). Courtesy Wisconsin Center for Film and Theater Research.

suppose I'd try to think up some questions to ask witnesses and then, if I didn't like the answer, ask another one."

A similarly pithy quotation intended to epitomize the speaker introduces each of the ten main characters. McCarthy, however, is allowed to introduce himself with a short speech in which he promises to fight the implacable communist menace until "victory or . . . death for this civilization." With a hint of irreverence de Antonio undermines the solemnity of the senator's rhetoric with quick reaction shots of Roy Cohn, who is playing with a pencil, and Welch, who is looking overcome with ennui. Cutting to Welch may have had the practical benefit of masking cuts in the audio, but it also reflects the keen sense of the ironic that de Antonio brought to editing.[14]

Selections from the hearings then begin in sequences approximately ten minutes long, with a bold intertitle across the screen
introducing each section. The first, "Charge and Countercharge,"
has Senator Stuart Symington, Democrat of Missouri, laying out
the problem in his patrician manner: "I suggest that the charges
are often forgotten. The charges were, did Senator McCarthy and
two members of his staff use improper pressure for Mister David
Schine [against] the army. The countercharge was that there was
blackmail on the part of the army and the use of Mister Schine as
a hostage."

We soon see twenty-six-year-old Roy Cohn responding to the
question of whether he had threatened "to wreck the army"
if Private Schine were not made "a general and [allowed] to
operate from a penthouse in the Waldorf Astoria." Cohn sits to
the right of McCarthy, who interrupts the proceedings at will
with his points of order. Alternating between the two camera
angles from which he had to choose, de Antonio repeatedly cuts
to show the senator in various poses—brooding and ineffectual,
jocular and strangely charming, thundering and unthinkingly
cruel. This allows McCarthy to become more than a midwestern
monster of the political right, stalking the eastern elite with his one
empty issue, as another leftist filmmaker might have depicted him.
Instead we see a tragic and hubristic figure, blundering ahead with
a giggling, childlike innocence of the human cost of his actions,
engaging in the "cold manipulation of the calculus of power," as
Robert Penn Warren said of a similar demagogue he created for
All the King's Men.[15]

Point of Order assumes a high level of knowledge about the
hearings and the political phenomenon known as McCarthyism,
whose origins are not addressed in even the most cursory fashion.
Unlike the reader of Richard Rovere's book on McCarthy, the
viewer of *Point of Order* will not learn "what he was and what
he did," and consequently the film makes a difficult introduction to the subject.[16] At the very least, the viewer does have an
opportunity to study the rhetorical style that brought McCarthy
to national prominence, with its tendency to wind itself around

the most ephemeral of issues, such as whether Schine owned a "fur-lined hood" for his army parka or whether the color of ink used on army charts to illustrate Schine's excess of free time was misleading. In response, the army brass proves itself just as willing to delve into minutiae on national television.

The generals counter with charges about a photo of Schine in a meeting with Secretary of the Army Robert Stevens—which a McCarthy aide had cropped to suggest an intimacy between the two men that did not exist. When no one can answer Welch's question about the origins of the altered photo, the Boston lawyer sarcastically suggests "a pixie." McCarthy then walks into what seems to be a trap, asking: "Would counsel, for my benefit, define—I think he might be an expert on this—the word *pixie?*" Welch responds: "I should say, I should say, Mister Senator, that a pixie is a close relative of a fairy? Shall I proceed sir? Have I enlightened you?" We hear laughter from the spectators in the Senate at the subtle allusion to the alleged sexual relationship between Cohn and Schine, while de Antonio cuts to Cohn, who is shifting uncomfortably in his seat.

McCarthy's fall comes soon thereafter in a section under the grim title "The Accusation." The senator suggests that a young member of Welch's law firm had been a member of the Lawyers' Guild—"the legal bulwark for the Communist Party," he says ominously. With the cadences of an actor (he would play a judge in Otto Preminger's 1959 film, *Anatomy of a Murder*), Welch defends his young colleague and utters his most damning criticism of the senator: "Until this moment, Senator, I think I never really gauged your cruelty or your recklessness. . . . Let us not assassinate this lad further, Senator. You've done enough. Have you no sense of decency, sir, at long last? Have you left no sense of decency?" De Antonio's selection of evidence has primed the audience to accept Welch's assertion (calculated though it sounds with repeated viewings of the film) that McCarthy was a man without scruples.

The film ends with McCarthy isolated, his colleagues leaving the room in apparent disgust for the ranting senator, a scene that actually took place in the middle of the hearings. The viewer of *Point of Order* would never know that the hearings ended with the senator being cleared of any wrongdoing. De Antonio reorders events to sharpen their meaning in his film, choosing to impose a symbolic ending that reflected the Senate's eventual condemnation of McCarthy, as well as de Antonio's moral condemnation, rather than the literal truth of the hearings.[17] This also is a form of what de Antonio described as "telegraphing to the audience that film is being manipulated," a Brechtian signal from the filmmaker to the audience that history is being constructed, that *Point of Order* has a point of view that the director never intended to hide.[18]

Bertolt Brecht was an important influence on de Antonio, as he was for anyone on the Left who attempted to dramatize history in the cold war era. Yet few other American documentarians can be reasonably compared to the playwright, even if de Antonio was not the only filmmaker of the sixties who found himself, unconsciously or not, in the Brechtian tradition. However, except for one critic's perceptive allusion to the "Brechtian aesthetic" of his films, de Antonio has never been understood in this light, one that illuminates his ideas about *Point of Order* in particular.[19]

The similarities between the two artists are striking. Brecht mocked the "well-made plays" of classical drama as "culinary theater" for bourgeois consumption and pushed for plays that would make audiences question their political assumptions. De Antonio applied this line of reasoning to the television and film industries, which seemed to foster a passive spectatorship in the 1960s. "T.V. is not neutral, it creates sickness and passivity," the filmmaker wrote with bitterness and the belief that its insidious powers of persuasion made "the pope look like a guy with a whistle and a basket and a cobra."[20] De Antonio's response was to use the images of television to construct a form of antitelevision that subversively celebrates its lack of neutrality and stimulates debate, as Brecht hoped his plays would do.[21]

Whereas conventional "Aristotelian" theater provides a cathartic experience for the audience, Brecht's epic theater was aimed at the mind rather than the heart, just as *Point of Order* requires audiences to make the effort of interpretation, a function of the narrator in most historical documentaries. In a lecture he gave toward the end of his career de Antonio explained his own work with a quotation he attributed to Brecht: "Our theater must encourage the thrill of comprehension and train people in the pleasure of changing reality. Our audiences must not only hear how Prometheus was set free, but also train themselves in the pleasure of freeing him. They must be taught to feel, in our theater . . . the triumph felt by the liberator."[22] No less grandiose coming from a filmmaker than a playwright, these words were more inspirational than pragmatic for de Antonio, who nonetheless attempted to translate some of Brecht's ideas into his filmmaking practice: his decision to structure *Point of Order* from a loose succession of scenes rather than a tight sequence of acts, his use of intertitles to disrupt narrative momentum, and his desire to engage the viewer in a dialectical process of interpretation rather than acquiescence—all evoke the spirit and practice of Brecht.[23]

De Antonio, however, eschewed the antiromantic, antiindividualist sentiment so often attributed to Brecht. Unlike Brecht, de Antonio possessed a streak of liberalism that undermined the Marxist perspective the filmmaker sometimes claimed for *Point of Order*. His political ambiguity is reflected in the artificial ending he imposed upon the film, an ending that suggests an aberrant quality to the junior senator from Wisconsin, as if he were a political pathology that could be isolated, then expelled from the body politic after the heroic diagnosis of Joseph Welch. Instead of being emblematic of the failure of democracy in the age of electronic demagoguery in which "we [are] all culpable in a sense," as de Antonio intended, McCarthy seems like an exceptional figure.[24] Ironically, then, the effect of what de Antonio intended as a "Brechtian ending" was to undermine the Brechtian aspect of the film. "Unhappy the land where heroes are needed," warns Galileo after submitting to the Inquisition in Brecht's play about the sixteenth-century astronomer, but *Point of Order* needed a hero in Joseph Welch to stop the implacable senator from Wisconsin, the sort of "heroizing" that is less Brechtian than characteristic of liberal ideology.[25]

Not surprisingly, reviewers were pleased to focus on this liberal aspect of the film. "A Love-Letter to Miss Liberty" was the title of an unctuous review in the *New York Post* by James Wechsler, one of many critics who seized upon the film as an opportunity to dance with a combination of sanctimony and spite upon the grave of the senator who had died in 1957.[26] The dancing began with an enthusiastic screening at the Museum of Modern Art in September 1963, after which the film opened at the Beekman Theater in Manhattan in January 1964.[27] Driving past the theater on snowy winter nights, de Antonio could see long lines of people waiting to see a movie he had more or less made in his living room.[28] *Point of Order* was a sweeping success, both with audiences and critics.

The quantity and quality of laudatory reviews that de Antonio's first film received were remarkable, helping to make it the most successful historical documentary to appear in U.S. theaters since World War II. "The greatest sustained drama . . . ever put on display," pronounced an overexcited writer for the *World Telegram*, whereas Dwight Macdonald more realistically described the film as "good cinema and better history," and Susan Sontag called it "the only successful spectacle shown this winter dealing with public issues." Brendan Gill of the *New Yorker* fawned over a "model documentary [which] should become a precious document of American history," and Stanley Kaufman lauded the film as "relentlessly gripping."

Time, Newsweek, Variety, and other mainstream publications agreed with Judith Crist of NBC's *Today* show when she said it was "one of the most impressive movies that's come out in a long time." Even Roy Cohn eventually acknowledged it was "without question the most important historical documentary of that period and perhaps any period," though he considered the film unfairly biased against him and threatened a lawsuit on more than one occasion. More than the reviewers who praised what they perceived as the impartiality of the film, Cohn understood that *Point of Order* was, as he said, "a cropped movie," an allusion to the "cropped photograph" of Schine that caused such controversy during the hearings.[29] De Antonio would have given him no argument.

The film landed a $100,000 advance from Walter Reade/Sterling Inc. to distribute the film, then played in 103 theaters in its first year of release.[30] With a stack of good notices and an invitation to show the film at the prestigious Cannes Film Festival, de Antonio found that he had become a minor celebrity. With a certain amount of irony he was appearing on television, the medium he so despised. Later in the decade he even debated Roy Cohn on talk shows hosted by Phil Donahue and William F. Buckley, Jr.[31] *Point of Order* was finally broadcast on national television in 1968, though not without alterations. "Time has passed," one network executive fretted, "and people have even forgotten who McCarthy and Cohn are."[32] So the network added an introduction, with the actor Paul Newman in a blue blazer explaining who the bad guys were, a strange preface to the first and last de Antonio film to appear on network television.[33]

Yet despite the immediate and continuing success of *Point of Order*, critics have been largely silent in regard to the film's relationship to the documentary tradition. No precedent seemed to exist for an historical documentary based on television footage and devoid of narration. Some critics inexplicably suggested that it "may not strictly be defined as a film," as *Variety* did when the film first appeared—de Antonio claimed that the New York Film Festival even rejected it on this ground.[34] But even if *Point of Order* stood outside the mainstream of past and present documentary, it was not sui generis.

Out of Synch

Point of Order must have seemed far from the cutting edge of nonfiction filmmaking in the sixties. Equipped with the latest breakthroughs in lightweight camera and sound technology, documentary filmmakers were creating exciting new forms of non-fiction cinema: cinéma vérité (film truth) and direct cinema, two distinct styles that looked the same to most audiences—candid, energetic, and as seemingly objective as a fly on the wall.[35] Viewers could follow John F. Kennedy behind the scenes in *Primary* (Robert Drew Associates, 1960), share in casual interviews with Parisians in *Chronicle of a Summer* (Jean Rouch and Edgar Morin, 1961), and wait backstage on Broadway with Jane Fonda in *Jane* (Robert Drew Associates, 1962). Yet de Antonio had no interest in this increasingly fashionable style of documentary filmmaking. Whether it was the celebrated work of Richard Leacock, David and Albert Maysles, D. A. Pennebaker, or what he later called the "watery stew" of Frederick Wiseman, de Antonio dismissed it all as "a childish assumption about the nature of film" that cloaked the filmmaker's political biases behind the supposedly unmediated gaze of the camera.[36]

Some, though not all, of these filmmakers were making extravagant claims to objectivity: "The film maker's personality is in no way directly involved in directing the action," said Robert Drew, while Richard Leacock asserted that "we were simply observers."[37] De Antonio was never simply an observer and doubted whether such a thing could exist. "Among the angelic orders," he said in mockery, "films are made by purple butterflies with cameras screwed into their gossamer wings, catching every iridescent jagger and flicker." For him film was "tug, pull, conflict, process"—an echo of Brecht's views on theater—and de Antonio expected an honest film to reflect this process on the screen without the veil of naturalism in direct cinema.[38]

This rift between de Antonio and his contemporaries was part of a larger divide in documentary practice, one that Thomas Waugh has noted. Contrasting *Point of Order* with Leacock's *Happy Mothers' Day*, also released in 1963, Waugh argues that these very different films offer a "strikingly clear paradigm of the twofold direction" open to documentary filmmakers in the 1960s: collage versus improvisation, thesis versus poesis, the probing of meanings versus the celebration of surfaces. Leacock's film about the local response to the birth of quintuplets in a South Dakota town is, Waugh says, "pure poesis, a cinema of great intimacy yet of almost baroque stylization. . . . [It] expresses its eloquent despair in the lyrical-populist Flahertian tradition: it sees the ultimate betrayal of the American ideal in ordinary townspeople, but rejoices in the equanimity and grace of the babies' mother." By contrast, de Antonio's film is in the vein of Eisenstein, "localizing the object of his despair at the very seat of power," with McCarthy, his cronies, and even his opponents coming across as "the personifications of a corrupt and oppressive system, just as his Soviet predecessor saw the Tsarist officers, the ineffectual Kerensky, and the fat kulaks and priests as embodiments of reaction."[39]

Most 1960s documentarians would choose to follow Leacock's model, and the result was a flowering of cinema verité, from which de Antonio kept his distance, remaining something of an iconoclast at least until the early seventies. Although he was at odds with many of his contemporaries, he could find like-minded political artists in an earlier era of filmmaking. For this reason *Point of Order* has been described as the first sign of a revival of radical film in the United States, although no one agrees on what was being revived.[40] The film scholar David James suggests a connection between de Antonio and the populist working-class films produced in New York in the thirties by the Workers Film and Photo League, Nykino, or Joris Ivens's Frontier Films.[41] Indeed, de Antonio shared the independent production and left-leaning politics of these groups, although his patience with collectivism and populism in both theory and practice would prove to be notoriously thin. Neither for nor about the working class, his films were addressed primarily to an elite audience of liberal urban intellectuals and college students, those middle-class souls who had the time, money, and education to frequent an alternative movie house. So perhaps a more important antecedent for the technique of *Point of Order* can be located in the work of the Soviet filmmaker Esfir Shub, who "had a comparable sense of the primary role of the film document as a raw material of historical

research," as Waugh puts it.[42] Though little known in the early
1960s, Shub figures prominently in Jay Leyda's *Film Beget Film*,
published in the same year that *Point of Order* was released. A
perceptive reader of the 1964 book might have recognized the
similarities between de Antonio and Shub, whom Leyda paints
as the towering figure of what he calls "the compilation film."
In films such as *The Fall of the Romanov Dynasty* (1927) Shub
reconstructed Soviet history from bits and pieces of newsreels,
home movies, and any other old footage she could locate.[43] This
method of constructing films was, as Shub's colleague Sergei
Eisenstein noted, "most suitable for the expression of ideologically
pointed theses," which may have been why de Antonio was drawn
to the form.[44]

But in 1964 he had not yet seen Shub's ingenious films, whose
pro-Soviet sentiment had made them unwelcome in the eyes of
U.S. Customs officials since their release three decades earlier.
Despite such obstacles, Shub's work had shaped the direction
taken by many U.S. documentarians. In the 1930s, for example,
she had a great influence on leftist filmmakers who cannibalized
newsreel footage and assembled it into new sequences with radical
implications—the essential idea behind *Point of Order*. Unfortunately, this brand of radical filmmaking became increasingly
difficult to finance or produce without harassment during World
War II and the ensuing intolerance of dissent that marked the
McCarthy era. Yet Shub's influence continued throughout this
era in an unlikely setting—in mainstream documentaries, such as
the monthly examination of current events known as *The March
of Time* (1935–1951), and in indoctrination films such as *Why We
Fight* (1942–1945), to name two examples that the film historian
Jack Ellis has suggested.[45] Later, this style of making movies from
archival footage would become a mainstay of historical documentaries on television in series such as *Victory at Sea* (1952–1953)
and *The Twentieth Century* (1957–1964).[46]

Unlike the "ideologically pointed theses" of Shub's or de
Antonio's films, commercial documentaries had little incentive
to engage in serious critiques of historical and political issues,

let alone something as controversial as McCarthyism. Only a few television programs had attacked the issue with any real energy before *Point of Order*, most notably Edward R. Murrow's trenchant "Report on Senator McCarthy" (1954) in the *See It Now* series. But Murrow was an uncommon journalist, and when CBS canceled his controversial program in favor of game shows and Westerns in 1958, Murrow's brand of independence became a thing of the past.[47] From then on, the networks kept their documentarians on a relatively short leash when covering political and historical subjects, and even the style of the filmmaking, especially the reliance upon the omniscient narration that so annoyed de Antonio, seemed to reflect this authoritarian atmosphere. With few exceptions, such as David Lowe's *Harvest of Shame* (1960), which Murrow narrated, television documentaries on political and historical subjects were beholden to official sources and had become "institutionalized, de-personalized" by the early 1960s, as the film historian Erik Barnouw has written.[48] Documentary had lost its bite.

Then along came the personal and political *Point of Order*, reviving the radical spirit of Soviet filmmakers such as Shub and the American documentarians of the thirties, carving something worth knowing out of the information overload of television culture.[49] This film makes a powerful statement about the effusion of images that comprises the public conception of recent U.S. history. "More people in the last 60 years have seen more different images on any one day," de Antonio complained, "than all the images seen by the people of the world in all preceding time."[50] De Antonio's culling of this material—the compilation technique of *Point of Order*—has deep significance in the early years of an era marked by "the disappearance of history," as Fredric Jameson has observed about the postmodern condition that afflicts Western capitalist economies. "Our entire contemporary social system has little by little begun to lose its capacity to retain its own past," Jameson writes, and "has begun to live in a perpetual present and in a perpetual change that obliterates traditions."

By making a compilation documentary from the television

record, de Antonio was in the uncommon position of actively resisting this trend by *re*presenting the past with an intelligence and independence not often found in the documentaries of the entertainment industry.[51] Even Roy Cohn, who sat twice through *Point of Order*, was painfully aware of its power as "an important myth-making factor" in the public perception of McCarthy's legacy. *Point of Order* made "McCarthy [come] through as the heavy villain, and I as his apprentice in the black arts—seeking to destroy everything from mere reputations to the armed forces of the nation," Cohn wrote, perhaps with a recollection of what McCarthy had once told him during a break in the hearings: "People aren't going to remember the things we say on the issues here. They're only going to remember the impressions," which for many viewers in the 1960s were filtered through the eyes of an upper-class Marxist like de Antonio.[52]

Media theorists as disparate as Noam Chomsky and Jean Baudrillard have taken issue with this optimistic brand of Brechtian resistance to the culture industry of television and Hollywood. For example, Chomsky reveals the ideological biases in a medium that has less interest in truth than in "manufacturing consent," a phrase he borrows from Walter Lippmann. This leaves little room for the alternative views that de Antonio began to offer with *Point of Order*. Although Chomsky himself actively supported de Antonio's later films, a sign that he believed in their potential to encourage change, his nearly conspiratorial conception of the media offers little hope to an underfunded independent filmmaker seeking to foster a democratic dialogue.

An even gloomier picture emerges from the work of Baudrillard, the skeptical postmodern theorist who doubts the efficacy of establishing an "anti-media" in the sense of both Brecht's and, by extension, de Antonio's work. If the media is "nothing else than a marvellous instrument for destabilizing the real and the true, all historical or political truth," as Baudrillard suggests, it can be neither the basis nor the forum for meaningful resistance. In other words, no matter how brilliantly and passionately constructed, *Point of Order* could never be more than another reflection of the simulation of reality that television and cinema produce. Baudrillard goes so far as to suggest that the most radical response to the media may be silence, which leads to the appalling notion that de Antonio would have been more subversive if he had avoided filmmaking altogether and stayed at home with a good bottle of wine (something he often did anyhow). Pessimistic in the extreme and insufferable to an optimistic Marxist such as de Antonio, Baudrillard's analysis throws the gauntlet down before political art in general, forcing it to defend its ability to convey alternative points of view to an audience in any meaningful fashion. The challenge is not easily met without a leap of radical faith, one that de Antonio was willing to make, as was evident in his decision to continue making films for almost three decades. In his willingness to fight, de Antonio took a position closer to one that the journalist Christopher Hitchens has articulated. Encapsulating the views of numerous media critics, Hitchens asks: "Might it not make sense to regard the mass communications industry as an area of contestation, in which the ruling class naturally holds most of the cards, but no definitively or universally predictable result can be arranged?"[53]

Compilation documentary allowed de Antonio to make the best of the cards he had been dealt, taking what the culture industry had cast off as worthless and putting it to progressive ends. In the "area of contestation" between conflicting representations of political reality, he would continue to rely on compilation as his primary weapon, even though he never made another true compilation film after *Point of Order*, something few critics have pointed out in their rush to categorize his style of filmmaking. His subsequent films blended archival footage with specially conducted interviews, creating a dialectic between past and present, and making him "the unique master of a compilation genre that he created and can call his own," as the film scholar Richard Barsam has observed.[54] De Antonio's later films would often be more complex, more compelling, more radical, but the elegantly simple idea behind *Point of Order* would remain at the heart of his filmmaking practice.

3

◄○►

Rush to Judgment
Genealogy of an Assassination

Prologue

"Oh, De, Jack Kennedy's been shot," said Andy Warhol on the telephone.

De Antonio was sitting in Jasper Johns's apartment, recuperating after knee surgery and not in the mood for practical jokes. He muttered something uncomplimentary into the phone and hung up.

Just in case, though, he hobbled over to the radio—Johns's apartment did not have a television—where he heard the news from Dallas. De Antonio rarely watched television, but on this occasion he asked a friend to bring over a portable so he could see the news coverage.

Not many of those watching had known Kennedy as he had. During his freshman year at Harvard he had shot billiards with a young man he remembered as "handsome, charming, vapid." He compared him unfavorably to the older brother, Joseph Kennedy, Jr., whom he knew slightly better. Nothing seemed to foreshadow his classmate's political success, except perhaps his ability to line up sufficient quantities of beer and singers for social events.[1]

During the two decades of Kennedy's political ascent, de Antonio remained skeptical. Even when Kennedy was elected president, de Antonio watched with a raised eyebrow. Unlike those who were intoxicated by the Kennedy mystique, de Antonio could only scoff at the desire to conceive of the Kennedy administration as a Camelot of any sort. Kennedy received faint admiration from de Antonio in one regard: he seemed more pragmatic, more flexible than a president driven by genuine ideals. Although de Antonio might find such qualities attractive in his friends or even himself, he saw idealism as a presidential liability because it led to moral certainty and intolerance of dissenting opinions such as his.[2]

Although he never perceived these traits in Kennedy, he saw them in the words and deeds of the investigators of the president's death. The readiness with which the news media accepted the lone assassin theory, even in the face of potentially conflicting evidence, was a particular source of concern. De Antonio resented what he considered to be the oversimplification of the events surrounding the assassination, especially the conviction of the Dallas Police Department, the FBI, and the Warren Commission that their case against Lee Harvey Oswald was unquestionable, that an ongoing public discussion of the available evidence was superfluous. One more sign of the failure of democratic capitalism, he thought, as he observed how "the police have become a law unto themselves."[3] In the weeks after the assassination de Antonio's doubts remained deep but unfocused, beginning to crystallize only when he attended a lecture by a lawyer named Mark Lane in January 1964.

Lane was just thirty-seven, though already a well-known New York defense attorney who had represented many civil rights demonstrators. He was arrested as a freedom rider in Mississippi soon after being elected as a reform Democrat to the New York legislature in 1960. His victory was due in no small part to the support of then-presidential candidate Kennedy, who was photographed next to the beaming attorney.[4]

In the weeks after the death of his political benefactor, Lane followed the media coverage with a lawyer's eye for detail. Yet he did not need a law degree to realize that much of the country was overlooking an obvious constitutional fact: the presumption of innocence for the accused until proved guilty. With the death of Oswald at the gun of club owner Jack Ruby, the nation had been deprived of a trial in which to hear evidence that did not support the "lone gunman theory" or in any way mitigated the charges against Oswald.[5]

Nor was the media interested in providing a forum for discussing both sides of the case. With the belief that "most Americans did not even want to listen to any theories that contradicted" the official story, the U.S. media unfailingly promoted the lone gunman theory in the months after the event.[6] Yet doubters emerged at the margins of public discourse almost immediately, questioning the work of the journalists, FBI agents, and other experts charged with explaining the crime. Books and articles gradually appeared by Thomas G. Buchanan, Edward J. Epstein, Penn Jones, Jr., Sylvia Meagher, Leo Sauvage, Josiah Thompson, and Harold Weisberg, as well as Lane. Lane was one of the earliest and most vocal critics of the point of view that came to be associated with the Warren Commission, the investigatory body created by Lyndon B. Johnson on November 29, 1963.[7]

When the Warren Commission began its investigation, so did Lane. By December 1963 he was at work on a document that in effect was a legal brief for Lee Harvey Oswald. After offering the article to the *Nation* and other mainstream liberal publications, all of which rejected such a controversial piece, Lane published it in the leftist *National Guardian* on December 19, 1963. Under the title "Lane's Defense Brief for Oswald," he began to present the case he might have made for Oswald, had he lived.

One person who read the article was Marguerite Oswald, the mother of the accused, who asked the lawyer to represent her son's interests before the Warren Commission. Her decision prompted FBI director J. Edgar Hoover to disparage Lane as someone "that anyone would not have retained if they were serious in trying to get down to the facts." Hoover even attributed the move to Mrs. Oswald's "emotional instability."[8] Nonetheless, the Warren Commission asked Lane to testify on two occasions, though it did not allow him to represent Oswald formally because an "impartial fact-finding agency," unlike a court of law, had no need for a "defense counsel."[9]

Marguerite Oswald, Lee Harvey Oswald's mother, in a still from *Rush to Judgment* (Judgment Films, 1967). Courtesy Wisconsin Center for Film and Theater Research.

During this extraordinary period of his life Lane came to know de Antonio, whom he had recently heard on the radio discussing the pending release of his film, *Point of Order*. In January 1964 Lane was giving almost nightly lectures on the assassination, one of which de Antonio attended. He contacted Lane the next day and over a sandwich and a drink explained his idea to film Lane's "brief for the defense." De Antonio made a convincing case, arguing that a film would give permanence and a wider audience to Lane's views, which the lawyer was gradually fashioning into a book. Even the French writer Émile Zola, de Antonio proclaimed, would have used film for his defense of Dreyfus had the technology been available.[10] Lane was in complete agreement. A film would have to be made but only after three conditions had been met: publication of the Warren Commission's report, publication of Lane's book, and the arrangement of financial backing for the film.[11]

Almost two years would pass before all three conditions were satisfied, but both principals used the time well. Lane finished his manuscript and after many rejections from American publishing houses found a willing publisher in the small and prestigious English firm, the Bodley Head. His book would appear in 1966 under the title *Rush to Judgment*, a phrase from Lord Chancellor Thomas Erskine in defense of the alleged assassin of King George III: "An attack upon the king is considered to be parricide against the state, and the jury and witnesses, and even the judges, are the children. It is fit, on that account, that there should be a solemn pause before we rush to judgment."[12]

Forced by circumstances to endure their own solemn pause, de Antonio and Lane benefited from the passage of time, gaining a modicum of historical perspective that hastier opinions lacked. Unlike reporters who seemed to require only one day after the publication of the twenty-six volumes of hearings by the Warren Commission to vouch for its conclusions, Lane closely studied the volumes for months. At the same time de Antonio became involved in two separate film projects that contributed directly to his ability to make *Rush to Judgment* into a film.

Two Detours: New York Politics and Bertrand Russell

The first project was a fifty-minute documentary about the New York City mayoral election of 1965. The idea was born during lunch at the Four Seasons Hotel in New York City when Marian Javits, wife of U.S. Senator Jacob Javits, introduced de Antonio to the BBC producer David Webster. Because of *Point of Order*'s success and de Antonio's familiarity with New York City, Webster wanted him on the as-yet-unnamed project. De Antonio liked the idea, especially because he needed a crash course in the numerous aspects of film production that he had not encountered in the making of *Point of Order*. For the first time he would work with a film crew in the field, shooting events as they happened, hoping to catch the mood in the streets and "to acquaint a then staid British audience with the hype and jazz of an American mayoral campaign."

Webster occasionally dropped by to check on the film's progress, but for the most part de Antonio was given a free rein with a very professional BBC crew—so professional, he thought, that they "never missed a point and were totally without imagination or drive."[13] With elitism undercutting his egalitarian instincts, de Antonio saw the crew as lower-class working stiffs, more interested in pensions than the political vision of their director, who wanted something "freeswinging and extremely difficult." Possessed by a mixture of inexperience and ambition, de Antonio wanted the crew to capture nothing less than the failure of democratic politics in America.[14]

The raw material was extraordinary. Throughout the summer of 1965 he shot interviews with candidates and observers: John Lindsay, Abraham Beame, William F. Buckley, Jr., Daniel Patrick Moynihan, Robert Kennedy, and Sammy Davis, Jr. Ambivalent, even skeptical about these individuals, de Antonio does not show them in the most flattering light. Interviewed in the living room of de Antonio's apartment, Moynihan struck the filmmaker as "fake and garrulous and witty and articulate." Kennedy did not come across much better; his reluctant support of Beame seems to foreshadow the opportunism he exhibited in de Antonio's later film about the 1968 presidential campaign, *America Is Hard to See*. The most bitter irony underlies the scene with the popular singer Sammy Davis, Jr., whose active support of a Republican candidate such as Lindsay was thought by some to be at odds with his Harlem roots. De Antonio caught the singer asking the musical question, "What Kind of Fool Am I?" at a Lindsay rally.[15]

After de Antonio and his crew captured these pithy images, the responsibility for the final shape of the film shifted to BBC editors in London. Disturbed by the possibility that some faceless bureaucrats would ruin his work, de Antonio scrawled a twenty-three-page letter explaining how he would edit the film. This letter, combined with the sheer mass of material shot by his crew, led the BBC to invite him to England in November 1965 to supervise the editing.[16] Now he could impose his personal style on the finished product, rather than allow the BBC to add its somber narration, which he despised for "explaining what is visually obvious." As he wrote in his lengthy plea: "It's my belief that using non-synch pix/track makes viewer focus/listen more attentively," meaning that he relished the tension created by the difference between what we hear and what we see—even at the risk of confusing the audience.[17] Epic theater in the Brechtian sense, this technique is supposed to startle the viewer into thinking about the subject critically, especially in the absence of a voice-over narrator.

By allowing de Antonio in the editing room, the BBC was sanctioning a more daring film. One shot showed candidate Lindsay handing a Coney Island hot dog to the camera, breaking the dramatic "third wall" and reminding the viewer of the film crew's presence—the sort of filmmaker-subject interaction reminiscent of *Primary* (1960), the Drew Associates cinema verité examination of John F. Kennedy and Hubert Humphrey's battle for the Democratic presidential nomination.[18] De Antonio made the film his own—ironic, complex, shorn of narration—but the BBC rejected his working titles (*Running to Win 1965* and *The Mayor of New York*) in favor of *That's Where the Action Is*. The title made him cringe, but he was pleased with the final product.

The film was not without problems. Writing more than a decade after the release of the film, Thomas Waugh criticized it for avoiding hard questions about urban decay and choosing instead to accept the sociological platitudes of Moynihan.[19] And as a critique of politics in the television age, the film left something to be desired and was far from the thought-provoking epic theater that it might have been. Though de Antonio includes political advertisements as an ironic commentary on the selling of candidates, his own film is susceptible to the pitfalls of "video politics." The most charismatic of the candidates, Lindsay, comes out of the film unscathed, as Waugh points out, because of photogenic qualities that even de Antonio could not undermine. *That's Where the*

Action Is was "a modest and promising second film," in which de Antonio began to develop a new style of filmmaking, which Waugh calls "the document-dossier" approach for its combination of interviews and explanatory footage. This style would form the heart of *Rush to Judgment* and greatly influence his subsequent films.[20]

While in London overseeing the editing of *That's Where the Action Is*, de Antonio had not forgotten about his plans for *Rush to Judgment*. Though he reserved a sufficient amount of time for social occasions involving "the beautiful long-legged English girls and the middle-aged American film person," he was also busy looking for someone to bankroll the film. Mark Lane was also in London, and working together they soon caught one pigeon who invested $10,000—an heir to the Buster Brown shoe fortune named Richard Stark. However, the real boon came from Lane's friendship with Ralph Schoenman, secretary of the Bertrand Russell Peace Foundation, who seemed to promise "free space and access to money" for their critique of the Warren report.[21]

Schoenman was a mixed blessing. That he was sympathetic to de Antonio and Lane's objectives was apparent as the three men walked the fashionable streets of Chelsea, plotting revolution and the film version of *Rush to Judgment*. But Schoenman also ran the foundation like "his private fiefdom," distributing "directorships and money and jobs with a mad hand," as de Antonio recalled. Despite this officiousness, Schoenman did de Antonio the favor of introducing him to Lord Russell, an encounter that brought about a second detour from *Rush to Judgment*.[22]

On an autumn afternoon in 1965 the entourage of de Antonio, Lane, and Schoenman "solemnly trooped to 34 Hasker Street to meet Lord Russell" at his London home. Then in his nineties, Russell came as close as anyone to receiving de Antonio's unqualified admiration, especially for the political opinions and activism that kept the philosopher embroiled in controversy. Russell had denounced the Warren report as well as U.S. involvement in Vietnam, for which he was rewarded with subtle allusions to senility in the English press. As if to counter such charges, de Antonio described Lord Russell as especially "keen and bright," his lucidity unquestionable. Undoubtedly, de Antonio was genuinely charmed by the eminent man, as he was by many English aristocrats with whom he maintained close friendships. On this afternoon in London de Antonio sat and listened to Russell "as his dry and passionate talk devoured the afternoon," just as T. S. Eliot had written a half century earlier after meeting the philosopher. If Russell's charm and wit were not enough to win over the filmmaker, he flattered de Antonio by mentioning how much he had enjoyed *Point of Order* on British television.[23]

On the basis of this sudden rapport between the two men, Russell invited the filmmaker to join the board of directors of the foundation. Lane was also asked, and soon the names of both were added to the short list of luminaries on the foundation's letterhead. Still, this was not the only reason for de Antonio's afternoon visit. He had in mind an unusual question for Lord Russell, one he could conceive of asking no one else: could he film his obituary while he was still living? Always keen to an irreverent idea, Russell agreed enthusiastically. The foundation and Lane's friend Stark agreed to put up the money, and they arranged for the filmmaker to spend three weeks at Russell's home in Wales in an effort to make a short documentary.[24]

De Antonio's idea was to attempt a portrait of an intellectual, a nonconformist, a peer who sought social change. Convinced that "filmmakers are generally numbskulls," de Antonio saw the venture as an ideal opportunity to display his uncommon combination of general erudition and filmmaking ability. But numbskulls, on whom he was dependent to make the film, began to appear almost immediately. The first was a member of his crew, a cameraman unstable both in temperament and in his ability to operate his equipment without wobbling.[25] And then de Antonio had to deal with the strong personalities of Schoenman and Lane. "The insane intrusion of Ralph Schoenman and the egotistical madness of Mark Lane prevented any of it from looking like anything other than Lane and Schoenman mugging on camera with Russell," de Antonio complained in his journal. As a consequence, what could have been a remarkable short film was reduced to a fiasco. Driven by what de Antonio called "that crazy hardline mad Marxism which produces nothing at all except hate and ego trips," Schoenman repeatedly diverted the interview to the question of the American torture of Vietnamese peasants. However, judging from the strange sixty-page transcript of the interview on November 22, 1965, de Antonio also asked questions about the American atrocities in Vietnam—though mostly he inquired about Russell's memories of Cambridge, his political courage, his views on A. J. Ayer, T. S. Eliot, and William Blake. De Antonio's dissatisfaction with the interview owed to his lack of control over the proceedings, for Lane and Schoenman asked the majority of the questions and Schoenman even offered answers for Russell, when the old philosopher's were not promptly forthcoming.[26]

Returning with the film to New York, de Antonio viewed the results with bitter disappointment. Unable to make the film he had envisioned, he decided to abandon the footage to Russell's foundation with the assurance that his name not appear on any future project that might use the material.[27] Professionally and personally, the experience was painful, and he recalled it as "the hardest thing I've ever done," his most profound failure. Slightly more than a year later, on November 29, 1966, he wrote to Russell, resigning from the foundation's board of directors because of Schoenman's mismanagement. Russell responded coldly, not at all pleased to hear the criticism, even though he was fully aware of his secretary's shortcomings.[28] Schoenman had been relieved of his secretarial duties in late 1966, a fact not made public until 1970 when an underground newspaper posthumously published Russell's "Private Memorandum Concerning Ralph Schoenman." In this memorandum Russell quotes from de Antonio's resignation letter to corroborate his own dissatisfaction with his secretary, though he does not use the filmmaker's name.[29]

Despite the acrimonious ending to his brief acquaintance with Lord Russell, de Antonio had laid the foundation for *Rush to Judgment* during his time in England. Stark, who joined the crew as assistant director, contributed $10,000, as he had promised. Valuable archival footage had been acquired from Visnews, an

English company. More important, de Antonio and Lane had nourished their contacts in London art circles. Lane claimed that Paul McCartney agreed to write a score for the film because " 'one day my children are going to ask me what I did with my life, and I cannot just answer that I was a Beatle,' " though nothing came of the promise.[30] A more tangible contribution, $30,000, came from Oscar Lewenstein, the producer of such films as *Tom Jones* and *Mademoiselle*, the playwrights John Osborne and John Arden, and the director Tony Richardson.[31] Some invested for reasons of conscience, others for the business opportunity. Finishing the deal with a drink at the Algonquin Hotel in New York, Richardson told de Antonio that he thought Oswald was "guilty as charged, but I think your idea is very commercial." If he was being ironic, the effect was lost on de Antonio.[32]

However, $30,000 was not enough to make the film, and de Antonio went about setting up a second corporation for the film, this one based in the United States. Through the financial support of sixteen individuals such as Anne Peretz, Peter Weiss, Harold Hochschild, and Robert Boehm, he raised an additional $45,000, bringing the final budget of the film to $75,000.[33] Finally, with money in the bank, de Antonio and Lane began to plan the film in earnest.

Making *Rush to Judgment*

On March 10, 1966, de Antonio flew alone to Dallas. In two weeks he acquired archival footage from WFAA-TV, a local television station, and arranged interviews with nearly twenty witnesses to the events surrounding the assassination.[34] Upon his return to New York he hired an inexpensive three-man film crew from San Francisco that would meet him and Lane in Dallas. Operating on a tight budget, de Antonio and Lane rented a car and drove to Texas in thirty-four hours, despite a wrong turn that sent them through Chicago.[35]

Once in Dallas they moved into the Tower Motel, not far from downtown. Lane had decided to use the pseudonym Robert

Mark Lane and Emile de Antonio during production of *Rush to Judgment* (Judgment Films, 1967). Courtesy Wisconsin Center for Film and Theater Research.

Blake while in Texas, even though his book had not yet come out. Already his name had achieved a degree of notoriety that he feared would arouse the suspicion of local authorities. This was more than mere paranoia: as early as June 1964 Lane had been added to the "lookout book" used at airports to notify the FBI of the whereabouts of certain individuals.[36] For the trip to Texas Lane had even suggested a disguise of fake hair and special glasses, which de Antonio considered silly and unnecessary, except to Lane's overdeveloped sense of theater.[37]

Yet even de Antonio was worried. He remembered a "physical fear of a sustained order" during the filming, especially after

locating Domingo Benavides, the closest eyewitness to the shooting of officer J. D. Tippet.[38] An interview was arranged for the
following day, and Benavides was promised $100 to compensate
him for the loss of a day's wages. That night the Dallas police
paid a visit to the Tower Motel. The detectives, who wore civilian
clothes and ten-gallon hats, inquired about Robert Blake and
wanted to know why "Blake offered that Mexican boy $100."
After unsettling everyone and conveying the impression that the
filmmakers were not welcome in Dallas, the detectives left. Only
de Antonio's persuasive if dubious arguments—"We're safer here
than we'd be flying home, because if they kill us here it would be
an obvious confession that there's something crazy going on"—
prevented the crew from quitting on the spot.[39] Just to be safe,
they decided to move to a hotel outside the city limits. And the
interview with Benavides never took place. He disappeared until
the filmmakers had left Texas.[40]

A low level of harassment continued throughout the shooting
in March and April. Local police would stop their cars and watch
the filmmakers conduct an interview, sometimes asking questions
that seemed motivated by more than idle curiosity. In this atmosphere the young and inexperienced film crew was nervous, so
when a truck backfired during an interview with one witness, the
sound technician fell to the ground, thinking it gunfire.

Strange occurrences, at least from the vantage of the filmmakers, seemed to plague the film. Interviews would be arranged, then
canceled for no reason. When pressed for an explanation, one
woman explained that she risked losing her job, that her supervisor told her that "if I say anything more about this, I've had it."[41]
Another witness agreed to the interview, only to back out while the
filmmakers were setting up their equipment.[42] De Antonio blamed
the FBI for "short-circuiting" the project whenever it could.
Indeed, FBI memoranda reveal that agents had been alerted to
the presence of the filmmakers in Dallas. However, no available
evidence supports de Antonio's assertion of FBI involvement,
which is richly documented in regard to his later films.[43]

Despite the problems, the trip to Dallas was a success. Before de Antonio and Lane returned to New York in May, they filmed more than twenty interviews, some with witnesses that the Warren Commission could not locate. De Antonio still needed archival footage, and as was often the case when he turned to the television networks for assistance, he was disappointed. Virginia Dillard, a film librarian at CBS, called him with the offer of some footage, including outtakes from a documentary on the Warren Commission. De Antonio expressed interest and set up an appointment to view the material that evening. The network would not let anyone examine footage alone, so from 6 P.M. until midnight de Antonio sat in front of a projector with a network employee, screening what he considered to be extraordinary footage. De Antonio believed it revealed how selective CBS had been with its evidence in order to support the Warren Commission's conclusions. Excited by what he saw, de Antonio signed a preliminary contract ordering specific sections of the footage and went home. The next day Dillard called, claiming to have made a terrible mistake. Not only was the footage not for sale but it was going to be destroyed.[44]

CBS broke the preliminary contract, de Antonio believed, because of his political orientation. The radical film collective Newsreel, he was told, experienced similar problems with the networks. If he had had more time, he might have pursued his legal options, as he was never reluctant to do. Instead he consoled himself with an outraged letter to the vice president of CBS News, who responded by saying that the network never sold such footage—even though de Antonio had paid $50,000 to CBS for exactly this sort of footage to make *Point of Order*.[45]

In view of such censorial tactics on the part of television networks, as well as his difficulties in Dallas, one can see how de Antonio came to view bureaucracies in a Kafkaesque light. These sorts of experiences gave substance to de Antonio's mildly paranoid political instincts, which led him to believe that U.S. institutions, such as law enforcement in the case of Kennedy's death, would willingly suppress evidence for political ends.

This view might have been alleviated somewhat had members of the establishment agreed to be interviewed. However, no one on the Dallas police force would speak to the filmmakers. De Antonio and Lane sent invitations to President Johnson as well as Chief Justice Earl Warren and members of his commission, such as former CIA director Allen Dulles and then-Representative Gerald R. Ford. Those who responded did so in the negative, which, according to one writer, was exactly what Lane and de Antonio wanted.[46] David W. Belin, junior counsel to the Warren Commission, received a letter in August offering him the opportunity for a rebuttal, "with the understanding that anything you say on camera will be used intact without cuts, additions, or deletions on our part."

But Belin viewed Lane's work as a "sham" and a "shrewd concoction of specious arguments based on misrepresentations of the overall record." He decided to agree to the interview and claims to have written nine letters stating his willingness to appear on film. His first eight letters produced nothing more than a belated postcard from de Antonio, and in the end Lane rescinded the offer. Even two decades later Belin remained distressed that he was unable to counter the "deception and misrepresentation that permeates the film production" of *Rush to Judgment*, though he does not mention specific charges or that the film was an indirect criticism of his own abilities and integrity.[47]

The summer of 1966 brought good news. In August Lane's book was published and swiftly became the number-one best-selling book that year in hardcover and the subsequent year in a paperback edition. Nothing if not grandiose, Lane wrote: "The American people had spoken by the millions," and de Antonio observed that it "sold as no anti-establishment book has ever sold." Norman Mailer hailed the work as "a classic" and the *New York Times* was equally positive. Moreover, public opinion was shifting away from the conclusions of the Warren Commission. According to a Harris poll on October 2, 1966, those surveyed rejected the "lone gunman theory" by a 3-to-2 margin. Only 1 in 3 had complete faith in the Warren report. Surely these developments would benefit the film, which was in the editing stage during the autumn of 1966.[48]

Unfortunately, de Antonio's relationship with Lane was beginning to erode. Lane's involvement with the editing was limited to occasionally stopping by the Movielab building at 619 West 54th Street for a cup of coffee, which left the work to de Antonio and his editor, Daniel Drasin, who had made the short film *Sunday*, which de Antonio had distributed.[49] As usual, money was also a problem. De Antonio and Lane had agreed to pay themselves $150 a week, but when this did not go very far, de Antonio secretly took $3,000 from the company as a bonus for raising the money in the first place. They were also throwing parties at the Chelsea Hotel as a business expense, not unlike the Hollywood filmmakers de Antonio so despised. For his part Lane had put his father on the company payroll as an accountant, which the old man was, though not a very good one, according to de Antonio.[50] Despite such squabbles, the film was finished in November 1966 and within a month they had found a distributor, Impact Films, for worldwide release.

Reading *Rush to Judgment*

On its surface *Rush to Judgment* is an unusually straightforward film in which we watch Lane drill holes in the Warren report. We listen to his observations and interviews with witnesses to the assassination, which the film then contrasts with readings from the text of the report and the film record as reflected in television news footage. Yet this simple structure effectively creates two texts and two levels of history. The first exists in the Warren report and is populated by an assassin named Lee Harvey Oswald, concerned members of the Dallas Police Department, and a trail of indisputable facts. The second text, based on Lane's book, offers a counterpoint to the first. It is populated by uncalled witnesses, strange coincidences, and uncertain conclusions.

The basic strategy of the film is to subtly mock the Warren report for its dead certainty about the events of November 22, 1963, making the testimony of Lane and his witnesses seem eminently reasonable in contrast. None of them claims to know what happened, none of them suggests conspiracy theories, even if the ominous tenor of the testimony does not preclude such thoughts. The witnesses share a common perspective, if only one of befuddlement. Unlike those giving the conflicting testimony in Errol Morris's documentary investigation of another, lesser-known Texas murder, *The Thin Blue Line* (1987), Lane and de Antonio's interviewees do not disagree with one another. Rather than multiple versions of the past proffered in *The Thin Blue Line* or in Akira Kurosawa's fiction film, *Rashomon* (1950), *Rush to Judgment* offers no specific version of the past except a refutation of the Warren Commission's. Thus instead of an historical narrative, the film possesses characteristics of what Michel Foucault calls a genealogy.

Embraced as a postmodern form of writing history, Foucault's concept of genealogy does not attempt to build a conventional account of what happened in the past, the sort of narrative at the core of most documentary films. Instead it focuses on "disqualified, illegitimate" knowledge from excluded or marginalized sources, such as the witnesses ignored by the Warren Commission. Lane and de Antonio used these sources to counter "the claims of a unitary body of theory which would filter, hierarchise, and order" (such as the Warren report) by examining "the singularity of surface events . . . small details, minor shifts and subtle contours," such as the remembrances of where someone stood, where they thought a puff of smoke appeared, and what they observed in a moment of crisis.[51]

"Genealogy is gray, meticulous, and patiently documentary," writes Foucault—and a better description of *Rush to Judgment* could hardly be made, though the film flirts with a genealogical sensibility rather than embracing it wholeheartedly.[52] When it reveals the contradictions and assumptions of the Warren report, *Rush to Judgment* suits Foucault's essentially deconstructive analysis. However, when it searches for a pattern in which to situate the events, if only by implication, it does not mesh with Foucault's notion of genealogy, which ignores hidden significances and totalizing theories of any sort. When, for example, newspaper editor Penn Jones provides a litany of strange deaths that have befallen various witnesses, one cannot help but think in terms of conspiracy theory. Although neither Jones nor anyone else in the film mentions a conspiracy, the film conveys a way of seeing the assassination in an unmistakably conspiratorial light. For example, as Lane solemnly reads between the lines of the Warren report, interpreting it like a Talmudic scholar, he fosters in the audience the suspicion that every errant detail in the investigation can be traced to malevolence. As a consequence the film gradually becomes a kind of mystery in which, despite Lane's resemblance to television attorney Perry Mason, the guilty party is never identified. Although mysteries are supposed to end with accusations and confessions, *Rush to Judgment* ends enigmatically, with Penn Jones gazing seriously into the camera and speaking with foreboding: "I think that all of us who love our country should be alerted that something is wrong in the land." His image slowly fades to black, the film seems to be over, but suddenly on screen is the district attorney for Dallas, Henry Wade. As he did in the first shot of the film, Wade spells the name of the accused for the benefit of reporters. This time "O-S-W-A-L-D" takes on a different significance than the benign clarification it seemed at first. If the film has hit its mark, it has embedded ambiguity in the viewer's mind.

To create this ambiguity the film uses several levels of persuasion, including one that is embedded in a style de Antonio described as "art brut."[53] Shot in black-and-white, *Rush to Judgment* looks as plain as a typed sheet of paper. One hears no music on the soundtrack, only voices and rustling wind from between the buildings of Dealey Plaza during several scenes, and the director noted with amusement the "almost boring quality of it (which I like)."[54] Because clumsiness has often been equated with verisimilitude, rawness with realness, the rough-hewn appearance of *Rush to Judgment* works in its favor by making it appear more "real." For example, one reviewer noted that the "just barely edited" quality of the interviews added to their believability.[55] Somewhere between psychology and aesthetics one can find the explanation for this phenomenon: a visual "fact" loses verisimilitude if it appears in too beautiful a light.[56] Recent television advertisements have exploited this phenomenon, using shaky handheld camera work to win the viewer's trust (and dollars) with the supposed authenticity of the documentary form.[57]

These qualities make *Rush to Judgment* an extreme example of documentary as a "discourse of sobriety," to use a phrase from the film theorist Bill Nichols.[58] However, the film drops its sober appearance on at least one occasion, stumbling ahead with an utter lack of cinematic polish, too awkward to take seriously. One scene shows Lane interviewing Joseph W. Johnson, the African American bandleader from Jack Ruby's Carousel Club, while Johnson plays the piano. "It'll be like Bogart in *Casablanca*," Lane had promised de Antonio, who was not amused. The interview, ridiculous though it appears, nonetheless contained useful information and had to be used in the otherwise somber film.[59]

Aside from the *Casablanca* scene and a few jump cuts used to condense interviews, de Antonio presents his case with a minimum of distractions. Unlike Bruce Conner's *Report* (1967), which delights in the "manipulation of strictly filmic possibilities" as it examines the assassination, *Rush to Judgment* eschews the formal experimentation of the underground films of the 1960s.[60] By separating the film's radical politics from its more mainstream aesthetics, de Antonio designed *Rush to Judgment* to appeal to a relatively broad audience. Yet a simple visual language is also suited to radical discourse, which depends on words, logic, and dialogue.[61] As was often the case with de Antonio's films, the words play a more important role than images.

We hear the voices of twenty-six individuals. From archival footage we hear (and see) Lee Harvey Oswald; Henry Wade, district attorney for Dallas; Jesse Curry, Dallas police chief; John Connolly, governor of Texas; Dr. Robert R. Shaw, who treated Connolly's wounds; and Detective James Leavell, who was handcuffed to Oswald when he was shot. Most of these voices are set in opposition to the twenty witnesses for the defense filmed by de Antonio. The stars include Acquilla Clemons, a witness (to the slaying of Officer J. D. Tippit) the Warren Commission could not find; Penn Jones, who alludes to strange happenings; and S. M.

Holland, who saw a puff of smoke from the grassy knoll far from Oswald's perch in the Texas School Book Depository. One of the most remarkable aspects of the testimony is the influence of the publication of the Warren report on individual memories of the assassination. Several witnesses, such as James Tague and Orville Nix, describe what they saw but sheepishly explain that they must be mistaken because the Warren report said otherwise. Even as the witnesses struggle to bend their memory to the official version, they shed doubts on the completeness of the report, especially because several interviewees were not even called before the Warren Commission.

The witnesses are convincing on a visceral level, even though their testimony might have suffered under expert cross-examination in an actual court of law. De Antonio certainly believed them, and he praised the people of Texas "who spoke up and told what they saw when it mattered and when it was dangerous to do so." "Hearing those American voices, unrehearsed, fumbling, trying to reach out and up to express the inexpressible," struck a chord in the filmmaker. The effect was as poignantly incommunicable as that of James Agee and Walker Evans's *Let Us Now Praise Famous Men*, a lyrical and populist aspect of the documentary tradition that de Antonio seldom mentioned.[62]

These voices have evidentiary value, as shown in the frequency with which subsequent films borrow footage from *Rush to Judgment*. Most interviewees are dead, their views best represented in the film. One witness, Lee Bowers, Jr., died five months after his interview was filmed, as the film ominously announces.[63] Moreover, Lane and de Antonio arranged the testimony as a defense lawyer might have—and the juxtaposition of the various witnesses is so persuasive that a jury would have had a tough time reaching a verdict on Oswald's culpability. Of course one could attack the film for omitting evidence that damages its case, but de Antonio would have shrugged his shoulders, so focused was he on the deeper meaning of the case.

He believed *Rush to Judgment* was not about the guilt or innocence of Lee Harvey Oswald, the inaccuracies of the Warren report, or even the merits of Lane's arguments, which are debated to this day.[64] As usual de Antonio's real concerns were structural, institutional, metaphoric. As one witness in *Rush to Judgment* says when asked about the Warren Commission's idiosyncrasies, "Well, I always thought it peculiar, but I thought that's the way they did business." This is exactly de Antonio's point: the deeds of the Warren Commission represented the rise of a police state in which the suppression of evidence was commonplace, rather than the exception to the rule. This is the real subject of *Rush to Judgment*: the "demystification of the police world" and its way of doing business.[65]

Exposing the inner workings of power was a critical part of de Antonio's work, as it was for Foucault, who articulated in greater detail the same themes as de Antonio's films.[66] The way in which the power of the state delimits knowledge, defines crime and punishment, and reacts to regicide are as much a part of *Rush to Judgment* as they are Foucault's important work, *Discipline and Punish*.[67] In a striking similarity of historical imagination, both de Antonio and Foucault sought to illuminate the hidden aspects of power, which they believed to function most insidiously when undetected or misunderstood.[68] But Foucault's theories leave little room for de Antonio's occasional bursts of optimism.[69] Calling himself a "Panglossian Marxist" for the blend of blind faith and dialectical materialism in his vision of history, de Antonio believed that justice could be done against all odds, even against the "tin gods and power structures" that propped up the Warren report.[70] A radical critique, the film was dangerous fare for film audiences accustomed to the bland politics of Hollywood.

Reception

Audiences got their first glimpse of the film at a small showing at Dartmouth College on January 12, 1967—theatrical premieres in the U.S. would be delayed until the summer, when it was shown at Carnegie Hall Cinema in New York City. The first large audience, however, was British: de Antonio had signed a contract with his former employers, the British Broadcasting Company, to air the film in England on January 29, 1967.[71] Promising a fair presentation of the film, the BBC paid the considerable sum of $30,000 for a single showing, thereby erasing much of the film's debt. The BBC also promised a balanced panel of experts to comment on the film, which would be interrupted four times for debate, making the program the longest live studio production in BBC history. But what transpired during those five controversial hours was entirely different.

De Antonio, acknowledging his coproducer's expertise, sent Lane to London for the occasion. But instead of debate, Lane could only defend: the four other participants turned out to be well-known supporters of the Warren Commission, including two of the commission's lawyers—David W. Belin and Arlen Specter, the flamboyant Philadelphia prosecutor who would become a U.S. senator in 1981. Even the set put Lane at a disadvantage: Lane was seated in what he described as a hole, while his fellow debaters sat in judgment above him on an elevated platform. To make matters worse, while on the air Lane realized that the other participants had another unfair advantage—a script, which no one would show Lane. During one commercial break Specter blasted the moderator for asking a difficult question—"We never went over that," he protested furiously, cowing the moderator into sticking to the script.

The moderator permitted the Warren Commission advocates, including Lord Devlin, who wrote a defense of its findings for the *Atlantic Monthly*, to trample Lane, who was barely given an opportunity to defend himself. The BBC even altered the film of *Rush to Judgment*, removing aerial footage of Dealey Plaza and replacing it with shots of a specially built model in the London studio. Elaborately detailed, the model's only flaw was that "in each crucial respect it was inaccurate," according to Lane.[72] The evening ended with one participant, Devlin, praying that President Kennedy's soul be left to rest in peace, presumably unbothered by the likes of Lane and de Antonio.

This drubbing had occurred on BBC-2, a channel that had an audience potential "so low that it cannot be rated," as de Antonio complained with some exaggeration.[73] Someone had watched that evening, for in the next week at least ten British newspapers discussed the program at length, many of them criticizing the BBC.[74] The *London Times* reported that disgruntled viewers had jammed the BBC switchboard: "Viewers Protest 'Unfair' During TV Marathon," ran the *Daily Express* headline. The *Daily Mirror* chastised the program's moderator for "clumsily silenc[ing] Mr. Lane whenever he tried to cross verbal swords with the rival lawyers."[75] The film had even changed the opinion of the *Guardian*, which had previously supported the Warren Commission: "Now it seems clear to almost everyone but the Warren Commission that it was indeed a rush to judgment."[76]

Reviewers in the United States were equally impressed when the film finally opened here in the summer of 1967. "If the purpose of this film is to rouse its viewers into having doubts about Oswald's total guilt," wrote Bosley Crowther of the *New York Times*, "then it eminently succeeds." *Rush to Judgment*, according to the *New York Post*, will "destroy your peace of mind" with the number of compelling questions it raises. The *New Yorker* called the film "arrestingly independent," and the *New York Daily News* commended the film's "cold, unobtrusive style," which made the film more persuasive than the book of the same title: "It is one thing to read written testimony, but something else to observe the witnesses' facial reactions to questions and hear testimony from their own lips." With some naïveté about the nature of film, this reviewer trots out the adage "the camera never lies" as evidence of the film's veracity.[77]

Yet positive reviews did not translate into a positive cash flow for the filmmakers. Impact Films, the U.S. distributor of *Rush to Judgment*, failed to complete a promised payment of $50,000, and de Antonio threatened a lawsuit to collect the money. The situation was bleak in England as well. Difficulties in obtaining a British distributor for theatrical release even prompted de Antonio to wonder if "the CIA is whispering down the secret corridors."[78]

De Antonio claimed in *Variety* that "some Texas exhibitors assert they've been threatened by certain individuals who claim they will 'break up their theatres' if the film is shown," even though publicizing these threats may have discouraged theaters from booking *Rush to Judgment*.[79] Another filmmaker might have turned to television, but the U.S. networks were not interested in such a controversial and rough-looking independent film. As a consequence the film did not reach the large audience it might have.

Everything about the film went sour after its bungled release, including the relationship between Lane and de Antonio. Though the two men had been close friends during the filmmaking, they had a falling out over the rights to the film's soundtrack, which culminated in de Antonio suing Lane.[80] By the late 1970s de Antonio loathed his former coproducer, mocking him as little more than a plastic invention of the media: "He must be the most despised figure the left has produced," he wrote after learning of Lane's connection to the group that committed mass suicide in Jonestown, Guyana, in 1979.[81] His loss of respect for Lane made it difficult to remember *Rush to Judgment* with fondness: the film began to seem harsh and didactic and Lane's camera presence a source of annoyance.[82] What de Antonio had once viewed as a landmark film seemed to him minor and immature in light of his later work.

Disillusionment with Lane's personality, however, did not bring de Antonio to abandon his interest in Kennedy's death. On the contrary, his theories about the assassination kept pace with Lane's, who went on to make a career out of criticizing the Warren report. Even as late as 1987 de Antonio added some videotape footage to his 1970 film, *America Is Hard to See*, about the 1968 presidential campaign of Eugene McCarthy, to discuss the subject.[83] The effect of a filmmaker's interrupting his work to comment upon the action is unsettling but not nearly as worrisome as what he had to say. In his Ivy League costume of khaki pants, blue oxford shirt, and blue blazer, de Antonio gazes uncertainly into the camera and explains that only in 1970, four years after the filming of *Rush to Judgment*, did he begin to realize the enormity of the conspiracy behind Kennedy's death. He then makes three claims familiar to any casual reader of "assassinology," as one writer called the genre of literature devoted to Kennedy's death.

De Antonio charges three groups with the crime: the CIA and anti-Castro Cubans; reactionary southerners with fears of Kennedy's racial attitudes; and anyone who wanted to expand the war in Vietnam and believed that Kennedy was becoming a dove.[84] Despite the obvious passion with which he asserts his opinions, de Antonio offers no evidence, not even a suggestion of how the three conspiracies operated simultaneously. Nearing the end of his own life, he was perhaps frustrated by the lack of closure in regard to the case. In order to resolve the matter he seems to have finally succumbed to the myth of Camelot, in which Kennedy's death becomes a "sacrificial offering . . . to the forces of bigotry, irrationality and fanaticism," a point of view that even a member of the president's inner circle, Theodore White, called "a misreading of history."[85] This is a sad performance by de Antonio, whose vague, bitter conjecture seems the product of someone other than the filmmaker who had once spoken with such eloquence and creativity about the assassination. As Noam Chomsky has observed, people "who want to change the world will do well . . . not to engage in groundless speculation as to what one or another leader might have done."[86]

When *Film Comment* devoted a special issue to *Rush to Judgment* at the end of 1967, de Antonio was effusive about the film's significance. He called it "the first time a film specifically attacks and confronts a major government position"; "the first time in which an actor in history becomes an actor in a film (Mark Lane)"; and "the first time a film is a plea for the defense." He also noted the film's "precise activist goal . . . to press for a re-opening of the case, with Mark Lane as counsel for Lee Harvey Oswald."[87] Though the desire to stimulate interest in the film may have inflated de Antonio's rhetoric, *Rush to Judgment* was without question "the first and the most famous documentary film challenging the findings of the FBI and the Warren Commission," according to Anthony Frewin, an expert on the visual record of the assassination.[88]

Before the release of *Rush to Judgment*, the film record had been entirely favorable to the conclusions of the FBI and the Warren Commission, from the newsreels quickly thrown together by the Pathé company in late 1963 to longer and more sophisticated films: the U.S. Information Agency's *Years of Lightning, Day of Drums* (1964), David L. Wolper's *Four Days in November* (1964), NBC's *The JFK Conspiracy: The Case of Jim Garrison* (June 19, 1967). Most significant was *CBS News Inquiry: The Warren Commission Report*, a four-hour documentary produced at a cost of nearly $500,000 and narrated by Walter Cronkite. Broadcast over four evenings in June 1967, the program was advertised as ending, "once and for all, any further doubts, rumors, and speculations."[89]

Nevertheless, as the release of *Rush to Judgment* in the same month made clear, the doubts and rumors had not been put to rest. Instead the controversy has raged for more than three decades, spawning more than two thousand books and films.[90] This torrent of speculation has overwhelmed the defenders of the Warren report, who constituted only 6 percent of the American public, according to an NBC poll in 1992.[91] The majority of the public no longer accepts "the notion that a misguided loser with a $12 rifle could end Camelot," as one writer bluntly put it.[92] This is the real legacy of films such as *Rush to Judgment*. After "nearly three decades of revisionist Kennedy-assassination investigation," the public has gained "a darker, more complex, less innocent vision of America," which is as confused about the assassination as ever, noted a writer for *Time*.[93] As Norman Mailer wrote in 1966, "The wealth of contradictory evidence now upon us from the rot-pile of Dallas permits any interpretation, any neat little path, to be cut through the thicket," which was made abundantly clear during the debate about Oliver Stone's film, *JFK* (1991).[94]

A self-proclaimed "cinematic historian," Stone spent $40 million to produce a three-hour epic detailing the secret history of the assassination.[95] Unfortunately, Stone elevated dramatic convenience above historical accuracy, creating characters and events to suit the theory that the CIA and anti-Castro Cubans were behind the shooting of President Kennedy. As in other Hollywood films from the 1970s and 1980s with conspiratorial bents (*Three Days of the Condor, Videodrome, Klute, The Parallax View*), Stone searches for what one critic calls a "geopolitical aesthetic," a way of seeing the world that can explain everything, including the inexplicable.[96] Stone has not always presented his film as history (at which it fails). He has also called it an "alternative myth to the Warren Commission myth," at which it succeeds magnificently. Yet even if *JFK* was "a lot closer to the truth than the Warren Commission was," as Stone claimed, it was also a lot closer to fiction than he cared to admit. This was not the case for the low-budget *Rush to Judgment*, where speculation does not extend to the point of fabrication.[97]

De Antonio died shortly before *JFK*'s release, but Mark Lane condemned Stone for "falsifying the record" and stealing scenes from *Rush to Judgment*, such as Lane's walk through Dealey Plaza with the witness S. M. Holland, which Stone distorted by re-placing Lane with Jim Garrison, the New Orleans district attorney played by the actor Kevin Costner.[98] Despite a few intimations of conspiratorial activity, *Rush to Judgment* is a very different type of film, in which a reticence to speculate about the precise nature of "the conspiracy" gives credence to the film's investigation of the Warren report's failings. "I don't know what happened, and I have no idea what happened," de Antonio said. "All I know is that whatever happened, was covered up."[99] *Rush to Judgment* made us less, rather than more, certain of what we know about the assassination and asked questions that we have been able to answer only with fictions such as Oliver Stone's *JFK*. Whether, as philosopher Jacques Derrida has suggested, truth passes more easily through fiction remains to be seen.[100]

DISTRICT ATTORNEY
PARISH OF ORLEANS
STATE OF LOUISIANA
2700 TULANE AVENUE
NEW ORLEANS 70119

JIM GARRISON
DISTRICT ATTORNEY

Rush to Judgment, has been extremely valuable to me. It played a large part in convincing me to begin the investigation of the conspiracy which led to the assassination of President Kennedy.

All America is indebted to Mark Lane. He held the door open until the rest of us decided to examine the Warren Commission Report critically.

JIM GARRISON

THE FILM RUSH TO JUDGMENT
NOW AVAILABLE TO THE PUBLIC.

A film by Emile de Antonio and Mark Lane

CARNEGIE HALL CINEMA

7th Ave. & 56th St.   PL 7-2131   SHOW TIMES 1 00, 2 50, 4 40, 6 30, 8 20, 10 00

Statement from New Orleans District Attorney Jim Garrison promoting *Rush to Judgment* (Judgment Films, 1967). One of the leading figures charging conspiracy in the assassination of President John F. Kennedy, Garrison was the investigator whose work inspired Oliver Stone's controversial *JFK* (1991). Courtesy Wisconsin Center for Film and Theater Research.

4

◄◇►

Vietnam
In the Year of the Pig

From White Hawk to Vietnam

Even before he completed *Rush to Judgment*, de Antonio was filling notebooks and boxes with research notes that would sustain him through a year of shooting with 35mm color film in dozens of locations across the continental United States. In 1966 he was planning a documentary film about Native Americans and the "loss of tribal dignity, [and the] retention of tribal dignity." His goal was to explore the conflict between Native Americans and the dominant culture and to examine "the plight of the [Native] American as a lost minority in an affluent society."[1]

However, the ambitious project never quite got off the ground, even after he narrowed its scope to focus on the plight of Thomas James White Hawk, a Dakota Sioux whose murder conviction was a source of great controversy in the mid-1960s. De Antonio communicated with American Indian Movement (AIM) leaders such as Dennis Banks, as well as with the actor Robert Redford, who seemed interested enough to finance the project. But the business relationship with Redford did not work out, and after looking into the various avenues for receiving grants for the project, de Antonio abandoned it in frustration. In one letter while he was researching this topic, he later wrote: "This is how good ideas die before their time. . . . No $." Although he was unable to bring this project to fruition over the next few years,

76

he was able to make a film about another indigenous people's resistance to U.S. culture.[2]

Like most of his friends on the Left in the mid- to late 1960s and a growing portion of the general population, de Antonio strongly opposed the U.S. involvement in Vietnam. When the Jesuit priest and peace activist Daniel Berrigan and the other members of the "Catonsville Nine" were imprisoned for destroying draft files in 1968, de Antonio sent out dozens of letters that appealed for money, "not in the name of charity but for a revolution which will change the values that have polluted our heads and rivers." Receiving a check to help underwrite their defense was small recompense to the Catonsville Nine, who went to prison for the principles of many, he pointed out in the letter, a copy of which he mischievously sent to FBI director J. Edgar Hoover.[3] De Antonio was also willing to go to jail to protest the war, and in a well-publicized act of civil disobedience he was arrested with the pediatrician Benjamin Spock and the actress Candice Bergen in the foyer of the U.S. Senate in 1972.[4]

Actions such as these were designed to focus media attention on dissenting views on the war, which was an even greater challenge in 1967. At that time only a few journalists had countered the administration's position in a meaningful fashion, while in general their colleagues in the press had "painted an almost one-dimensional image of the Vietnamese and Vietcong as cruel, ruthless, and fanatical," as Daniel Hallin put it.[5] The few dissenting voices were drowned in a sea of homogenized information that flowed from television, which de Antonio recognized as a serious danger: "Power no longer resides in the universities, as it once may have, but in the television aerial."[6] This did not mitigate his disgust with his social peers, the middle-aged Harvard- and Yale-educated policy makers in the Kennedy and Johnson administrations—he singled out McGeorge Bundy and Arthur Schlesinger, Jr., for special scorn—who "like most intellectuals when they play politics . . . were much more cruel in their capacity to treat people as abstractions."[7]

But television was always the great demon from de Antonio's

perspective, and he distrusted the medium's presentation of the war. "Variations on the official line" reported "in a vacuum," was how Neil Compton described the television coverage of the war, and two decades later this sentiment was echoed when the historian Bruce Cumings noted that from watching television one would think the war had no historical context, no discernible past.[8] In part this was by design, part of the need to maintain the uncontroversial, noncritical perspective that sponsors and sometimes even the White House demanded from the television networks.[9] With only a few noteworthy exceptions—CBS's *Morley Safer's Vietnam* (1967) or *Inside North Vietnam* (1968) by Englishman Felix Greene—television had tended to support the administration's position up until 1968 and more often than not thereafter.[10] From his pre-1968 vantage, de Antonio was especially concerned about the ubiquitous nightly news, which was sending a stream of fragments, devoid of context, into the living rooms of American households. This had the unfortunate effect of familiarizing viewers with images of war to the point of mundanity: "By making [the war] quotidian, television made it go away. I wanted to bring it back." He wanted to give the viewers "our recent history right smack in the face, like a napalm pie," as a writer for *Newsweek* later described de Antonio's film.[11]

The cinema had offered few improvements on this situation, as few American films—fictional or not—attempted to make sense of the U.S. involvement in Vietnam. After *The Ugly American* (1963), Hollywood avoided the subject until the release of John Wayne's celebration of mindless virility in *The Green Berets* (1968), whose commercial failure forestalled other movies on the subject until the mid-1970s.[12] A relentlessly didactic movie that Wayne initiated and codirected, *The Green Berets* takes pains to illustrate the point that one beefy sergeant makes at the beginning of the film. "It doesn't take a lead weight to drop on my head," he says as the audience ponders this image, "to recognize what's involved here is communist domination of the world."[13]

This perspective was also the basis for official apologies for the war in films such as the Department of Defense's *Why Vietnam?*

(1965). Required viewing for all GIs shipping out to Vietnam, and with ten thousand prints in circulation in a variety of other contexts, it was the first documentary about Vietnam that a large number of Americans saw.[14] Far less popular was the U.S. Information Agency's enormous production of *Vietnam! Vietnam!* (1966), whose title sounds more like a musical than a celebration of Pax Americana. Directed by John Ford and narrated by Charlton Heston, *Vietnam! Vietnam!* sums up the rationale behind these official documentaries on the war, which was to convince people "once and for all of America's noble intentions and heroic deeds in that faraway land."[15] Newspapers, television, and films such as *The Green Berets* and *Why Vietnam?* worked together to reinforce the prejudice that " 'they' were not like 'us,' and for that reason deserved to be ruled," as Edward Said wrote in a different context.[16] This sort of orientalism—a way of seeing that was implicitly violent, out of context, and reductive—was at the heart of these official representations of Vietnam.[17]

Some American documentarians attempted to avoid such views, though the pre-1968 list is short. Eugene Jones's *Face of War* (1967) offered a more complex, if conservative, view of the U.S. involvement in Vietnam. Like the documentaries from World War II, such as John Huston's *Battle of San Pietro* (1945) or NBC's *Victory at Sea* (1952–1953), *Face of War* focused on the hardship and courage of ordinary soldiers without examining the larger issues at stake and on the human cost to the GIs but not the Vietnamese.[18]

De Antonio found more sophisticated portraits of Vietnam in foreign documentaries. Pierre Schoendorffer, the French war photographer, captured footage that de Antonio greatly admired in *The Anderson Platoon* (1966). Joris Ivens released *The Seventeenth Parallel* and contributed to *Far from Vietnam* in 1967, a work by Chris Marker, Jean-Luc Godard, and other notable French avant-garde directors. Though he admired their motivations, de Antonio regarded the collaborative project as too vague, "a failure in structure as well as in execution."[19]

Although he was able to view some of these foreign films in

his research for his own work, many other films existed that he was probably unable to locate, always a problem for students of documentary film. The Canadian director Beryl Fox made three films that criticized the U.S. role in Vietnam and that predate or parallel de Antonio's film: *The Mills of the Gods* (1965), *Saigon* (1967), and *Last Reflections on a War* (1968). The Japanese filmmaker Junichi Ushiyama documented U.S. atrocities in *With a South Vietnamese Marine Battalion* (1965).[20] Also, the Soviets, East Germans, Cubans, and the North Vietnamese themselves had made a variety of documentaries, though they were rarely available in the United States and never aired on television. Even when U.S. Customs did not prevent the importation of such films, they were used in limited contexts, such as when NBC broadcast part of *Pilots in Pajamas* (by East Germans Walter Heynowski and Gerhard Scheumann, 1967) with the phrase "communist material" superimposed on the images. U.S. television ignored even the documentary on the antiwar movement from the BBC's *World of Action* series, which had won an award at the Cannes Film Festival.[21]

Because these cinematic models on the subject of Vietnam were not readily available to de Antonio on television or in theaters, his voracious reading habits proved useful for clarifying his understanding of the war and leading him into the dissenting current of U.S. historiography. Writing in the sort of critical voice that marked de Antonio's films and often aligning themselves with the New Left, younger scholars were bringing politics into the writing of history with unprecedented passion, expressing dissident views on U.S. foreign policy and tracing the roots of U.S. aggression in the Pacific.[22] This was a step in the right direction but still not enough for de Antonio, who complained that "our revisionist history, William Appleman Williams aside, has not been revised enough in finding the lines and history of our insane destructive actions which are bringing about the fall of our imperial structure."[23]

This sort of radical critique was what two professors, John Atlee and Terry Morrone, had in mind in 1967 when they called the Museum of Modern Art with a question: who could best make a critical and intellectual film about the war in Vietnam? The museum suggested de Antonio, who was busy working on a screenplay about a desert cult in Alamogordo, but he agreed to meet the professors at the Algonquin Hotel in New York. Inspired by what they had to say, he took the project and pushed it into something far more ambitious than whatever the professors might have envisioned.[24]

Radical Scavenging:
The Logistics of Antiwar Filmmaking

As with all films, the first order of business was financial. To finance a major antiwar film without institutional support, however, requires creativity, cunning, and connections—all of which de Antonio had in abundance with his uncanny ability to stroke the egos and consciences of Left-leaning capitalists, something he had demonstrated in the courtship of Elliot Pratt's fortune for *Point of Order*. From his previous films and days in the New York art world, he had gained many connections to potential investors, and his social register was enhanced by the woman who became his executive producer, Marjorie ("Moxie") Schell, a wealthy New York activist who also had many friends among the affluent supporters of the peace movement.[25] They made a good team, even though raising the money required a great deal of time and effort, which would have been better spent doing research in archives or conducting interviews. De Antonio was forced to alternate filmmaking with fund-raising in a routine that he summarized as "shoot, sync up, research, travel, run out of money, another fund raising foray, and once more, more film."[26]

Once again he relied on the satirical entrepreneurial spirit that had kept him well fed without an ordinary job for much of his life. Sometimes his schemes were unsuccessful, such as when he called on Andy Warhol to donate one of his electric chair paintings to help finance the Vietnam project.[27] Undeterred by

Warhol's reluctance, de Antonio went outside his immediate circle of acquaintances in his hunt for patrons—"easy touches," he called them—which he described with the diction of Hemingway. Moxie Schell was his "guide and stalker," making the connection so that the eloquent artist could make "the kill." Once his powers of persuasion had brought the pigeon's checkbook to the table, a misfired question could result in little more than a free meal in a fancy restaurant. So with tongue-in-cheek he claimed to rely on his experience in duck blinds and skeet ranges to know when to make his pitch, and more often than not, the "great American safari team" of Schell and de Antonio tracked down the funds he needed.[28]

One of their biggest scores was Harold Hochschild, president and chairman of the board of American Metal Climax (now Amax, Inc.), who invited the producers to lunch in the Rainbow Room Grill. As the various courses were served, de Antonio—who even wore a tie in a rare return to the sartorial splendor of his youth— agonized over the exact moment to spring the question. Just before the coffee he realized "it had to be then, so it didn't come too late with a rush at the end." As he began to speak, he imbued his presentation with the sort of high moral tone he hoped would assuage the conscience of a very rich old man. He guessed right, for Hochschild liked what he heard and waited for him to name his amount. "Just like a wing shot. I didn't even look at Moxie," de Antonio recalled. "I said $10,000. He didn't say anything. He pulled out a checkbook and wrote it. Right there. For him it was right, on target. $15,000 would have brought a no. $5,000 would have produced $1,000.[29] The filmmaker seemed to take an aesthetic satisfaction from the exchange, from mastering the delicate art of withdrawing cash from a patron.

Sometimes the plea for funds was less than artful. Ann Peretz threw off his hustler's rhythm when she appeared in flat shoes and a worn cardigan, looking more like a graduate student or a baby-sitter to de Antonio than the heir to the Singer sewing-machine fortune. Then she surprised him by agreeing quickly to the sales pitch, cutting off "the performance . . . in the middle of a line of blank verse," as he recalled. The apparent cynicism of his description is misleading, for he was sincere in his conviction that he alone could make the sort of film that was needed, especially because the peace movement was "too full of tears, sobs, untutored arrogance and feelings without thought or knowledge" to do the job itself. Despite his own more tutored arrogance, his sincerity and self-confidence were not lost on Peretz, who wrote a check for $10,000 with such nonchalance that de Antonio kicked himself for not asking for more. Now he would need to entice a slew of smaller investors, for whom Schell began to arrange dinner parties with the express purpose of selling shares in the film at $560 a piece.[30]

These efforts paid off, bringing in more than $100,000, no small sum for an independent nonfiction film production in 1967–1968. In addition to Peretz and Hochschild, investors included many celebrities: the fashion photographer Richard Avedon, comedian Steve Allen, conductor Leonard Bernstein, actors Paul Newman and Robert Ryan. As he had with *Point of Order* and would with *Millhouse*, de Antonio received the support of heirs to the Rockefeller fortune: Laura Rockefeller Case bought ten shares and Marion Rockefeller Weber bought two in what was named the Monday Film Production Co.[31] Curiously, de Antonio often condemned Robert Flaherty for accepting Standard Oil's financial backing for *Louisiana Story* (1948), although de Antonio was willing to fund his own films with the same oil money when it was filtered through the hands of more progressive heirs.[32]

Of course no one can ascertain the personal and political reasons behind these investments, but de Antonio knew how to use U.S. tax laws to make an investment seem practical. At the end of each film he would donate to a university the footage he had collected, thereby allowing one major investor to take a large tax deduction on the value of the footage. In the case of his extensive collection of footage on Vietnam, Cornell University became the beneficiary of this manipulation of the tax code, which put the U.S. government in the ironic position of encouraging the heirs of robber barons to finance a left-wing film.[33]

With the money coming in, the film about Vietnam came to-gether quickly and without serious problems—at least compared to his experiences in producing *Point of Order* and *Rush to Judgment*, not to mention his later films such as *Underground*. And as with most of his films, the making of this film involved a series of colorful and sometimes risky adventures that only a dedicated independent filmmaker would endure without the expectation of a sizable payday.

He began simply enough with books, which he read vora-ciously throughout the second half of 1967. Unlike many film-makers, he conducted serious research and was willing to read nearly two hundred books on Vietnam in French and English. The next step was to line the walls of his office with nine-foot rolls of corrugated paper that he got from a friend who owned a box factory. These scrolls were perfect for constructing elaborate time lines and research notes on Vietnamese history as far back as the Han dynasty. Here on the walls of his office a vast picture of his vision of Vietnam emerged, a sort of first draft of his film based on words and still photographs.[34] It was the first step toward "a kind of political collage of voice," as he called his unique style of filmmaking, one that he intended would reveal the complexity of the wars in Vietnam.[35]

The next step was to acquire footage that reflected his per-sonal vision of Vietnam, and he began "radical scavenging"—his term for the process of obtaining material from diverse sources and means—in the United States.[36] Television outtakes, which he called "the confessions of the system," were one of many types of footage he examined, and he acquired footage from Paramount, United Press International, and Twentieth-Century Fox.[37] WABC television in New York sold him material but then tried to change its mind, claiming, "We didn't know what kind of film you were going to make."[38] Sometimes he received covert assistance from sympathetic employees of the corporate media, such as the young television producer at NBC who provided stolen footage of material shot in Vietnam with the actor Raymond Burr, though little of this footage appeared in the final film.[39] A young woman at the Sherman Grinberg Film Library went out of her way to alert de Antonio to the existence of a particularly damning outtake of Colonel George S. Patton III describing his men as "determined and reverent. . . . But still they're a bloody good bunch of killers," then grinning half-boyishly, half-maniacally.

With customary aplomb de Antonio even tried to procure footage from the Department of Defense (DOD), exchanging letters in 1968 with the chief of the Audio-Visual Branch of the Directorate for Defense Information of the office of the assistant secretary of defense whose responses were as circuitous as his title.[40] Of course the DOD was not interested in treating de Antonio's project with the encouragement it showed to films that supported U.S. involvement in Vietnam; at this time, for example, it was subsidizing the production of John Wayne's *The Green Berets* with more than $1 million worth of equipment and technical support.[41] The military's lack of cooperation was neither surprising nor serious, for de Antonio had already brought together a strong collection of visual sources on Ho Chi Minh, Richard Nixon, Lyndon Johnson, Dean Rusk, General Curtis LeMay, John Foster Dulles, and many others. Some filmmakers might have been content to make a film from this abundance of material alone, but de Antonio was adamant about locating material that had never been seen in the United States, if anywhere. So from the end of 1967 through the early months of 1968, he traveled to various archives in Europe. In East Germany and Czechoslovakia, where he was a guest of the state, he was able to obtain large selections of film from television archives, including four films made in North Vietnam by the German director Peter Ulbrish, and a Soviet film by Roman Karmen that reenacted the battle at Dien Bien Phu.[42] The archive in East Berlin was an ominous place guarded by barbed wire and machine guns, but the East Germans treated him with generosity, he recalled. The same was true in Prague, where representatives of the National Liberation Front provided him with footage, and a nervous American defector named David Leff interviewed him on Czech radio. De Antonio also spoke at a gathering of Czech filmmakers, including Milos Forman, who would go on to direct

One Flew Over the Cuckoo's Nest (1975) and who attacked de Antonio for his bitter criticism of the U.S. government's policy in Vietnam. Other evenings, he recalled, were reserved for drinking wine in cafes with students and admiring beautiful young women, though his rakish proclivities were held in check by the presence of a new wife, Terry Moore, who had recently become his fourth partner in marriage.[43]

His most dangerous act of radical scavenging took place in France. In the course of researching the film he had become acquainted with Paul Mus, a professor of Buddhism at Yale University who had negotiated with Ho Chi Minh for the French in the forties. Mus wrote his friend Pierre Messmer, then the French minister of defense, on de Antonio's behalf, requesting permission for him to become the first foreigner to examine the film stored in the French military archives at Fort d'Ivry. Never before available to an American filmmaker, the footage was extraordinary, the work of many gifted cameramen who had documented more than fifty years of the French involvement in Vietnam.[44] For several days de Antonio perused the archival material with astonishment, but the opportunity was too good to be true. His access to the archive was suddenly canceled without explanation—de Antonio suspected that someone, perhaps the CIA, notified the French authorities about his radical plans for the material. On his last day in the tantalizingly rich archive, faced with the possibility of getting nothing at all, he chose to steal the one shot he wanted most, a telling image of Ho tossing a cigarette from the gangplank of a French battleship in 1945 after his negotiations with the French broke down. It was a subtle gesture of frustration that, to de Antonio, exuded "dignity, wit, intelligence in every gesture." Asking the sympathetic young guard to leave the room for a moment, he cut the shot from film, stuck it in his raincoat pocket, and walked boldly past the gates, never to return. Risking what he suspected might be several years in a French prison, he obtained no other material from the French military archive.[45]

Ironically, getting material from sources closer to where the war was being fought was less dangerous. Peace groups in Tokyo sent him footage, and initially he intended to travel to Japan, pick up a Japanese film crew, and fly to Vietnam.[46] Though the trip to Vietnam never materialized, Mai Van Bho, Hanoi's ambassador in Paris, assisted de Antonio when the two men met in Paris. Permitted to make a negative of *The Life of Ho Chi Minh*, an official film biography, de Antonio went through legal channels to import the negative into the United States, which required a shipping agent and an application with the Federal Reserve Bank that listed every investor in the film and promised that he was not trading with the enemy by offering payment.[47] After a three-week delay de Antonio was pleasantly surprised to have the importation approved, because his material from East Germany—9,774 feet of 35mm negative—had been detained for almost two months.[48]

Throughout the process of accumulating archival footage, he was also arranging for and shooting interviews. In the United States he interviewed the peace activist and Jesuit priest Dan Berrigan, who had just returned from meeting with Pham Van Dong, the prime minister of North Vietnam; Roger Hilsman, who had been director of the Bureau of Intelligence and Research at the State Department until 1963 when he became assistant secretary of state for Far Eastern Affairs; David Halberstam, the former *New York Times* correspondent in Saigon; and a remarkably candid senator, Thruston B. Morton, Republican of Kentucky. Other interviewees included a Green Beret deserter named John Towler and academics such as David Wurfel, a professor of political science.

In France he interviewed Philippe Devillers, who had served in Vietnam and edited a journal about Southeast Asia, and Jean Lacouture, who had written a biography of Ho Chi Minh. Finally, in England he nearly interviewed Anthony Eden (now Lord Avon), the former prime minister of England whom the filmmaker had charmed at a small dinner party in New York. Lord Avon said that he and his wife had twice watched *Point of Order* and voiced his opposition to the U.S. policy in Vietnam. When de Antonio described the film he was then assembling and requested an interview, Lord Avon responded with generosity, inviting him to his country home in England and arranging for his camera crew to lodge at a nearby pub. Before the scheduled date, however, Lord Avon wrote a short note to cancel the interview on the advice of his doctors—though de Antonio suspected he was acting on the advice of Washington, especially when he learned that the earl was well enough to be interviewed for Marcel Ophuls's documentary on the Holocaust, *The Sorrow and the Pity* (1970), not long afterward.[49] In general, though, de Antonio could not complain about the quality or quantity of interviews he had managed to conduct, for he had enough voices from the establishment to deflect any criticism that the film was simply radical propaganda.

With archival and interview material piling up in his office, de Antonio could begin the monumental task of editing more than forty hours of material. Every piece of film was time coded and edge numbered as it arrived in New York, but the sheer mass of material was still daunting. In June 1968 he wrote to his friend, the film historian Jay Leyda, about reaching the critical point of deciding the length of the film: "Do I go for a four hour film and say screw everybody or do I trim sail and shoot for a reasonable 1 hour 52 minutes?" His fascination with obscure images of Ho Chi Minh and others made it difficult to edit the film—"I can't let go of a single frame . . . and every foot cut out hurts. *C'est ca.*"[50] Every time he made an important edit, he did so with the entire film in mind, which meant viewing it from start to finish to see how the change affected the whole.[51] He agonized about the ending of the film in particular. At first he thought of using some old footage of the Viet Minh charging at the camera on a deserted road, but he dropped it in favor of what he considered a more American ending, a more "suitable ending, a politically coherent ending."[52] As de Antonio later described it, he sought to relate the Vietnam conflict to U.S. history, in particular the American Civil War.

The final dilemma was about the title. Although he had initially considered *The Vietnam Wars*, which clearly reflected the film's emphasis on continuity between the French and U.S. involvements, he decided on the confusing but rhetorically powerful *In the Year of the Pig*. A play on the Chinese calendar, which has

Emile de Antonio, late 1960s, probably during the production of *In the Year of the Pig* (Monday Films, 1969). Courtesy Wisconsin Center for Film and Theater Research.

89

no year of the pig, it was chosen before Mayor Richard Daley and his Chicago police were known as pigs to the counterculture and was more about politics than police: "In this film 'pig' means French colonialism and American intervention," he said.[53] The title, which the film does not clarify, was the source of some confusion, and the filmmaker never fully explained why he chose the phrase, which had a certain resonance when an influential underground newspaper was dubbing 1968 "The Year of the Cop" or "The Year of the Barricade."[54] He shed some light on the nature of the pig in his journal in 1978, writing about Vietnam and the legacy of the U.S. involvement there: "stunted, permanently stunted forests, the dead fields, how long dead, can they be brought back to life? . . . The pig has gone and what he has left is ruin of soul and country. . . . The USSR[,] much as I hate its prisons[,] serves a hypocrisy less mean than ours."[55] Violence and hypocrisy—that was the pig, according to de Antonio. Whether Americans would go to the theater to see it in action was another question.

He finished the film in the fall of 1968, but deciding on the next step raised new problems. The initial showing in Boston was dependent on the good graces of a New York stockbroker whose antiwar views led him to put up the $15,000 necessary for the occasion.[56] Even a distribution deal with Pathé-Contemporary films, a division of McGraw-Hill, was troublesome enough to require threats of legal action from de Antonio's attorneys.[57] Presumably, the distribution company put up the money for subsequent openings in a few other major cities, though the film still had difficulty finding theaters willing to screen it. As a result of such problems, *In the Year of the Pig* premiered in Boston on February 26, 1969, and opened in other cities over the course of the next ten months, finding the bulk of its audience in the students and faculty of universities.

As early as October 1968, de Antonio's production company sent a form letter to campus leaders to promote the film. The letter explained the nature of the film as "a new kind of political theatre" and noted de Antonio's willingness to appear on campuses in conjunction with it, something that would increasingly become a part of his efforts to promote his work.[58] By November 1969 the film had been shown at a variety of colleges, including Harvard, Hobart, Yale, Wesleyan, and Dartmouth, and on the day of the first antiwar moratorium, October 15, 1969, it played in at least twenty theaters across the country. Though de Antonio could not appear personally at every one of these showings, he was a tireless and eloquent lecturer on behalf of his beliefs.

In the Year of the Pig was more readily accepted outside the United States, playing in theaters in London and Paris for eight weeks and on television in other European countries. U.S. television continued its customary indifference to de Antonio's films, but programmers in Finland, Norway, Denmark, Sweden, Belgium, Holland, East Germany, and Hungary were eager to broadcast the film. When it finally came to Greece several years later, it became "an enormous hit," as de Antonio put it, with five theaters in Athens sharing three reels of film, using motorcycles to shuttle the reels back and forth throughout the evening.[59]

Overseas distribution was often arranged in an informal manner that allowed de Antonio to exercise his prejudice against distributors with purely commercial motivations, those who "would be equally interested if the film were about fucking in Borneo." For example, he wrote to a political activist named John Percy with a simple business proposal: if he would advance $500 to de Antonio for the rights to promote and distribute the film in Australia, the two men would split the earnings equally after repayment of the first $500. De Antonio also encouraged Percy to attempt to sell the film to Australian television, for which he suggested a nightlong debate much like the one the BBC had created around *Rush to Judgment*, though little came of these grandiose plans for Australia.[60]

Putting politics first resulted in meager profits despite good notices. After *In the Year of the Pig* had been in theaters for more than two years, its distributor reported that it had earned back less than a quarter of the initial investment.[61] Yet in public de Antonio claimed the film had done "fantastically well" for its distributor, that it had played fifty theaters during the moratorium when the real number was about twenty. One can only speculate that these exaggerations were for the benefit of future investors who might read financial trouble as a sign that the film was not reaching an audience.[62] Another strategy would have been to present his inability to make money as a virtue, casting himself as a martyr and his film as too dangerous to attract a mainstream audience. Such an assertion would not have been unfounded, because part of the problem with the film's earnings can be traced to various forms of censorship.

In fact, censorship of the most primitive variety plagued *In the Year of the Pig*. The night before the film was to open in Los Angeles, someone broke into the theater and vandalized the screen, spray painting a peace symbol and hammer and sickle above large letters that read "TRAITORS" and "PROLONG THE WAR YOU SLOBS KILLED 40,000 GOOD MEN!" The theater used a photograph of the graffiti in an advertisement with the caption: "IF WHAT YOU DID TO OUR SCREEN = YOUR INTOLERANCE OF DISSENT, THEN WE ARE INDEED IN THE YEAR OF THE PIG." De Antonio reported that, in an Orwellian twist, the employee who had booked the film was fired for having done so.[63]

Bomb threats hampered the opening night in Chicago, where *pig* seems to have been misinterpreted as a reference to the local police force.[64] An art house in Houston was afraid to show the film, forcing it to move first to the Jewish Community Center, which also changed its mind, then to Rice University, where the film was shown despite the threat of fire bombing.[65] Other forms of censorship were less barbaric but equally effective, such as when a theater in de Antonio's hometown of Scranton, Pennsylvania, canceled the film's appearance without explanation, quietly replacing it with Ali MacGraw and Ryan O'Neal in *Love Story*.[66] And as late as 1971 the film had not played in Washington, D.C., where "the good 'liberal' theater-owners have refused to show it," as de Antonio claimed, because it was "un-American."[67] Despite these problems, the film was seen in enough urban and college theaters to receive a small pile of glowing reviews.

De Antonio's press release for the film quoted Noam Chomsky and Dr. Benjamin Spock as pronouncing the film "Magnificent!" in unison. An editorial in the *Boston Globe* declared "it should be seen," while the reviewer for the *New York Times* called it "stinging, graphic and often frighteningly penetrating." The *Washington Post* claimed it would be worth seeing even after the war, so much did it reveal about the nature of U.S. power, while the *Harvard Crimson* called it "more than a collage of poignant footage. It is a document of what is happening this minute in our heads and someplace not so far away." Writing in the *New Yorker*, Pauline Kael called the film "remarkably persuasive," and even mainstream periodicals such as *Newsweek* echoed this praise. Dwight Macdonald praised its rare combination of "solid scholarship with technical brilliance." Even the right-wing *National Review* made no attempt to refute the film's charges, choosing instead to comment absurdly on how the premiere of the film revealed the essential similarity between Hanoi and New York City in 1969.[68] The contemporary critics' point of view was summed up in a 1994 book: "Without a doubt, in any other war but Vietnam, [*In the Year of the Pig*] would have been considered sedition rather than being praised by the film community and the viewing public."[69]

Perhaps the strangest accolade came from the Academy of Motion Picture Sciences, which nominated *In the Year of the Pig* for an Academy Award, one of the only radical films so honored in the history of that institution. In his introduction of the various nominees for best documentary, the dancer and actor Fred Astaire appeared embarrassed to read the film's name, or at least de Antonio thought so.[70] The film was competing against more standard documentary fare: films about wolf men, the Mexico City Olympics, one by the Office of Economic Opportunity, and a winner that Astaire could proudly announce, *Arthur Rubinstein— The Love of Life* (Bernard Chevry, 1969).

In the Year of the Pig also received excellent reviews and sizable crowds in Europe. De Antonio happily reported the "good and great reviews in London," and the film was soon voted the

Publicity material for *In the Year of the Pig* (Monday Films, 1969). Courtesy Wisconsin Center for Film and Theater Research.

"most important film" at Festival dei Popoli, Florence, with lesser awards at the Leipzig Film Festival and the Cannes Film Festival.[71] It was one of the few American films on Vietnam that was seen all over the world.

Perhaps more important than the praise the film received was its efficacy as an organizing tool, for in addition to lecturing with the film on dozens of campuses in the United States, de Antonio donated showings to raise consciousness as well as money. It was shown in 1969 at the Conference of Concerned Asian Scholars in Cambridge, Massachusetts, and at a special screening for the staff of *Time*.[72] It was also screened for the International Board of the Methodist Church, the Society of Friends, and the American Friends Service Committee, and at a benefit for the Catonsville Nine; an antiwar group, Clergy and Laymen Concerned, presented it at benefits in churches in nearly twenty cities. At one time it was playing twenty-four hours a day in a coffeehouse near Fort Dix, New Jersey.[73]

Always willing to put politics above profits, de Antonio was glad to donate a showing of the film to a good cause. In November 1969 he turned the film's opening night in Chicago into a benefit for the Chicago Seven defendants, who included Abbie Hoffman, Jerry Rubin, Dave Dellinger, and Tom Hayden. Four police cars, their red lights flashing, were parked in front of the Three Penny Cinema when de Antonio arrived, and he noticed the tension between the police and the peacenik crowd, as contemporary writers might have dubbed it. Inside the atmosphere was far different, almost triumphant, as people cheered the film, elating the director. Afterward he went to a party thrown in honor of him and his film. He was accompanied by the oral historian Studs Terkel, who admired *In the Year of the Pig* so much he hoped de Antonio would make a film out of his book *Division Street*.[74]

This politically charged atmosphere was also present when the film appeared in Paris for eight weeks. The French newspapers gave the film generous reviews, despite the occasional act of vandalism in which "stink bombs" were thrown into the theater— "one of the sincere forms of criticism which has followed my work," wrote de Antonio with some amusement.[75] No such criticism was present on opening night, however. Behind the French radicals and American expatriates in the audience of the Cinéma Git-Le-Coeur were three quiet Vietnamese who said nothing as the last reel ended and the press began to ask questions. After some time one of the Vietnamese pressed forward and spoke to de Antonio alone. Presenting a card that identified him as Nguyen Thanh Le, the director of information for the Democratic Republic of Vietnam's negotiating team and someone with whom de Antonio had exchanged letters, he praised *In the Year of the Pig* as the best he had seen on Vietnam. In appreciation of de Antonio's efforts, Nguyen presented him with a ring made from the metal of a downed U.S. plane; de Antonio gave it to Moxie Schell when he returned to New York. The ring was too big for her finger, so she had Tiffany's line it with silver to create a small token of radical chic.[76] Perhaps his youthful desire to be a pilot made de Antonio uncomfortable with the idea of wearing the wreckage of a U.S. plane as a trophy.

But de Antonio was comfortable in developing a relationship with the Vietnamese, as he had been doing since early 1969 when he began exchanging letters with Nguyen. Throughout 1969 he requested various books and articles from Hanoi, such as works on Ho Chi Minh that were unavailable in the United States at the time: Turong Chinh's *The August Revolution* and Vo Nguyen Giap's *A Heroic People*.[77] In June 1969 he also made plans with Nguyen for another film on Vietnam that would include thirty minutes each of Ho Chi Minh, former premier Pham Van Dong, and Vo Nguyen Giap, who had been the commander of the Viet Minh in the victory over the French at Dienbienphu in 1954. Each would offer statements rather than interviews, with Ho speaking in English for the first time to an American audience. He would also be shown informally—smoking, talking, drinking tea—which "would be a very great psychological contrast to the rigidity of the U.S. presidential addresses," de Antonio promised.[78]

The letter received a cautious but favorable response from the Vietnamese, but the project was soon derailed by those he called the "incompetent, pot befuddled filmers of the New Left," de Antonio's slur against those whom the Vietnamese trusted to approve the project in the United States. These included members of the radical film collective Newsreel and a leading antiwar activist, Dave Dellinger, who insisted on making the film a collective venture. To de Antonio this was absurd in that it presupposed an equality of talent and ideas that could never exist—at least when he was in the room. Arguing in the offices of Dellinger's *Liberation* magazine on Beekman Street in New York City late in the summer of 1969, de Antonio wanted control over the project, which meant choosing his own cameraman—Ed Emschwiller, who later shot much of *Painters Painting*. None of his suggestions were acceptable to Dellinger and company, forcing de Antonio to give up his hopes for the project. Only posthumously would Ho have a chance to speak in English to audiences in American theaters with the release of de Antonio's 1976 film, *Underground*, which included footage of Ho speaking to a Vietnamese camera crew.[79]

De Antonio would have relished the opportunity the film would have provided to meet with the Vietnamese leader. Praising Ho's "extraordinary combination of poetry and courage" after his death in September 1969, de Antonio wistfully agreed with Paul Mus's assessment of Ho in *In the Year of the Pig*—"In the history of this century, he will be the great patriot"—and de Antonio's only consolation was the approval that the Vietnamese delegation in Paris had shown his film.[80] Yet as much as the warmth of the Vietnamese response heartened him, he had not made the film for them but for his own people, "to show Ho Chi Minh as a Marxist hero, to reveal how we betrayed those honorable moments of our own past."[81]

With frustration he wished his film could change public opinion and government policy: "How can a film be nominated for the Academy Award, be the subject of major newspaper editorials, be very well reviewed and still be unknown to most of the American people?" The film, he believed, had exposed the real history of the U.S. involvement in Vietnam two years before the revelations of the Pentagon Papers, which the public clamored to read. So in

1971 he wrote to U.S. Representative Philip Burton, Democrat of California, to request a special screening of *In the Year of the Pig* in Congress. Burton was unable to accommodate this bold request, probably aware that most of his colleagues would have little interest in a Marxist critique of the war in Vietnam.[82]

"Deconstructing" Vietnam

In the Year of the Pig begins with an eerie silence. Half the screen is black; the other half shows the face of a Civil War casualty, a private from the 149th Pennsylvania Infantry immortalized in stone. After several seconds the title appears on screen, accompanied on the soundtrack by a crescendo of a roaring engine that suddenly sputters as if it had run out of fuel. Roar, sputter, silence is the rhythm of the soundtrack as the picture alternates between black leader and a series of images: a gravestone of an American Revolutionary soldier with the inscription "When I heard of the revolution, my heart enlisted"; a GI in Vietnam with "Make love, not war" painted on his helmet; an old Vietnamese man bowing in deference as he runs from the cameras.

Then the soundtrack changes, and instead of the engines we hear a hypnotic, almost sickening, whine. Difficult to identify, it is a recording of several helicopter rotors whose metallic whirling forms the basis of a new crescendo that reaches a peak so loud that projectionists rush to turn down the volume. While this sound continues unabated, as if to blast extraneous thoughts and preconceptions from the mind, a series of images slowly appears on screen.

First is a monument from World War II. Then the screen goes black. Then we see the self-immolation of Thich Quang Duc.[83] Black screen. A still photo of a gunner weighted down with grenades. Black screen. A still photo of a small Vietnamese child smoking a cigarette. Black screen. Then Augustus Saint-Gaudens's memorial to Colonel Robert Gould Shaw and the black troops of the Fifty-fourth Massachusetts Infantry. Black screen.

Then silence as Vice President Hubert Humphrey quotes from Scripture: "Blessed are the peace-makers."

Once again we hear the hissing of helicopter rotors, this time in accompaniment to John Foster Dulles's spinning a globe aimlessly. Then silence as Humphrey describes the necessity of making peace and President Johnson points out that the American people "never had it so good." Black screen. Then the title of the film appears for the second time, marking the end of the film's introductory montage, a mysterious foreshadowing of the themes of the film. After this point begins a more conventional history of Vietnam in the early part of the twentieth century: the film identifies speakers and follows a chronology.

This bleak and powerful narrative starts with images of French colonialism before the Second World War. We see a re-vealing sequence of white-suited French officials berating their rickshaw pullers—a scene the filmmaker called "the equivalent of a couple of chapters of dense writing about the meaning of colonialism."[84] Then, as if in contrast, comes a film hagiography of Ho Chi Minh—the George Washington of his country, as Senator Morton acknowledges to the camera. The next sixteen minutes examine the French fight to regain control of Vietnam after the Japanese occupation, a period in which, as Paul Mus, the pro-fessor of Buddhism at Yale, explains, "every time Ho trusted us, we betrayed him." We also see a Soviet reenactment of the battle of Dienbienphu—from Roman Karmen's *Vietnam* (1955)—that is offered as documentary footage.

The next twenty-three minutes cover the transition from French to U.S. involvement and continue through the U.S. sup-port of Ngo Dinh Diem from 1954 to 1963. John Foster Dulles puts forth the domino theory, and Senator Joseph McCarthy warns, "If we lose Indochina, we'll lose the Pacific and become an island in a communist sea." Various observers discuss the origins of the National Liberation Front (NLF), emphasizing its legitimacy and autonomy in contrast to the evident corruption of the Diem regime. After covering the fall of Diem, de Antonio spends seventeen minutes on the debate among policy makers in the United States that culminated in full-scale U.S. intervention circa 1965.

Throughout the film de Antonio shows the official version of events in a skeptical light. For example, he juxtaposes conflicting accounts of the Tonkin Gulf episode: as U.S. officials defend their response to the "attack," a Navy sonar operator from the U.S.S. *Maddox* offers another story, one that supports the assertion of Senator Wayne Morse, the Oregon Democrat, that the American bombing of North Vietnam is outright aggression. In another juxtaposition General William Westmoreland defends the treatment of prisoners by U.S. military personnel, just before a former private in Vietnam testifies that "prisoners were executed in our outfit as a standard policy."

The next section (fifteen minutes) examines the violence done to the Vietnamese peasants and countryside as the U.S. involvement escalates. This is one of the many sequences that function as an antidote to films such as *The Green Berets*, also completed in 1968.[85] De Antonio's film implicitly scrutinizes the racism of John Wayne's epic by using footage of U.S. soldiers on a Vietnamese beach complaining about the local women—"they're slant eyes, gooks; they're no good." General Mark Clark describes his military opponents as "willing to die readily, as all Orientals are. . . . I wouldn't trade one dead American for fifty dead Chinamen." A machine-gun–wielding helicopter pilot blithely grins and announces the ominous name of his ship: "Birth Control." Although the film illustrates how the U.S. military has dehumanized its opponents, de Antonio did not want to do the same thing to the U.S. soldiers fighting there.

As someone who had spent time in the armed forces during the Second World War, he had a great deal of sympathy for the soldiers of all ranks in Vietnam, a quality not universally shared by his peers on the Left. Even Colonel George S. Patton III, who refers to his men as "a bloody good bunch of killers" in the film, seemed to de Antonio a basically "good guy" with whom he would enjoy socializing in other circumstances, though de Antonio believed Patton's comment dramatized "how totally irrelevant we are to a decent world."[86] This hints at the complexity of de Antonio's position, which makes his film more than a simple inversion of *The Green Berets* in which one should applaud the downing of U.S. planes, as one Columbia University audience did to his dismay.[87] Instead of inversion, de Antonio sought to "deconstruct" the fragile logic that supported these attitudes and policies. Though he had little interest in deconstruction as a critical practice, one he dubbed "arcane" a decade after its emergence in the late 1960s, he later claimed to be "wholly aware of the various structures and deconstructures" in his film on Vietnam: "I deconstructed the accepted images [of the war] to create a positive result, a pro-Vietnamese construction. . . . The deconstruction of those images was effected by placement, by sound or music and, for example, the images of officers of the French Foreign Legion in Saigon in 1934 which were seen in U.S. and French newsreels and had a deconstructive meaning in 1967."[88]

Did de Antonio make a "deconstructive" film in the Derridian sense? The literary scholar Barbara Correll argues that he did. In an article entitled "Rem(a)inders of G(l)ory: Monuments and Bodies in *Glory* and *In the Year of the Pig*," Correll homes in on the deconstructive aspect of de Antonio's film, using Edward Zwick's movie about the Fifty-fourth Massachusetts in the Civil War as a counterpoint.[89] She argues that rather than reproducing the "reality effects" of official historical discourse, *In the Year of the Pig* "both exposes the construction of an official history and reflects upon that construction." This allows viewers to study the "stuttering" of power and the link between " 'violence and metaphysics in which the Self exists at the expense of the other." De Antonio presents the viewer with new possibilities for interpreting old events and reminds the viewer of the "heterogeneity, difference, and violence" in the discourse and reality of Vietnam. This forces the viewer to overcome the selective remembering that has characterized debates about the war.

Although Correll made a good case for seeing *In the Year of the Pig* as a model of deconstructive filmmaking, de Antonio's

approach has more in common with Marxist ideological criticism
than a Derridian project. Looking for inconsistencies between
official utterances and the truth is an old-fashioned muckraking technique, not an example of deconstructive effort to unveil
multiple truths, and perhaps it is in his quest for *the truth* that
de Antonio is at his most Marxist, most modernist, and least
deconstructive. This important distinction is lost in Correll's
article, although she alludes to it in a footnote: "While irony,
juxtaposition and disjuncture do not necessarily add up to a
'deconstructive meaning,' I argue (not immodestly) for attention
to de Antonio's post-structuralist leanings or affinities. . . . It is,
of course, profoundly ironic, given the current history of their
debates, that Marxist and post-structuralist positions are reduc-
tively collapsed in neo-humanist polemics."[90] Correll sought to
locate the "points of affinity" between these positions without
effacing the differences between them, yet the effect of reading her
"neo-humanist polemic" is to lose sight of de Antonio's Marxism.

Certainly, we should not dismiss the possibility of nonfiction
films in a deconstructive mode. The critic Brooke Jacobson and
the filmmaker Jill Godmilow have located "deconstruction" in
documentary films that undermine the appearance of objectivity
and leave us with ambiguous "open text" that demands interpretation, something that could certainly be said of de Antonio's
films.[91] Without a narrator's guidance the viewer of *In the Year
of the Pig* must connect the cinematic dots in a pattern that the
film only suggests. Moreover, the film includes many instances of
self-reflexive techniques, such as when we hear the filmmaker's
voice as he conducts an interview, or when interviewees look into
the camera without discomfort, contributing to the sense that de
Antonio does not want to hide the seams of the argument he is
constructing.

As the historian Bruce Cumings has argued, "De Antonio,
'mere' filmmaker, intuited the position of 'metahistorians' like
Michel de Certeau and Dominick LaCapra," who have emphasized the fictional and ideological influences on the construction
of historical "truth."[92] Such points are interesting to consider,

but I believe Cumings may be overstating the philosophical self-awareness of the filmmaker. Though de Antonio may have thrown around *deconstruction* in his later description of *In the Year of the Pig*, I would suggest that he was using the term more loosely—even inaccurately—as a metaphor for Marxist ideological criticism in particular, if not radical critique generally. Ascribing too much significance to de Antonio's films is as problematic as ascribing too little. De Antonio was more of a muckraker than a theorist, and his tools tended to be old-fashioned rather than philosophically au courant. For example, one of his most effective tools was humor, which he used to mock the powerful, a technique as old as Aristophanes.

The humor in *In the Year of the Pig* is the grim jesting of a satirist aimed at the official logic of the war. After the fifteen-minute section on the damage done to the people and land of Vietnam during the escalation of U.S. troop presence, the film includes a short Department of Defense propaganda film under the title "Communist Guerrilla Becomes U.S. Ally." This campy charade, the short story of a defecting North Vietnamese soldier who turns in his ignoble past for the American way of life, cannot help but elicit a guffaw from more cynical viewers—especially with a lush Mahler symphony pouring from the soundtrack. Generally, the black humor of *In the Year of the Pig* is more subtle, as in the next section, a seven-minute discussion of the 1967 election. In an Orwellian turn of phrase, Premier Nguyen Cao Ky defends his suppression of freedom of speech and of the press as necessary to prevent "confusion and division," as several commentators and images that suggest otherwise call into question the legitimacy of his statement.

The final section (seventeen minutes) examines the situation in the late 1960s and the prospects for the future. Harrison Salisbury of the *New York Times* describes the ravages of the war on the civilian population and observes that a multitude of North Vietnamese civilians have died in bombing raids on "military" targets. Pushing his romanticized and heroic portrait of the North Vietnamese, de Antonio goes on to emphasize their fortitude in its various manifestations, from their will to fight for as long as necessary to their ability to function as a society despite the interminable bombing. Daniel Berrigan sums up the situation as symptomatic of "the last days of Superman," as the United States is unable to achieve victory or to understand what it is losing. Then Paul Mus explains to the American audience: "You are not the first people who destroyed villages in Vietnam, unfortunately. And so, they are used to that, and it's a great tradition that the village is not lost even when it disappears from the surface of the ground." These are the last words of the film. In a strangely appropriate Chinese box structure it then ends much as it began— images of American GIs, now wounded, in agony, being carried to waiting helicopters. A scratchy version of the "Battle Hymn of the Republic" begins to play, and the screen fills with the image of the same Civil War statue that began the film, the same half-black screen, "to show, in my mind anyway," as de Antonio said, "that our cause in Vietnam was not the one that boy had died for in 1863."[93] So ends the film.

What has the audience just experienced? "The genius of de Antonio," wrote the *Harvard Crimson*, "is that he realizes that we see the actual war as a sort of documentary film." With a similar sentiment Theodor Adorno once described the effect of representing reality through the media: "Men are reduced to walk-on parts in a monster documentary-film."[94] This is exactly what de Antonio wanted to challenge, even if it required the ironic use of documentary film itself as a sort of "antifilm," a continuation of the Brechtian strategies he used in *Point of Order*. To break the viewer's passivity and emphasize the distance between the images of television and the statements of observers on one hand, and the reality of war on the other, de Antonio returned to his Brechtian technique, which "irritates the viewer into thought," as one reviewer noted.[95] And consider his use of sound, which was always important to him, though nowhere more than in a film for which his crew had recorded 70 percent of the sound, though only 35 percent of the images.[96] With what Pauline Kael described as "unusually good sound-editing," he created a seamless flow of voices and sounds to form a narrative line on the soundtrack.[97] Yet at times it is difficult to determine who is speaking, because the film identifies the speakers only when they first appear. When we hear their voices later in the film, the filmmaker—whose memory was probably more powerful than his audience's—gives no identification.

Other material on the soundtrack requires the viewer to recognize an unfamiliar sound at the risk of missing the point being made. De Antonio commissioned the introductory "helicopter concerto" from a student of John Cage, Steve Addiss, who also adapted several songs to be played on traditional Vietnamese folk instruments known as the dan bao and the dan tranh.[98] When the dan tranh's one trembling string plays "The Marseillaise" after the defeat of the French at Dienbienphu, the irony is as unmistakable as the tune. But the initial helicopter concerto, with its grating rotors and sputtering engines, is more difficult to identify without the image of a helicopter on screen. Only those who know the sound from experience can fully appreciate the full effect of the concerto, as made evident by the Vietnam veteran who instinctively ducked when he heard it at the beginning of the film, whereas many audience members were mystified.[99]

Such limitations of the historical documentary, even in the complex form that de Antonio uses, are important to remember when assessing the accomplishment of this type of film. Not only was the soundtrack a source of some confusion for the audience, from its initial screenings in 1968 to one I attended in 1992, but so were the images. As de Antonio's associate producer, John Atlee, wrote in an excellent in-house analysis of the film in 1968, it has a "disjointed collage effect" that did not suit the taste of many viewers at early screenings. More seriously, Atlee called the film "politically shallow" for not looking for systemic causes of the war—as a self-described Marxist filmmaker might be expected to do—or for ways to prevent such policies from being repeated. Atlee seems to have missed the point, for de Antonio was not making a Marxist critique, despite whatever he said, but a relatively brief film essay, a polemic on the irrationality of the war that at

times was guilty of the same quick treatment of complex issues
that dooms television to superficiality.[100]

An acknowledgment of these limitations should not undermine
the merit of *In the Year of the Pig*, however. Writing about the film,
de Antonio described his desire to create an "intellectual weapon"
against the U.S. involvement in Vietnam, "to make a movie that
was not a lecture, not a scream."[101] He succeeded in making an
important film at a time when the perspective of an intelligent
dissenter was desperately needed on screen. As Studs Terkel wrote
to de Antonio, "I still can't get *In the Year of the Pig* out of my
mind. . . . Now more than ever we need it."[102] Still, the filmmaker
was not satisfied—"Everyone praises it," he complained in 1971,
even though "no one seems to understand how it was made."[103]
Today he might complain about how few remember the film at
all, especially among the college-aged students who once filled
auditoriums to see his work. If they have any familiarity with the
work, it is from pieces that have resurfaced elsewhere in popular
culture, such as the use of an image from the film on a 1985 album
cover for an English pop group, The Smiths.[104]

Nevertheless, even if the film has slipped to the edge of our
cultural memory, *In the Year of the Pig* should be remembered as a
groundbreaking part of the filmography of Vietnam, especially because its influence on other films was significant. In an important
book dedicated in part to the memory of de Antonio, Bill Nichols
commends *In the Year of the Pig* for pioneering a way to examine
the relationship of past and present in a documentary and cites
eight films that show the influence of de Antonio's technique of
contrasting archival footage with interviews: *With Babies and
Banners* (Lorraine Gray, 1977), *The Wobblies* (Deborah Shaffer
and Stuart Bird, 1979), *Seeing Red* (Jim Klein and Julia Reichert,
1984), *The Life and Times of Rosie the Riveter* (Connie Field,
1980), *Solovki Power* (Marina Goldovskaya, 1988), and *Hotel
Terminus* (Marcel Ophuls, 1987).[105]

But Nichols does not discuss the film that *In the Year of
the Pig* most directly influenced, a better-known documentary
about Vietnam entitled *Hearts and Minds* (Peter Davis and Bert
Schneider, 1974). De Antonio resented this film and its producers

on several counts: their hiring of his editor from *In the Year of the Pig*; their use of similar and sometimes identical footage; their manipulation of interviews such that one interviewee, Walt W. Rostow, former national security adviser to Lyndon Johnson, took the filmmakers to court and obtained a restraining order forcing the deletion of a two-minute segment of his interview—all to produce a version of de Antonio's film that was palatable enough to mainstream America to win an Academy Award for best documentary in 1974.[106] De Antonio's animus cannot be attributed to simple professional jealousy, even if he was envious of the recognition that *Hearts and Minds* received, for such emotions never stopped him from applauding a film he admired, such as *Invitation to the Enemy* (Christine Burrill, Jane Fonda, Tom Hayden, Haskell Wexler, and Bill Yarhaus, 1974). What he so detested about *Hearts and Minds* was its "japing, middle-class, liberal superiority" toward the subject, "its contempt for America," which was particularly offensive from a film made at a time when the war was winding down and the risks to the filmmakers were smaller.[107]

He called the film "heartless and mindless," which was almost as cruel as his assessment of Francis Ford Coppola's Vietnam epic, *Apocalypse Now* (1979). He could only laugh at this "semi-literate" rendering of Conrad's *Heart of Darkness* with Marlon Brando as Kurtz: "in the heart of darkness we find a creampuff, a fat, bald, middle-aged creampuff spouting Eliot."[108] He complained that *Apocalypse Now* had nothing to do with the reality of Vietnam or the reality of America. Whether his own film did is a matter of opinion; what is certain is that it opens a window on the filmmaker's vision of the United States.

America Is Hard to See

In describing the beginning of *In the Year of the Pig*, I have pointed out how images move past the viewer's eyes like photos from a scrapbook, like recollections of "what has been good in U.S. life . . . as well as what was going awry in [Vietnam]," as the filmmaker wrote.[109] And at the end of the film we see images of the self-inflicted agony of the Americans fighting there, as the "Battle Hymn of the Republic" provides an ironic commentary on the moral differences between the American Civil War and the Vietnam War.

Between these two extremes lies a film about America whose setting is Vietnam, a film that "isn't just 'about' that war but rather about deep-seated American doubts of their future function as Americans," as one reviewer noted.[110] Even the distribution of those with speaking parts in *In the Year of the Pig* reflects this American focus: forty-six men and women (mostly men) from the United States; ten Europeans, mostly French; thirteen Vietnamese, from both the North and South. Furthermore, the film's emphasis—on the way in which the Vietnam experience reflected turmoil in the United States—can be seen in de Antonio's subsequent film, which functions as a domestic mirror of *In the Year of the Pig*.

This next film, *America Is Hard to See* (1970), takes its title from a poem of the same name by Robert Frost. As I discussed in the introduction, in this poem Columbus navigates along the coast of the "New World" with uncertainty, which seems to stand for the confusion of contemporary Americans:

> America is hard to see.
> Less partial witnesses than he
> In book on book have testified
> They could not see it from outside—
> Or inside either for that matter.[111]

Senator Eugene McCarthy, whose candidacy for the presidential nomination of the Democratic Party in 1968 is the subject of the film, chose *America Is Hard to See* as the title of the book he was writing about the campaign. When his publisher rejected it as uncommercial, opting instead for *The Year of the People*, an unintentional echo of *In the Year of the Pig*, de Antonio decided to use Frost's phrase as the title for his film.[112]

America Is Hard to See depicts the failure of liberalism in 1968 from the vantage of a filmmaker whose hopes to do something meaningful "within the system as we know it" rested upon one "decent, complicated intellectual," as he described McCarthy.[113] Tracing the McCarthy campaign from its humble start to its disappointing finish at the Democratic National Convention in Chicago the following summer, de Antonio built the film from the usual archival footage and specially conducted interviews. We see McCarthy himself, as well as supporters and observers such as the playwright Arthur Miller, economist John Kenneth Galbraith, former Johnson speechwriter Richard Goodwin, and antiwar activist Martin Peretz, whose wife helped finance the film.[114]

Released one year after *In the Year of the Pig*, this film continues de Antonio's critique of the U.S. role in Vietnam. It begins with the words *In the gap of credibility* written across a photo of President Johnson and his cabinet, then launches into a short reiteration of the themes of *In the Year of the Pig*, emphasizing the "arrogance of power," to use the phrase of Senator William Fulbright, the Arkansas Democrat. Included in the film are excerpts from the Department of Defense's bizarre documentary from 1965, *Why Vietnam?* that provide the opportunity for McCarthy to repudiate that film's comparison of Ho Chi Minh to Hitler.

However, the bulk of *America Is Hard to See* concerns the inner workings of a presidential campaign, a process that seems, from an insider's vantage, to be designed to minimize participatory democracy. De Antonio's admiration for the quixotic spirit of McCarthy's grassroots efforts, as well as for the wit and intelligence of the candidate, is evident throughout the film.[115] Though his film avoids the mawkish heroism of *Mr. Smith Goes to Washington* (Frank Capra, 1939), de Antonio attempts to paint the candidate in the hues of Adlai Stevenson's statement about McCarthy: "There is no more eloquent representative of what is good in American life."[116] But no matter how eloquent the candidate, how idealistic the campaign, the machinery of politics pushes aside our urbane and modern Jimmy Stewart and the rest of "what is good in American life." The film ends on the sour note of Hubert Humphrey's giving thanks to Lyndon Johnson as

Humphrey accepts the Democratic presidential nomination—a pessimistic ending to an otherwise hopeful film.

Like de Antonio's other "positive" films such as *Underground*, the filmmaker seems to be slightly lost without an obvious target for his anger, and perhaps this explains why the film received inadequate distribution and few reviews. Too often his efforts to praise the virtues of Senator McCarthy come across as halfhearted and unpersuasive, rendering McCarthy as bland as the film's caricatures of Humphrey and Robert F. Kennedy. The reviewer for *Cinéaste*, one of the few film journals to take note of the film, complained about this shortcoming and trashed de Antonio for taking "a tedious and disingenuous look at his subject" and for refusing to explain "in what way Eugene McCarthy could represent a significant alternative to his supposedly more conservative antagonists in the Democratic Party."[117] The reviewer was particularly incensed that the film would present "a standard politician as a daring rebel," though de Antonio acknowledged as much in interviews related to the release of the film. "*America Is Hard to See* represents a dramatic change in my work because it is a very positive statement about one man and his work in America in the 1960s," he said, willing to ignore the leftist skepticism about McCarthy because de Antonio recognized something of himself in the candidate—another idealistic intellectual in whom he saw hope for changing U.S. politics.[118] Yet the disappointment of the film's ending reveals something darker than was evident to the *Cinéaste* reviewer, something that is fundamental to de Antonio's vision of America, which blends hope and despair in equal measure. The real importance of this otherwise minor film is as a complement to de Antonio's previous film. When viewed in combination with *In the Year of the Pig*, one can discern the basic outline of this vision.

"As I became more involved in film, the great seams of the American Empire began to give way more and more, revealing the hollowness of the centre," he confided in a 1972 letter.[119] Each of his films added a chapter to his informal study of the decline of the American empire, and in this sense he saw himself as a cinematic Gibbon of his age, at least in the sense that Gibbon's great history of the Roman Empire was a "creation of strong feeling and great mental vigor rather than psychological depth . . . [imbued with] grief at the extinction of values dear to the enlightenment."[120] Driven by the same secular passion for rationality as Gibbon, de Antonio produced a body of work that fits this description equally well. Because he is placed so quickly in an amorphous, if vaguely leftist, category of "radical filmmaker," it is easy to overlook the strain of cultural conservatism in his thinking, one that is reflected in his films, as I will discuss, and his choice of literary heroes: Gibbon, Santayana, and Eliot. Each wrote from a cosmopolitan, often expatriate, perspective that de Antonio claimed for himself, although he spent most of his life only a few hours from where he was born: "Yes, I am cut off. It was my father who introduced me to that god awful word which Santayana liked too: déraciné."[121] This perspective accounts for both his fascination with what it meant to be American as well as the detachment that enabled him to attack his homeland with such vitriol.

In her review of *In the Year of the Pig* in the *New Yorker*, Pauline Kael recognized these aspects of the film: "de Antonio obviously means to suggest a basic rottenness in Americans, and an America which is anti-life."[122] Certainly, one can find hints of this cultural pessimism throughout his films, and explicitly in his journal, where he paints a melancholy portrait of a country that killed Native American women and children "to make room for plodding farmers who were in turn run off the land by the banks and agribusiness." Where was honor? What gods, what dreams could live in such a place? Unable to answer these questions, he announced his agreement with Allen Ginsberg that it is time to say Kaddish for America.[123]

Yet Kael's understanding of de Antonio is incomplete, for he also admired America "when it can be found," as he said, when it is not "hard to see." He believed that his work was "always in opposition but not necessarily in hate, for at bottom I love America as well as hate what it's doing and what is happening."[124] The object of his patriotic impulses was in the past, when he believed the country had been different, that its innocence had once been genuine, that the authors of the Bill of Rights were made of different stuff than Richard Nixon and Lyndon Johnson.[125] De Antonio expressed these views, often obliquely, in his films and, more privately, in his writings. Quoting Melville in his journals of the late seventies, de Antonio wistfully described America's chance to be the river of the blood of all the people of the earth and with bitterness reported that instead we became "a flashy urinal."[126] Then he referred to Hemingway's statement that America was ruined after the Civil War—hence the images at the beginning and end of *In the Year of the Pig*—when "all the robber barons became our souls," as de Antonio phrased it.[127] This was the same conflict of idealism and materialism that Santayana dissected in *Character and Opinion in the United States*, a book that had a profound influence on de Antonio, who no less than Hemingway or Santayana saw the turning point of American culture in the Civil War.[128]

In fact, the essence of his vision of the United States can be traced to his childhood tears over the "faint little men who had fought in the Civil War [standing] before my grammar school assembly in 1929." Weeping at the sight of their blue uniforms and tattered campaign ribbons as a boy, he remembered their names throughout his life.[129] He believed, perhaps naively, that the nobility of those men could be recaptured in the contemporary struggle for social change and that he had no alternative but to work and hope for a radical renewal of America.[130] This hopeful romanticism undercut his conservatism, making it possible for him to believe in the beneficence of change, even the necessity of revolution, in a way his literary heroes had never allowed.[131] If the virtues of America were hard to see, if the spirit of revolution was frustrated at every turn by the "police state" he so detested, they might be glimpsed in his romantic vision of the Vietnamese, who were resisting the onslaught of U.S. culture with a vehemence he could only admire. If Ho Chi Minh was the George Washington of his country, as we learn from Senator Morton in the film, in a metaphoric sense Ho was a founder of de Antonio's America as well.

5

◄o►

The Incursion into
Richard Milhous Nixon

Chasing Checkers and Other Political Animals

In 1970 de Antonio was working at his office in the
Movielab building in New York City with his editor, Mary Lampson, and staff members Marc Weiss, Tanya Neufeld, and Nancy
Ogden. The project at hand was the editing of *Painters Painting*,
de Antonio's film about the major figures of American art at
midcentury—Willem de Kooning, Andy Warhol, Robert Rauschenberg, Clement Greenberg, Jasper Johns, Barnett Newman,
Frank Stella, and others. The office phone rang and de Antonio
heard a "voice from the past," whose anonymity he subsequently
preserved. All he would say in public was that the voice belonged
to an old contact at one of the television networks, someone who
knew him from his research on an earlier film.

"We've just ripped off the whole Nixon library at the XYZ
network and we'll give it to you if you'll make a film out it,"
the voice told him. "XYZ" turned out to be NBC, where the
voice claimed to have a friend employed in the editing room
that prepared television obituaries for dignitaries such as Nixon.
Much of this material was unavailable to the public through legal
channels; it would be a windfall for de Antonio, whose antipathy
toward Nixon was deep and long-standing. But if he accepted the
offer, he would be receiving stolen goods, a misdemeanor in the
State of New York that carried a penalty of a year in jail. He

113

warily asked the voice: "Are you [for] real? How much do you want?" The caller wanted nothing in return. The only condition was that de Antonio had to decide in the next twenty minutes.

He hung up and considered the implications of the call. He didn't need a lawyer to understand the legalities. He had broken the law for the sake of his films before, such as when he stole footage from a French military archive for *In the Year of the Pig*. For de Antonio the real question was one of ethics—not his own but those of the television networks, whose policies regulating access to their archival footage had long infuriated him. As a documentary filmmaker he had an obvious need for such footage, access to which was often denied for seemingly arbitrary reasons. No reason would have satisfied de Antonio, of course—he firmly believed the visual record of U.S. history belonged to the public. From this vantage, then, he felt a moral obligation to "liberate" the material, as he put it, and he called back to accept the offer, putting aside the completion of *Painters Painting* for the time being.

The call had been secretive, but the melodrama did not end there. On the phone he had been instructed to meet the "liberators" in front of a large apartment house on 16th Street. He walked there and found three young men; one pulled a key from a hiding place in the dirt. He soon learned that the key opened a garage on 11th Street, east of First Avenue in Manhattan, that was filled with cans of film taken from the NBC film library.

Now the liberators' guise of noble political motivation began to fade: one did want money—$1,000—for traveling. Another admitted to having wrecked editing equipment during the film heist. However, from de Antonio's perspective, the quality of the footage made up for the excesses of its bearers, and he arranged for the material, 220 cans of 2,000-foot rolls of film, to be left in the foyer of his building in the middle of the night. He and Mary Lampson sequestered themselves in their offices for the next three days, working almost without rest to make new negatives of the material, paranoid that at any moment the FBI would appear to seize the film, which was marked with numbers and other identifying material from NBC. After cataloging the stolen footage, de Antonio decided to keep only the material on Nixon, which included a rare copy of the Checkers speech; the rest, such as material on the Native American occupation of Alcatraz, he delivered to the Cuban embassy to use in its films—"thereby breaking two laws," as he later told one audience with some amusement.[1] He may have also had no use for material that was favorable to Nixon, who had been praised by some Native American activists for his handling of the Alcatraz occupation.[2]

Had the material been about any other politician—John F. Kennedy, Lyndon Baines Johnson, Hubert Humphrey—de Antonio would have shown little interest. But his fascination with Nixon went back to the early fifties, to the Alger Hiss case in particular. De Antonio claimed to be "depoliticized" during this period, yet he nonetheless managed to follow the Hiss case closely. Though de Antonio was not certain of Hiss's innocence, he believed that the evidence did not warrant the conviction that Nixon and the FBI had obtained.[3]

From that point on de Antonio saw Nixon as "a disjointed, sleazy and . . . self-serving scoundrel patriot," a symbol of everything he despised in American politics. "I hated him," de Antonio wrote in his journal, though over time he claimed to transfer his scorn more to what Nixon signified than the man himself. De Antonio, the former English instructor and always voracious reader, began to conceive of Nixon in terms of literature: as Molière's Tartuffe, as Robert Musil's Man Without Qualities, as a Richard III too filled with personal insecurities and Protestant guilt to enjoy his power. Nixon was "the villain in Horatio Alger who made good by consummate hypocrisy, who claimed pluck and luck when it was in fact the cheapest opportunism divorced from principles." In a more succinct, if Rabelaisian, metaphor of Nixon's perversion of the Protestant ethic, de Antonio described him as "Horatio Alger with his thumb in his ass."[4]

Because de Antonio saw Nixon as an apt symbol of the American political system, he was unavoidable for a filmmaker who with each successive film was creating an alternative history of the United States during the cold war era. He viewed Nixon as the only major figure in American life who "runs the whole length of the Cold War and ends up in power."[5] Politically, he linked Nixon to another early cold warrior, one who had long since fallen from grace—Senator Joseph McCarthy, the subject of his first film, *Point of Order*. De Antonio saw Nixon as a smarter, more cautious—and hence more dangerous—version of McCarthy. To make a film attacking Nixon would be a worthwhile project and would complement his other films on American political figures, such as *Point of Order, That's Where the Action Is*, and *America Is Hard to See*. Yet it would also be more difficult, because Nixon was in office, with the power and political savvy to cover his errors. De Antonio had learned this firsthand in 1968, when he attempted to locate a copy of Nixon's Checkers speech of September 23, 1952, in which the vice presidential candidate saves his place on the Republican ticket by conflating suspicious campaign contributions with the gift of a dog named Checkers.

During the 1968 presidential campaign, de Antonio began looking for a copy of the speech as a way of alleviating his boredom and bitterness at watching what he expected to be a Nixon victory. It was "one small way in which I could stick it in Nixon's ass without necessarily helping Humphrey," wrote de Antonio, who viewed Humphrey as "contemptible and empty, with an expansive heart, a liberal heart, when his self-interest wasn't endangered." If he could locate a copy of the Checkers speech and screen it at independent movie theaters or perhaps on college campuses, he thought it could spark opposition to Nixon among younger voters.[6] He was not the first person to find himself "chasing Checkers," as he put it. The writer Gore Vidal, as a member of John F. Kennedy's campaign team in 1960, had tried unsuccessfully to obtain a print. "We thought it would be marvelous to use for Kennedy," Vidal said, "and we tried everything we could think of to get hold of it. But it was as if it had never existed."[7]

De Antonio called various television networks in search of the print. On August 23, 1968, NBC claimed to have a copy and was pleased to sell it, though its release would have to be approved—a mere formality. Send in a purchase order, de Antonio was told. Then on August 26, an NBC attorney, Paul Johnson, called the filmmaker. NBC had made a mistake; the network could not release such material without permission from the sponsors of the original broadcast, the Republican National Committee. De Antonio reached someone named Gus Miller at the RNC, who was not pleased to hear from him. No, absolutely not, Miller said, not without permission of the "client," who turned out to be Nixon himself. Calling Nixon's law offices, de Antonio spoke with a lawyer named Barbara Baiter, who said she would consider the matter and get back to him. She never did.[8]

Rebuffed in every legitimate request for the material, de Antonio decided that "some words are better than no picture," so he and a writer who had worked as assistant director on *In the Year of the Pig*, Albert Maher, transcribed portions of the speech and wrote a brief introduction recounting Nixon's tactics to suppress the Checkers footage. De Antonio initially offered the article to the *New York Times* and other major media outlets, but none were interested in even a letter to the editor on the subject.[9] Undaunted, he offered the transcript to an underground paper in Manhattan, the *New York Free Press*, which published it as a cover story a month before the election. The article was insignificant to the election's outcome, but it is important nonetheless because it was de Antonio's first step toward making a feature-length satirical documentary about the president, an attack that would the "first incursion into Richard Milhous Nixon," as one writer phrased it.[10]

Considering the ordeal de Antonio went through in his attempt to poke fun at Nixon, one might conclude that the political climate was such that satire of a sitting president was unacceptable and unsalable. Nothing could have been further from the truth; de Antonio's satirical hostility toward the president was just one example of a burgeoning subgenre of political satire with an unusual severity of ad hominem attack.[11] Perhaps Lee Harvey Oswald is to blame, for satirists of John F. Kennedy suffered a serious career setback with the assassination, which made it difficult to mock the slain leader for profit. A reservoir of resentment must have accumulated during the mourning of Kennedy, for shortly after Johnson ascended to the presidency he became the object of especially bitter satire. The most notorious example was Barbara Garson's play *Macbird!* which ran off-Broadway for several months in 1967, before moving to London—ever the impresario, de Antonio played a small role in the play's British success by encouraging its production in letters to friends in London theater circles. A broad parody of Macbeth, *Macbird!* caricatured Johnson as the mastermind behind Kennedy's death.[12] The novelist Philip Roth described *Macbird!* as the closest thing in the American tradition of political satire to "the brutal and impious manner of Aristophanes."[13]

In the wake of Garson's play, and with the new acceptance of a vitriolic style of political satire, de Antonio was not the only intellectual to find an ideal target in Richard Nixon, who had reemerged from political hibernation to capture the presidency in 1968. The new climate of creative irreverence included some of the best writers and artists of the era, all of whom were inspired by hostility toward Nixon. The abstract-expressionist painter Philip Guston shifted to representational mode for the first time in his career, spending the summer of 1971 preparing caricatures of Nixon and his cabinet that he described as "very serious, but funny . . . vituperative." In the same year Gore Vidal wrote a play, *An Evening with Richard Nixon*, using only Nixon's actual words to illustrate his essential boorishness, to use Vidal's description. Woody Allen also planned a "little funny documentary" about Nixon in 1971. It was entitled *The Politics of Woody Allen*, and PBS refused to broadcast the half-hour film at the last minute, fearing budgetary reprisals from the administration. But most similar to de Antonio's mode of thinking about the president was Philip Roth's popular novel *Our Gang*, which appeared about the same time as the film de Antonio was making about Nixon.[14]

De Antonio and Roth shared a way of thinking about Nixon that is reflected in Roth's choice of epigraphs for his book: a quote about lying from Jonathan Swift's "A Voyage to the Houyhnhnms" and, more significant, several lines from George Orwell's essay from 1946, "Politics and the English Language." When conceiving of the Nixon film, de Antonio too focused on what Orwell identified as "the decay of language" in politics, which "is designed to make lies sound truthful and murder respectable, and to give an appearance of solidity to pure wind."[15] Indeed, one film critic later perceived this Orwellian aspect of de Antonio's work on Nixon, writing that "when [Nixon] uses words like 'democracy,' 'freedom,' and 'progress,' they take on immutable, ideological connotations that have nothing to do with a nation undergoing continual change."[16] Or, as de Antonio said, returning as he often did to a Platonic metaphor: "The man's a figment of his own rhetoric, a cave of winds."[17] Much in the same vein, he often paraphrased the German philosopher Karl Jaspers, claiming that "anything can be said as long as it signifies nothing."

Roth makes a similar point in his satirical novel, which reveals a great deal about the intellectual climate in which de Antonio was operating, one in which few boundaries were placed upon the political satirist. *Our Gang*'s protagonist is a villainous character named Trick E. Dixon, described on the book jacket as "a hypocritical opportunist such as might be found in a comedy by Molière." The connection to literary tradition appealed greatly to de Antonio, for he often spoke of Nixon as "Tartuffian." Perhaps *Tartuffe* was a natural leap for an educated mind to make when confronted with the spectacle of Nixon; or perhaps de Antonio borrowed it from Roth, even though he began work on his Nixon film almost a year before Roth's *Our Gang* appeared. Undoubtedly, the sentiment embodied in their work was very similar, though Roth, to a greater extent than de Antonio, believed "good taste" was irrelevant and claimed: "To ask a satirist to be in good taste is like asking a love poet to be less personal."[18]

Whether it was good politics was also irrelevant to a novelist who believed satire to be "essentially a literary, not a political act," a point of view that frees satirists from concern about the potential political impact of their work. This school of satire, in which de Antonio sometimes fits, makes satire a symbolic release, a creative expression of outrage at Nixon's duplicities, or, as Roth said, a manifestation of "the imaginative flowering of the primitive urge to knock somebody's block off."[19]

The difference, of course, is that de Antonio faced a different, and perhaps larger, set of obstacles than a writer such as Philip Roth. His métier was film, and his idea—a satirical political documentary—had no clear antecedents. In the history of American documentary no one had demonstrated the desire or the gall to make a film subverting the authority of a sitting president. Furthermore, to make a satirical documentary—two seemingly antithetical modes of discourse—raised a variety of aesthetic problems. By definition satire makes no claims to objectivity, the mythical veil in which documentary had often shrouded itself. De Antonio attempted to solve this paradox by retaining an emphasis on historical factuality while jettisoning claims to objectivity—the same rationale that many New Journalists use. The two forms are less at odds than they might seem at first glance, for if documentary was the "creative expression of reality," to use the oft-quoted definition from the documentary pioneer John Grierson, then satire should be within its boundaries.

For the time being, the greater obstacle for de Antonio was the nature of the medium itself. Film is expensive, even for low-budget filmmakers. By 1970 an independent filmmaker was obliged to raise a considerable sum of capital, in this case more than $100,000. The irony was not lost on de Antonio that he needed the fund-raising skills of an entrepreneur and the sympathetic ear of very rich individuals in order to make a radical film.

To finance the as-yet-unnamed project, de Antonio began casting his net for potential investors. As was his practice on earlier films, he formed a new corporation for the Nixon film, the Whittier Film Corp. (an allusion to Nixon's alma mater), thereby receiving a new exemption from the sales tax of the State of New York.[20] Then he started to solicit funds, though he had neither the patience nor properly suppliant attitude to request money from grant-bestowing agencies and other institutions, which probably would have looked askance at his project anyway. Consequently, he had little choice but to do as he had always done, which was to rely on the patronage of rich friends and associates, some of whom he met through family members. For example, his brother, Carlo, a doctor in Encino, California, provided the name of a prospective investor, a medical colleague named Richard Saxon. On June 2, 1970, de Antonio wrote a long letter to Saxon, explaining his modus operandi as a political filmmaker. Prefacing the candid and sardonic letter by asserting that "this is not a solicitation for you to invest," he then proceeded to solicit Saxon's investment, conceding that "left-wing documentary films are generally money losers, not winners." In fact, he "couldn't think of a worse investment," in part because the distribution of such films is "usually performed by the inept and occasionally by inept crooks." Attempting to be fair to his prospective investor, de Antonio explained that most of his backers came from "the very rich," which was why he did not invest in his own films.

Asking for money was a necessary evil of making films, and he had made it into a art form, one in which he refused to grovel or even plead. Instead, his letters soliciting financial support made their case with the simplicity and brevity of someone who has better things to do, using an almost aggressive directness rather than the beseeching tone one might expect. In his letter to Dr. Saxon, de Antonio explained the nature of the investment and its drawbacks, then suggested the doctor locate fifty to one hundred politically sympathetic professionals to form a foundation that could become "a powerful political force in the arts and many other areas." The letter concluded with two characteristically cheeky observations: that the foundation would allow doctors and other professionals to begin acting like intellectuals rather than "members of the A.M.A. or the Bar Association," and that "their wives should probably run it." Whether Saxon followed up on this scheme is unknown; he was, however, persuaded to make a small investment of one share ($1,000).[21]

Needing to secure a larger investment, de Antonio returned to the blue bloods who had made possible his earlier films, looking for the sort of person who could afford to purchase ten or twenty shares. On August 5, 1970, he wrote a short letter to Stewart R. Mott, explaining that he was doing a film biography of Nixon and had been "lucky enough to obtain the only print of the 'Checkers' speech." Mott was, as de Antonio scrawled across the letter, "$$, daddy is largest General Motors stockholder." Then, returning to the sociable style that resulted in his first financial coup, the $100,000 check written by Elliot Pratt over lunch for *Point of Order*, de Antonio suggested that Mott and he meet to have a drink and talk about the film. This time the pitch failed; according to extant records, Mott did not invest.[22] However, others were persuaded by de Antonio's considerable charm. By the end of August 1970 the Whittier Film Corp. included the future publisher of the *New Republic*, Martin Peretz, and his wife, Anne Peretz, who bought $48,000 worth of shares; four other major investors, including James Hoge, editor of the *Chicago Sun-Times*, and his wife, Alice Hoge, also a journalist, who together contributed $10,000; and several individuals holding one share each. As president of the corporation, de Antonio granted ten shares to his editor, Mary Lampson, as an inducement to continue working for him for far less than was commonly paid to union editors.[23] The total capital raised was approximately $88,000, enough to begin the film but not quite enough to complete it.

Only a few more investors joined the list, but their contributions were significant. In late 1970 de Antonio indicated that the actors Elliot Gould and Dustin Hoffman were likely to add $15,000, though records do not make clear whether this ever transpired.[24] The last significant investment came from heirs to the Standard Oil fortune—though this time not Elliot Pratt, *Point of Order*'s angel.

Laura S. Rockefeller Case and Marion F. Rockefeller Weber, daughters of Laurence Rockefeller, and Abby A. Rockefeller, daughter of David, had bought shares in *In the Year of the Pig*. For the Nixon film, whose title de Antonio kept secret throughout production, the Rockefeller heirs also made sizable investments, buying stock in de Antonio's production company and providing loans. In 1974 the journalist Jack Anderson revealed the

Rockefeller involvement in de Antonio's film; Anderson claimed the family put up $37,000 of the film's cost of $200,000. More likely, the Rockefellers contributed in the vicinity of $23,250 of the total cost, which was closer to $110,000.[25]

Thus de Antonio was able to raise sufficient funds in a short period of time; he was a rare independent filmmaker in his ability to raise money quickly but equally rare for eventually repaying his investors. On February 22, 1972, de Antonio sent $2,500 to Laura Rockefeller Case, promising to repay the remainder of her loan of $11,000 (with 4 percent interest) in the next year. In May he satisfied this obligation and thanked her, noting that "without your loan, the film could not have been finished."[26]

Aside from the financial woes that continually beset any independent filmmaker, de Antonio faced several creative and logistical dilemmas. The first problem was deciding who to interview, then persuading that person to go on-camera. Although he could have made a film simply from editing the stolen archival footage in the pure compilation technique of *Point of Order*, once again he planned to conduct interviews to interweave with the archival footage. In addition to being a satire, his film would be a sort of biography; as always, he researched extensively, closely reading accounts of Nixon's life, developing a bibliography of relevant material. Several of his prospective interviewees had written books about Nixon, with Garry Wills being perhaps the best known. Others were friends, colleagues, political opponents. What he needed from such people was something beyond the "dryness of political books," because "the trick is to find people, to get them to agree to talk and to talk freely."[27] Though not as frustrating as looking for witnesses to the Kennedy assassination, as he and Mark Lane had done for *Rush to Judgment*, finding people who met those conditions was no small task.

Though de Antonio tended to select interviewees who would put his sentiments into words, in effect providing him with a series of narrative voices that told the same story he might have told himself in voice-over narration, he also attempted to find subjects with whom he disagreed. However, their words were more likely to appear in the final film if they suited his larger argument in some way. In the case of the Nixon project, interviewing the subject himself was out of the question, as was interviewing Nixon's staff, his friends, and his family. If the film were about President Ronald Reagan, his less loyal children might have spoken on camera, but de Antonio did not even attempt to cajole interviews from Nixon's family and associates. Nonetheless, de Antonio pursued some individuals with a tenacity that was usually not rewarded.

His most unlikely target was Governor George C. Wallace of Alabama. De Antonio intended to obtain an inflammatory interview from the governor in order to use the far right (Wallace) to bruise the moderate right (Nixon). In his letters de Antonio sidled up to the southerner with praise for his "refreshing candor" and congratulations on his reelection in the gubernatorial race of 1970. De Antonio was sincere in complimenting Wallace's direct way of speaking, which he contrasted to Nixon's obfuscatory rhetorical style, especially because de Antonio viewed the substance of the two politicians as essentially the same. De Antonio did not try to hide his left-wing credentials; rather, he explained, "in fairness . . . to Governor Wallace . . . I'd like to point out that my political beliefs are completely dissimilar to his." He offered to bring a film crew to Alabama to shoot an interview lasting no more than forty minutes. Unfortunately, after two months of exchanging negotiatory letters, Wallace declined the opportunity.[28]

Perhaps a greater loss was Helen Gahagan Douglas. The former Broadway and opera star was elected to the House of Representatives in 1944. A New Dealer, she attracted the support of California liberals as a result of her support of labor and outspoken criticism of the House Un-American Activities Committee (HUAC), though she was not liberal enough to support Henry Wallace's Progressive Party in the 1948 election. In 1948 she and Nixon squared off in the race for the U.S. Senate, and Nixon tarred his opponent with a half-million copies of the infamous "pink sheet"—he had Douglas's voting record printed on pink paper to insinuate that she was soft on communism. De Antonio obtained one of the ancient pink sheets and filmed it to use in conjunction with newsreel footage of Douglas, as an example of

Tricky Dick's campaign technique. Ideally, he would have had an interview with the former member of Congress as well, but she was not interested.[29]

Nor was Ring Lardner, Jr., a blacklisted screenwriter who had been brought before HUAC but who had little desire to speak about Nixon on film, though he "enthusiastically" supported the project. Another no came from Dr. Arnold A. Hutschnecker, Nixon's psychiatrist, who might have provided psychological insights into the president's personality, a line of inquiry later brought to public attention by works such as Eli S. Chesen's *President Nixon's Psychiatric Profile: A Psychodynamic-Genetic Interpretation.*[30] However, the most elusive interviewee, the one whose absence de Antonio most regretted, was Professor Albert Upton.

Upton had been Nixon's English teacher at Whittier College in the early thirties; he had introduced the young Quaker to Tolstoy and directed him in student productions. In one play, John Drinkwater's *Bird in Hand*, Nixon was cast in the lead, a part he played successfully except for one aspect: he was unable to cry on cue. Real tears were simply not forthcoming, so Upton explained to his pupil, "If you just concentrate real hard. . . . I think you can cry real tears." The trick worked. Upton had told the story in print on a number of occasions; he would even tell it to de Antonio in person at his home in California but not with the camera or tape recorder rolling. As a consequence of Upton's refusal, de Antonio lost an opportunity to provide an obvious link between Nixon's acting ability and his manipulation of the television audience. For example, although Nixon may have been genuinely frightened and angry, de Antonio viewed Nixon's emotional performance in the Checkers speech as contrived and mawkish. Indeed, Nixon was reported to have said of the speech: "I staged it." And the Hollywood producer Darryl Zanuck seemed to confirm Nixon's skillful Checkers performance, wiring the vice president to say it was "wonderful."[31]

Finally, de Antonio hoped to interview the writer who was producing some of the most insightful and intelligent analyses of Nixon's career—Garry Wills. Wills's soon-to-be acclaimed book,

Nixon Agonistes, was still in galleys as de Antonio began his research, but his interest was piqued by what he called Wills's "brilliant" essay, "Nixon's Dog," in *Esquire* in August 1969.[32] This essay later became chapter 5, "Checkers," in *Nixon Agonistes*, an account of the speech that so fascinated de Antonio.[33] De Antonio wrote to Wills on June 17, 1970, asking to see galleys for his book and requesting "a brief filmed interview." Wills politely declined the interview, explaining that he was "not a performer," that he even refused his publisher's requests to publicize his book with television appearances. Wills suggested that de Antonio might contact John Cronin, a priest who wrote speeches for Nixon throughout the 1950s. In his refusal to be interviewed Cronin was more firm, less polite, and subtly protective of his friend in the White House.[34]

Yet for every refusal de Antonio located someone who was willing to speak on film; de Antonio's sister-in-law, Madeline de Antonio, Carlo's wife, was instrumental in finding several of these interviewees. Because she lived in Encino, she was in a good position to track down Nixon's oldest friends and enemies from his years on the West Coast. Throughout the second half of 1970, as he was beginning the film, de Antonio repeatedly wrote Madeline for assistance in finding information or arranging interviews. He asked whether she could locate footage in which "Joe McCarthy speaks for Nixon in 1950 campaign," and a copy of "Tom Braden's pamphlet on Nixon and the Hughes Tool Co.," which described a $200,000 loan made to Donald Nixon, brother of the then vice president, by one of the largest defense contractors. In a bit of the cloak-and-dagger that appeared so often in the making of his films, de Antonio assigned code names to potential interviewees for the purposes of his correspondence. Predicting Madeline's response, he wrote: "Don't smile too broadly at code names. When I was in Dallas for *Rush to Judgement* about half of the people who agreed to cooperate refused after the passage of a little time," which he attributed to pressure from "FBI, police etc."[35]

Whether this secrecy was helpful is unknown, but de Antonio was able to obtain several good interviews. Marjorie Hildreth

Knighton, the president's prom date at Whittier College, reminisced pleasantly but rather unproductively for the camera; asked to think of an anecdote about her old boyfriend, she drew a blank, unable to think of anything. The effect, as a reviewer later wrote, was "Transylvanian, as if the man had passed in front of the mirror and not created a reflection."[36] Other interviewees were politicians familiar with Nixon's career. Burton, the Democratic member of Congress from San Francisco and a striking film presence, recounted incidents from Nixon's defeat of Helen Gahagan Douglas. The best interview, however, was with Jerry Voorhis, whom Nixon had defeated for Congress in 1946.

Voorhis was concerned about sounding like "sour grapes," but eager to have an opportunity to denounce his old foe, for whom he had little regard. The interview took place in July 1970 at Voorhis's office in Chicago, where he had moved from California. The wistful old man told of the tough political lessons he received from the Nixon campaign team, such as anonymous phone calls made to voters throughout his district—the caller would announce, "Voorhis is a Communist" and hang up, part of a campaign that Nixon's biographer, Stephen E. Ambrose, characterized as a "vicious, snarling approach that was full of half-truths, full lies, and innuendos" about Voorhis's alleged left-wing sympathies. Ironically, Voorhis had written the Voorhis Act of 1940, a conservative piece of legislation that required the registration of all Communists in the United States, something de Antonio would not mention in the final film.

Pleased with the interview and Voorhis's general helpfulness, de Antonio wrote to reassure him that "your appearance is excellent, your manner sympathetic, clear, rational and kind. At the same time, the facts are there. I can't understand why more journalists haven't found them."[37] De Antonio had little respect for journalists as a group but greatly admired the exceptions whose independence of mind reflected his own. He sought out such individuals for his films.

Unable to get Garry Wills, de Antonio was able to interview some intelligent Nixon watchers among the press. Fred Cook, author of many political books, asserted Alger Hiss's innocence in the face of Nixon's politically motivated accusations, a point that de Antonio did not feel obliged to counter with his own reservations about the issue. The *New York Post*'s James Wechsler, who had described *Point of Order* as "a love letter to Miss Liberty" in 1964, discussed aspects of Nixon's early career, such as the events leading up to the Checkers speech. Jack Anderson spoke about the Hughes Tool Company's loan to Nixon's brother. Jules Witcover, author of *The Resurrection of Richard Nixon*, described Nixon's strategy for coming back from defeats in the presidential election of 1960 and the California gubernatorial race of 1962 to win the presidency in 1968. Still, de Antonio's favorite interview was with Joe McGinniss, author of *The Selling of the President, 1968*.

In 1968 McGinniss, then a young journalist, had set out to write a book about the role of advertising in presidential campaigns. He approached the Humphrey camp and was rebuffed, because they understandably preferred to keep such information out of the public view. Before giving up, McGinniss tried the Nixon campaign, and much to his surprise, the Republicans consented. In fact, they were "happy to cooperate," as long as he did not publish anything until after the election. Consequently, McGinniss was privy to an inside view of the mechanics of modern American politics, the sort of manipulation that de Antonio wanted to tie to Nixon in his film, though he knew it applied equally to all candidates. In late 1970 de Antonio interviewed this "handsome young Irish American," as he called McGinniss, at his farmhouse in New Jersey. The crew shot ten rolls of films—one hundred minutes of material—which became only four minutes in the final film. As de Antonio said, "I take the hundred minutes and in a sense I re-write those hundred minutes into what I really want him to say in the film," a technique that reveals a filmmaker with a clear idea of what he wants to create.[38]

His clarity of vision helped him know not only who to interview but what else he would require to make a good film about Nixon. He wrote the University of Oklahoma for photographs of Helen Gahagan Douglas, and to ABC newsman Ted Koppel, requesting footage of the opulence of Nixon's campaign retinue. De Antonio lied and said ABC had sold him some other Nixon material; still, the request was denied. Other material he obtained with a larger prevarication, that he needed footage to "give some talks at universities" on various imaginary subjects. And though the *Washington Post* denied permission to film Herblock's famous political cartoon of Nixon climbing out of the sewer from September 25, 1952, de Antonio procured from the *St. Louis Post-Dispatch* a Fitzpatrick cartoon entitled "Variations on a Theme" from April 28, 1954. The drawing shows Nixon playing piano under a candelabrum of smoking guns that are emitting the words *War in Indochina*. Finally, for the purposes of posters advertising the film, de Antonio was happy to pay $300 for the rights to a David Levine caricature of Nixon and Spiro Agnew, Nixon's vice president, that had appeared in the *New York Review of Books*; it showed a shifty-eyed Nixon, and Agnew as a faceless egghead, and captured the spirit of a project that was gradually making the leap from de Antonio's imagination to film.[39]

With the materials collected and interviews conducted, de Antonio and Mary Lampson set about editing the still unnamed film in early 1971. But it would be a film without an audience if they did not soon find a distributor. Considering the unusual and controversial nature of this film, de Antonio's difficulties in securing adequate distribution are not surprising. During the year the film was in production, he hoped it would be distributed by Don Rugoff, whose company was called Cinema V. Rugoff had given de Antonio the impression that he would accept the film "sight unseen," but after viewing the final print, Rugoff delayed for five weeks, then passed on the opportunity.

De Antonio also hoped for a larger commercial release and in June 1971 wrote to the Hollywood producer Bert Schneider to solicit an investment of $7,500 to finish the film. He told Schneider, "It is funny and it is political and it may have an audience." His past films, he wrote, would have been "modest money winners" had they received more effective distribution, something he hoped Schneider might provide. Schneider, who later produced *Hearts*

An advertisement for *Millhouse: A White Comedy* with a drawing by David Levine (Whittier Film Corp., 1971). Courtesy Wisconsin Center for Film and Theater Research.

and Minds (1974), the documentary de Antonio reviewed brutally for its unacknowledged resemblance to *In the Year of the Pig*, was apparently not interested, so de Antonio turned once again to his old friend and first distributor, Dan Talbot of New Yorker Films.[40]

Talbot accepted. Their contract specified 50 percent of the net profits to Talbot, 50 percent to de Antonio's Whittier Film. As one writer noted, each of de Antonio's films was distributed differently, and no pattern existed as to how the profits were divided. De Antonio's share was sometimes less than 50 percent when he had received an advance from a distributor, all of which points to the financial vulnerability of independent filmmakers.[41] But these issues were irrelevant if the film could not attract an audience.

Appropriately enough, the film opened in Washington, D.C., for a one-night showing on June 17, 1971, exactly one year before the Watergate burglary, at the American Film Institute, not far from the White House. Needless to say, this was a coup for de

Antonio. In the previous year an AFI staff member, Michael Webb, had proposed to de Antonio a retrospective of his films at the AFI Theater in October 1970. De Antonio consented but with one condition: that the AFI Theater be the site of the world premiere of the Nixon project. De Antonio chortled that the U.S. government was now in the position of sponsoring the opening of a radical film. The further irony, which completely escaped the filmmaker, was that the AFI, despite its official-sounding name, was unrelated to the U.S. government.[42]

The film at last had a title: *Millhouse: A White Comedy*. However, doubts nagged the filmmaker, prompting him to screen the film a week before the opening with his wife, Terry, whose laughter and comments assured him that "it would be fine, and I trust her judgement."[43] He had little reason for concern—even members of Congress and an FCC commissioner, Nicholas Johnson, attended the raucous opening night, though the eight-hundred-member audience was comprised mostly of young government workers, college students, and a smattering of elderly Nixon haters.[44] One member of Congress, Henry S. Reuss, a Democrat from Wisconsin, "was nearly doubled over in mirth."[45] Such responses should have allayed any trepidation the director might have had about the film, and with relief he described an audience "spilling into the aisles, laughing the way they do for *A Night at the Opera*, cheering at the end."[46] Afterward, Jack Anderson told him that he would write a column in his defense, should the film be subjected to pressure from the government. Though this later became important, for the time being de Antonio was enjoying the successful completion of *Millhouse: A White Comedy* after a year's work.

Understanding *Millhouse*

Millhouse: A White Comedy is a strange title that requires explanation. Why the added letters to Milhous, the president's middle name? the filmmaker was often asked. After attempting to diffuse the question with a paraphrase from the literary critic William Empson—"only an idiot would explain an

Protesters outside a theater showing *Millhouse: A White Comedy* in 1971, location unknown (Whittier Film Corp., 1971). Courtesy Wisconsin Center for Film and Theater Research.

intentional ambiguity"—de Antonio would relent and offer several reasons. He wanted a title that was "h-e-a-v-y" and thought "Millhouse" semantically heftier than "Milhous." The misspelling also functions as a rather weak Joycean pun, connoting images of a political "mill" grinding out bland ideology. Finally, the subtitle, *A White Comedy*, declares the film's subjectivity—it is not titled "A Documentary of the Political Life of Richard Nixon"—and ironically alludes to the film as a black comedy whose subject is both the quintessential Caucasian, in de Antonio's perspective, and a resident of the White House. Though not the most straightforward title, the derisive misspelling of the president's name and the glib subtitle well suit the irreverent tone of the film, a satire of equal parts Marx brothers absurdity and Strangelovian blackness. To these elements de Antonio adds touches of Molière, Dos Passos, and even John Cage, creating an unusually complex and unique example of political theater.

In the very first scene of *Millhouse* we see a close-up of a lifeless, rubbery face that appears to be part of a disembodied head of Richard Nixon. Trumpets blare. Soldiers salute. The presidential head then floats across the room to join a headless but well-dressed body. As a ghoulish beautician grooms the political Frankenstein, we realize that this is Nixon's wax likeness being prepared for display at Madame Tussaud's museum. By beginning the film this way, de Antonio indicates rather heavy-handedly that he will be taking apart and reassembling not so much the man but the artificial media creature, "Millhouse." Both Molière's *Tartuffe* and de Antonio's film share a central theme of the confusion of appearance and reality, which forms the basis of hypocrisy. To unmask the hypocrite and expose the fraudulence of the modern-day Tartuffe, de Antonio places himself in the role of Molière's noble character, Cleante, who sees through the hypocrite's guise and avers:

> My only knowledge and my only art
> Is this—to tell the true and false apart . . .
> Nothing seems more odious to me
> Than the disguise of specious piety.[47]

De Antonio uses ironic juxtaposition to reveal the "disguise of specious piety," in one instance: the unacknowledged rhetorical debt of Nixon's acceptance speech at the 1968 Republican convention to the earlier "I Have a Dream" speech by Dr. Martin Luther King, Jr. Wittily blending the two speeches on the soundtrack, while focusing visually on the legion of prosperous white supporters in the convention hall, de Antonio reveals the way in which Nixon mimicked the cadences of King's sincerity and idealism. The scene includes images of black rioters being tracked by police dogs and tanks, footage shot not far from the Miami convention center—a further contrast, black and white as it were, between Nixon's rhetoric and American reality.

Millhouse, like *Tartuffe*, encourages its viewers to ask how such blatant hypocrisy could go unchecked. The true nature of these characters, Nixon and Tartuffe, would surely be evident to any observer. Yet Tartuffe's wickedness nearly goes unpunished; his downfall requires a deus ex machina in the form of the king's intervention at the very end of the play. Similarly, Nixon's fall required a deus ex media in the form of Watergate, an ending of which *Millhouse*, completed in 1971, is deprived. Throughout the film one can only wonder how someone as untelegenic as Nixon could use the medium to his advantage throughout his political life. Yet the great myth of his pre-Watergate career was that he received "bad press" or was inept on television. With the exception of his much-discussed subpar performance during the 1960 debates with Kennedy, television was more often Nixon's ally, one he used skillfully to his advantage. Using his compilation technique of drawing together a variety of newsreel and other archival footage, de Antonio offers ample evidence of this skill but none greater than Nixon's performance in the Checkers speech.

Mawkish and crude as it may seem today, or to *Millhouse*'s audiences in 1971, the Checkers speech was television genius in its time (1952), and it saved Nixon's career. De Antonio described Nixon's ability to dramatize his plight as "a prime asset in today's media manipulation."[48] Nixon himself must have been aware of this aspect of the speech because he attempted to keep copies of it from the public. De Antonio inserted much of the speech into the middle of the film, inverting Nixon's plea for sympathy into a soliloquy of self-damnation. According to reviewers, the appearance of Checkers himself was an occasion for high-camp vaudeville, inducing fits of laughter in the audiences, who appreciated what de Antonio called its "bizarre and grotesque humor."

"A movie in the tradition of the Marx brothers," as the poster claimed, *Millhouse* relies frequently on Marx brothers irreverence and silliness. De Antonio admired the anarchistic spirit of Marx brothers films such as *Duck Soup*, and in *Millhouse* he aims for a similar brand of antiauthoritarianism. "The icons of authority make me reach for a hammer," he once claimed. "But then I am as much Dada as I am a Marxist." In his journal he assembled an impromptu collage from one page of the score to John Cage's *Atlas Eclipticalis, French Horn 5, Percussion 4, Cello 7* (1961) and a photograph of a young Nixon leaping in the air.[49] This sort of dadaism appears also in *Millhouse*, such as in the opening scene at the wax museum. More often, though, the comedy is broad, and at times sophomoric.

More or less following the chronology of the subject's life as any biography might, *Millhouse* pauses to mock rather than celebrate—a humorous inversion of the television program *This Is Your Life*. For much of his film de Antonio uses the structure of Nixon's memoir, *Six Crises*, which was divided into sections: "The Hiss Case," "The Fund" (leading to the Checkers speech), "The Heart Attack" (Eisenhower's), "Caracas" (where his vice-presidential goodwill trip turned sour), "Khrushchev," and "The Campaign of 1960." In *Millhouse* the appearance of large titles on screen signals another crisis begun or passed, often accompanied by horrible renditions of the sort of martial music that Nixon enjoyed.

At the end of Nixon's May 1955 trip to Caracas, the words *Fin de Crisis* appear, a sarcastic reference to Nixon's memoirs. De Antonio's version of this trip is one of the more droll moments in the film. After Nixon reminds the United States to stop thinking of Latin America in terms of the "salsa, the rumba, and the cha-

cha-cha," his motorcade is shown being attacked by "communist-directed mobs," as a stentorian newsreel narrator assures us. Any concern for the vice president's safety in the face of this violence is undermined by the advertising jingle chosen for the soundtrack—"I'm Chiquita banana and I'm here to say . . ."— an amusing allusion to the dominance of U.S. foreign policy in Latin America by the likes of the United Fruit Co.[50]

Coexisting rather uneasily with this silliness is an ominous black comedy that echoes Stanley Kubrick's apocalyptic satire, *Dr. Strangelove, or: How I Learned to Stop Worrying and Love the Bomb* (1964). Many scenes elicit astonishment and anger along with a guilty chortle: Nixon urging the death penalty for drug dealers; Nixon calling Hubert Humphrey "a dedicated radical"; Nixon addressing a group of supporters in his home town of Whittier, California: "There used to be orange groves here, lemon groves, avocado trees. . . . Now they're gone—replaced by homes, buildings, industry. That's progress! That's America!" Nixon rather unpresidentially ogles the vibrations and contortions of a voluptuous go-go dancer at a White House reception, while Bob Hope offers homophobic observations. With President Eisenhower seriously ill in the hospital, Nixon exhorts his supporters, "Let's win this one for Ike!" after which de Antonio deviously cuts to a now well-known scene from the 1940 football melodrama *Knute Rockne—All-American*, in which actor Pat O'Brien tells his discouraged football players to "win this one for the Gipper." We see the Gipper lying in his hospital bed; he is played, of course, by none other than a young Ronald Reagan. As the layers of irony further intertwine from the perspective of the contemporary viewer, de Antonio illustrates the grotesque and unoriginal quality of Nixon's political rhetoric, which reduced the candidate to echoing the lines of old movies, just as he did the speech of Dr. King.[51]

This barrage of media images moves at a speed that sometimes leaves the viewer behind. At its best, this technique, which Dos Passos used so effectively with newspaper headlines in his *U.S.A.* trilogy, can produce small epiphanies of historical understanding. At its worst, however, the technique can confuse and bore, causing the narrative of *Millhouse* to move ahead fitfully, while the viewer wonders, "What was that all about?" Most often this happens when de Antonio attempts to pack too much visual and aural information into a scene, overwhelming us with details that rush across the screen. Part of the visual chaos, however, is a result of de Antonio's vision of history.

He believed that although one can find a discernible narrative, history remains fundamentally chaotic. This is not the point of view of many historical documentarians, who tend to oversimplify history in the service of ideology, dramaturgy, or time limitations. De Antonio gives a looser rein to his historical material, welcoming complexity and contradiction as inevitable parts of the story. This allows the viewer, as the film critic Bill Nichols has pointed out, "to reassess an initial set of statements in light of a second, discrepant set" of statements. Such juxtapositions bring the viewer into an active role of interpretation rather than the spectatorial passivity that moving pictures so commonly induce.[52] The use of this technique in *Millhouse* can be confusing for viewers accustomed to a simple chronology, but for the most part it allows the viewers' curiosity to propel the narrative.

And where does all this lead? Dropping its various masks of Tartuffian farce, black comedy, and Marx brothers zaniness, *Millhouse* at last reveals an agitprop heart in its final ten minutes, becoming an antiwar film not unlike *In the Year of the Pig*. The political activist Dick Gregory exhorts a crowd of protesters; someone reads a quote from Mao about guerrilla warfare; statistics on South Vietnamese casualties flash on the screen; and Nixon promises that under no circumstances will he be affected by college students protesting the war in Vietnam.

At this point, de Antonio makes one of the film's clearest political statements. While Nixon speaks altruistically about the U.S. involvement in Vietnam, de Antonio superimposes a list of companies that benefit from a noncommunist Vietnam: Coca-Cola, Firestone, IBM, Hilton International, Chase International Investment Corp., Colgate Palmolive. In his review of the film the conservative columnist William F. Buckley, Jr., wrote that the scene implies that anyone "in Vietnam who uses rubber or brushes his teeth is doing so in order to further American imperialistic interests," which he construes to be tantamount to claiming that "Albert Schweitzer was a scout for the medical cartels."[53] Though a persuasive conservative critique of the film could be made, Buckley did not provide it, for his reading misses the point of de Antonio's work, which, more in the mode of Brecht's plays, operates on a symbolic rather than literal level. But viewers of de Antonio's work can easily misinterpret the politics of a film that lacks voice-over narration and often makes its points in abstract metaphoric terms.

By virtue of its subject, *Millhouse* is a highly political film, but the nature of its politics is difficult to determine. Scenes such as the one that raised Buckley's ire make a harsh critique of capitalism, linking it to a highly destructive foreign policy, but is this stance in keeping with de Antonio's occasional claim to be "a Marxist social critic"? *Millhouse* does not even mention the issue of class and would probably not satisfy the simplified Marxist aesthetics that have been described as "vulgar Marxism," a point of view caricatured by the Soviet official who criticized Sergei Eisenstein's *The Old and the New* because the peasants in the film were not smiling quite enough.[54] Perhaps this explains why *Millhouse* was not welcomed in the Eastern bloc or in the Soviet Union, where it was as unsettling to the government as the plays of Bertolt Brecht. Indeed, the politics of *Millhouse* are more in line with those of Brecht's plays: both offer an elitist critique, "a view from above" as one critic said of Brecht, and, while short on specifics, encourage in general a humorous, anarchistic stance toward the world. Besides, a constructive social vision is not the responsibility of the satirist; discrediting Nixon is task enough for one film.[55]

The angry politics of *Millhouse* make for good propaganda, but can that propaganda coexist with the work of a historian, which de Antonio sometimes called himself? If so, what sort of history does *Millhouse* provide? Historians debate at great length the differences between traditional written history, in both its academic and journalistic forms, and its film counterpart, the historical documentary. De Antonio was always an unusually literary-minded filmmaker, both in his research and the way he conceived of his subject. When *Millhouse* was completed, he spoke of it in terms of literature—Molière, Horatio Alger—as if it were a book. Judging his work as it might appear on the page, one could point out that a transcript of *Millhouse* might have difficulty finding a publisher, let alone an audience, because it would contain little new information about Nixon and does not have the depth of analysis that written history can provide.[56]

Nevertheless, this is not the manner in which to assess a film, even one so bookish in its influences. Despite his literary rhetoric and conceptions about the film, de Antonio executed *Millhouse* cinematically, and therein lies the film's value: in the visual information, the half-forgotten images, the television outtakes, the montage sequences, the ironic interplay of sound and image. For this reason *Millhouse* offers a unique historical portrait, an audio-visual presentation that functions differently than written history because, as de Antonio wrote in May 1971, "more important than the words are the images, not images that illustrate the point but images that are the point."[57]

Reception of *Millhouse*

However critics have interpreted *Millhouse*, they have had little bearing on one fact: audiences like the film. *Millhouse* set a new house record at the New Yorker Theater, where the film began its commercial run in New York in September 1971, slightly more than two months after the opening night. Even a year later the film showed sufficient box office appeal to be revived at the New Yorker during the month before the presidential election of 1972, where it grossed $43,549 in five weeks, a respectable sum for a Hollywood film of the day and an astronomical one for a political documentary. Whittier Film Corp. received $10,225.41 from this engagement alone.

In the argot of Hollywood, *Millhouse* had legs, attracting a small but significant audience for a long period of time. From October to December 1972 the film appeared at fifty-seven colleges and universities.[58] Nixon's reelection dimmed enthusiasm for the film, and bookings decreased to sixty-one theaters for 1973, but in the wake of the Watergate investigations and scandal, the film acquired a second wind, playing 116 theaters during 1974. In light of this relative popularity *Millhouse*'s stockholders most likely recouped their investment, though the financial records of the Whittier Film Corp. are incomplete in this regard. With the exception of *Point of Order*, *Millhouse* became the most widely shown of de Antonio's films, especially after he signed a contract on September 12, 1971, with the Video Tape Network, a subsidiary of National Talent Service, to show the film on videotape, primarily at universities and colleges: the advance was $15,000, with the Whittier Film Corp. receiving 35 percent of the gross receipts.[59]

Television presented a greater obstacle. Unfortunately, de Antonio could not interest the American television networks, toward which he was generally antagonistic for their failure to show the work of political dissenters. Nor was the Public Broadcasting System interested in such overtly political, if not partisan, fare. The film did appear on European television, where de Antonio's work was always more readily accepted. However, as noted earlier, it was not shown in Eastern Europe, where de Antonio was frequently invited to visit as a guest of state—he had been a judge at the East German Film Festival, the most important in any communist country. When in the mid-1970s de Antonio questioned why East German television showed so little interest in *Millhouse*, he was told by an East German anchorman, "You don't understand at all. . . . We despise your cold-war liberals like Kennedy, but Nixon we understood because he understood us. We would never play a film that was against Nixon." As for the Soviet Union, de Antonio claimed that the Soviets disapproved of his mild preoccupation with cinematic technique as too formalist, but, more significantly, he believed that Soviet television would never broadcast films that "reveal governments doing things wrong . . . because it could make people think, why don't we make films like that over here."[60]

In the United States much of the film's promotion occurred on a small scale—advertisements, personal appearances, and posters advertising the film with the slogan, "A movie in the tradition of the Marx brothers." Evidently, the advertisements misled some people who were not appreciative of this sort of humor. The Fine Arts Department chairman of Bethel College in Indiana, appropriately named Myron L. Tweed, had expressed interest in bringing the film to his campus but complained that the anti-Nixon advertisements were "very presumptuous" and suggested that the filmmakers "seriously consider a more positive tone in your advertising if you expect to market your product."[61] Of course de Antonio scoffed at terms such as *market* and *product*, which seemed more appropriate for Hollywood movie making, but was not beyond promoting his films with his favorite form of advertisement—himself. He seemed to enjoy the attention of being interviewed, especially after playing the role of the interviewer so often in making *Millhouse*. Loquacious and controversial, he was invariably a good interview.

His itinerary for promoting the San Francisco Bay Area opening of the film is typical. Arranged by a public relations firm, the schedule for October 6–7, 1971, provided the filmmaker with numerous opportunities for self-promotion. He taped interviews with a television station and four different radio stations; had a press conference with reporters from *Rolling Stone*, United Press International, and various student and leftist papers such as the *Berkeley Barb*, *People's World*, and the *Daily Californian*; and then had a press lunch with five film critics from large circulation papers, including the *San Francisco Chronicle*.[62] Not surprisingly, the opening night sold out in San Francisco.

The political nature of the film did cause problems, however. Some radio and television stations were unwilling to interview de Antonio, claiming that equal time would have to be awarded to Nixon supporters. San Francisco affiliates of ABC and CBS television canceled scheduled interviews on the dubious ground that de Antonio's appearance would obligate them to offer equal time to the president. CBS television refused to air commercials for the film; newspapers in Los Angeles refused to print the Levine drawing in the *Millhouse* advertisement; some refused to print the word *Nixon* in the advertisement. Richard D. Kuratli, the owner of the Bluebird Theater in Denver, reported another form of censorship based on the same principle. After making $4,000 from *Millhouse* from October 22 to November 4, 1971, Kuratli attempted to arrange special showings of the film on various college and high school campuses in the Denver area. But when school administrators learned that the film was not about the manufacture of cereal products, they invariably canceled the film, often at the last minute. The only explanation offered was that the schools could not present *Millhouse* without "presenting another viewpoint that was 100 percent PRO NIXON."[63]

Despite such setbacks with censors, the film was soon appearing in dozens of cities, and the critical reception was mostly very generous. Perhaps the most important U.S. reviewer, Vincent Canby of the *New York Times*, fawned over the film, calling it "superior fiction, as implacable as *An American Tragedy*, as mysterious as *You Can't Go Home Again*, and as banal as *Main Street*," by which he did not intend "to say that it's not true, but rather that it shares with fiction the kind of truth that is greater than the sum of its factual parts."

Some newspapers covered the film on the editorial pages, as if it were a political event not to be trusted to film reviewers. The *Boston Globe*, for example, a relatively liberal newspaper that had kindly reviewed de Antonio's previous films, published a favorable article by its Washington Bureau chief, Martin F. Nolan. In words that would later appear in advertisements for the film, Nolan facetiously wrote: "The movie is all-talking, all-singing, all-dancing, all-Nixon." Finally, *Time* magazine examined what it termed de Antonio's "cinematic acupuncture," and found Nixon emerging as "the kind of bunko artist of whom W. C. Fields always ran afoul," a comment that must have delighted the filmmaker, who greatly admired the old vaudevillian.[64]

Foreign perspectives were also generally positive, perhaps because a greater physical and political distance from Washington may have allowed British and Canadian reviewers to appreciate *Millhouse* without fear of offending the president. The *New Statesman* claimed that the film incites "hard laughter," a reaction "somewhere between a rictus and a spit." Canadians, who had often exhibited a particular soft spot for satirizing U.S. presidents, blanched at de Antonio's harshness. *Millhouse* was screened at the Stratford Film Festival in September 1971, the National Film Theater of Canada in April 1972, and at various commercial theaters in Canadian cities. The *Toronto Star* said *Millhouse* "destroy[s] Nixon's new image," and the *Ottawa Citizen* called the film "instructive"—but both reviews complained of the film's lack of subtlety.[65]

Other reviewers opposed the film on ideological grounds. Buckley's *New York Times* piece appeared because he so detested the film that he requested equal space from *New York Times* to counter Canby's enthusiastic review of September 24. Five weeks later the *Times* published Buckley's article under the headline "Leave Your Wits at the Entrance." Like many journalistic reviewers, Buckley parades his ignorance of the documentary tradition while regarding *Millhouse* as an occasion to air his altogether dissimilar political views. Several other reviewers seemed to echo Buckley's point that de Antonio was overeager to "cash in an anti-Nixon chip" at any expense and that the satire was unduly harsh. One reviewer for the *San Francisco Examiner* took this position, lamenting the release of a film with such "venom for our leaders," as the review was entitled. The writer complained that *Millhouse* "implies (and presumably betrays) some degree of fairness," though this could only be said by someone who had neither seen the film nor read de Antonio's public statements.[66] Similarly, reviewer Stuart Kline of WNEW-TV claimed the film violated "the cardinal rule of hatchet jobs," which was to give the subject all the credit he or she deserves, "*then* give it to him in the neck."

A more informed group of naysayers also expressed concern

about the film's severity. The theater critic Stephen Koch defended Nixon as "endlessly shrewd" and complained that "the besetting vice of Nixonart," as he categorized the current work of de Antonio, Gore Vidal, and Philip Roth, "is to presume the sympathies of the audience and shamelessly play for the gallery." For Koch the film was an ambitious failure because it did not capture the humanity of the man—a failing "so symptomatic of the left in general"—though he did not explain how a satirical film might expose vice and folly with tepid appeals to humanity. Ironically, de Antonio would have agreed with Koch's assessment of Nixon as "endlessly shrewd." Unfortunately, his film did not adequately convey de Antonio's belief that Nixon was, as the director observed in an interview, "a very clever, complicated man. Much of what he has done has been absolutely brilliant, and he has courage, he has guts, he had tenacity. I admire that."[67]

The failure to communicate even this begrudging respect for his political enemy disturbed some reviewers who otherwise admired de Antonio's work. Roger Ebert pointed out in the *Chicago Sun-Times* that "cheap shots" create sympathy for Nixon and limit the film to "preaching to the converted."[68] And James A. Wechsler in the *New York Post* called the director a "gifted, spirited maverick" but asked, "On whom is the joke?" De Antonio had interviewed Wechsler to get an explanation of the nature of the secret fund that had made the Checkers speech necessary, so Wechsler naturally had a keen interest in the film. With some disappointment he weighed the entertainment value of the film to "hard-core anti-Nixonites" against the film's inability to change the vote of mainstream Americans: "One had the uneasy sense that large segments of de Antonio's documentary, hilarious as they seemed to most of the assemblage at the New Yorker theater on Manhattan's W. 85th St., could evoke reverent attention on some streets in Manhattan, Kansas."[69] Even the progressive *Village Voice*, which presented a generally laudatory review, criticized the film on these grounds, complaining that *Millhouse* encourages complacency, if not a sense of smug superiority, about Nixon that would do little to prevent his reelection.[70]

In his zeal to skewer Nixon, de Antonio may not have paused to consider the political ramifications of his film. When confronted with such issues, he tended to raise the flag of art for art's sake, or least his sake, claiming that he made films for himself alone, the world be damned. Yet the evident pleasure he took from the public appreciation of his work, even the Academy Award nomination of *In the Year of the Pig*, makes this attitude seem more defensive than genuine. In fairness to a filmmaker working without the hindsight of historians, no one could have foreseen the ramifications of such a novel work—*Millhouse* had few models, after all.

Philip Roth has pointed out that watching Aristophanes did nothing to change Cleon's policies in ancient Greece, but satire can have an influence beyond the stage or screen. For example, Norman Mailer attacked Gore Vidal's *An Evening with Richard Nixon* for being so excoriating that it might backfire and foster sympathy for the president, thereby pandering to critics of what was described by a later administration as a "cultural elite." Vidal acknowledged this but thought it applied more to Roth's *Our Gang* and de Antonio's film: "The crueler they are, the more people want to support him. They just create sympathy for him." De Antonio might have responded to this critique with an idea he frequently expressed: "I didn't make this film to elect Democrats," which was a good thing because Nixon had little difficulty in 1972 against Senator George McGovern, whose campaign staff had expressed interest in using *Millhouse* as a campaign tool.[71] No matter how amusing or politically useful they might have found it, the Democrats had the political savvy to maintain a safe distance from the film.[72] De Antonio, however, claimed this was due to his reluctance to support Democrats, who in 1972 did ask him to create a short film "debate" between McGovern and Nixon. Using archival footage of Nixon, who had refused a live debate throughout the campaign, and McGovern's filmed answers to questions, de Antonio tried to compile something favorable to his potential employer, McGovern. To the filmmaker's dismay he realized as he viewed an early version of this footage that McGovern was somehow losing the imaginary debate: Nixon simply knew better how to use television. Disgusted, de Antonio dropped the project, probably to the benefit of the Democratic Party.

Smaller political groups, however, did use the film as an organizing tool. New Hampshire Peace/Action screened *Millhouse* in the months before the presidential primaries of 1972. Early in the same year de Antonio received an appeal from Maria Jolas, an American expatriate living in Paris and the widow of Eugene Jolas, editor of *transition* magazine and one of the great litterateurs of Paris in the era of Joyce and Pound. Maria Jolas requested the use of *Millhouse* in conjunction with a speaking engagement by Jane Fonda, who was then protesting the war in Vietnam. De Antonio granted her request magnanimously: "I don't make films for $ and there[fore] I can be fairly carefree in my gestures," meaning that he was willing to donate the film for the occasion. Always with an eye toward future projects, he asked Jolas if she was acquainted with the "Paris Hobbits," a group that clandestinely circulated radical materials all over the world but particularly to U.S. servicemen. The question served a double purpose, implying also that the Hobbits might distribute *Millhouse*.[73] Though mostly small groups such as these were interested in using *Millhouse*, making the film's political impact minimal, the film attracted considerable attention from the highest political circles in the United States.

The Response of the Nixon White House

From the filmmaker's point of view the best review *Millhouse* received was from the film's subject, at least indirectly. As de Antonio wrote, the White House reacted "as if I had given a Trident [missile] to Albania."[74] The appearance of the film, and the small ripple of publicity it made in the press, caused a good deal of consternation at the Nixon White House, and the administration reacted on several fronts, all of which reveal a remarkable abuse of political authority in order to curtail dissent—even to the point of engaging in the sort of political espionage that precipitated the Watergate crisis.

In March 1969 John Ehrlichman, then the domestic affairs adviser to the president, asked John Caulfield, a former New York City police officer, to set up a "private security entity in Washington for the purposes of providing investigative support for the White House." Caulfield, with an assistant, Tony Ulasewicz, was charged with investigating Nixon's political "enemies" from a variety of backgrounds: Senator Edward Kennedy, Rabbi Meir Kahane, the Smothers brothers, the presidential impersonator Dick Dixon, and Representative Richard H. Poff, a Virginia Republican. When the columnist Joseph Kraft wrote a piece that rankled Nixon, the president ordered the FBI to tap the phone of the newspaperman. When FBI director J. Edgar Hoover refused, Nixon had Caulfield place the tap. The president was aware of the illegality of these actions, which he later characterized as a "very, very unproductive thing" for the purposes of his political career.[75]

The White House did not curtail these forays into political espionage, however. In early 1971, when public opinion polls showed the Democratic front-runner, Senator Edmund Muskie of Maine, beginning to pose a serious threat to Nixon's reelection, the administration's collective level of paranoia was further heightened. As a response to this threat, the White House kept closer and closer tabs on its perceived enemies through the efforts of several men known euphemistically as the "plumbers," such as Caulfield. The effort was well organized with approval from high within the administration; White House memoranda implicate Chief of Staff H. R. Haldeman, which makes the president's involvement probable, though not verifiable.

A memo dated August 16, 1971, to Ehrlichman from John W. Dean, the president's counsel, illustrates the extent of the surveillance campaign. Dean described a system in which key members of the staff "should be requested to inform us as to who they feel we should be giving a hard time." Then the administration could determine "how we can best screw them (e.g. grant availability, federal contracts, litigation, prosecution, etc.)."

Following up on Dean's request, special White House counsel Charles Colson sent Dean a list of twenty "enemies," the seed of a longer, stranger list, mostly compiled by two of Colson's subordinates, Joanne Gordon and George Bell. The original "priority list" contained many individuals of significance, after which Colson added his own acerbic comments: Number 8, Morton Halperin, "leading executive at Common Cause: a scandal would be most helpful here." Number 13, Congressman John Conyers, "emerging as a leading black anti-Nixon spokesman. Has a known weakness for white females." Number 17, Daniel Schorr, Columbia Broadcasting System: "a real media enemy." Number 19, the actor Paul Newman: "Radic-Lib causes."[76] Eventually, the enemies list swelled to contain more than two hundred individuals and eighteen organizations, from a handful of genuine radicals to dozens of respected members of the establishment, such as the presidents of Yale, Harvard Law School, the Massachusetts Institute of Technology, the World Bank, the Rand Corporation, and Philip Morris.

The compilation was neither methodical nor accurate. Professor Hans Morgenthau made the list because he was confused with Robert Morgenthau, the former U.S. attorney in New York City.[77] One individual who was not technically on the list, though he believed himself to be because he had been subjected to a greater level of investigation than those who were on it, was Emile de Antonio. Caulfield later testified under oath that "the only time I ever asked the bureau to conduct a check on any individual who was not a prospective employee of the White House or the Administration was Mr. de Antonio." Though Caulfield might have minimized his role in the White House's political surveillance to protect himself, the statement does point to the seriousness with which the White House regarded de Antonio.[78]

One of the eight hundred audience members viewing *Millhouse* on opening night at the AFI Theater, and presumably one whose laughter was more restrained than those "rolling in the aisles," was a secretary named Anne Dawson, who had been sent by her supervisor, Jack Caulfield.[79] Another Caulfield employee, Ulasewicz, "the president's private eye," watched a later showing of the film—alone in a theater where he had to fend off homosexual advances, as he claimed in 1990. Why he added this unlikely detail is unknown, though he might have been attempting to question the virility of de Antonio's liberal student audience with this homophobic observation.[80]

The White House had learned that de Antonio had somehow obtained a copy of the Checkers speech; the administration also had learned that some portion of the speech appeared in the film. Dean later reported that Haldeman "sent us frequent questions" about the film: "Would it hurt us with the youth vote? Could we stop it?"[81] Whether Haldeman or someone else sparked the flurry of memos regarding *Millhouse* remains unclear. The memoranda, however, present a small drama of a government's attempting to control political dissent.

The first extant memo, from Caulfield to Dean, is, like all the memoranda, written on White House stationery; the heading of the memo reads "SUBJECT: EMILE DE ANTONIO, PRODUCER OF THE FILM 'MILLHOUSE: A WHITE COMEDY.' Dated June 25, 1971, one week after the opening night in Washington, the memo instructs Dean to read an enclosure, a *Washington Post* story on the film, and "the FBI report on de Antonio."[82] Shortly after the opening, someone in the White House had launched the investigation into the film. Caulfield recommended monitoring the film's progress, "taking particular note to determine if Larry O'Brien [Democratic National Committee chairman] is stupid enough to get behind it"—in which case Caulfield proposed "a Nofziger job on De Antonio and O'Brien." Franklin "Lyn" Nofziger was a White House staffer who worked in public relations; Caulfield's testimony on March 23, 1974, before the Senate Watergate committee revealed that "a Nofziger job" meant leaking embarrassing information to the media—in de Antonio's case, from his FBI file.[83]

On August 10, 1971, Caulfield sent another memo to Dean, this time regarding de Antonio and Talbot's showing of the Checkers speech as a theatrical short at the New Yorker in May. "I will have someone take a look at the Washington showing of the Checkers speech . . . with a view towards determining if [it] is a shady money-making scheme or a politically directed attack—or both." Caulfield encouraged Dean to advise Haldeman and Bill

Timmons, the new congressional liaison, on the matter. Others in the White House monitored the situation. Mort Allin, who prepared daily news summaries for the president, sent Haldeman a memo on October 6, noting an advertisement for *Millhouse* in the *New York Review of Books* and rental fees for the Checkers speech.

But tracking *Millhouse* was primarily Caulfield's task. On October 13 he sent a panicky message to Dean. "This matter seems to be building. You are reminded that a significant derogatory dossier is in the possession of the bureau vis a vis de Antonio." Once again he recommended using such information at "a propitious moment"—such as if the Democratic Party showed support for the film.

Two days later, October 15, Caulfield proffered more specific suggestions. A recently published article in *Variety* appeared to verify that the Democrats were interested in using *Millhouse* as a campaign tool, causing Caulfield to believe "it is time to move" before the "massive distribution of the film" to college theaters. What Caulfield had in mind was the release of de Antonio's FBI file to "friendly media" and "discreet IRS audits of New Yorker Films, Inc., de Antonio and Talbot."[84]

Caulfield sent his man in New York, Ulasewicz, to see Talbot at his "sloppy one room operation with one secretary." On October 20 Ulasewicz reported the results to Dean. The lengthy communiqué contained biographical information ("member of Stop the Draft"). However, he obtained no information that linked the Democratic Party to the film, and Caulfield expressed some relief that the film's distribution "appears to be in the hands of amateurs." Not to underestimate the threat, however, he reminded Dean that the film "is getting considerable play in the liberal press" and that de Antonio had been interviewed by the well-known reporter Martin Agronsky for CBS's Washington, D.C., affiliate, WETA-TV. Perhaps more worrisome was the threat that the film would become "a cause célèbre," especially if the White House interest in the film were made public. "Resultingly, any action taken vis a vis D'Antonio [*sic*] or Talbot should be weighed carefully and well hidden. This includes my previous comment re D'Antonio's background and our capability at IRS."

Caulfield's warning hit its mark. The last thing the White House needed was a new liberal cause célèbre in the wake of the sensation caused by the publication of the so-called Pentagon Papers in the summer of 1971. Dean had also received a memo from White House staffer Fred F. Fielding that echoed Caulfield's concerns. Dean later claimed the administration only "planned to leak [de Antonio's FBI dossier] if the movie became a hit [or] if the Democratic Party sponsors showings. Neither occurred," at least by mainstream standards of film success.[85]

What was in the FBI dossier to make it seem such a potent weapon? It documented de Antonio's left-wing activities, but he never made a secret of his politics. Any of his interviews from this period were full of forthright expressions of his radicalism. Perhaps his short-lived membership in the Communist Party during the 1930s had caught the attention of the White House; this might have caused some embarrassment to the Democrats had they given official sanction to the film. Caulfield may have envisioned headlines reading "Democrats Use Propaganda Film by Ex-Red," but this never came to pass.

One point should be made clear: de Antonio was not technically on the enemies list, though he believed his name appeared there, which would have made him the only filmmaker so represented. Nevertheless, he was treated more like a political enemy than nearly anyone on the actual list. Angry though it made him, he took a certain amount of pride in being subjected to so much scrutiny: "It was the biggest honor I've ever been accorded. It's better than having received an Academy Award."[86] Being on the enemies list seemed to become something of a left-wing credential for de Antonio, as it was for some others on the list, and he would refer to it often in interviews—more fodder for journalists looking to canonize him as a radical saint. Government harassment may have even created beneficial publicity for later de Antonio films, raising his stature from "iconoclastic" filmmaker to "dissident" or "persecuted" artist.

Even so, the publicity was small compensation for being the target of such a personal attack by the White House. Undoubtedly, few filmmakers have been so hounded by the U.S. government, especially from such a high level. Then again, few artists have gone as far as de Antonio to antagonize a president, even though shortly after the film's premiere de Antonio acknowledged that he had some sympathy for the politician—"He's an extremely shallow man, a man who bruises very easily."[87] One may only wish the president had seen the film that bore his name.

During and after the Watergate crisis, when *Millhouse* was acclaimed as prophetic, de Antonio was occasionally asked why he did not make a film about that final spectacle. Everything he had to say about Watergate was in *Millhouse*, he replied, meaning that the seeds of Nixon's political destruction lay in his lifelong insecurity. But this answer was slightly disingenuous, because the Watergate crisis seemed to befuddle de Antonio. His enemy disgraced, he might have gloated or interpreted the crisis as a hopeful sign that the democratic process was throwing out the scoundrels, that justice was being served. Instead, he saw the scandal as an accident, as an example of "cruelty in history [that] falls over itself" but in effect changes little. "Tartuffe ends in his San Clemente riches rewriting history but his world goes on," he wrote cynically in his journal, and *Millhouse*, after all, was about a system of politics, not simply a personality.[88]

That nothing had changed after Watergate was glaringly apparent to de Antonio in the years after the scandal. He ridiculed Hollywood's response to Watergate, at least as he perceived it in films such as *All the President's Men*, the saga of Bob Woodward and Carl Bernstein's book of the same title. Reviewing the film for the *Yipster Times*, de Antonio blasted "Mrs. Graham's Galahads," in reference to their employer, Katherine Graham, the publisher of the *Washington Post*; blasted the self-congratulation of the liberal media; and blasted Vincent Canby's description of the film as "the thinking-man's *Jaws*."[89]

Emile de Antonio in his New York studio, early 1970s. Courtesy Wisconsin Center for Film and Theater Research.

Another reason for cynicism was Nixon's efforts, beginning in the late 1970s, to rehabilitate himself as a public figure—not the first time he had rebounded from ignominy to celebrity. When the ex-president was scheduled to address the Union at Oxford University in 1978, de Antonio sent a satirical warning to the university: "Garlic won't do. The crucifix and holy water won't help. Watch Shelley's tomb during the daylight hours. . . . That Transylvanian visitor who ruled my country . . . is among you." Ironically asserting the concept of equal time, which had caused the cancelation of several U.S. television interviews with de Antonio, the filmmaker asked that Oxford screen *Millhouse* before Nixon's speech. It did not.[90]

Perhaps de Antonio felt some small consolation in watching the subtle changes in perception brought about by *Millhouse*. John Updike observed in 1974 that *Millhouse* "makes plain" that Nixon was "the least charismatic, most painfully self-conscious politician since the invention of newsreels. His television appearances were the pitiable ordeals of a man at war with himself." This interior war, de Antonio would have us believe, surfaced in Nixon's language as the empty rhetoric of political convenience. Making one small incursion into Richard Nixon, *Millhouse* shows that, as Allen Ginsberg said, "the war is language"; the sentiment echoes Orwell's "The Politics of the English Language," which had greatly influenced de Antonio.[91] To a president who boasted of closing his ears to the voice of dissent, de Antonio responded by listening with extreme care.

One might question the value of a film such as *Millhouse* by asking, as Philip Roth did of his novel *Our Gang*, "So what?" Roth provides an eloquent defense of his novel and, by extension, of *Millhouse*: "To make indecorous, vituperative comic art . . . is to demonstrate that there is a world of feeling and ideas and values that remains unimpressed by the Official Version of Reality."[92] Like an enormous Bronx cheer at a sober political rally, *Millhouse* both spiced up and laughed at the monotone of American political discourse.

6

◄○►

Art, Politics, and *Painters Painting*

Perspective

After being a minor player in the New York art world for almost two decades, de Antonio decided to make it the subject of his next film, after *America Is Hard to See*.[1] The decision came as something of a surprise, if not a disappointment, to those who expected him to continue exploring the pressing political issues of the late 1960s and early 1970s.[2] Why would a radical filmmaker make a "feature-length commercial for the art establishment?" asked one critic who viewed *Painters Painting* (1972) as an aberration in the development of de Antonio's film career.[3] This interpretation, however, does justice to neither the filmmaker nor the film, which was better characterized by one of its participants, gallery owner Leo Castelli. While de Antonio's camera explores the famous Castelli Gallery, we hear its proprietor speaking on the telephone: "I have de Antonio here. . . . He's making a film, you know, like the McCarthy film but without McCarthy." Or, as the filmmaker wrote to one of his critics: "*Painters Painting* is more political than you seem to think. Art is power."[4]

De Antonio had a complex view of this power. He loved the painting of the New York School and its offspring as the "one thing that makes me comfortable in postwar America," the one place where alienation and dissent were intelligently and passionately expressed. Yet at the end of the sixties de Antonio's favorite

155

paintings were increasingly accused of sins—elitism, apoliticism, commodification—that were at odds with his political radicalism. The problem was an old one: as the artist Robert Smithson said in 1970, the rat of politics always gnaws at the cheese of art. Caught between art and politics, taste and conscience, de Antonio responded with a personal film that walked the tightrope between these polarities rather than give in to one or the other. While *Painters Painting* does not pretend to resolve this dilemma, de Antonio's experience with the project sheds light on one of the thorniest issues confronting a political filmmaker during this period.[5]

The idea for the film came from Terry Moore, the young poet who married de Antonio in the mid-1960s.[6] Part of the avant-garde scene in New York, she had acted in Claes Oldenburg's happenings and was a close friend of painters such as Frank Stella. When de Antonio was at a loss for what to do after *In the Year of the Pig* (1969) and *America Is Hard to See* (1970), and before he had the materials that sparked *Millhouse* (1971), she suggested he make a film about painting, clearly one of his favorite topics. Few filmmakers had the background and the connections to make a serious and personal film about art in New York in the fifties and sixties. What other filmmaker had dated Helen Franken-thaler, produced concerts for John Cage and Merce Cunningham, arranged commercial jobs for Robert Rauschenberg and Jasper Johns, helped Frank Stella find a gallery, and been credited by Andy Warhol with inventing pop art? Warhol had even made a film about him (*Drink*, 1963), and de Antonio's portrait was one of Stella's "Purple Series" of abstract paintings (*D*, 1963). But de Antonio was reluctant and relented only when Moore pointed out the perfect locus for such a film.[7]

Henry Geldzahler, then curator of twentieth-century arts at the Metropolitan Museum, was planning a major show of American painting from 1940 to 1970 as part of the museum's centennial celebration. De Antonio obtained the exclusive rights to film the show by drawing on his friendship with Geldzahler, as well promising the curator $3,000 up front and 10 percent of the profits.[8] Important paintings had come from collections all over the world in a journey made precarious by their enormous size, fragility, and insurance costs. For these reasons de Antonio believed "Henry's show," as the press referred to it, was the last best chance to survey the accomplishments of the New York School. From October 18, 1969, to February 1, 1970, Geldzahler adorned the walls of the Metropolitan with "New York Painting and Sculpture: 1940–1970," which included 408 works by forty-three artists, among them Barnett Newman, Frank Stella, Jasper Johns, Willem de Kooning, and Robert Rauschenberg. With excitement de Antonio wrote: "Where once the Rembrandts and Titians hung, now hangs the School of N.Y.; one painting by Frank Stella is 42 feet wide."[9]

De Antonio's agreement with the Metropolitan was to film at night under the watchful eyes of three security guards. With a talented cameraman, Ed Emschwiller, who was already making a name for himself as an experimental filmmaker, and a budget of nearly $100,000 in the form of a confidential loan from Frank Stella, de Antonio and his crew spent many nights in the empty museum during the winter of 1969–1970.[10] A former painter with an obvious sensitivity to the medium, Emschwiller used 35mm color film in the museum, the first color film to appear in de Antonio's work. One could not film the canvases of "colorfield" painters such as Jules Olitski in black-and-white, though the guards seemed to think that such paintings should not be filmed at all. "It's awful," said one as he pointed to an Olitski, before offering to let the filmmakers into the galleries where the Old Masters were stationed.[11] De Antonio counted a small victory for his powers of persuasion when, at the end of the shoot, the same guard turned to a de Kooning collage and said, "You know, that's not too bad."[12] The rapport between the museum staff and the filmmakers was useful on several occasions, such as when the guards looked the other way while Emschwiller covered the metal frames of certain works with gaffer tape to minimize their glare.[13]

Filming the paintings was one thing. Getting the artists to discuss them was quite another. De Antonio began to cajole

Emile de Antonio directing *Painters Painting* with Ed Emschwiller filming (Turin Films, 1972). Courtesy Wisconsin Center for Film and Theater Research.

interviews from his friends and acquaintances for *Painters Painting: New York*, as the film was originally entitled. He ended up
with the most important living painters of the New York School—
he ignored most sculptors for the sake of simplicity. These artists
seemed eager to discuss their works in a serious film, as if they
agreed with Willem de Kooning, who had written:

> There's no way of looking at a work of art by itself
> It's not self-evident
> It needs a history; it needs a lot of talking about:
> It's part of a whole man's life.[14]

Ten other painters were willing to provide "a lot of talking" about
their work: Robert Motherwell, Kenneth Noland, Larry Poons,
Frankenthaler, Johns, Newman, Olitski, Rauschenberg, Stella,
and Warhol. Jackson Pollock and Hans Hofmann, though they
were long dead, would also be discussed at some length.

De Antonio also wanted to interview the collectors, dealers,
and critics, and he called on the movers and shakers of modern
art in New York: Castelli, whose gallery represented many of
the aforementioned artists; Geldzahler; Thomas Hess, the former
editor of *Art News*; Philip Leider, the critic for *Artforum*; Hilton
Kramer, the *New York Times* art critic; William Rubin, curator of
the Museum of Modern Art; and the collectors Robert and Ethel
Scull. Of the two most prominent critics of the New York School,
Harold Rosenberg and Clement Greenberg, de Antonio chose the
latter even though he was the only interviewee who insisted on
being paid ($100). Both de Antonio and Greenberg believed that
it was important that the individual artist learn from tradition, to
paraphrase T. S. Eliot.[15] Both had been Marxists in the thirties,
and though Greenberg had become far less radical, de Antonio
still viewed the critic as brilliant.[16] Rounding out the cast were the
architect and collector Philip Johnson and the sculptor Phillip
Pavia; de Antonio included Pavia simply because the filmmaker
liked what he had to say.

De Antonio claimed not to see people in color, so they filmed
the interviews in the more economical 16mm black-and-white

Ken Noland in a still from *Painters Painting* (Turin Films, 1972). Courtesy Wisconsin Center for Film and Theater Research.

even though they had used 35mm color film at the museum.[17]
This process went smoothly through the spring of 1970, though
de Antonio had to postpone several interviews while "overcome
with dizziness," his euphemism for the after-effects of a night of
drinking, sometimes acquired after an interview with friends such
as Rauschenberg and Johns. For his interview with Rauschenberg
de Antonio had posed the artist on a tall ladder in front of a
large window in his studio, a former orphanage, but the artist
had soon descended for whiskey and poker with the filmmaker.
Barnett Newman drank vodka like water throughout his interview
and produced a variety of colorful aphorisms for the camera
("Aesthetics is for me what ornithology must be for the birds.").
The interview turned out to be his last, though shortly after his
death the film crew returned to capture some remarkable footage
of the works in his studio.[18]

De Antonio had great respect for Newman and excluded any
painter from the film for whom he could not say the same. He was
unwilling to arrange interviews with Mark Rothko (de Antonio
called him "boring"), Cy Twombly ("his work is narrow, it is
based on the Palmer Method of penmanship"), Larry Rivers
("isn't worth it"), and the minimalists Donald Judd and Robert
Morris ("beasts"). The artists Adolph Gottlieb and Clyfford Still
and the collector Nelson Rockefeller met his criteria but were
unable to be interviewed. De Antonio knew the prominent young
critic Barbara Rose, who had married his friend Frank Stella,
but decided not to interview her because her criticism was "all
on the surface, perceiving who belongs to what but never who
to whom in a sense of past and role."[19] His friend John Cage
might have appeared to speak about his influence on Johns and
Rauschenberg, but de Antonio considered only his music—for the
soundtrack (the same music, ironically, that had been performed
fifteen years earlier at the concert de Antonio had produced). In
the end, however, the filmmaker decided not to use it, though Cage
would be a focal point for de Antonio's final film, *Mr. Hoover and
I* (1989), as well as a short film de Antonio planned in 1983 under
the title *John Cage at the Whitney*.[20]

Robert Rauschenberg in a still from *Painters Painting* (Turin Films, 1972). Courtesy
Wisconsin Center for Film and Theater Research.

Outtakes best reveal de Antonio's casual interviewing technique for what would soon be entitled *Painters Painting*, because he preferred to edit out his questions except when someone
such as Jasper Johns wanted him to share the discomfort of the
camera's gaze.[21] Interviewees were supposed to repeat the gist
of the question so their responses could stand on their own, but
some had difficulty following the rule, let alone answering the
questions. When the filmmaker was interviewing de Kooning in
his extraordinary studio, which Philip Johnson had designed, de
Antonio asked him what he meant by the phrase "style is a fraud."
De Kooning replied, "Gee, I forget now. That was a long time ago.
You know, people change their minds too. And it is out of context

now."[22] The painter's forthrightness was a welcome contrast to the self-important pontification for which artists are sometimes known.

For his part de Antonio emphasized context in his subsequent questions. What he wanted to know in general was "why they did what they did when they did it, how they did it . . . who collected it? why? [who] curated it? who bought and sold it and what did that mean?"[23] To answer these questions he compiled and selected from one hundred hours of filmed interviews. He could have made an eight-hour documentary—he had no commercial limitations on its length—but he kept to the two-hour length of his previous films, even if it meant the omission of interviews with the artists Josef Albers, Louise Nevelson, John Chamberlain, and other fascinating subjects.[24] Two hours was enough for the film to accomplish what de Antonio wanted, for it to say everything he wanted it to say. Though not the literal voice of the film in the same sense as the art historian Kenneth Clark in his series *Civilisation* (1969), de Antonio was equally in control of what was being said.

Foreground

Painters Painting interweaves illustrations with conversation: in one of the most effective conjunctions of camera and canvas in cinematic history, the film presents a tour of "Henry's show" from the perspective of Emschwiller's deft tracking shots, which are combined with the oral histories elicited by de Antonio. As a memoir of his acquaintance with the major artists of his time, a casual sociology conducted from the perspective of a critical insider, *Painters Painting* is a subtle examination of the art world.

Some of the film has the casual tone of gossip, but much of it is an attempt at serious discussion of several recurring themes. Much is made of the way in which these painters expanded the definition of art, especially salable art. When de Antonio asked Warhol why he made the transition in the late fifties from commercial art to becoming a painter, Warhol coyly replied, "Well, you made me a painter, De." The filmmaker laughs and yells "Cut!" but the camera continues to record their conversation. De Antonio questions him further, causing Warhol to feign a defensive tone: "That is the truth, isn't it? You used to gossip about the art people, and that's how I found out about art. You were making art commercial, and since I was in commercial art, I thought real art should be commercial, because you said so. That's how it all happened."[25] Most of the responses were less surprising to the filmmaker. Rauschenberg discusses how he spent three weeks erasing a de Kooning drawing, forming a ghostly blank canvas that is now highly valued. Johns laughingly tells of being inspired to make *Painted Bronze (ale cans)* (1960) after hearing de Kooning claim that Castelli would sell even cans of beer. Ethel Scull describes how Warhol began her famous portrait in a coin-operated photo booth on 42d Street in New York City. Warhol even dryly notes that his assistant had been doing all his painting for the last three years, a statement that seems to unsettle de Antonio.

Other conversations reflect the technical emphasis of the film's title, though not much actual painting occurs. Poons demonstrates how he crops an enormous canvas. Sitting on the floor of his studio with a Cuban cigar, Frank Stella explains with striking lucidity how he composed one of his paintings. But most of the talk is about something more than the type of brush or the choice of color. Rauschenberg says, "You have to have time to feel sorry for yourself to be a good abstract expressionist." Johns discusses his relationship to dada; Motherwell describes the heroic impulse behind the large canvases. And above all these conversations looms the Olympian presence of Clement Greenberg, who celebrates the accomplishment of Pollock as coolly as he dismisses pop as "easy stuff." With great subtlety de Antonio frames these conversations in decidedly political terms.

The film begins on an obliquely political note, with an image of a pale yellow rectangle divided evenly by several stripes. The title *Painters Painting* appears in two of the vertical panels on the rectangle, whose creator remains unidentified. The stripes of Stella's early paintings come to mind, as does Rauschenberg's

atypically monochromatic *White Painting* (1951). Over the course
of a minute the camera recedes from the surface of the painting,
which is revealed to be the wall of an enormous building, the
skyscraper headquarters of Ma Bell in New York. As this visual
game proceeds, we hear the critic Philip Leider speaking about
the relationship between American painting and the society that
produced it: "We made portraits of ourselves when we had no
idea who we were. We tried to find God in landscapes that we were
destroying as fast as we could paint them. We painted Indians as
fast as we could kill them, and during the greatest technological
jump in history, we painted ourselves as a bunch of fiddling
rustics." By juxtaposing these elements of sound and image, de
Antonio seems to offer the building as a cultural self-portrait
in which the face of corporate America has become the face of
the people—and his comments at this time seem to support this
reading.[26] To the extent that painting reflects national identity,
which de Antonio believed despite the protests of artists such as
Stella, the canvases of the New York School reflect the failure of
American culture that de Antonio asserts in each of his films.[27]

From this narrow perspective the implicit subject matter of
both the New York School and *Painters Painting* is the disarray of
U.S. society, much as the Marxist critic John Berger had observed
the "disintegration of our culture" in the work of Pollock.[28] The
large size of these canvases and the energy, if not violence, of
their imagery made them obvious metaphors for American society.
Motherwell makes this point in the film shortly before we hear
Frankenthaler describe the anger that made her want to fling
paint at the canvas. Not surprisingly, then, the film ends much as it
began, with an another observation of the cultural significance of
modern art. The final words belong to Newman, who emphasizes
the importance of "human scale" in art—"and the only way you
can achieve human scale is by the content." We do not see him
as he speaks these words for the second time in the film. Instead,
de Antonio repeats the ironic juxtaposition of the beginning of
the film, and we watch as Emschwiller's camera sweeps across the
faces of people walking through an exhibit of modern art. Their

confusion is evident—human scale has not been achieved and "the general public is just as disinterested in advanced art as ever," as the artist Will Insley said in another context.[29]

Yet between the two censorious extremes of the film lies a good deal of nuance. These paintings may reflect the failure of U.S. culture, but they also contain "the spirit of America, that which is good in it," as de Antonio said.[30] Throughout the film de Antonio's obsession with the issue of authentic "Americanness" is evident in his questions, though it is sometimes deflated by comments such as Newman's, spoken in the deliberate cadences of an actor: "I recognize that I am an American, because I am not Czechoslovak, and my work was not painted in Czechoslovakia or in Hungary or in India."

Newman and the other painters fit neatly into de Antonio's vision of romantic dissent, a form of heroic resistance to bourgeois culture. De Antonio looked at the New York School and saw his own anger, optimism, and creativity. He gives Newman a prominent role, not surprising given the painter's political activism and beliefs. Newman was once asked about his famously minimalistic canvases, and the artist replied that if the meaning of his paintings were understood, "it would mean the end of all state capitalism."[31] Yet Newman would not sacrifice the inherently elite notion of quality to political expediency, and his paintings were rarely understood in the way he had intended. This is where de Antonio parts with the Left to meet the New York School, an apostasy that confused his more political admirers.

The *New York Times* aptly described de Antonio as "as flaming a radical as ever donned a dinner jacket," and the contradiction between his tastes and his politics was nothing new.[32] Nor was it unique to de Antonio, because the art world as a whole was beginning to reel from a crisis involving the politicization of art. At least in theory, the New York art scene had intentionally separated art from politics since World War II, although it had many members with roots in the radical politics of the thirties (Pollock, Newman, Greenberg, Ad Reinhardt, etc.).[33] Critics such as Greenberg and artists such as Newman and Motherwell made it clear that artists should not comment directly upon political issues in their work, in the manner of Ben Shahn, for example.[34] Arshile Gorky, more conservative than most of his peers, was so blunt as to dismiss propagandistic art as "poor painting for poor people."[35]

In the wake of the Vietnam War, however, this attitude began to fall out of fashion, and the question of relevance was being raised as often as the question of aesthetics.[36] Political statements became louder and larger—witness the creation of the *Peace Tower* in 1966 in Los Angeles with the support of Rauschenberg, Motherwell, and Stella.[37] The New York art scene began to include groups such as the Artists Meeting for Cultural Change and the Maoist-inspired Anti-Imperialist Cultural Union. Some said the painting of the New York School was standing "in the way of all expression that is appropriate to our times," and in 1970 *Artforum* responded to these concerns with a symposium entitled "The Artist and Politics."[38] The hallmarks of modernism—a belief in aesthetic autonomy and an empirical standard of quality— were gradually being replaced by the postmodernist critique of originality, tradition, and apolitical art.[39] Artists left the canvas altogether and began conducting surveys about political issues, moving dirt in the desert, evaporating water, dancing with coyotes—the concept had replaced the canvas. This was the intellectual climate in which de Antonio conceived *Painters Painting*.

To the surprise of his political acquaintances, his film ignored these new developments and focused on the "elitist" New York School. Implicitly in his film and explicitly in conversations, de Antonio came to the defense of modernism.[40] "Other Marxists never understood," he said, "that a genuine U.S. art was created in the period covered by *Painters Painting*," that this art was an authentic form of resistance to the boring bourgeoisie.[41] And if that failed to convince his critics, he explained with a shrug, "Life cannot be all politics. I am not Lenin."

Yet de Antonio often sounded guilty about the "elitism" of *Painters Painting*, even pentitent for not addressing the issue of art versus politics "in a solid Marxist way."[42] "Perhaps it's something I have to do to get it out of my system," he said about making *Painters Painting*, as if the project could taint the purity of his politics.[43] He had faced a similar problem as an instructor of literature whose favorite poets were Eliot and Yeats, both far from the Left, neither of whom had been purged from his system. But as a result of the film, de Antonio's contradictory views about painting were thrust into the spotlight.

De Antonio wanted to have it both ways. In political forums he was the rebel making the claim to be "more interested in what Mao's doing than in the art of my friends" and calling the New York School the "work of the enemy"—"Their work, in my opinion, is totally uninvolved with the nature of social struggle going on in this country."[44] Yet in other circles he defended their work and disparaged the next generation of artists, which wore its politics on its sleeve. Observing the art works exhibited by the "the young, the new, the blacks, the women," he was unmoved except to note that art should be "about quality, not good wishes and intentions."[45] Nothing could be more ill conceived, he pointed out with anger, than the art that resulted from the good intentions of communist governments with which he otherwise agreed in principle, if not often in practice. De Antonio's program notes for the world premiere of *Painters Painting* on May 26, 1972, at the American Film Institute Theater in Washington, D.C., said that "the arts have always been the worm in the apple of socialism." This was not the first occasion on which he had expressed his distaste for what he called the "bad religious art" of the Soviet Union and other communist countries.[46] He seemed to identify with the fate of Pablo Picasso, about whom he wrote in his introductory letter to the fugitives of the Weather Underground in 1974: "Picasso was a good man, a good Marxist and a great painter even if the French and Soviet [Communist] Parties didn't understand it." One could easily substitute "de Antonio" for "Picasso," "American left" for "French and Soviet Parties," to understand how de Antonio perceived his situation.[47]

Torn between art and politics, de Antonio suffered what he described as "the agony of the revolutionary artist." Even more worrisome to him was the possibility that political art was irrelevant to the real political struggles in the world. As Auden had written on the death of Yeats:

> Ireland has her madness and her weather still
> For poetry makes nothing happen.

The same could be said of painting. If the greatest political artwork of the century, Picasso's *Guernica* (1937), had no measurable influence on subsequent events in Spain, de Antonio could not be certain that his work had changed a single mind, that a film such as *In the Year of the Pig* had shortened the Vietnam War by a single day.[48]

But de Antonio knew that art could serve an indirect political role in overcoming the sense of alienation from mainstream American culture that had attracted him to the New York School in the first place. The intellectual defense of this position goes back at least as far back as Hegel and Schopenhauer, and its later proponents included Jean-Paul Sartre, Theodore Adorno, Herbert Marcuse, Meyer Shapiro, and Clement Greenberg—all of whom pointed to the emancipatory potential of "art for art's sake."[49] Marcuse's voice is the relevant one for de Antonio, for during the production of *Painters Painting* he was reading the influential philosopher's latest work, *An Essay on Liberation* (1969), with approval—"Our freedom is still best defined by Marcuse," the filmmaker wrote in a letter in 1970. De Antonio was probably aware of how Marcuse describes art as bringing about "the rebirth of radical subjectivity," a liberating change of consciousness.[50] Art cannot be predetermined by politics. While de Antonio sought the "terrible clarity of art" and "the pursuit of the abstract ideal," he never made this argument explicitly, though he offered proclamations based on the same line of reasoning: "As for the dilemma between art and politics, I still believe in an art of quality and radical politics. The two are not incompatible."[51] This was an emotional rather than intellectual response, because in practice he separated the two realms with no explanation about how they might function together.

Marcuse based his argument on some questionable assumptions as well. As Janet Wolff shows in her book *Aesthetics and the Sociology of Art*, Marcuse depended too much on metaphysical claims that cannot otherwise be validated. Where is this Archimedean point of liberation, this transcendent vantage of aesthetic bliss? Such a point really does not exist in splendid isolation from the concerns of the real world, a point made clear in works that discuss the ideological undercurrents of art and literature. In his influential study, *Orientalism*, Edward Said demonstrates "the dependence of what appeared to be detached and apolitical cultural disciplines upon a quite sordid history of imperialist ideology," an observation that the art historian Serge Guilbaut later applied to the painting of the New York School.[52] However, *Painters Painting* does not acknowledge Guilbaut's thesis, one that a Marxist such as de Antonio should have considered long before Guilbaut's wrote his book: that the success of the paintings of the New York School was linked at some level to the ideology of the cold war. For a filmmaker whose real subject was the history of the United States during the cold war, this is a glaring omission.

To make this point would not have required an attack on his friends in the art world. Indeed, the best defense of the painting of high modernism might be made on the basis of the work of Said, who claimed that a work of art becomes more worldly, dynamic, and valuable when it reveals the connections between art and empire. De Antonio once made the guilty admission that "imperial art is exciting," but he did not ask why this was the case. His desire to fill the role of the "revolutionary artist" made such questions a threat to the doctrinal purity that a tentative Marxist could never attain.

Beyond whatever psychological import this dilemma may have had for de Antonio, one can see that it was representative of a larger issue regarding the definition of meaningful art, whose boundaries had been set by the tenets of modernism for most of de Antonio's life. To transpose Said's ideas to the present discussion, an emphasis on the autonomy of aesthetics became a limitation rather than a freedom of modernism, for it deprived modernism of the vocabulary it needed to come to terms with the shifting political currents of the sixties.[53] As a consequence, in 1968 a critic such as Nicolas Calas could complain that modernism was overlooking many meanings of a work of art.[54] But what were the alternatives? The obvious ones in the political culture, such as the ill-defined category of Marxist aesthetics, held little appeal for artists such as de Antonio, who scoffed at what he called the determinism of Marxist aestheticians and maintained that "almost all the politically committed art is garbage," a strange and ironic admission from a political filmmaker.[55]

Some artists were finding a solution to this problem in the practice of a new aesthetic, one that would gradually move under the rubric of "postmodernism," which some have called an anti-aesthetic.[56] For example, Sally Banes has located the roots of post-modernism in the makers of happenings and other performance artworks who were leaving the canvas in order to unite political and artistic radicalism in art that mimicked everyday life.[57] A term even more complex than modernism, *postmodernism* in the visual arts has tended to recast problems as virtues: if art lacks universal meaning, then flaunt its shifting place in the "political economy of the sign," to use Jean Baudrillard's phrase. If elitism offends your audience, make art that mocks the notion of individual artistic ge-nius or blurs the boundary between art and mass-produced junk. If commodification is inescapable, then ironically test the limits of commodification. Although these concepts may have offered some resolution to de Antonio's art-and-politics dichotomy, he simply was not interested or was not aware of them. His vision was essentially romantic, individualistic, rebellious, and firm in its belief in the power of creativity and the efficacy of resistance. From such a vantage postmodernism appears too passive in its acceptance of the ills of late capitalism, as Harrison and Wood have argued, too easily and willingly subsumed "under the sign of information/entertainment," as Baudrillard has called it. At heart de Antonio was a product of the thirties who believed that art was more than a game, that it was a place where truth and beauty could exist in a way that affirmed a sense of meaning in life.[58] These were qualities he saw in modernism, even if it mystified the general public in the manner that his film suggests.

This is not to say that the film is uncritical of modernist painting, that "culture is exonerated of any entanglements with power," to borrow Said's felicitous phrase.[59] Even without the barbed satire of *Millhouse*, some critiques one might expect from de Antonio are present when *Painters Painting* gently mocks the commodification of art in the hands of "the culture of leeches, crooks, conmen and hucksters."[60] As someone who bought Stella's *Reichstag* for $300 and sold it for $175,000, and sold a handmade Christmas card from Johns for $10,000, de Antonio was well acquainted with the business side of art.[61] Artists such as he and his friends had a legitimate reason to seek financial security, and to prove his point he quoted Zola: "Money had emancipated the writer, money has created modern letters." On the other hand, greed should be kept within certain limits of taste, because "painters wear their wealth as badly as their patrons," as he noted in regard to the opulent lifestyles of his friends Warhol and Stella.[62]

In *Painters Painting* de Antonio reserves his scorn primarily for the collector Robert Scull, whose egotism and vulgarity required little emphasis from de Antonio's editors (Lampson assisted by Cinda Firestone). Unlike the cruel juxtapositions of *Millhouse*, this film offers a restrained critique of people such as Scull, whose bumbling quest to depict himself as the Medici of pop causes the viewer to question the seriousness of any work that so pleases this parvenu. De Antonio does not go out of his way to make the man appear ludicrous, as he did in *Millhouse*, because he respected Scull on one count: he knew what to buy.

The portrayal of de Antonio's good friend Leo Castelli is even more subtle.[63] Sitting comfortably behind his desk in his gallery, Castelli discusses the wild inflation of prices on the art market with a bemused detachment and scoffs at the notion that dealers determine the taste of the art world. His depiction seems less critical than wary, as if the prominence of businessmen in the art world were unavoidable. Indeed, this aspect of the film possesses

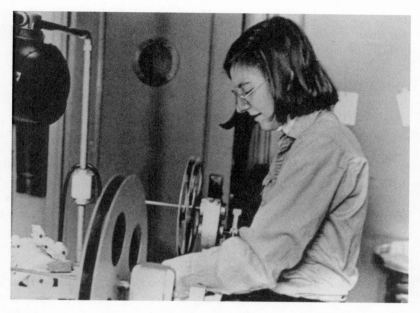

Cinda Firestone, assistant editor of *Painters Painting* (Turin Films, 1972). Courtesy Wisconsin Center for Film and Theater Research.

an air of resignation, which receives its perfect expression when the camera captures an angry young man of the radical Artists' Workers Council demanding a voice for artists in the Museum of Modern Art. "When will the museum serve the artist rather than the Rockefellers?" he asks with a note of militancy. The director of the museum, John B. Hightower, responds calmly: "I don't see that happening."

Though scenes such as this question the influence of commerce upon art, the film also offers a defense against simplistic critiques of the art world. Mitch Tuchman, curator of twentieth-century art at the Los Angeles County Museum, contends that *Painters Painting* makes clear that modernism "was no art world monolith," a view put forward by Tom Wolfe's best-selling *The Painted Word* (1975). Tuchman points out how *Painters Painting* reveals the inaccuracy of Wolfe's "factitious burlesque of cut-throat Svengalis, Jewish critics lustily brawling, while mesmerized armies of besmocked drones obediently fabricated off-the-rack canvases to critical specifications." De Antonio always detested Wolfe, perhaps because *The Painted Word* approached modern art with the irreverence that was expected from the filmmaker.[64]

In fact, hostility of another sort had motivated him to make *Painters Painting*: he detested previous films about art, which he dismissed as too arty, too reverent, too dependent upon "brainless zooms on Apollo's navel." He considered these documentaries as little better than implausible Hollywood films such as *Lust for Life* (1956) with Kirk Douglas as Van Gogh or *The Agony and the Ecstasy* (1965) with Charlton Heston as Michelangelo.[65] Beyond these sarcastic observations, he seemed unaware of the history of films on art, even though by the time he was making *Painters Painting* hundreds of serious short and feature-length films on art had been released. In addition to ignoring worthy films such as Alain Resnais's short documentaries, *Van Gogh* (1948), *Gauguin* (1950), and *Guernica* (1951), and Henri-Georges Clouzot's *Le Mystère Picasso* (1956), de Antonio preferred to ignore the fact that de Kooning, Johns, Rauschenberg, Pollock, and Hoffman had all been the subject of short films before *Painters Painting*.[66] However, few films in this substantial filmography had accomplished what de Antonio wanted to do.

The film historian Richard Barsam noted the genre's "child-like innocence" and "idol worship" toward its subject, neither of which interested de Antonio, who wanted to make a film as sophisticated and creative as the work it described.[67] To this end he quoted Schlegel's assertion that great works of art criticize themselves: "The work of criticism . . . is superfluous unless it is itself a work of art as independent of the work it criticizes as that work is independent of the material that went into it."[68] While *Painters Painting* does not meet this lofty standard, it came closer than most documentaries on art.

The minimalist sculptor Carl Andre wrote to de Antonio in 1980, commending him on the "extraordinary unity of style that

allowed each of the principles to be very much him or herself—
that kind of transparency of style is so rare, like Turgenev," the
sort of literary reference that de Antonio's films often evoked.[69]
One might also see the film as a sort of memoir, not unlike the more
explicitly autobiographical *Mr. Hoover and I* (1989), as an artistic
self-exploration in which he was able to examine the apparent
contradiction between his tastes and politics. He was certainly
pleased with *Painters Painting*, which even years later he called
his best work.

Others seemed to agree with this assessment—if not his best
film, it was at the very least "an unprecedented art historical
document," as one admiring academic gushed.[70] Tuchman, often
an insightful critic of de Antonio's films, noted that Emschwiller's
camera pan across a Johns collage was one of the finest such
camera movements in the history of cinema.[71] The participants
in the film seemed to appreciate de Antonio's depiction of them,
a sentiment not universal among his subjects. Henry Geldzahler
thought it impossible to teach a course on modern art without the
film, which was based on his show, and Warhol swore to the fidelity
of the film's depiction of the art world. Though Newman died
before the film was completed, he had watched his own interview
on an editing machine with delight. Mainstream reviewers were
generous to the film as well, if a little disappointed in its rambling
structure and lack of obvious point of view. Stanley Kauffmann
called it "a lovely gift" for anyone interested in contemporary
art, probably the first time the adjective *lovely* had been used in
conjunction with a de Antonio film. Few reviewers were aware of
the personal conflict in which it had embroiled its director, and
few noticed the retrospective quality of the film.[72]

De Antonio emphasized this aspect of the film in interviews
soon after its release. "After Stella and Poons, who is there?" he
asked rhetorically about the exhaustion of American painting.[73]
The comment appeared in a *New York Times* article about the
filmmaker and did not go unnoticed, at least in New York City.
"What an appalling point of view!" the *Village Voice* scolded
in response, certain that such pessimism would cause "many

sensitive art students to switch to dentistry or forestry."[74] While this rebuke must have caused him to laugh at its inanity, de Antonio was a pessimist about the prospects of contemporary art. With little sympathy for conceptual art and other trends of the 1970s, he seemed to regret what Warhol called the death of painting, which was compounded by the literal death of Barnett Newman.[75] "Painting has always been dead," de Kooning tells de Antonio with optimism, "but I was never worried about it," though others share a sense of finitude that enlivens the discussion in the film, making the interviewees both wistful and articulate about the history of their community. As Irving Howe wrote, "There comes that tremor of self-awareness which no one would have troubled to feel during the years of energy and confidence. A tradition in process of being lost, a generation facing assault and ridicule from ambitious younger men—the rekindled sense of group solidarity is brought to a half-hour's flame by the hardness of dying."[76] Or, in the case of *Painter's Painting*, a two-hour flame.

De Antonio's interest in painting did not die with the release of his film or with his immersion in the crucible of "revolutionary agony," in which he felt torn between the worlds of serious art and serious politics. For the time being, flush with the experience of filming at the Metropolitan Museum of Art, he wanted to repeat his *Painters Painting* experience in early 1972 with the Picasso exhibition at the Museum of Modern Art. His idea was to film the show on the night before it opened, then to fly to France with a film crew to interview Picasso himself, the most celebrated artist in the world. Unfortunately, his prospective interviewer and only entrée to the artist was William Rubin, the MOMA curator who appears briefly toward the end of *Painters Painting*. For reasons of his own—de Antonio suspected a desire to increase the value of a forthcoming book on Picasso—Rubin was reluctant to help the filmmaker with this project. Derailed even more quickly than his project on Bertrand Russell, the Picasso film never left de Antonio's imagination.[77] The closest he came to repeating his

Emile de Antonio, photographed by Thomas Bergman, son of Ingmar, October 1973.
Courtesy Wisconsin Center for Film and Theater Research.

accomplishment in *Painters Painting* was to plan a short film
on John Cage's 1982 show at the Whitney Museum. However,
other filmmakers would extend the tradition of *Painters Painting*,
as Barbaralee Diamonstein did in *Inside New York's Art World*
(1980), which de Antonio viewed as derivative of his own film.[78]

Painters Painting was also the source of two books. De Antonio signed a contract in 1985 to write the biography of his friend
Leo Castelli. As if to make explicit the theme of *Painters Painting*,
this book would have been about "power and money in art,"
but after conducting many hours of interviews he gave up the
ambitious project.[79] The second book was also entitled *Painters
Painting* and was the result of de Antonio's collaboration with
the art critic–curator Mitch Tuchman in culling a coherent oral
history from the seven hundred pages of transcribed interviews

conducted for the film.[80] "I think your book is terrific," wrote
Jasper Johns, and de Antonio agreed, viewing it as the second
emblem of his accomplishment of bringing together such a remarkable cast.[81] But the book barely echoes the voices heard so clearly
in the film—Rauschenberg's labored drawl, Newman's dramatic
cadences, Stella's clipped eloquence—and its real value lies in
the creativity of Tuchman's thematic arrangement of the material
and in de Antonio's long introductory essay, the best writing of
his stunted career in prose.

De Antonio's "great dilemma" between politics and art, unre-
solved in *Painters Painting*, followed him into later controversies,
such as the one surrounding Richard Serra's *Tilted Arc* (1981–
1989). On March 8, 1985, de Antonio testified at a public hearing
regarding the question of Serra's sculpture, which the U.S. government had commissioned and then wanted to remove after only
a few years. An enormous steel wall set in the middle of Federal
Plaza in Manhattan, *Tilted Arc* was not what federal employees
expected from a public monument. Here was a clear case of the
public versus the art world, but in a reverse of the battle lines
of the sixties, the conservatives now called for art with public
relevance while the avant-garde stood behind the autonomy of art.

Aligning himself with the avant-garde, de Antonio protested
the government's actions as a form of censorship reminiscent of
Stalin. While de Antonio showed his continuing willingness to take
a public stand on controversial issues, his words had little effect.[82]
Despite the testimony of de Antonio and many others in the art
world, the site-specific sculpture was dismantled—in other words,
destroyed—in 1989.

Such was the state of art in the eighties. De Antonio believed
that Newman and Stella had brought painting to a conceptual
impasse, and the filmmaker had little more than sympathy for
performance artists who drilled holes in their bodies in the name
of art, as he once quipped.[83] On occasion, however, he did find
painters who interested him, such as Guyana-born Andrew Lyght
in the late seventies and African American Jean-Michel Basquiat,
the rising star of the 1980s art world who died at twenty-eight of

Jean-Michel Basquiat and Emile de Antonio, 1984. Courtesy Wisconsin Center for Film and Theater Research.

a drug overdose. De Antonio's support for their work seemed to contain an element of atonement for his lack of interest in the art of "outsider" groups during the 1960s—*Painters Painting* has no faces of color and only one woman, Frankenthaler (though de Antonio did hire talented women such as Lampson and Firestone to edit the film). Not to slight the accomplishments of Basquiat, though some critics have been eager to do so, de Antonio may have been motivated by a degree of guilt about the conservative characteristics of *Painters Painting*. If this was the case, his first act of penance was his next film, which delved into everything *Painters Painting* had ignored, submerging de Antonio in the youth culture and radical politics of the Weather Underground.[84]

7

—◄o►—

Underground

Melodrama

Between swims in the cold ocean waters of the Atlantic coast in the summer of 1974, de Antonio sat on the beach holding a red-covered book: *Prairie Fire: The Politics of Revolutionary Anti-Imperialism: Political Statement of the Weather Underground.*[1] The thin volume with the long title had been published in secret a few months earlier. Though the mainstream media dismissed its authors as "distracted former students who sustained revolutionary pretensions with sex, ideology and a dream of violence," *Prairie Fire* sparked de Antonio's curiosity about the Weather Underground, its members' motivations, and their histories. "I mean what the hell is an essentially white, middle-class revolutionary group doing in America?" he wondered.[2]

The roots of the Weather Underground were firmly in the politics of the sixties, specifically in Students for a Democratic Society (SDS). Gaining more than 100,000 young adherents in its brief life, SDS was at the center of the counterculture as well as the political revival known as the New Left. Often with eloquence, rarely with violence, its members fought the draft, protested the war in Vietnam, marched for civil rights, and held "teach-ins." But at the SDS National Convention in June 1969 the organization fell into disarray over internal differences and split into various factions, including one known initially as "Weatherman."

181

Taking their name from a Bob Dylan song that says, "you don't need a weatherman to know which way the wind blows," Weatherman abandoned SDS and embarked on its own course, quickly moving beyond nonviolent protests to the Maoist sentiment that "political power comes out of the barrel of a gun."[3] In October 1969 its members put their words into practice, fighting the Chicago police with chains and clubs in what became known as the "Days of Rage."[4] Such actions alienated many of their former SDS colleagues, especially as the violence escalated into a "life-or-death revolutionary struggle for freedom."[5] Death came soon enough: in March 1970 three members of the Weather Underground blew up a stylish Manhattan townhouse and died while building antipersonnel bombs.[6] The survivors literally crawled from the wreckage of the townhouse, fled from the police, and went underground to continue a slightly different form of revolutionary violence.[7]

Now known as the Weather Underground, this small cadre of revolutionaries became a "freelance bombing collective" with approximately thirty-seven members, twenty-two of whom were sought by the FBI for various offenses.[8] As targets they chose what they considered to be the symbols of U.S. imperialism, buildings such as the Pentagon, the U.S. Capitol, and the New York City Police headquarters, where their bombs were planted in restrooms and set to explode at night in order not to injure anyone.[9] With the support of an above-ground network, they completed more than two dozen bombings between 1970 and 1975, secretly printed *Prairie Fire* and a bimonthly magazine, and even coordinated the prison escape of counterculture guru Timothy Leary, who had been convicted on a drug charge. They were "a radical underground, which, though small and shaky, was unique in United States history," as one member recalled—yet the FBI, much to its embarrassment, could not find them.[10] De Antonio thought he could.

He began in 1974 with a call to Robert Friedman, the editor of the progressive *University Review*, a magazine that had published one of de Antonio's scathing film reviews.[11] Friedman had

given the filmmaker his first copy of *Prairie Fire* and claimed
to know its authors. "Let me make a film about them" was the
message de Antonio asked him to convey to the Underground.[12]
Evasive at first, Friedman decided to deliver the message, and
a week later he had one for de Antonio. The Underground was
interested, even flattered by the offer because "it was like they
had made it big," as one Weatherman dryly noted. Not wanting
to be sandwiched between commercials for soaps and cars, the
Underground claimed to have rejected lucrative television offers
not unlike those that would be satirized in the film *Network*
(1977), where real revolutionaries are given their own television
show called "The Mao Zedong Hour." However, to members of
the Weather Underground, de Antonio represented something
different, far from the commercialism of U.S. television.[13] "You
are internationally respected. . . . You have earned your reputation thru [*sic*] making good, revolutionary films," they later
wrote to him. Still, their caution required further evidence of his
suitability. To his mild annoyance they requested something on
paper describing what sort of film he had in mind, which seemed
to him more in keeping with a shrewd Hollywood producer than
a band of young radicals.[14] Overlooking this contradiction, he
decided to write a proposal, which would be a welcome diversion
from his personal problems, the worst of which was that his wife,
Terry, was dying of leukemia in the fall of 1974.[15] After visiting her
at the hospital one night, he sat in front of a soundless television
with a bottle of Glenlivet and typed out his thoughts about the
Weather Underground.[16]

A revealing document written in his staccato prose style, the
proposal described his background, his films, his politics. As
tokens of his sincerity, he offered unusual pieces of information
about himself, such as his boyhood refusal to bow his head for
school prayers. This was all part of his sales pitch to the Weather
Underground, though his main selling point was his work. A "well-
made film," he explained, would amplify the group's revolutionary message, if not drown out the message of President Gerald
Ford, which de Antonio curtly summarized as "fuck the people,

fuck the environment, fuck everybody."[17] Though the language seems chosen for the benefit of the tough-talking young radicals, the sentiment was genuine de Antonio.

In the letter he went on to praise the Underground's bombings as a "masterstroke of political theater which not only reveals the police state but that it's possible to beat it." Still, political theater was one thing, the risk of hurting someone quite another, and he was secretly pleased that the group was moving away from violence, which was how he, like many people, interpreted the publication of *Prairie Fire*.[18] Although he presented himself to the Weather Underground as "anti-pacifist," and its bombings undoubtedly fascinated him, he was generally against bringing violence into politics.[19] "Political violence . . . counters the violence of the state but to be more inhuman than the state is to lose both battle and war," he wrote in his journal in this period, echoing Gandhi.[20] On the other hand, de Antonio believed the media had simplistically reduced political violence to fit inside "trendy Wonder Bread reality sandwiches . . . one-sided, sensationalist, all about 'cr[a]zed terrorists' and bombers."[21]

De Antonio was not alone in his criticism of media coverage of political violence in the mid-1970s, though his conclusions were far outside the mainstream. Politicians made frequent mention of the relationship between the media and what was generally categorized as terrorism.[22] In 1977 former president Gerald Ford blamed "lavish media attention" for encouraging such violence, while Andrew Young, then the U.S. ambassador to the United Nations, complained that "the First Amendment has got to be clarified by the Supreme Court in light of the power of the mass media" to cover terrorism.[23] Despite these criticisms, U.S. journalists were able to report on terrorism with far fewer restrictions than their foreign counterparts. The British government had enacted the Prevention of Terrorism Act in 1974, which could require journalists to "notify authorities before they have contact with groups engaged in violence, to report any unplanned contact, and to provide copies of materials to the authorities."[24] With the U.S. news filled with references to a confusing array of violent organizations, from the Black Liberation Army to the Symbionese Liberation Army, the issue of political violence was a source of considerable pressure on journalists and politicians alike in the mid-1970s.[25] In short, de Antonio could not have chosen a more controversial time to start a film on the Weather Underground.

On the other hand, this air of controversy made the Weather-people—who had outgrown the gender-specific "Weathermen"—all the more eager for some positive publicity, which they assumed de Antonio would provide. To continue pushing the possibility of a film toward fruition, they instructed Friedman to arrange a meet-ing between the filmmaker and the Underground with elaborate safeguards against being followed by the FBI. The Weatherpeople were adamant about security precautions, almost to the point of comedy. When the day of the meeting arrived, Friedman picked the filmmaker up at the Museum of Natural History in New York City. "They'll be glad you're wearing sneakers," Friedman told de Antonio as they drove through the city. "No way to sneak a transmitter into a heel."[26]

Not even Friedman knew the meeting place. His only in-structions were to leave de Antonio at a certain phone booth in Brooklyn, where de Antonio was to wait for the phone to ring. He answered with his code name, Frank, and was told to go three blocks toward the canal and stand on the corner for five minutes . . . then cross the street and walk to the bridge . . . then stand there.[27] He did what the voice instructed, and the melodrama continued as a man approached and told him to walk to a nearby cafe and look for a woman holding a *Newsweek*. A police car drove past as de Antonio walked toward the cafe and he realized how nervous he was. Stepping into the cafe, he met "Alex" and "Nina," which were also code names, and at last the security ritual was complete. With a laugh and a sense of relief, he sat down with Jeff Jones and Eleanor Raskin of the Weather Underground.

He liked them immediately. They struck him as "bright, streetwise, pragmatic and uneducated" kids. After some light-hearted discussion about the possibilities of a film, the Weatherpeople raised a serious issue. If de Antonio were served with a subpoena, would he promise not to cooperate with the government's efforts to find the Weather Underground? He replied that under no circumstances, even if immunity were given, would he cooperate with a grand jury. Jones and Raskin inquired about the other crew members—would they also be willing to go to jail? De Antonio vouched for them, though the Weather Underground wanted to meet each crew member before filming. The crew would be unusually small for security reasons, and de Antonio had one person in mind whom he could trust.[28]

De Antonio wanted Haskell Wexler, a celebrated cameraman who had won Oscars for his work on films such as *Who's Afraid of Virginia Woolf?* (1967). Wexler had made a great deal of money from his work on popular films and sophisticated television commercials for companies such as Royal Crown soda, but he had another side to his professional life that attracted de Antonio's attention. Wexler had made serious political documentaries on subjects such as Vietnam, Chile, and Brazil, as well as an innovative feature film, *Medium Cool* (1969), which was set in part at the Democratic National Convention of 1968. Its distributor, Paramount, considered the film too controversial for widespread distribution.[29]

De Antonio had only one doubt about Wexler: his lifestyle. His Malibu beach house, Cadillac limousine, and Mercedes with a $1,500 paint job became lodged in de Antonio's imagination as symbols of what was wrong with the Hollywood Left.[30] Wexler's initial reaction to the project did little to reassure de Antonio, who had flown to California to recruit the cameraman for the project. "I didn't know anything about the Weather Underground except what I read in the papers," Wexler said, and what he had read sounded too violent for his taste.[31] As for de Antonio's proposal to make a film about the Underground, Wexler said, "I wished it were on something else." However, his sense of adventure and de Antonio's persuasiveness overcame Wexler's reservations, and he agreed to meet with the Weather Underground to see for himself what the project would involve.[32]

After a breakfast that de Antonio ironically described as yogurt, honey, and vitamins on a silver tray, the middle-aged radicals went to meet the young revolutionaries at a meetingplace near the Los Angeles County Museum. They sat on a park bench and waited until Jeff Jones arrived alone to begin discussing the film. When someone sat on a nearby bench, the filmmakers became alarmed. However, Jones remained calm and attempted to reassure his jittery companions by saying, "I'm very comfortable. Are you?"[33] Years of living underground had taught Jones when to be worried about police surveillance and when to relax.

Jones was more worried about the security of the Weather Underground in regard to the making of the film, and he quizzed Wexler about methods of shooting the film without showing their faces. The FBI had not seen the fugitives for the better part of five years, making it easier for the Weatherpeople to move aboveground, where they could take ordinary jobs under assumed names. Ski masks were an obvious solution, but both de Antonio and Wexler rejected the hostile impression they made— "We didn't want to make them look like they had just robbed the local A&P," said de Antonio. Wexler was left to think about this security problem as the meeting ended, with the Weather Underground satisfied with the cameraman's integrity.[34]

The Weatherpeople then decided that the film crew should include a woman.[35] De Antonio was not accustomed to having demands placed upon his filmmaking decisions, but he agreed and called Mary Lampson, who had worked on his last three films. He was talking in a low and excited voice, she remembered, "and making the most of a very dramatic situation." Still, like Wexler, she was not easily persuaded to join the venture.[36]

"We will form a collective and work together as equals," he promised, which was difficult to believe coming from someone she had known as "very egocentric, strong and often pig-headed."[37] She also worried about the Weatherpeople, whom she described as "outlaws, fugitives, revolutionaries."[38] Despite her work on controversial films such as *Millhouse* and Cinda Firestone's *Attica* (1971), Lampson did not share the politics of the Weatherpeople.

"I thought they were crazy" from what she read about them, though she was also willing to meet with them to find out for herself.[39]

Accompanied by de Antonio, Lampson met Jones and Raskin on a deserted street in New York City. Pairing off, Lampson walked with Jones, explained her doubts about the Underground and expected the inevitable ideological rebuke. But much to her surprise, Jones welcomed her criticism and hoped the film would be a dialogue. "They wanted us to challenge them and they wanted to challenge us," Lampson remembered.[40] This tolerant attitude won her over, and, as de Antonio wrote in his journal in the cadences of clichéd prose, "We were now a film team."[41]

Underground

Only six months had elapsed since de Antonio had read *Prairie Fire* on the beach; now, on April 27, 1975, the filmmakers sat in Los Angeles, nervously waiting for a phone call with directions to the safe house, a location secure from FBI detection.[42] They waited for almost forty-eight hours, their fragile confidence in the Weather Underground slowly replaced by fears and doubts: would the group be armed? What would happen in the FBI discovered them?[43] De Antonio knew that the Symbionese Liberation Army had been "wiped out in L.A. like a search and destroy scene from Nam" in a hail of more than eight thousand rounds of ammunition in May 1974, and he feared the same for the Weather Underground.[44] Finally, the phone rang, and they received the first step of their elaborate directions. They loaded one of Wexler's cars, "a beat-up Chevvy [*sic*] wagon, king-size," with so much equipment that the undercarriage scraped against the pavement.[45]

The first stop in the cloak-and-dagger routine was a gas station where further directions were taped beneath a pay phone. These pointed the way to another pay phone with even further directions through dead-end streets, a maneuver intended to reveal anyone who might have been following their car. After negotiating a labyrinth of dark streets and deserted areas, they at last found Jeff Jones, who got behind the wheel of their station wagon. To keep the location of the safe house a secret, Jones asked the filmmakers to put on sunglasses that had been painted over with nail polish. "I knew I was losing control," de Antonio thought as he put on the glasses he described as grotesque, so he suggested that the sight of several passengers in identically preposterous disguises might attract police attention. Jones agreed. De Antonio could remove his glasses but had to keep his eyes shut.[46]

They arrived at the safe house after a half-hour of driving and began to unload the station wagon. The house was empty and the setting stark; the boarded-over windows put de Antonio into a pessimistic mood. "I knew it would be bad," de Antonio recalled. "Haskell was too cavalier." They set up the equipment and went to bed for a sleepless night. Up at dawn on April 30, 1975, de Antonio and Wexler wondered who their actors would be, who the Weather Underground would choose as representatives. Then Jones walked through the door, followed by Billy Ayers, Bernardine Dohrn, Kathy Boudin, and Cathy Wilkerson—most of the best-known members of the Weather Underground.[47]

These counterculture celebrities made a strong first impression. Dohrn, a lawyer by training, "fused the two premium female images of the moment: sex queen and streetfighter," at least in the active imagination of one male observer.[48] Her photograph graced the FBI's "Ten Most Wanted" list for years, and de Antonio called her the "underground Jeanne d'Arc." Ayers was the soft-spoken son of the president of Commonwealth Edison of Chicago and had been active in educational reform. Even more reticent was civil rights organizer Boudin, the daughter of a well-known lawyer for progressive causes. Wilkerson, whose father owned the townhouse where the Underground's bombs had exploded, had worked in the national office of SDS. When he met her in the safe house, de Antonio sensed "strong human and sexual vibrations."[49] Jones was a radicalized southern California surfer, the "Leninist all-American boy," as de Antonio saw him, who had promoted the film project within the Weather Underground.[50] If a sense of radical chic counted for anything, the film was off to a promising start.

Everyone exchanged tense greetings as they took seats around a table. "Then, all at once, everyone just totally and spontaneously started to laugh and clap their hands," so relieved were they to be together, finally making the film. But once the cameras were in place, this relaxed atmosphere evaporated. Though the Weatherpeople were unaccustomed to being in front of cameras, their real source of anxiety was having so many Weather Underground luminaries in one place. It was the most dangerous thing they had ever done, according to Jones.[51] This burden was on the filmmakers as well. "Every mistake they make leads to their arrest or death," de Antonio said with a heavy sense of responsibility for the welfare of his new acquaintances.[52]

To conceal the identities of the Weatherpeople, Wexler had decided to film them through a sheet of opaque gauze called a

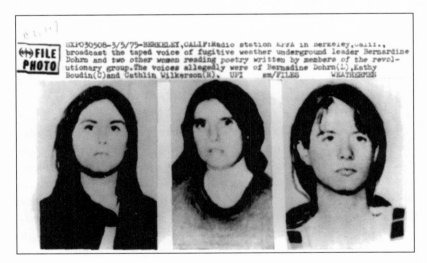

Bernardine Dohrn, Kathy Boudin, and Cathy Wilkerson in a still from *Underground* (Turin Films, 1976). Courtesy Wisconsin Center for Film and Theater Research.

scrim, which he hoped would reveal a sense of their features without giving away the details. But the scrim also formed a barrier between the filmmakers and their subjects. Wexler was uncomfortable shooting his camera at the hazy images, and the hazy images were uncomfortable behind the wall of translucent fabric. How could he convey the sense of "sitting there with Robin Hood," de Antonio wondered, without showing their faces?[53] To make matters worse, the Weatherpeople insisted on speaking in an impersonal language, hitting de Antonio with "salvo after salvo of meaningless bombed out words and lines" buried in monologues that outlasted Wexler's ten-minute rolls of color footage at $120 per roll. What the filmmakers did not know was that the Weatherpeople had vowed not to interrupt each other as a gesture of their communitarian values. When this became known to de Antonio, he sought to redirect their abstract speeches into more personal histories. Film was inevitably voyeuristic, he said, seeking to explain his interest in them as "vehicles" of their politics.[54] Nevertheless, the Weatherpeople resisted, unwilling to make a sensational exposé of life in the Underground, and the day ended on this unproductive note.[55]

On the second day of the shoot the Weatherpeople decided to rearrange the set. Getting rid of the scrim, they would now speak directly to the filmmakers while Wexler focused on a mirror hanging on the wall. This method, which revealed nothing more than a reflection of their backs, made the Weatherpeople feel more comfortable. Another problem was the attitude of the filmmakers, who were too sympathetic to the plight of their new friends to disagree even gently with their radical pronouncements. "Please participate more, challenge us," Bernardine Dohrn said.[56] Aware that the Weatherpeople had put themselves at risk by agreeing to make the film, de Antonio held his natural combativeness in check and sat passively while they spoke with great earnestness and with the "encrustations of a ritualized Marxism," to use Barry Katz's phrase.[57] The Weatherpeople described the inevitability of revolution, the beauty of communism, their solidarity with the civil rights movement, their sense of loss over the three who died

Emile de Antonio, Haskell Wexler, and Mary Lampson during the production of *Underground* (Turin Films, 1976). Courtesy Wisconsin Center for Film and Theater Research.

in the townhouse explosion, the anxieties of life as fugitives. For the first time they described how they bombed the U.S. Capitol on March 1, 1971, causing $100,000 worth of damage.[58] With some reticence they did their best to answer de Antonio's primary question about them: what were they doing in the United States in 1975?

At the end of the day the Weatherpeople and the filmmakers parted as friends. The Weatherpeople presented de Antonio with a quilt emblazoned with the words "THE FUTURE WILL BE WHAT THE PEOPLE STRUGGLE TO MAKE IT," which appears in the film several times. Then the filmmakers loaded their car, endured the various security precautions, and left the Underground. With enormous relief they realized that the FBI had not followed them.[59]

Then the Weather Underground suggested a third day of filming. Jones and Boudin wanted to be filmed in public, as if to flaunt their ability to elude the FBI. De Antonio did not approve of the idea, especially when he was told that he was not invited on the excursion. In order to submerge his forceful personality into the spirit of collectivity, he was instructed to stay home while Wexler and Lampson accompanied Jones and Boudin to Martin Luther King Hospital in Los Angeles, where young African American doctors were striking for an increase in community service on the part of the hospital. Any effort to remain inconspicuous was immediately undermined. Wexler, who arrived in a wide-brimmed hat and carried his expensive film equipment, parked their car close enough to be noticed by anyone who cared to write down their license plate number. Lampson shouldered a Nagra sound recorder. De Antonio believed that the Los Angeles Police Department was taking photographs of the picket line, while a rotating video camera scanned the crowd from the roof of the hospital. The filmmakers stayed only a few minutes, long enough for Jones and Boudin to speak with a few people on film, and left without incident.[60]

Surveillance

They hoped no one had noticed the eccentric-looking film crew, but within forty-eight hours a car appeared in front of Wexler's house in Hollywood. Its occupants pretended to be changing a flat tire, but they were "a couple of guys looking so much like cops, you wouldn't believe it," as Wexler said.[61] The clean-cut motorists seemed less interested in fixing their car than peering through binoculars at Wexler's home, an activity they performed quite openly. One even stood in the middle of the street and snapped Polaroid photos. Afraid that the FBI would seize the undeveloped film and put an end to the project, de Antonio wanted to process the film immediately so that he could make certain that they had adequately distorted the Weatherpeople's images. He wanted to be certain the film contained nothing of use to the FBI.

Wexler supervised the film processing, while de Antonio was in charge of the soundtrack, which needed to be transferred

from the original quarter-inch tape to a 16mm magnetic track
before it could be edited. But de Antonio suspected that film
labs and sound "transfer houses" maintained close connections
with the U.S. government, which provided substantial business.[62]
Concerned that a technician might hear something suspicious, de
Antonio concocted an elaborate ruse that played to the stereo-
type of southern Californians, pretending to have footage of "a
new kind of transactional analysis" in which the patients discuss
intimate matters. Trying to look "both zany and deadly serious,"
he explained that no one but he could hear the material. The lab
seemed to accept his story and let him spend the better portion of
two days making the transfer.[63]

As for the film, Wexler decided that the least conspicuous
option was to use his regular lab in Los Angeles where he processed
footage for television commercials. The day after he dropped off
the film an executive from the lab called, concerned that the film
was defective. "You can't see the faces," he fretted, but Wexler
told him to continue processing the film as it was. When the lab
finally delivered the results of the filmmakers' three days underground, they were not pleased. Despite all their precautions—the
scrim, the mirror—clear glimpses of the Weatherpeople appeared
on the film. "Sanitizing" the film became their immediate priority.

De Antonio was annoyed with Wexler. "Had he worried about
it as much as the dollars he makes in commercials he would have
tested the scrim" beforehand.[64] Back in New York de Antonio and
Lampson went over the film, practically frame by frame, painting
over the faces of the Weatherpeople whenever they could be seen.
"That's better than any mug shot!" Lampson would point out,
and they'd apply the paint. After many hours of tedious labor
at a film company on East 45th Street, they reshot the negative
using the painted-over print. De Antonio went to his house in the
country and started a fire in which to destroy the original film: "I
drank and stirred the ashes of our risks and failures and stayed
for hours, poking small segments of film until it was all burned."[65]
Every scrap of film had to be destroyed, especially after de Antonio received a letter from a friend in the American Civil Liberties
Union of Southern California, warning him that the FBI had

access to a new computer process called "image enhancement," which could clarify the cloudy images of the Weatherpeople.[66] Even with such precautions, the FBI somehow found the film to be helpful: when agents eventually watched the film, they were able to see the Weatherpeople with sufficient clarity to note their resemblance to available photographs.[67]

The FBI was active on other fronts as well. Agents investigated de Antonio's friends, including Antoinette O'Connor, with whom he was close after the death of Terry Moore earlier in the year. Although O'Connor had nothing to do with the film, the FBI examined her background at length, questioning friends in Texas she had not seen for years. For the sake of security the filmmakers had decided not to meet again with the Weather Underground after the filming, but de Antonio believed the FBI was waiting for them to make contact with the fugitives. Then, he believed, the FBI would have killed the Weather Underground members because "they had to" for making the FBI "look like fools for five years."[68]

The FBI surveillance was not simply a figment of the film-maker's imagination. In 1979, after he obtained his files under the Freedom of Information Act, de Antonio found suggestions the sound-editing company, Sound Services, Inc., had provided the FBI with a copy of the soundtrack. Evidently, the owner of the lab had not believed de Antonio's story about "transactional analysis" and had reported his suspicions to the FBI. In a letter of March 7, 1976, to the U.S. attorney general, Edward H. Levi, FBI director Clarence Kelley noted that "a cooperative individual in Los Angeles was willing to make a copy of the voice tapes available to us."[69] The ACLU of Southern California filed suit on de Antonio's behalf against the firm on September 16, 1980, alleging violation of federal copyright law as well as its contract with the filmmaker.

But in early May 1975, de Antonio had only suspicions, not evidence, that the FBI was investigating his involvement with the Weather Underground. When his phone line crackled "like crisp Sunday morning bacon," he naturally wondered whether it was a sign of electronic eavesdropping, which was not unusual for the

FBI agents assigned to the WEATHERFUGS (Weather Underground fugitives) case.[70] Agents did in fact request de Antonio's financial records from American Express, Master Charge, VISA, Chemical Bank, and the New York Telephone Co. On May 14, 1975, the Los Angeles office of the FBI sent a teletype to Washington and fourteen other offices that described "investigative developments" in regard to de Antonio—including his reservations to fly from Los Angeles to New York.[71] One agent who investigated the Weather Underground from 1970 to 1977 came forward in 1981 and claimed that the agency intended to steal a copy of *Underground* from the filmmaker's studio but was unable to pick the lock; however, this story is not verified elsewhere.[72]

The FBI office in Los Angeles also compiled a long list of potential charges against the filmmaker: "Rebellion or Insurrection," "Advocating Overthrow of the Government," "Unlawful Possession and Receipt of Firearms," "Explosives and Incendiary Devices," "Anti-Riot Laws," and "Unlawful Possession of Destructive Devices." While de Antonio later scoffed at the litany of charges, noting with amusement that he was too convivial for such things, the subtle signs of the FBI's attention were taking a toll on him.[73]

The psychological pressure increased throughout May 1975, until one night de Antonio called the FBI and asked, "Would you get your fucking gumshoes off my back please[?]" As if in reply to his comment, two FBI agents appeared several days later at his Manhattan offices. The agents asked him where they could serve a subpoena on his wife, Terry—"A graveyard on Long Island," he told them.[74] Flustered, the agents left, only to return with a subpoena requiring the filmmaker to appear in U.S. District Court in Los Angeles on June 12, 1975. He refused to be interviewed by the agents, and he was left to read the document, which instructed him to "bring with you any and all motion picture film, including, but not limited to all negatives, working copies and prints, and all sound tracks and sound recordings made in connection with the filming of such motion pictures, concerning a group known as the Weathermen or Weather Underground."[75]

The Subpoena

The subpoena became an immediate cause célèbre, touching a nerve in the Hollywood community and evoking images of the McCarthy era, when the exigencies of anticommunism circumscribed the subject matter of films. "This flagrant violation of the First Amendment rights of freedom of the press and speech ranks with the witch-hunts against Hollywood in the 1950's," proclaimed Ramona Ripston, executive director of the ACLU of Southern California, who immediately came to the filmmakers's defense as a part of the ACLU's mission to protect the First Amendment.[76] She blasted the government for using journalists and documentarians as "informers" and arranged for a well-publicized press conference in Los Angeles on June 6, 1975, one week before the filmmakers were to appear before the grand jury.

At the center of the press conference were the three film-makers, who vowed not to cooperate with the grand jury in any fashion. Robert Wise, president of the Screen Directors Guild, solemnly read a statement of support, which said Hollywood had an obligation to fight the subpoena as a form of censorship: "We're bound to speak up and not turn our backs."[77] Influential elements within Hollywood seemed to recognize the connection between the civil liberties of these relatively obscure filmmakers and their own. As Wexler noted with pleasant surprise, his peers realized that "it had to do with *their* films."[78]

At the ACLU press conference the filmmakers made public a petition supporting their right to make a film about any subject "and specifically [their] right . . . to make a film with and about the Weather Underground Organization." Thirty-two well-known film people signed the document, including the actors Warren Beatty, Mel Brooks, Sally Field, Rip Torn, Shirley MacLaine, and Jack Nicholson. Others were producers and directors of both mainstream and independent films: Henry Jaglom, Cinda Firestone, William Friedkin, Terrence Malick, Arthur Penn, Elia Kazan, Peter Bogdanovich, and Bert Schneider, who was instrumental in getting signatures. Beneath the illustrious names from

Hollywood were fourteen individuals distinguished by their work in other fields, including various academics, as well as Daniel Ellsberg, who had leaked the Pentagon Papers.[79]

Perhaps the most surprising omissions from the list of Hollywood politicos were the actress Jane Fonda and her husband, the former SDS member Tom Hayden—both of whom had seemed to support the Weather Underground in the past.[80] But Hayden, who was preparing to run for the U.S. Senate the next year, needed to distance himself from his radical roots. He refused to sign the statement, and instead produced a document that the filmmaker regarded as "so vague, so broad, so electoral-hypocritical" as to signify nothing.[81] De Antonio was disgusted with Hayden and attacked him as a "little tennis-playing fraud" and, more creatively, a "liberalpseudorad."[82] Several months later Fonda sent him a conciliatory letter with the plea, "I hope we can be friends again," but de Antonio did not respond.[83]

Ironically, de Antonio had no more respect for the Hollywood liberals who did come to his defense. Just as he privately mocked the Hollywood Ten of the McCarthy era with a surprising lack of empathy, he scoffed at the Hollywood activists of the seventies such as Schneider. Without a word of gratitude, he dismissed them all as "coke-snorting, Beverly Hills snob-Marxists," though he made a surprising exception for Kazan, who had been a friendly witness before HUAC in 1952.[84] De Antonio respected Kazan's courage in signing the petition even though it seemed to run counter to his past cooperation with the government and his reputation as "the former pigeon who squealed," as de Antonio indelicately put it.[85]

Of course the filmmakers needed something more substantive than the symbolic support of Hollywood's elite. To add legal substance to the celebrity cachet of their petition, they hired three prominent lawyers to represent them: Michael Kennedy; Leonard Boudin, the father of the Weather Underground member Kathy Boudin; and Charles Nesson, a professor at Harvard University Law School.[86] What made the case unique to these lawyers was the timing of the government subpoena. While in the past the First

Amendment had been invoked to protect completed documentary films, the status of an unfinished film raised a new issue. From the point of view of the filmmakers, the government was interfering with freedom of expression, in effect placing its foot on the typewriter, to use a journalistic analogy that Nesson suggested. Or, as Haskell Wexler said, "What the government is demanding is our notes."[87]

Leonard Boudin described the subpoena as an unprecedented case of "prior restraint," a concept drawn from the First and Fourteenth Amendment and often invoked to guarantee the freedom of the press to publish and disseminate information, especially of a political nature. In its famous 1971 decision the U.S. Supreme Court had accused the government of trying to exercise prior restraint in its efforts to prevent the publication in the *New York Times* and the *Washington Post* of classified documents popularly known as the Pentagon Papers.[88] De Antonio wanted this protection to extend to documentary filmmakers, who he believed should have the right to film anything at all, without the specter of prior restraint.[89]

The legal defense of the filmmakers also rested on the contention that the subpoena represented an abuse of the grand jury system. Traditionally the first step in a criminal proceeding, the grand jury had been devised as a "screening device . . . to protect people from improper prosecution," as Leonard Boudin observed.[90] Yet in this instance, the ACLU claimed, the grand jury was being wielded like a "blunderbuss" by a government unable to locate the Weatherpeople. Charles Nesson explicitly questioned the use of a grand jury for police, rather than investigative, functions: "They're not trying to solve a crime, they're trying to catch somebody, and that's not any grand jury function I ever heard of."[91] De Antonio put forth another explanation for the subpoena, claiming its real intention was to block the completion of a film that would embarrass a government whose vast resources had failed to locate a network of fugitives that a middle-aged film director had found with little difficulty.[92]

The combination of several prominent attorneys with weighty

legal arguments, dozens of celebrities willing to put their names on a petition, and three utterly uncooperative filmmakers must have had the intended effect. The government backed off and withdrew the subpoena without comment on the eve of the ACLU press conference.[93] Though the government could issue a second subpoena if it chose, an option it considered as late as May 1976, Attorney General Levi seemed to prefer a tactical retreat from what the FBI described as "wide newspaper publicity." When Levi "squashed" the subpoena, as the FBI memoranda describe it, he partially granted de Antonio's wish that documentary filmmakers receive the same First Amendment protection accorded to journalists. Though the law had not changed, documentary filmmakers now were "considered part of the 'news media' " at least as far as the FBI was concerned, as the director of the FBI wrote in reference to the case.[94]

The withdrawal of the subpoena was hailed as a victory for freedom of expression. Under the headline "Protecting Filmmakers," the editors of the *Boston Globe* criticized the subpoena's "chilling effect on the filmmaker's ability to lawfully gather information."[95] De Antonio called the episode "the most significant case of prior restraint in the history of this government," and allowing for his hyperbole, the assertion makes sense in the context of the history of documentary film.[96] The subpoena resulted in "the first time [that] First Amendment privilege has arisen in the case of a documentary filmmaker," as Charles Nesson wrote, and it had been resolved in favor of the filmmakers.[97] Outside the films that made his name, this was probably the most significant achievement of de Antonio's career.

Not everyone was pleased with the government's withdrawal of the subpoena. On July 30, 1975, one enraged member of Congress, Democrat Larry McDonald of Georgia, stood before his colleagues in the House of Representatives and denounced "the notorious Emile de Antonio" and the "Hollywood crackpots" who supported him in making a "propaganda puff piece on these criminals" in the Weather Underground. McDonald lamented the government's decision to withdraw the subpoena under pressure from "a whole crew of Hollywood's radical chic colony," whose names he read into the *Congressional Record* as a "dishonor role."[98] When de Antonio heard the remarks, he responded with a viciously sarcastic letter to the representative in which he announced his intention—utterly imaginary—to stage a musical revue of the American right in which "J. Edgar Hoover will play a transvestite with a pink notebook" while members of the John Birch Society "copulate in the Capitol with members of the Daughters of the American Revolution."[99] Despite the fury of de Antonio's satire, McDonald's criticism was relatively isolated. In the wake of Watergate and the end of the war in Vietnam, the public seemed far more concerned about the potential abuse of government authority than the supposed misdeeds of documentary filmmakers.

In this regard the subpoena episode reflected a wider phenomenon of public dissatisfaction with the FBI. The bureau was on the defensive, as made evident when Attorney General Levi instituted reform measures in April 1976, though these would later be overturned by the Reagan administration.[100] Public pressure also led FBI director Clarence Kelley to announce the most extensive reorganization of the bureau since 1945, partially in response to the first criminal investigation in its long history.[101] In 1978 four prominent members of the FBI, including former FBI director L. Patrick Gray and former acting associate director W. Mark Felt, were indicted on charges stemming from the conduct of agents assigned to the WEATHERFUGS case. The charges against Gray were dropped, and Felt and another agent were found guilty in 1980 of authorizing raids without warrants, though they were pardoned as "loyal public servants" by President Reagan in 1981.[102] That the subpoena was on the other foot was an irony that de Antonio must have appreciated.

"The Film the FBI Didn't Want You to See"

Late in the summer after the withdrawal of the subpoena, the filmmakers were finally able to return to work on the film. Haskell Wexler moved on to other projects, leaving de

Antonio and Lampson to finish the film in New York City, only a few blocks from the Museum of Modern Art's retrospective of de Antonio's films.[103] Unfortunately, the celebratory spirit of that occasion did not carry into the editing room, where de Antonio was becoming increasingly frustrated. Structuring a film from the Underground footage seemed impossible because the Weatherpeople "didn't want to say very much" to the camera.[104] To strengthen the story he decided to incorporate footage from other documentaries, more than he had ever used before. He turned to some of the best radical films of the late sixties and early seventies, films such as Mike Gray and Howard Alk's *The Murder of Fred Hampton* (1971), Cinda Firestone's *Attica* (1971), Saul Landau and Irving Saraf's *Fidel* (1969), Chris Marker's *The Sixth Side of the Pentagon* (1969), and Stephen Lighthill's *Berkeley Streetfighting* (1970).[105] Combining these borrowed images with the footage from Wexler's camera, de Antonio and Lampson had an eighty-eight-minute finished film on November 7, 1975.[106]

All these activities—from the editing equipment to purchasing footage from other films—strained the film's pitifully tight budget of approximately $55,000. Being unable to reveal the nature of the film made it difficult to raise funds in advance, forcing de Antonio to break his rule against investing in his own projects. He spent more than $5,000, not quite half of what Wexler contributed, while the remainder of the budget came from a handful of rich individuals with political motivations, as was customary for de Antonio's films.[107] No one expected to make a fortune from the film, and de Antonio even hoped that profits could be given away to radical causes.[108] In fact, some profits were illicit because de Antonio had neglected such niceties as paying royalties for using some well-known songs on the soundtrack. Although folksinger Phil Ochs drunkenly granted permission for his song "The War Is Over," he died before he signed a release, and songs by Nina Simone and Bob Dylan were used without permission or payment.[109] Yet skimping on such legalities made it possible to create an ambitious film from meager resources.

Underground is without question an ambitious film. The

Mary Lampson and Emile de Antonio, October 6, 1975, New York City. Courtesy Wisconsin Center for Film and Theater Research.

filmmakers skillfully intertwine personal narratives of the five Weatherpeople with a visual history of anti-imperialism, which is broadly defined to include everything from the Flint sit-down strike of 1936 to the civil rights movement, from Fidel Castro's musings on revolution to the death of the Black Panther leader Fred Hampton. Much of the film celebrates the success of 1960s radicalism, especially in regard to Vietnam: military helicopters are pushed into the sea while Ochs sings "The War Is Over" on the soundtrack; antiwar veterans toss their medals onto the steps of the U.S. Capitol while a crowd cheers. In the most powerful and unprecedented scene Ho Chi Minh addresses the American people in English while he walks among his countrymen.[110]

Despite the merits of its impressionistic history, the promise of *Underground* is largely unrealized. Because the filmmakers were reluctant to challenge the Weatherpeople, it lacks the critical edge of de Antonio's muckraking, adversarial films.[111] Where a dialectic between various levels of the text existed in *Rush to Judgment* and *In the Year of the Pig*, *Underground* has only one didactic point of view: the silhouettes of the Weatherpeople present a systemic critique of U.S. imperialism, to which de Antonio and Lampson add complementary, and sometimes uninspired, illustrations. For example, when Bernardine Dohrn mutters the word *enemy*, de Antonio flashes a shot of Chase Manhattan Bank on screen without the irony and wit of his earlier films. As a consequence the film is curiously flat, lacking the narrative tension that gave force to the images of *In the Year of the Pig*, mystery to *Rush to Judgment*, and humor to *Millhouse*. Such shortcomings risk making *Underground* a "righteous, heavy political rap illustrated with a few pictures," as a radical film of the Newsreel collective was unhappily described.[112] Unfortunately, the invisibility of the cast of *Underground* exacerbates this problem.

Forced behind the gauze scrim, the humanity of the Weather Underground is lost in the fabric. "We're trying to reach through it," says Jeff Jones as he presses his hand against the opaque material, but what we see is tantalizingly abstract and inscrutable. Unable to see the faces of the Weatherpeople, a viewer might easily be put off by their rhetorical stiffness, their youthful self-importance as revolutionaries, or what one reviewer called their "bumbling" and "elementary" Marxist analysis.[113] Spliced with more evocative shots of Malcolm X and members of the American Indian Movement, whose faces are of course visible, the Weatherpeople are at a cinematic disadvantage that their words cannot overcome.

Because viewers are unable to see the "subject" of the film, their attention is likely to shift to the other figures on screen, the filmmakers who appear frequently. For this reason *Underground* is in part a film about filmmakers and their ultimate authority over their "subjects." As Wexler aims his lens into a mirror, he captures a telling image of a pyramid in which the filmmakers form the upper portion while the Weatherpeople sit on the floor below the filmmakers. Unshaven and weary in his rumpled Oxford shirt, de Antonio gazes coldly at the young didacts, as unimpressed by their rhetoric as Lampson seems enraptured. At the peak of the pyramid is Wexler, strongly evoking Dziga Vertov's *Man with the Movie Camera* (1929) with his one eye closed, the camera perched on his shoulder, wielding authority over what his machine records. To the credit of the film, the filmmakers openly discuss these issues of representation with the Weatherpeople, providing a refreshing sense of self-consciousness and honesty. This collaborative and reflexive aspect of *Underground* put it in the vanguard of nonfiction filmmaking in 1976.[114]

Underground ends as it begins: with a sentimental song about the world's coming together in harmony and a crude drawing of a rainbow symbolizing the Weather Underground. But if "there's a new world coming," as Nina Simone sings on the soundtrack, the film announces its arrival somewhat halfheartedly. It was intended to unify and inspire the radical Left in some small way, but *Underground* seems strangely elegiac, its celebratory tone

Mary Lampson interviewing a member of the Weather Underground in *Underground* (1975). Courtesy Wisconsin Center for Film and Theater Research.

undermined by an implicit but obvious question: if radicalism has been forced "underground," what is to be celebrated?[115] De Antonio seems to have given the matter little consideration, and even he acknowledged it was a confused film.[116]

This ambiguous and controversial film was a natural source of fascination for film critics. The filmmaker and critic Alan Rosenthal decided that it was not "a particularly good film . . . but it is a unique film," while Waugh made the opposite claim, that *Underground* was a major film but not unique.[117] One of the most knowledgeable writers on the subject of documentary film, Waugh linked *Underground* to a variety of little-known antecedents: Joris Ivens's *Borinage* (1933), an examination of a Belgian miners' strike, and *Indonesia Calling* (1946), both filmed under duress even greater than the hazards of filming *Underground*; Fernando Solanas's *The Hour of the Furnaces* (1966–1968); and the short film *Tupamaros* (1973), which was filmed clandestinely by the Swedish filmmaker Jan Lindquist with fugitive revolutionaries in Uruguay. None of these films would have been possible without the courage of the filmmakers, a quality that, as Waugh points out, makes *Underground* subversive in a way that few "underground" films of the 1960s had ever been. Nonetheless, Waugh lavishes more praise on the ordeal of the filmmaking process than the film itself.[118]

Waugh was not the only reviewer willing to overlook the film's problems in light of the circumstances under which it was produced. A highly positive review in the *New York Times* noted that despite "crippling difficulties," the shortcomings of the film—the rhetorical excesses, the visual monotony—were handled with "skill and integrity."[119] Other mainstream reviewers did not qualify their praise, which seems surprising in light of the revolutionary posturing of the Weatherpeople. *Underground* may be "one of the most important political documents of the 1970's," wrote the *Boston Globe*, while *Variety* commended the film's "committed investigative reporting." The *Los Angeles Times* applauded a "remarkable, deeply disturbing documentary," as did the *San Francisco Chronicle*, which called it "extraordinary, intriguing, bizarre, troubling and not unenlightening."[120] Small radical periodicals naturally supported the film as "a serious and purposeful account of the Vietnam war and its aftermath," a "major film," and a "film of ideas" though "not meant for entertainment," which was something on which every critic could agree.[121]

Despite these laudatory reviews, confusion about the distribution of the film hampered its release.[122] As three different distributors vied for the film, interest in it evaporated even among the few theaters that might book a radical film with faceless revolutionaries. Moreover, de Antonio's hopes that television, either PBS or CBS's *60 Minutes*, would air the film were short-lived.[123] *Underground* was too controversial even for film festivals: the Cannes Film Festival rejected the film because of a specious technicality, prompting de Antonio to suspect the hand of the censor at a time when the "French are having student strikes and this film calls for a Communist revolution."[124]

As a consequence *Underground* was a film without an audience. If it was "The Film the FBI Didn't Want You to See," as its advertisement proclaimed, the bureau could relax (just as the Nixon White House staff did when it realized the limited box office appeal of *Millhouse*).[125] Neglected ever since by the general public and film scholars alike, *Underground* failed because it did not reflect the drama of its own creation, the cardinal sin of a work of art. In his review of *Underground* the film critic Stanley Kauffmann summed up the situation aptly when he proclaimed "hats off" to the people who produced a documentary against such odds—but "hats on again" for the film.[126] However, the importance of *Underground* is in its production history, not its box office failure. Without slighting the contributions of Wexler and Lampson, de Antonio deserves recognition for the boldness of his idea to make a film with revolutionaries—not just about them, as he put it.[127] To have endured circumstances that would seem to be the product of a spy novelist's imagination, to have resisted the FBI, and to have rallied a significant portion of the media and entertainment establishment behind "the first, feature-length, clandestine film ever made in this country" was no small feat.[128] Few other filmmakers would have been willing to make the film; few others could have navigated the obstacles it presented.

The Weatherpeople, for their part, remembered the film as an "amazing project," a new form of collective filmmaking, even though their collective was falling apart.[129] *Underground* was said to have exacerbated the problems within the organization, to have been part of a "weather inversion," a term Dohrn applied to an elaborate plot to raise money and improve the public image of the Weather Underground for those who wished to leave the organization. In a 1994 interview Dohrn told me she never made this claim, which had appeared in an obscure publication.[130] Certainly, the Weatherpeople were divided on the issue of whether to surface, and "the film fell right in the middle of this," as Jeff Jones wrote.[131] For personal and political reasons that remain unclear, Dohrn was even forced to denounce the film as "a crime against the national liberation movements, women and the anti-imperialist left" by a faction of the Underground that soon expelled her and other founding Weatherpeople.[132]

De Antonio was furious: how could he have made a sexist, racist film when three of the five Weatherpeople in the film were female and much of the film trumpeted the legacy of the civil rights movement? He scoffed at the notion that his film was part of a Weather Underground strategy for "inversion." Bill Ayers agreed. The film had not split the Weather Underground—the end of the war in Vietnam in 1975 was what left the organization without its primary raison d'être.[133] For a variety of personal and doctrinal reasons, most of its remaining members would surface within the next several years, in some cases to face criminal charges: for example, Cathy Wilkerson was sentenced to three years for possession of dynamite at the time of the townhouse explosion.[134] In the mid-eighties, the most reticent figure of *Underground* was thrust to the foreground when Kathy Boudin was arrested for her role in the widely publicized Brink's robbery murders in Nyack, New York, on October 20, 1981.[135] From her small celebrity in *Underground* she moved into an intense media spotlight where journalists could fulfill mainstream America's dark fantasies about young radicals and turn the events at Nyack into a morality tale about the tragic legacy of the 1960s. While one could argue just as easily that her actions were emblematic of nothing more than her own poor judgment, the timing of her arrest worked against this interpretation: the conservative impulse in U.S. politics that put Ronald Reagan in the White House in 1981 included an eagerness to repudiate "the sixties" in all its forms, even at its most unrepresentative. Attuned to the conservative tide in U.S. politics, journalists cast the tragic events at Nyack as symptomatic of the failure of the entire Weather Underground, if not the Left in general.[136]

The real story of where the former Weatherpeople ended up was much less sensational and salable than the Brink's robbery, and very few reporters tried to show how the "revolution" had continued in a less dramatic fashion—Ayers and Dohrn returned to educational and legal reform, respectively, while Jones became a writer. *Underground*, an unseen film, was the solitary exception to this monolithic portrayal of a complex phenomenon.

Yet even de Antonio, who continued to be friends with the Weatherpeople, privately expressed regrets about his involvement with them.[137] "I can't make all of th[i]s public now but someone is going to have to know the truth," he wrote in 1978, venting his anger at the younger generation of radicals, their "mad elitism," their lack of a "real understanding of america [*sic*]," their lack of a "theoretical base."[138] This hostility toward the young radicals reflects a shift in his political attitudes, one that echoed Herbert Marcuse's earlier criticism of the New Left and its "ritualized language, its aesthetic puritanism, its propensity to engage in desperate acts of terrorism or 'revolutionary suicide,' and above all, its masochistic, self-destructive anti-intellectualism."[139] Though this realization came to de Antonio several years after Marcuse's statement, he expressed it in no uncertain terms: "I dropped weather politics after making the film," he wrote, sounding like a middle-aged man who had foolishly dabbled in the fashions of the young.[140]

His fascination with revolutionary violence dimmed as he realized the price of the Weather Underground's methods.[141] Perhaps their bombings were not such clever "masterstrokes of political theater" after all, as he had written in his first letter to the Underground.[142] A bombing may relieve political frustration in some symbolic fashion, but it "harms the practitioners as much as it harms those who stand in their way," as the long-time activist David Dellinger wrote about the Weather Underground. De Antonio would gradually perceive the wisdom of Dellinger's position.[143] Consequently, his next film explored a group with goals and motivations similar to the Weather Underground's but with far different methods: the nonviolent Catholic Left. *In the King of Prussia* (1983) is also about bombs—but its protagonists, peace activists known as the Plowshares Eight, were dismantling rather than planting them.[144] De Antonio even considered making a fiction film about the thin line between political violence and pathological behavior during the early eighties, though the project never moved beyond the idea stage.[145]

Flirting with revolutionary violence comprised a brief chapter in de Antonio's political development, one that had pushed him beyond the cant of the Weather Underground to a more nuanced understanding of political resistance that reflected Jean-Paul Sartre's statement: "Revolution is not a single moment in which one power overthrows another. It is a long moment in which power is dismantled. Nothing can guarantee success for us, nor can anything rationally convince us that failure is inevitable. But the alternatives really are socialism or barbarism."[146]

Buried without explanation in one of de Antonio's journals from the late seventies, this quote embodies a fundamental aspect of the filmmaker's vision of America. It implicitly acknowledges and accepts the Gramscian notion of a slow cultural "war of position" against the forces of hegemony, an intellectual project that aptly describes de Antonio's film career.[147] He had given the Weatherpeople every opportunity to convert him to their way of thinking. Yet once convinced that their methods led into an intellectual dead end, he retreated to his own "party of style and wit and hate" to regroup for his next cinematic offensive on American complacency, one that would bring him ever closer to home in his search for something worth fighting for.[148] But even in his caustic and anarchistic party of one, the essential optimism of his vision of the United States remained intact.

8

◄○►

Films of the Eighties

Docudrama in King of Prussia

King of Prussia is the unusual name of a small city in eastern Pennsylvania. With its evocations of eighteenth-century military conquest, the name might seem ill suited to the calm and prosperous town, if not for the presence of a nondescript building belonging to the General Electric Corp. Here, without the knowledge of most local residents, General Electric manufactured a protective nose cone for the Mark 12A nuclear warhead.

This quiet state of affairs ended on an early September morning in 1980, when eight men and women conducted a dramatic act of civil disobedience to focus public attention on the destructive capabilities of the weapons. Calling themselves "the Plowshares Eight" after the Old Testament's injunction to beat swords into plowshares, these activists from the vanguard of the Catholic peace movement drove into the almost empty parking lot of the GE plant as the sun was rising and the shift was changing. Pushing aside the lone guard at the door of the building identified only as the "Re-Entry Systems Division Operational Manufacturing Center," the activists quickly followed a plan they had been practicing for several months. They ran to the room where the nose cones for the Mark 12A were tested, pulled hammers from beneath their coats, and struck the protective shell of the unarmed missiles. They poured vials of their own blood across secret documents and ripped blueprints to shreds; then the eight chanted prayers and waited for the police to arrest them.

They had envisioned their trial as a public forum in which to discuss the threat of nuclear annihilation, but the media showed little interest in the case. Whatever incentive the media might have had to cover the trial was dealt a fatal blow when Judge Samuel Salus disallowed a "justification defense," a legal strategy that would have cast the defendants as victims acting in self-defense against the lethal threat posed by the Mark 12A. Unwilling to listen to the expert testimony of Nobel Prize winners and other eminent scientists that would have supported the action of the defendants and attracted the media, the judge pointedly told the activists, "Nuclear warfare is not on trial here—you are!" By these standards the case was open and shut for the prosecution, for the defendants never denied having entered the GE plant to sabotage the nose cones. As a consequence they received a guilty verdict with stiff sentences of five to ten years for burglary, criminal mischief, and conspiracy.[1]

De Antonio might not have heard of the case if it had not included two well-known members of the Catholic Left. Daniel and Philip Berrigan, two brothers who had been priests for most of their adult life, had been nominated six times for the Nobel Peace Prize. They were celebrated in some circles and reviled in others for mixing political activism with the customary duties of the priesthood. Their creative opposition to the Vietnam War, which included the symbolic burning of draft files with homemade napalm, landed both in prison for several years. De Antonio had raised money for their legal defense in 1970 and even asked Daniel Berrigan to appear in his film about Vietnam, *In the Year of the Pig*. De Antonio was particularly attracted to Daniel Berrigan because he expressed views that paralleled his own. "American power is locked into its method, its sleep-walking, its nightmare, its rampant and irreversible character. No change in the personnel of power seems to bring about any serious change in the functioning and direction of power, in the misuse and grinding under of human beings," wrote Berrigan, echoing the views de

Antonio put forth in *In the Year of the Pig*. The words could just as easily have come from de Antonio, even if his cinematic jeremiads emerged from a darker and more puritanical belief that "everyone is infinitely corruptible," as he once said.[2]

The similarity of their outlook is also reflected in Daniel Berrigan's verse, which had been nominated three times for the National Book Award. In 1972 Berrigan had written this verse under the title, "America Is Hard to Find," a deliberate allusion to "America Is Hard to See":

> Hard to find; lost not found rare as radium rent free
> uncontrollable uncanny a chorus
> Jesus Buddha Moses founding fathers horizons
> hope (in hiding)
> Hard to find; America[3]

Disillusioned by the violence of the Weather Underground, de Antonio found hope—and a reclamation of the purity of America's mythic past—in the civil disobedience and personal courage of the Berrigan brothers. Putting aside his lifelong bias against the church, as well as his frustrated plans with former CIA employee Philip Agee for a movie based on his best-selling exposé of "the company," *CIA Diary*, de Antonio decided to make a film about the trial of the Plowshares Eight.[4]

As always, the first step was raising money, though never before had he faced such reluctance to participate in a film. The problem was not the subject of the film as much as the stars. Between their opposition to abortion and their support for the Palestine Liberation Organization, the Berrigans alienated the two groups that had contributed the bulk of de Antonio's funding in the past: rich progressive women and rich liberal Jews.[5] According to the filmmaker, these two groups had contributed most of the $1.2 million he had spent in producing documentaries since 1961. He had few other sources of funding, in part because he refused to work in the typical channels of independent filmmaking. Fearing the loss of creative control he believed would result from accepting foundation money, he shied away from the few granting agencies that assisted independent filmmakers. Further limiting his options was his hostility toward the Public Broadcasting System, which he derided as the "Petroleum Broadcasting System" for the corporate underwriting that he held responsible for PBS's unwillingness to televise challenging political films such as his own.[6] In desperation de Antonio even turned to friends in the arts community for assistance, as he had for earlier films, and attempted to wangle $15,000 out of Robert Rauschenberg in exchange for some blueprint drawings that the artist had given him two decades earlier.[7] However, he was not able to raise much capital in this manner, and in the end he was forced once again to violate his own cardinal rule of filmmaking—"never invest your own money"—and spent more than $200,000, nearly going broke in the process.

This budget was four times larger than that of *Underground*, which he had shot on film just six years earlier, yet for the first time in his career he decided to cut costs by switching the format of the project from film to less expensive videotape. Though his motivation for this switch to video was overwhelmingly financial, he concocted some rationalizations for the choice of format; he pointed, for example, to videotape's suitability to the rough-looking aesthetic that had marked his films since *Point of Order*.[8] Documentary filmmakers had seen the utility of the inexpensive and easily reproduced format for more than a decade, as demonstrated by George Stoney's Alternative Media Center in New York City, cooperatives such as Video Free America, or individuals such as Alan and Susan Raymond, who took the techniques of direct cinema to video for *Police Tapes* (1976). Yet few feature directors had the audacity—or perhaps the desperation—to shoot in video, a format used primarily for television, and then transfer the lower-quality video image to 35mm film for the wide screen. One exception was the celebrated Italian director Michelangelo Antonioni's adaptation of Jean Cocteau's *The Mystery of Oberwald*, a little-known work that de Antonio encountered during its appearance at the New York Film Festival in 1981. With new works such as Antonioni's expanding his sense of what was possible with videotape, de Antonio decide to try the less expensive format.

At first, de Antonio intended to make a short and simple film from the trial itself. "It'll take a month to edit and it'll be like some fucking TV thing," he predicted with some impatience.[9] He undertook the costly legal maneuver of petitioning the Pennsylvania Supreme Court for permission to film the actual trial and lost, for what he suspected were political reasons. He learned he could film a murder trial but nothing as controversial and political as the trial of the Plowshares Eight.

"Fuck the trial, I don't need it," he proclaimed. "I'll make a script out of the trial." By quoting, condensing, and omitting a great deal, he reduced the eleven-hundred-page transcript of the trial to a sixty-page screenplay. Setting up this sort of historical reconstruction was de Antonio's first and last foray into the realm of docudrama, a genre that had long been used for historical subjects. Usually understood as a semifictional interpretation of real events, docudrama creates "stories based on fact but performed by actors and scripted from both documentaries and conjecture," to use a succinct definition from Bill Nichols.[10]

Though de Antonio never publicly acknowledged it, he was joining a tradition of reconstructing events for the camera that was as old as cinema itself. For instance, in 1899 the film pioneer Georges Méliès had used reconstruction in short films based on newspaper reports of the Dreyfus Affair.[11] Robert Flaherty, the most influential American documentarian of the early twentieth century, also used the technique—generally without the audience's awareness—in *Nanook of the North* (1922) and *Man of Aran* (1934), two of his most famous works. Even newsreel series such as *The March of Time* made extensive use of reenactments. So prevalent was the technique in early documentaries that the film scholar Dan Streible has claimed that "actuality footage" was the *exception* in nonfiction film—at least until technological improvements soon after World War II increased the mobility of camera and sound equipment.[12]

These sorts of technological limitations were not a factor in de Antonio's decision to explore docudrama, but he had one motivation that his cinematic predecessors would have recognized immediately: the problem of access. Long before the Pennsylvania Supreme Court turned down de Antonio's request to film the trial of the Plowshares Eight, political filmmakers had turned to docudrama when they were shut out of courtrooms and factory floors as events unfolded.[13] As early as 1926, pro-labor films such as *The Passaic Textile Strike* had made use of reenactment, and leftist American filmmakers of the thirties did the same— Leo Hurwitz and Paul Strand for *People of the Cumberland* (1938) and *Native Land* (1942), for example.[14] Docudrama had a political cast in England as well during this era. For example, the influential filmmaker John Grierson restaged numerous aspects of his documentaries in order to emphasize an underlying social message.[15]

De Antonio was stepping into a docudrama tradition longer and more noble than he realized, yet he expressed no interest in the work of his predecessors or in learning from Grierson, Hurwitz, Strand, and other political filmmakers who had created films of lasting beauty and importance. What may have blinded him to this admirable side of docudrama was its more recent connotation, one that it had acquired from American television. In the 1970s docudrama had become a big business for U.S. network television. Programming executives seized upon the concept as a means of attracting huge audiences to subjects that de Antonio had already explored in his inimitable and unmarketable fashion— *Tail Gunner Joe* (compare with *Point of Order*), *The Trial of Lee Harvey Oswald* (*Rush to Judgment*), *The Ordeal of Patty Hearst* (*Underground*), *Blind Ambition* (*Millhouse*)—as well as others that he had not, such as *King, Clarence Darrow*, and *The Amazing Howard Hughes*. Historical accuracy was not always the hallmark of these popular projects, which tended to sensationalize their subjects for the sake of ratings. Of course de Antonio despised these works as much as anything else on television and had no interest in a slipshod "reenactment" that was only loosely based on actual events. What de Antonio had in mind was closer to the earnest historical reenactments of an earlier era, not the slick dramatization of commercial television.

In keeping with the older tradition of docudrama, de Antonio wanted the participants in the trial to play themselves. Not surprisingly, the prosecution declined this offer as quickly as the Plowshares Eight accepted. As a consequence de Antonio was forced to assign some parts to professional actors willing to work without pay, such as Martin Sheen, the star of films such as *Badlands* (Terrence Malick, 1973) and *Apocalypse Now* (Francis Ford Coppola, 1979). De Antonio had met the celebrated actor when Sheen had signed the petition against the FBI subpoena of *Underground* in 1975. When de Antonio wrote to him in 1982 and solicited his involvement in the Plowshares project, Sheen responded instantly and generously, giving $5,000 to the project and donating a week of his acting skills to play the most difficult role—Judge Samuel Salus.

Several dozen cast and crew members came together on a Thursday in July 1982 with a daunting schedule before them—three days to tape everything—because the defendants wanted one free day before they had to appear in court on Monday for sentencing and incarceration. The nonactors, who comprised the majority of the cast, were not expected to memorize their lines flawlessly, only to show up on time and speak in the proper sequence. The bulk of their lines came during a reenactment of the trial, which was shot entirely in an unusual set constructed for the occasion. In a theater space adjacent to St. Peter's Episcopal Church on West 20th Street in Manhattan, de Antonio constructed a set that evoked an experimental play more than a Pennsylvania courtroom.[16]

The most pressing of the handicaps confronting de Antonio was time. Just one brief rehearsal was possible, and it would be videotaped if it went well, though this was unlikely because he had no real experience in directing this sort of project. Somehow the shoot was finished on time, and as most of his actors were taken to jail, de Antonio could at least slow down as he edited the videotape. He worked almost alone, hiring only an editor, Mark Pines, to make the cuts he wanted. In several places de Antonio added music donated by a noted popular musician, Jackson Browne. "Crow on the Cradle," a mild ballad performed by Browne and Graham Nash, represented only the second time de Antonio had used contemporary music in his work (*Underground* was the other). Previously, he had associated this sort of soundtrack with popular documentaries of the sixties such as Charlotte Zwerin and David and Albert Maysles's *Gimme Shelter* (1970) or D. A. Pennebaker's portrait of Bob Dylan, *Don't Look Back* (1966), a category of films that de Antonio denigrated without reservation.[17]

Editing went slowly. De Antonio took more than seven months to achieve what he wanted from the unfamiliar electronic editing equipment. An interviewer asked him during the editing whether he knew how he was going to structure the film. "Nope," he replied. "I've never done this before. But isn't that part of the fun? You take those chances, and you can come out looking like a fool or you can come out feeling that you've done something good." Finally, at the end of the seventh month, he was ready to transfer the one-inch videotape to film at a cost of $25,000 in Los Angeles.[18] From start to finish the project was unorthodox and exceeded the limitations of his scant film training, low budget, and tight shooting schedule. These shortcomings are readily apparent in the end result, a film of ninety-three minutes that seems much, much longer.

After an auspicious beginning in which a graffiti artist scales a wall to spray-paint the title, *In the King of Prussia*, on the wall of a building, the narrative focuses primarily on the reenactment of the trial. The courtroom action plods along with little momentum, though the situation improves when de Antonio cuts to external scenes, which he shot in the observational style of direct cinema. For example, we see the demonstrations outside the courtroom and the brief expert testimony that Judge Salus refused to hear from various luminaries: George Wald, the Harvard biologist and Nobel Prize winner; Richard Falk, a professor of international law at Princeton; Robert Jay Lifton, a psychiatrist and author of a book on the survivors of Hiroshima; Daniel Ellsberg, who had released the Pentagon Papers a decade earlier; former U.S. attorney general Ramsey Clark; and David Dellinger, a long-time peace activist and member of the Chicago Seven. Salus had agreed to give de Antonio an interview, but the judge changed his mind at the last minute, leaving only Martin Sheen's portrayal of him in the film.[19] Unfortunately, Sheen exhibits more passion than believability in the role of the judge, who comes across as sweaty, irrational, and dull witted as he shuffles and straightens papers on his desk like a parody of a news anchor. The broad strokes with which the opposition is painted continue across the prosecution. The caricature of the prosecuting attorney as a rabid dog adds little to what might have been a complex portrayal of a legal bureaucrat who relishes his work. The result is less dramatic than clumsily propagandistic, a shortcoming of political filmmaking that de Antonio generally transcended.

In addition to the weaknesses exhibited by the cast, *In the King of Prussia* suffers from the limitations of the video format. Michelangelo Antonioni's experiment with video offers a useful point of comparison, for he explored the visual nuances of video in *The Mystery of Oberwald* in a manner far beyond *In the King of Prussia*. Antonioni, for example, attempted to manipulate the color of images in a subtle effect that would have been far more difficult with film. Unfortunately, neither de Antonio nor his cinematographer, Judy Irola, had worked with video before, and their lack of experience resulted not only in a poor quality and composition of image but also a muddied soundtrack.[20] The poor quality of production not only makes *In the King of Prussia* difficult to watch but provides both commercial and public television networks in the United States with a convenient excuse for not broadcasting a dissenting point of view.

In this regard the film demonstrates the central problem of the political artist, one that de Antonio had generally negotiated with success: that of keeping politics and art in balance, neither descending into formalist experimentation that would obscure the political meaning of the film nor allowing aesthetic considerations to be completely subsumed in a humorless sort of cinematic pamphleteering. For example, the greatness of *In the Year of the Pig* lies in the push and pull of competing points of view, as de Antonio interweaves complex montages with straightforward polemics, moral righteousness, and black humor.

But de Antonio could find nothing humorous, even darkly so, in the subject of nuclear annihilation. As a consequence *In the King of Prussia* seems monolithic, an unrelenting jeremiad about impending doom that rarely achieves the cinematic power that coursed through de Antonio's earlier work. The best scenes occur when de Antonio is not directing every move, such as when the defendants are allowed to speak spontaneously rather than forced to struggle with their lines or their rudimentary blocking. Exhibiting the only intimation of dramatic flair among the nonactors, Daniel Berrigan eloquently relates his experience in a cancer ward in a New York hospital to the grim effects of radiation from a nuclear blast. Equally effective are the scenes that capture unscripted events outside the courtroom, such as when the local police are shown squabbling with the defendants who had returned to the site of their original protest. Another effective scene appears toward the end of the film: the camera follows an actual juror from the trial to his job at a local garage, where he expresses his sympathy for the defendants and acknowledges that "most people didn't know until this trial came out that they were building nuclear weapons up there" (at the GE plant). The film ends on a strong note, with footage from the steps of the courthouse of the various experts for the defense, though their voices are barely audible in the muffled recording. After hearing the verdict, Ramsey Clark stands outside the courthouse looking disappointed and describes the sentencing of the defendants as "an incredible miscarriage of justice."

The clear and noble message of the film reflects a profound respect for human life and a fear of nuclear proliferation. "I want people to think that it is absolutely insane to continue the nuclear arms race," de Antonio said, though he fails to remember his own assertion that a good film "reveals without preaching, without tears, without 'balance.' "[21] Though no one would accuse

In the King of Prussia of balance, the preaching and tears ensure a maudlin quality that de Antonio had never exhibited before *Underground*. Much to the surprise of anyone who watches de Antonio's films in chronological order, *In the King of Prussia* substitutes the unbearably earnest singing of "Kumbaya" for the cold dialectical analysis of his earlier films, which set charge and countercharge in opposition for the audience to interpret. Unfortunately, *In the King of Prussia* preaches with such fervor that the unenlightened are likely to feel as excluded and bewildered as an atheist at a fundamentalist revival, a predicament to which de Antonio might have related. Unlike other narratives that had been marshalled in support of peace movements—classic antiwar books such as Erich Remarque's *All Quiet on the Western Front* (1929), or the scenarios of nuclear holocaust in books and films such as Nevil Shute's *On the Beach* (1955) or Jonathan Schell's *The Fate of the Earth* (1982)—*In the King of Prussia* does not do justice to the solemnity and necessity of its message.[22]

Perhaps the greatest influence of the film was on the filmmaker. "Wow, a juicy conversion yarn," he exclaimed sarcastically about working with the Berrigans: "Middle-aged life-long non-believer finds Christ while filming priests and nuns. An edifying take. Christ!"[23] The sarcasm of the comment may betray some self-consciousness about his earnest, if temporary, conversion to the Gandhian spiritual resistance of the Berrigans. He admired the Plowshares Eight as heroic dissenters whose actions were unambiguously worthy—this time de Antonio did not suffer the moral qualms he expressed about the violence of the Weather Underground. "Up until recently," he told the *Philadelphia Inquirer*, "I have believed that social change is brought about through violence . . . at the end of a gun," an echo of the Maoist sentiment expressed by the Weather Underground. As he watched the Berrigans, whose willingness to translate their beliefs into action had remained constant for several decades, de Antonio began to soften his position. "They do exactly what they say. I never knew a Marxist who would do that over a long period of time."[24] At times he preferred Philip Berrigan's self-effacing attitude to what de Antonio considered to be the egotism of Daniel Berrigan, but the filmmaker's excitement over finding true believers in the church of dissent was profound, enough to prompt some autobiographical self-mockery.[25]

Sheen echoed this sentiment when he described his days with the Berrigans as "as close to bravery as I'm ever likely to come" and even wrote to Judge Salus to plead for a merciful sentencing of the defendants.[26] Working with de Antonio was also a source of pride for the actor, who told *American Film*: "Frankly, I've worked with three directors whom I consider important: Terrence Malick, Francis Coppola, and Emile de Antonio."[27] Sheen maintained a warm friendship with the director for the next several years and even offered his services for future projects, such as the possibility of playing de Antonio in his long-planned autobiographic film, a role in which the actor Rip Torn also expressed interest. For the time being, however, de Antonio was primarily concerned with getting *In the King of Prussia* to as wide an audience as possible.[28]

This was accomplished with some success in Europe where the film won prizes at festivals in Berlin, Belgium, and Locarno, appeared on television in much of Europe, and generated favorable comments such as this one from the Manchester (U.K.) *Guardian*: "one of the most important American films in recent years." In the two nuclear superpowers of the cold war, however, the response was far more measured. The Soviet Union showed no interest in allowing the film about civil disobedience to be shown within its borders, whereas American television was able to ignore the film on the grounds that it was too one-sided and too crudely produced to broadcast. Like de Antonio's previous films, *In the King of Prussia* did make its way into art houses in the United States, where it garnered mixed reviews in mainstream and alternative periodicals. Writing in the *New York Times*, Janet Maslin congratulated de Antonio for eschewing Hollywood techniques but complained that his film, whose "plainness border[s] on the bland," did not offer a strong alternative. Other reviewers for major newspapers and magazines commended his effort, although they expressed impatience with the long speeches that Daniel Berrigan and others make in the film. De Antonio justified these by claiming that "if people are too bored to look at Berrigan for ten minutes, let them get out of the theater. I'm not going to change it, speed it up, make a cut, just to make it palatable for them."[29] The defiance in this comment may hint at a defensiveness about the film in general, which, like *Underground*, did not meet the standard set by the work of his most fertile period of creativity, the years marked by *In the Year of the Pig* (1969), *Millhouse: A White Comedy* (1971), and *Painters Painting* (1972). Though he never said as much and may have believed otherwise, *In the King of Prussia* represented his second disappointment in a row, surely an ominous sign for a filmmaker in his mid sixties.

As for the Plowshares Eight, they achieved a short-lived success when they successfully appealed the decision of Judge Salus in 1984. However, after a protracted legal battle the Pennsylvania judiciary reversed this ruling, and Salus was allowed to resentence the defendants in April 1990. Nonetheless, most defendants ended up serving less time than their original sentences had stipulated. A more lasting victory for the goals of the group occurred in the court of public opinion. The publicity surrounding the de Antonio film seemed to awaken public interest, which had slumbered through the trial, for the Plowshares Eight inspired more than one hundred peace activists to commit thirty-three acts of civil disobedience in the name of the "Plowshares movement," and "directly influenced thousands of arrests at [nuclear] facilities" over the next decade.[30] *In the King of Prussia* was directly responsible for at least one protest after the video opened in Minneapolis on November 3, 1982—three hundred activists held a protest at the gates of a local plant that was producing military hardware. That his hastily shot, underfinanced, awkward-looking film might have played a small role in fostering such actions would undoubtedly have pleased de Antonio, whose politics remained clearly to the left even as his spiritual conversion waned. By 1985 he was writing to friends and explaining that at the age of sixty-five, "I am not religious, I don't believe in an after life, etc."[31] Evidently, the

Gandhian spirit of the Catholic Left had not taken root very deeply, so easily was it displaced by his old animosities. More interested in settling old scores than seeking or granting absolution, he moved toward his final project, a cinematic memoir of a tumultuous life of dissent.

Mr. Hoover and I: Documentary as Autobiography

"No twentieth-century man has meant more to his country than Hoover," said Ronald Reagan, then governor of California, about the FBI director upon Hoover's death in 1972. "A loss to the nation and cocksuckers everywhere," de Antonio sneered a few years later. "I can't get over Hoover—ever."[32] His bitterness seemed to increase with age, though he consoled himself with an old Sicilian proverb: revenge is a dish best eaten cold.[33]

This deep animosity was based on more than the obvious ideological differences between a bureaucrat with little respect for civil liberties and a radical artist with little respect for anything else. De Antonio had personal reasons for hating the FBI, which he believed—often with good reason—had harassed him throughout his career. During the years just after Hoover's death de Antonio was battling the FBI through the Freedom of Information Act (FOIA) for the files the bureau had kept on him since he was a teenager at Harvard, where he had attracted its attention by joining left-leaning groups such as the Young Communist League, the John Reed Society, and the American Student Union. The pages of his files began to trickle in after he began litigation in 1975 with the assistance of Charles Nesson, the Harvard Law professor who had helped fend off the attempted prior restraint of *Underground* and who now guided him through the various layers of bureaucratic obfuscation. Testing the limitations of the FOIA, de Antonio learned about the "field office gambit," which forced someone requesting files through the FOIA to follow a paper trail through the filing systems of dozens of FBI field offices. Though what he received was substantial, the ten thousand pages were rife with deletions and black markings over many passages, sometimes entire pages, which led him to conclude that the FOIA was a publicity ploy in which "there is no freedom and no information."[34]

What he received, however, was sufficient to raise both his ire and his curiosity. One page from his file reported his youthful answer when asked what he wanted to be when he grew up—"an eggplant," he had joked to a companion over lunch, unaware that he would read the line fifty years later in a more somber context. He learned that before his twentieth birthday he had been slated for "custodial detention" as part of a program Hoover had hatched to gain permission for the FBI to incarcerate individuals whose "liberty in this country in time of war or national emergency would constitute a menace to the public peace and safety of the United States Government," as the bureau director put it.[35] Reading the files made de Antonio see himself from the strange perspective of the U.S. government, whose memoranda seemed to cast him as a prospective agent for the Soviet Union with a willingness to do "things even Lenin would have been afraid to do," as de Antonio said in astonishment. He was barely able to recognize himself in this biographical fun-house mirror because he knew his potential for espionage was limited by his personal eccentricities. "I talk too much, I drink too much, I've been married six times," he said with a laugh in his last film; "I'm not the right kind of person to be a spy."[36]

If the de Antonio of the FBI files had little to do with the actual man, he wondered whether he could make a film that would underscore the inaccuracy and ludicrousness of the government's understanding of his life—*A Middle-Aged Radical as Seen Through the Eyes of his Government* was how he tentatively entitled the project. He envisioned drawing on the material in the files to fashion dialogue and casting Martin Sheen, Rip Torn, or one of the few other actors he respected to enact scenes from his life. In the manner of a one-man play the film would be shot in a skylighted sound stage with "no props, no gimmicks . . . wandering, discursive, mad, true, my enemies done in, my loves, my work, nothing cut out."[37] At least as early as 1978 he began planning this project, which would evolve into many forms during the next ten years. "I find I'm lucky to have lived as long as I have since I don't make films quickly and I began doing them late," he said, a comment with particular relevance to this final project.[38] Finally, in 1986 the BBC's Channel Four agreed to finance a project that bore little resemblance to *A Portrait of a Middle-Aged Radical* as it was originally conceived. The BBC wanted de Antonio's life and work to be the subject of a conventional documentary under the direction of Ron Mann, a young documentarian whose film about writers such as Charles Bukowski, *Poetry in Motion* (1982), had been dedicated to de Antonio for the advice he had provided.

The BBC project would be based primarily on interviews with those who knew de Antonio and his work, though he never expected unqualified praise for his life—"I'm a good guy and a bad guy . . . my politics have remained good for much of [a] long life and I have also been a shit to many different people."[39] To arrange these interviews de Antonio wrote letters to childhood friends from Scranton and to acquaintances in Italy, asking them to reminisce on camera and hoping to film the gravestones and old houses of his ancestors. To discuss his work he wanted to converse on screen with Bill Nichols, his favorite film theorist, and with his friend from the Swedish Film Institute, Anna-Lena Wibom, "who showed me where I belonged [in film history], who showed me Esther Shub [*sic*], who gave me my first foreign retrospective." Whether for reasons of time or funding is unclear, but the project was never realized in this ambitious form.[40] Instead de Antonio turned the project into something more economical, another exercise in radical scavenging in which he found himself making a movie out of whatever he could find, whatever he could not stop thinking about.

J. Edgar Hoover was one such obsession, for the more de Antonio thought about him, the more he wanted to desecrate the memory of the dead bureaucrat. Focusing on Hoover also made sense in light of de Antonio's previous inquiries into the nature of cold warriors. In this regard the film that would be entitled *Mr. Hoover and I* would form the last part of a trilogy on the hypocrisy and demagoguery of U.S. politics; the first part of this accidental trilogy examined Joseph McCarthy in *Point of Order*, while the second scrutinized Richard Nixon in *Millhouse*. The new film would also connect with *Rush to Judgment*, de Antonio's examination of the origins of the police state bureaucracy for which he held Hoover responsible.

Using film to dissect the Hoover legend also seemed appropriate because the medium had made Hoover's reputation in the first place, as a nation starved for heroes during the depression swallowed Hollywood's depiction of Hoover as "Public Hero Number One" in a series of movies that glamorized the mythical "G-man."[41] Taking Hoover to task comprises half of *Mr. Hoover and I* and includes some harsh commentary from de Antonio. He attacks Hoover's alleged love affair with his assistant Clyde Tolson, though de Antonio cared less about the supposed homosexuality than the hypocrisy that kept it secret. He excoriates Hoover's middlebrow tastes, comparing them with the cosmopolitan style that de Antonio attributes to figures from the American past: "Can one imagine Tom Jefferson or Tom Paine, George Washington or Abraham Lincoln dining and conversing on art and liberty with John Edgar Hoover and Clyde Tolson?" he asks in amazement.

However, this assault on Hoover has less force than it might have had, coming as it does at a time when Hoover's legacy had been battered in the wake of Watergate and other embarrassments to the Washington establishment. Moreover, de Antonio's dissection was less precise than it had been in earlier works such as *In the Year of the Pig*, for the claims he made about Hoover were often little more than historical gossip, more speculative and polemical than scholarly—something closer to Philip Roth's vision of Nixon in hell in his comic novel, *Our Gang*.[42] In alluding to Hoover's alleged homosexuality, de Antonio sinks to the mudslinging level of McCarthyism and the film does not benefit. Given the number of gay friends in the New York art world to whom he owed a great deal, de Antonio should not have pressed this point with such moralistic delight, as if he had caught the top cop with his pants down and Clyde Tolson somewhere nearby. Allegations of such hypocrisy may have appealed to a nation made cynical by

Watergate, but historians such as Richard Gid Powers have been far more reluctant to categorize Hoover's sexual leanings than best-selling biographers and television documentarians with audiences to entice. In 1993 PBS's *Frontline* series of documentaries included *The Secret File on J. Edgar Hoover*, which attempted to provide evidence for the same prurient charges that de Antonio made in *Mr. Hoover and I* in 1989. However, a reviewer for the *Journal of American History* described the evidence as consisting "exclusively of unsupported allegations" and including astounding tales of a cross-dressing Hoover clutching a bible in a most unlikely fashion while having sex with men too young to join the FBI. Both this film and de Antonio's would have been well served to step around such homophobic territory and to focus on the real and documentable abuses that can be traced to Hoover, such as his sabotage of the civil rights movement, which far exceeds the significance of whatever sexual practices he might have enjoyed.[43]

Fortunately, *Mr. Hoover and I*, as de Antonio would entitle the film, was less about Hoover than about the "I," and whatever merit it has comes from its autobiographical aspect, not its historical insight into the life of J. Edgar Hoover. De Antonio had been rehearsing his autobiographical musings for at least a decade, beginning in the mid-1970s in a journal of observations and recollections. If not quite an autobiography, his journal was a first step toward such a work, for its focus was inward—on his personal and professional history—with an awareness of the limitations of self-analysis: "Truth is all in these pages and there is so much to hide, to slant, to prepare a past which will deal with itself as the present, the endless falsification in the name of truth." Even as he scoffed at the vanity that made "every man his own tawdry Rousseau," as he put it, he continued to add volume after volume to the project, which became a rich source of information about his life and work.[44] These journals were also good practice for the writing of an autobiography, but the métier in which he best expressed himself was always cinema.

"To the best of my knowledge, no one has ever made a feature length autobiographical film before," de Antonio claimed, demonstrating his selective knowledge of film history.[45] If one excludes

the allusive self-referentiality of films such as Federico Fellini's
8 1/2 (1963) or Robert Flaherty's *Louisiana Story* (1948), few
well-known examples of film as autobiography come to mind.[46]
But avant-garde filmmakers—Jonas Mekas, Hollis Frampton,
Jerome Hill, Stan Brakhage, and James Broughton—had been
making autobiographical films for several decades, making the
form "one of most vital developments in the cinema of the late sixties and early seventies," as the film theorist P. Adams Sitney has
asserted.[47] In his dissertation on the subject of autobiographical
cinema, Jim Lane mentions in passing de Antonio's project as part
of a wave of similar films during the eighties: Mark Rance's *Death
and the Singing Telegram* (1983), Ross McElwee's *Sherman's
March* (1986), Su Friedrich's *The Ties That Bind* (1987), and
Arlene Bowman's *Navajo Talking Picture* (1989).[48] One might
also include celebrated films such as Michael Moore's *Roger and
Me* (1989) and *Swimming to Cambodia* (Jonathan Demme, 1987)
with monologuist Spaulding Gray.

For the documentarian one benefit of this self-reflexive mode
of filmmaking is ethical: putting yourself at the center of the film
avoids "the tradition of the victim" that had long plagued documentary films, especially those that focused on homeless waifs,
degraded workers, and exotic foreigners.[49] Another astute film
critic put the matter this way: "The time when an artist could
take photographs of strangers, usually poor or in some other way
removed from the mainstream of America, and justify the action
as the inherent right of the artist, is, I believe, ending."[50] Rare
in the documentary tradition, de Antonio's films had depicted
few downtrodden victims, a result of his scorn for the classics of
observational cinema such as Frederick Wiseman's *Titicut Follies*
(1967), an examination of the brutality of life in a mental hospital.
Unwilling to point his camera at those less powerful than he, de
Antonio's solution was to make films about presidents, senators,
generals, bureaucrats, and himself. Obsessed with the structural
rather than the anecdotal, he returned again and again to the one
salient fact of his vision of postwar American life: the existence
of the cold war and its attendants such as Nixon, McCarthy, and

Hoover. While making films about the powerful minimized the ethical quandaries that documentary often raises, now he was making a film on the subject he could most ethically represent—himself.[51]

Taping an outline of his "script" to a lighting fixture with key words to prompt his memory, he decided to just talk to the camera. "It wasn't as if I was reading off a [Teleprompter]. I'd just look and see the word and that would get me going," he recalled. "I'm not sure that I have much camera presence but by hearing myself do a take, I'd do it over again and eventually manage to get it O.K." Unaware of the amount of acting that de Antonio put into his performance, one critic said, "If films were made in Photomats, they might look like this: a man seated before a stark white background, harsh light glinting on his forehead and spectacles, extemporizes."[52]

However, de Antonio was giving a practiced performance, one he had been giving all his life. Still, *Mr. Hoover and I* provided him with a formal opportunity to look back on his life and work in the manner of the *Künstlerroman*, a novel that traces the development of an artist such as James Joyce's *A Portrait of the Artist as a Young Man*, Thomas Mann's *Buddenbrooks*, or Henry Miller's *Tropic of Cancer*. De Antonio even seems to echo the angry tone of Miller's work, in which the novelist claims: "This is not a book. This is a libel, slander, defamation of character. . . . This is a prolonged insult, a gob of spit in the face of Art, a kick in the pants to God, Man, Destiny, Time, Love, Beauty." It is in this spirit that de Antonio attacks Hoover in a manner that displays more animosity than accuracy, all of which is designed to show the malevolent and bureaucratic pettiness of the original "G-man" who "ran the secret police of my country . . . [and] exercised his power with spite." With disdain the filmmaker recounts the media manipulation that surrounded the shooting of the depression-era bank robber John Dillinger and condemns the FBI harassment that allegedly caused the actress Jean Seberg, whose lovers included a member of the Black Panthers, to commit suicide in 1979.

Intertwined with these ruminations is footage originally shot for Ron Mann's *Poetry in Motion* (1983). It shows De Antonio with John Cage, who had inspired de Antonio's earliest films, discussing chance and other matters in the composer's kitchen as he prepares a peculiar-looking loaf of bread for the oven. Vincent Canby, writing in the *New York Times*, detected "something sweet and (in retrospect) sad in his demonstrably easy relations with Mr. Cage . . . and with his somewhat younger wife, who seems clearly to delight in his mild attempts to act as if he were difficult and crotchety."[53] Then de Antonio is shown speaking in front of an audience at Dartmouth College, a typical example of the lectures he gave with great success. Some humorous footage from *Millhouse* also appears, showing Hoover's discomfort while President Nixon stands before an audience and jokes about his rejection by the FBI in the late thirties. Then de Antonio recounts the FBI harassment that beset the production of *Underground*. Whatever the flaws of this essentially autobiographical film, it makes an excellent introduction to the world according to de Antonio.

Mr. Hoover and I is stark, simple, direct, not the average fare for commercial theaters in the United States, and it had more trouble finding a home in theaters than any of de Antonio's previous films. *Mr. Hoover and I* even had difficulties in Europe, where sound problems caused the BBC, which had commissioned the project, to postpone the film's appearance until the last day of 1989. In the United States the problems were even greater: the film was less widely distributed than any of de Antonio's previous films and limited to appearances at a few festivals. Somehow— perhaps in recognition of de Antonio's stature as an éminence grise of documentary—the film attracted favorable notice in a few influential periodicals. Canby, a long-time admirer of de Antonio's films in the pages of the *New York Times*, called the film "an amusing companion piece to the many films he made about other people and their causes. At last the film maker is seen front and center." *Variety* praised the "thought-provoking 'meta-film'" as reminiscent of Orson Welles's later work such as *F for Fake* (1973), a quasi-autobiographical film that contains both documentary and fictionalized scenes.[54] One of de Antonio's best explicators, Mitch Tuchman, wrote about *Mr. Hoover* in *Film Comment* with his customary insight: "The artist who through long practice develops a fruitful and congenial style may eventually strip every contrivance from that style, and craft a work both characteristic and revealing. . . . *Mr. Hoover and I* is such a work." Another reviewer noted that de Antonio's enthusiasm for the monologue runs throughout the film—"much funnier and smarter than anything in Spalding Gray's *Swimming to Cambodia.*"[55]

Aside from these isolated reviews, the film attracted little notice from critics or audiences alike, which de Antonio had predicted: "This film, although it won't be seen by very many people, is an attempt at subversion," he says in the middle of *Mr. Hoover and I*. Perhaps a negative review in the influential *Village Voice* undermined its appeal in the critical New York market. For some reason the *Voice* had never shown much interest in de Antonio, a long-time resident of Greenwich Village. Its reviewer took *Mr. Hoover and I* to task for not applying the compilation technique of *Millhouse* to J. Edgar Hoover. Watching de Antonio on screen for the better part of two hours seems to have tried the patience of the *Voice*'s writer, who complained, "He is charming, he is witty, he is tiresome," though "tired" seems more accurate and certainly more generous to a filmmaker at the end of a long life in dissent as well as his tenth full-length film since 1964.[56]

Despite this weariness de Antonio manages to end his final film on an optimistic note: "We're on the verge of a new kind of social change. We will be aware of that form as it takes place." Then his stately presence recedes from view and the film flickers to a close, the last will and angry testament of a seventy-year-old rebel. De Antonio died of a heart attack in front of his home in New York in December 1989—the greatest radical filmmaker of the cold war died just weeks after the fall of the Berlin Wall and the symbolic end of hostilities between the United States and the Soviet Union. Appropriately enough, *Mr. Hoover and I* received one of its first screenings at a memorial service for the filmmaker, where his last testament became, as Mitch Tuchman has observed, his valediction.[57]

"The great theme of American autobiography," writes the critic Herbert Leibowitz, "is the quest for distinction, a quest that has shaped and deranged American identity throughout our history." Obsessed with the sins of power, blessed with the artistic and entrepreneurial skills to execute his creative vision of American history and his place in it, de Antonio achieved a level of distinction throughout his life. Nowhere is this more apparent than in his parting shot—a last stab at cultural criticism, old enemies, and self-examination alike. In this regard *Mr. Hoover and I* makes a worthy memorial to the filmmaker, who achieves the sort of distinction in this film that may elude his better-known adversary, a caricature of a bureaucrat less interested in justice than power.

De Antonio had planned one "last filmic thrust against the emptiness of *Jaws, 2001,* [and] *Star Wars,*" against the banality of Hollywood blockbusters, one last attack on the hypocrisy of those in power. "Although not as flashy or funny as *Roger and Me,*" one critic wrote just after de Antonio's death, "*Mr. Hoover and I* presents a similar dialectic between personalities and ideologies—one populist and libertarian, the other corporate and bureaucratic."[58] This dialectic between de Antonio and those in power was always present in his films, but it was generally implicit: only in his final film did it emerge full force. With the filmmaker at center stage *Mr. Hoover and I* offers an important contribution to the art of autobiography. Although some writers on the subject of cinematic autobiography have perceived its mere existence as a threat to the written memoir, others have seen the cinematic representation of self as a source of hope. The film theorist Michael Renov has argued this latter position, claiming that autobiography, "far from being an endangered species, shows new signs of life" as a cinematic subgenre.[59] Nowhere is this more apparent than in *Mr. Hoover and I,* a film that captures the unique timbre of de Antonio's voice and reminds us of his lasting importance as a radical filmmaker in cold war America.

Epilogue

In this book I have used the phrase "America is hard to see" to describe the difficulty of making films about such a sprawling subject, one that has forced filmmakers into the clichés that have earned the scorn of professional historians. But Emile de Antonio took an unusual approach to the past in his literate and thought-provoking films. Probing a deep but narrow aspect of American culture, his historical imagination focused on two sides of the same issue: the hypocrisies of the powerful and the frustrations of the dissenters. On one side was *Point of Order, Rush to Judgment, In the Year of the Pig*, and *Mr. Hoover and I*; on the other was *America Is Hard to See, Painters Painting, Underground*, and *In the King of Prussia*.

De Antonio claimed that beneath each of these films "there lies a hope that the world can change."[1] Yet even when he professed this sort of romantic utopianism, the object of his political desires often seemed more in the conservative past than the radical future. In fact, when one examines de Antonio and his films, the pattern that emerges often puts him at odds with a category such as "left-wing filmmaker" or "radical documentarian," as he was generally labeled by journalists and film critics.

Consider the following contradictions in the views of this notorious iconoclast: he was a self-described Marxist whose films make almost no mention of class and were funded by the rich; a progressive whose films often ignore issues of race and gender; a leftist who never embraced the counterculture of the New Left as much as its politics; a democrat who despised much of popular culture; an atheist looking for moral and even spiritual solutions

235

to political problems. He is not easily pigeonholed except as something of a paradox, as a revolutionary conservative who would have turned the world upside down to restore the moral and artistic virtues of an earlier age. Despite these contradictions, he was a political artist of uncommon power and one of our society's select individuals with "the leisure, the facilities, and the training to seek the truth hidden behind the veil of distortion and misrepresentation, ideology, and class interest through which the events of current history are presented to us." This passage comes from Noam Chomsky's essay, "On the Responsibility of Intellectuals," though it might also describe the sensibility that has long been at the heart of the documentary tradition.[2] No American filmmaker contributed more to this tradition in the second half of the twentieth century than Emile de Antonio, a man who pursued the truth with a tenacious sense of purpose.

Even when he did not find it, his films presented a unique and invaluable perspective on some of the thorniest issues of American life during the cold war era. Despite a shortage of funds, a lack of technical expertise, and various forms of censorship, he was able to express his controversial views to thousands of people in a remarkable series of films: *Point of Order* (1963), his powerful distillation of the 188 hours of Army-McCarthy hearings; *Rush to Judgment* (1967), the first and most judicious in a long line of films to question the Warren report; *In the Year of the Pig* (1969), a groundbreaking antiwar film that put the U.S. involvement in Vietnam in a historical context and received an Academy Award nomination; *America Is Hard to See* (1970), a muted protest against the political machinery that prevented Eugene McCarthy, a "decent, complicated intellectual" in the eyes of de Antonio, from winning the Democratic nomination in 1968; *Millhouse: A White Comedy* (1971), a brutal and hilarious examination of Richard Nixon's career and character; *Painters Painting* (1973), a series of rich and subtle interviews with the luminaries of the New York art scene; *Underground* (1976), a tantalizing but essentially disappointing examination of contemporary American revolutionaries; *In the King of Prussia* (1983), a stiff and somber

docudrama about the trial of the Plowshares Eight; and an engaging autobiographical film, *Mr. Hoover and I* (1989), which
dissected the FBI's longtime persecution of de Antonio.

I have attempted to explain how these films came into being,
how contemporary film critics interpreted them, and how we
might interpret de Antonio's films today. De Antonio changed the
landscape of American documentary filmmaking—tearing away
the cherished myth of objectivity, minimizing the use of voice-
over narration, reviving the compilation documentary as a tool
of radical filmmaking—and focused his lens on the powerful
rather than the downtrodden. His significance goes beyond these
contributions, however. Alan Rosenthal has claimed that "de
Antonio's importance lies in the intelligence he has applied to
an examination of the politics of the sixties, and his ability to
get a critically left view seriously considered by a complacent
middle-class liberal audience."[3] His films "raised America's political consciousness," Vincent Canby wrote in the *New York
Times* in 1990, "and enriched its documentary heritage with a
series of works that weren't quite like those of any other film
maker."[4] Perhaps his most astute critic, Thomas Waugh, described him as possessing "the rich creative energy, the obstinate commitment to rationality and to change, and the clearsighted historical consciousness which have made him one of
the major American filmmakers of our time."[5] A bold assertion about a largely forgotten body of work, these words gain
credence when one considers the retrospectives of de Antonio's
work that have appeared at the American, Swedish, British,
and Danish Film Institutes, the Pacific Film Archive, and the
Cinémathèque française. Long after the initial release of his films,
these events have brought de Antonio's work to the attention of a
small group of kindred spirits, some of whom have been inspired
to emulate his mode of political filmmaking in films such as *With
Babies and Banners* (Lorraine Gray, Lyn Goldfarb, and Anne
Bohlen, 1977), *The Wobblies* (Deborah Shaffer and Stuart Bird,
1979), *The Life and Times of Rosie the Riveter* (Connie Field,
1980), *Seeing Red* (Jim Klein and Julia Reichert, 1984), *Hotel*

Terminus (Marcel Ophuls, 1987), and *Solovki Power* (Marina Goldovskaya, 1988).[6]

Indeed, de Antonio's influence can still be seen in the recent development of a small school of irreverent and intellectually aggressive filmmakers: Mark Archbar and Peter Wintonick, who produced a clever study of de Antonio's old ally, *Manufacturing Consent: Noam Chomsky and the Media* (1992); Michael Moore, whose *Roger and Me* (1989) was one of the highest-grossing documentaries on a subject other than rock music; and Kevin and Pierce Rafferty, whose compilation of unaired television footage of the 1992 presidential election, *Feed* (1993), was built from exactly the sort of outtakes that de Antonio called "the confessions of the system." These films have far more in common with de Antonio's ironic meditations on political power such as *Millhouse* or *Mr. Hoover and I* than the mainstream documentaries that are usually welcome on public television.

A useful point of comparison is the work of Ken Burns, the skillful filmmaker behind PBS's extraordinarily popular series *The Civil War* (1989). Anecdotal, ostensibly objective, and dramatic in the calculated vein of Hollywood, Burns's mode of writing history on film is the antithesis of de Antonio's structural concerns, dialectical narrative, and desire to make films in which the drama arises from a deeper historical understanding rather than the excitement of a cavalry charge. The fundamental problem with Burns's films is that "the history imparted is by and large traditional, conventional history," as the historian Leon Litwack has observed, "and it is usually safe, risk free, upbeat, reassuring, comforting history . . . [these are] exercises in self-congratulation."[7] With PBS and most of the new cable venues for nonfiction film more interested in comforting mythologies than harsh realities of the sort de Antonio examined, his legacy would seem confined to the most stalwart independent documentarians willing to operate far outside the system.

Although the situation for documentary might appear grim, I find some consolation in the intriguing possibilities that exist outside the normal modes of film production and distribution.

Consider, for example, the new forms of documentary that are developing on the Internet. In many ways the Internet could be the perfect place for the heirs to de Antonio's brand of radical scavenging: it is inexpensive, it is instant, it is difficult to censor (so far), and it is widely disseminated (and increasingly so). Individuals with dissenting views can respond immediately to events as they unfold, disseminating a large quantity of information with an unprecedented speed. No need to seduce the rich into underwriting a good cause or plead with a granting agency over many months. No need to buy film, rent equipment, hire a crew. Compared even with video production, Web page creation is punk—it's do-it-yourself information technology for anyone with access to a computer and some affordable software. Just type it up, scan it in, and upload a Web page. Digitize video and audio clips, and revise the site as new information comes available. One can build dossiers of existing documents, rearranging, editing, and commenting upon them, just as de Antonio was doing with film footage.

Although most of the early Web-based programs were soap operas with titles like *Lost Elvis Diaries* and *101 Hollywood Blvd.*, the potential for producing serious documentaries in this format is exciting.[8] The Witness On-Line Documentary Series, for example, has used "streaming video" technology to produce multipart programs on topics such as ethnic tensions in the former Soviet Union.[9] Other companies are translating existing film for Web-based distribution, making available old television footage—including Nixon's Checkers speech and short scenes from the Army-McCarthy hearings—that appeared in de Antonio's films.[10]

Although the small picture and poor resolution of Web-based programs still resemble television in its infancy, the differences between what is possible on the Web and what is possible with contemporary film or video will diminish with time. At first the Web was silent and still—few moving images, few sounds. But already an increasing number of Web sites contain video and audio files and will soon offer something analogous to what we have known as cinema. By creating new possibilities for documentary expression, Web-based digitized video, available on line at little or no cost, raises the power of alternative media to have a real (if immeasurable) influence on public discourse. At the dawn of the millennium, the potential of the Web is far from realized, and we may see the emergence of even more sophisticated radical Webmasters in the next few years. De Antonio himself may appear in this new medium as technology allows. Already he exists on CD-ROM in an annotated version of *Painters Painting*, and his other films may find a new life on line. When they appear in this new format, they will set a high standard for anyone attempting to use the Web with the same critical intelligence, depth of research, and clarity of presentation that de Antonio brought to film. Meeting this standard would politicize the Internet in a significant new way.

I am sanguine about such possibilities but do not want to over-estimate the emancipatory potential of new communication tech-nologies. Cautionary tales are not difficult to find in the history of mass media. For example, in 1932 Bertolt Brecht envisioned radio as a vast participatory communication system that would link citizens together to work for progressive ends.[11] He did not foresee the rapid commercialization of radio, a process that may occur with even greater ferocity on the Internet. The concern is valid, but so is the chance that remarkable new forms of documentary expression will flourish in cyberspace. Without question, we are at a critical juncture for exploring such opportunities.

The confluence of video and computer technologies is creating a major shift in the way we obtain information, one in which the moving image will play a critical role. In his latest book, the media theorist Mitchell Stephens describes the emergence of something he calls "the new video," an expansive phrase that includes video and film with certain characteristics. The new video is information intense. It breaks our cinematic gaze into shards and reassembles it into new patterns; it makes use of quick edits, multiple layers of information, and unexpected juxtapositions to allow us to see more than is available at any one time, to say much more in a shorter time than ever before. As such, it can capture "more of the tumult and confusions of contemporary life than tend to fit in lines of type."[12] Although the new video began in places like MTV and hip advertising campaigns, its elements are rapidly spreading throughout the medium.

I believe de Antonio was a pioneer of the new video revolution. Even though the pace of his films was often slow and contemplative, he was prescient in his recognition of the power of the image in the age of television and sought to harness this power for something more than the selling of soft drinks and senators. When he broke apart the television footage of the Army-McCarthy hearings to assemble *Point of Order*, he was redirecting the power of television to his own ends. And as the chapter on the production of *In the Year of the Pig* mentioned, when de Antonio found images of arrogant French colonials arriving by rickshaw at a Saigon café, he recognized their value for his critique of what was happening in Vietnam: "To me, that said everything you could say about colonialism without ever saying the word. If anything shows the primacy of the image over the word, what the image can reveal, it's the image of those rickshaws. It's the equivalent of a couple of chapters of dense writing about the meaning of colonialism."[13]

In the two decades since de Antonio made this observation, the image has continued its ascendancy over the word. Mitchell Stephens argues that we are witnessing the next great transformation in communication technologies since Gutenberg and that we must confront the inevitable "rise of the image and the fall of the word," to quote the title of his book, that began with the Kennedy assassination and the war in Vietnam.[14] Something happened during the television coverage of those events: the moving image seduced us with a thoroughness that cinema or early television had never managed. De Antonio must have intuited this because he took on both critical events, attempting to change the nature of the seduction from the commercial transaction of the nightly news or the *Green Berets* to the intellectual exchange of *Rush to Judgment* or *In the Year of the Pig*. In these films and others he refused to speak down to his audience, resisting the notion that visual information must be simple. Standing in opposition to the blandness and reductiveness of the mainstream television media, de Antonio used documentary to tell complex stories about abstract issues.

At his best de Antonio offers a complex cinema of self-criticism, one that engenders critical thinking about the underside of America and its past. More than a story that can divert or illuminate, his version of history is a chaotic place where ideologies compete for the mantle of truth, where conflicting interpretations are set in opposition for the audience to resolve. For students of history looking for a viable alternative to the simplifications of the historical drama, the television docudrama, and mainstream documentaries, de Antonio's films are a valuable resource for two reasons. The first is the wealth of historical data his films contain, from oral histories of modern art and the war in Vietnam to obscure images of 1960s radicals fighting in the streets. The second is the manner in which his documentaries teach audiences how to watch film in general. Sewing together various points of view without the benefit of explanatory narration, de Antonio pushes an audience into an active rather than passive mode of viewing, one that encourages viewers to interpret visual information with an awareness of and suspicion toward the political values embedded in any cinematic text. The importance of learning to analyze visual information in the age of television cannot be underestimated. "Any society which commits itself . . . to preserving the freedom of expression for news agencies and public figures must also assume the responsibility to prepare the public to critically evaluate the messages they receive," the historian John E. O'Connor has written. "There is no more appropriate place for this sort of training, this opening of minds, than the history classroom," where de Antonio's films might find a new audience receptive to his creative mode of filmmaking.[15]

Persuasive, trenchant, analytical, his films retain the power that made them cultural events in their own right.[16] Even today his work is unsurpassed in helping us to understand American society at a crucial time in its history, when political realities were often obscured from view and Robert Frost could claim that "America is hard to see." An apt metaphor coined in the midst of the cold war, it has outlived that anxious era, just as it will outlive the next, remaining with us as long as we look for America, in all its myriad forms, through a haze of media distortion and political chicanery. Never acquiescing to this situation, always hoping to recapture the promise of American democracy as he saw it, de Antonio became the foremost cinematic chronicler of cold war America and one of the most provocative film essayists of the century. Yet more important than his place in film history is his lesson for those attempting to understand the United States in the latter half of the twentieth century. *America is hard to see*, but the task is not impossible. With the clarity of vision and force of conscience that he brought to documentary, he showed how we can place America in a new light, sometimes harsh, often brilliant, and always penetrating.

Notes
Selected Bibliography
Filmography
Index

Notes

Introduction

1. Gary Crowdus and Dan Georgakas, "History Is the Theme of All My Films: An Interview with Emile de Antonio," *Cinéaste*, Spring 1982, p. 21. (All other citations to the Crowdus and Georgakas essay are from their chapter of the same title in Alan Rosenthal, ed., *New Challenges for Documentary* [Berkeley: University of California Press, 1988]; this quotation appears in an introductory note for the original article that was not reprinted in Rosenthal.)

2. *Point of Order* was completed in 1963 and had its first public showing that September, but it was not released commercially until January 1964.

3. Thomas Waugh, "Beyond Vérité: Emile de Antonio and the New Documentary of the Seventies," *Jumpcut*, no. 10–11 (Summer 1976): 33–39.

4. The poem was first published as "And All We Call American," in the *Atlantic Monthly*, June 1951, then as "America Is Hard to See" in Frost's collection *In the Clearing* (New York: Holt, Rinehart, and Winston, 1962).

5. Research into how documentary affects viewers' attitudes is not well developed. See John Corner and Kay Richardson, "Documentary Meaning and the Discourse of Interpretation," in John Conner, ed., *Documentary and the Mass Media* (London: Arnold, 1988), 140–60.

6. This approach is described in John E. O'Connor, *Image as Artifact: The Historical Analysis of Film and Television* (Malabar, Fla.: Kreiger, 1990), 132–33.

7. Kristeva is quoted in Jonathan Culler, *Structuralist Poetics: Structuralism, Linguistics, and the Study of Literature* (Ithaca, N.Y.: Cornell University Press, 1975), 139.

247

8. Bill Nichols, *Representing Reality: Issues and Concepts in Documentary* (Bloomington: University of Indiana Press, 1991), 132.

9. Earlier attempts to produce studies of de Antonio—either in print or film—were unsuccessful despite numerous promising beginnings. In the early 1970s the filmmaker's sister-in-law, Madeline de Antonio, made the first attempt, though it did not get far beyond the outline stage. The second was in 1975 when Mitch Tuchman proposed a book to New Republic Books. Although Tuchman went on to write several fine articles about de Antonio, his book never appeared. Ten years later Arno Luik, a German writer, proposed a similar book-length overview of the filmmaker, but nothing was published.

Ideas for films about de Antonio suffered the same fate. Finnish filmmaker Peter van Bach recorded several hours of interviews with de Antonio on 16mm film in the mid-1980s with the intention of making a documentary on his life, but van Bach never completed the project. In the late 1980s producers Scott Robbe and Chiz Shultz started planning a film called *Emile de Antonio: A Vision of Conscience*. With de Antonio's approval Robbe went so far as to request $170,000 from the Corporation for Public Broadcasting, Channel Four (U.K.), and the MacArthur Foundation, but once again nothing came of the project. Most recently, in the early 1990s a group based in Austin, Texas, including Douglas Kellner, Ali Hossaini, Jamie McEwen, and Richard Linklater (the *Slacker* director who counts de Antonio as a major influence on his own approach to filmmaking) proposed an ambitious documentary about de Antonio's life and films. Despite many hours of planning and a well-crafted proposal, this film never came to fruition.

10. Waugh, "Beyond Vérité"; another worthy contribution to the scholarship on de Antonio was Robert C. Ladendorf, "Resistance to Vision: The Effects of Censorship and Other Restraints on Emile de Antonio's Political Documentaries" (master's thesis, University of Wisconsin–Madison, 1977).

11. Waugh, "Beyond Vérité," 36.

12. Ibid., 39.

13. Ray Carney, "Looking Without Seeing," *Partisan Review*, Fall 1991, 716.

14. For an interdisciplinary approach to a contemporary fiction filmmaker, see Ray Carney, *American Dreaming: The Films of John Cassavetes and the American Experience* (Berkeley: University of Cal-

ifornia Press, 1984); for the phrase quoted and a discussion of the general dearth of scholarship on the topic of independent filmmaking, see Carney, "Looking Without Seeing," 716; on the problems of being an independent political filmmaker in the United States, see Peter Steven, ed., *Jump Cut: Hollywood, Politics, and Counter Cinema* (New York: Praeger, 1985), 16–17.

15. In 1973 de Antonio began sending boxes of his papers to the Wisconsin Center for Film and Theater Research at the State Historical Society of Wisconsin. He had spoken on the Madison campus on various occasions and admired the political radicalism associated with the university. For this reason he thought it would make an ideal home for his large archive.

Chapter 1. Life Before Film

1. De Antonio, Journals, vol. 7:143.

2. Donato Bonardi, *Biographical Highlights of Dott. Prof. Cav. Francesco de Antonio* (Alessandria, Italy: Gazzotti, 1915), 1; de Antonio, Journals, vol. 5:30; vol. 7:145.

3. De Antonio, Journals, vol. 5:3; Frederick L. Hitchcock, *History of Scranton and Its People*, vol. 2 (New York: Lewis Historical Publishing, 1914), 154–55.

4. De Antonio, Journals, vol. 5:32.

5. De Antonio, notes for an autobiographical film, probably 1989, 17; see also Emile de Antonio and Mitch Tuchman, compilers, *Painters Painting: A Candid History of the Modern Art Scene, 1940–1970* (New York: Abbeville, 1984), 16.

6. De Antonio, Journals, vol. 7:143; Terry de Antonio, "An In-Depth Talk with Emile de Antonio," *Shantih International Writing*, Winter–Spring 1972, 17–19.

7. De Antonio, Journals, vol. 7:41–42.

8. FBI Report no. III-32581, November 11, 1943; de Antonio, notes for an autobiographical film, 16; de Antonio to Anna Rappe, November 1, 1973.

9. De Antonio to Rappe.

10. De Antonio, Journals, vol. 5:147.

11. *Daily Kansan* (University of Kansas, Lawrence), April 23, 1985; FBI Report III-32581.

12. De Antonio, Journals, vol. 9:36, describes his parents' wishes; vol. 6:80 is the source of the "sensitive, proud, uneasy boy" quotation.

13. De Antonio to his sister Ursula de Antonio, n.d. [1943]. He exchanged numerous letters with Ursula during the 1940s and 1950s, but after that point his main sibling contact was his brother Carlo, who became a medical doctor and lived in the Los Angeles area.

14. De Antonio, Journals, vol. 7:13.

15. De Antonio to Rappe; de Antonio, Journals, vol. 6:78, 82–83; the American Student Union had formed in 1935 from a merger of communist and socialist groups, though it was mainstream enough to embrace the New Deal. See Harvey Klehr, *The Heyday of American Communism: The Depression Decade* (New York: Basic, 1984), 317; on the social aspects of the Communist Party, see Vivian Gornick, *The Romance of American Communism* (New York: Basic, 1977); de Antonio mentions his monocle affectation in his final film, *Mr. Hoover and I* (1989); FBI File 100-630, September 14, 1948.

16. De Antonio made this statement in his film *Mr. Hoover and I* (1989), almost a half century after his college days, and may have been projecting some of his later views onto his youthful self. His real relationship to the Communist Party, like that of many leftists in the 1930s, was probably more complex.

17. De Antonio is quoted in Robert C. Ladendorf, "Resistance to Vision: The Effects of Censorship and Other Restraints on Emile de Antonio's Political Documentaries" (master's thesis, University of Wisconsin–Madison, 1977), 9; de Antonio to Rappe; de Antonio to "Bix" [Townley Bixler], n.d. [1939].

18. On de Antonio's anti-Soviet attitudes see de Antonio to Rappe; de Antonio to Inga [?], March 11, 1970; de Antonio, Journals, vol. 9:86. See Michael Wreszin, *A Rebel in Defense of Tradition: The Life and Politics of Dwight Macdonald* (New York: Basic, 1994).

19. De Antonio to Jim Frosch, February 25, 1970; *Dallas Morning News*, April 5, 1968.

20. Quoted in de Antonio to David Mitchell, July 13, 1967.

21. See, for example, the *Baltimore Sun*, November 18, 1937; *Harvard Crimson*, February 25, 1964.

22. Reginald H. Phelps (assistant dean in charge of records, Harvard University) to [?], August 10, 1943, which appears as part of FBI file 100-630; de Antonio, Journals, vol. 9:35.

23. De Antonio, Journals, vol. 9:37.

24. Ibid., vol. 4:24. The archive contains no mention of when or why de Antonio and Ruth Baumann were divorced; probably she left him after two or three years and he was too embarrassed to talk about it.

25. Ibid., vol. 6:88.

26. FBI Report no. III-32581; see also de Antonio, Journals, vol. 7:88; de Antonio to Ursula de Antonio, n.d. [1943].

27. De Antonio to Anna-Lena [Wibom?], August 7, 1972; de Antonio, "How It Began," typescript chapter for a never-published book on the filming of *Underground*, probably from 1976.

28. De Antonio, Journals, vol. 4:35.

29. Ibid., vol. 9:39; vol. 6:51.

30. *London Evening Standard*, clipping dated only as 1964.

31. De Antonio, Journals, vol. 4:n.p.; vol. 6:46. Although the exact amount of the inheritance is not mentioned anywhere, de Antonio talked about it in a way that implies that it was significant. However, it was not so large that he could not squander it by the mid-1950s, when he found himself plagued by angry debtors.

32. FBI file 105-45304, January 18, 1961.

33. De Antonio to Ursula de Antonio [1948].

34. The *Dartmouth* (Hanover, N.H.), November 11, 1977.

35. He mentions his attempts to write in a letter to Ruth Baumann de Antonio, June 1946.

36. De Antonio, Journals, vol. 7:139.

37. Connolly used the term *hominterm* to describe certain "psychological revolutionaries, people who adopt left-wing political formulas because they hate their fathers or were unhappy at their public schools or insulted at the Customs, or lectured about sex." Connolly is quoted in Ian Hamilton, "Spender's Lives," *New Yorker*, February 28, 1994, 72.

38. De Antonio, Journals, vol. 6:3.

39. Leo Castelli, telephone interview by the author, March 14, 1994. During the 1980s de Antonio made about $400,000 by selling early paintings by Jasper Johns and Frank Stella that the director had received either as gifts or for small sums (de Antonio to Madeline de Antonio, March 11, 1987).

40. De Antonio to Madeline de Antonio, July 10, 1956; de Antonio's work as an agent is also discussed in Fred Lawrence Guiles, *Loner at the Ball: The Life of Andy Warhol* (New York: Bantam, 1989), 119.

41. Guiles, *Loner at the Ball*, 119.

42. De Antonio, Journals, vol. 6:3.

43. Tanya Neufeld, "An Interview with Emile de Antonio," *Artforum*, March 1973; Patricia Bosworth, *Diane Arbus: A Biography* (New York: Knopf, 1984), 161.

44. Bosworth, *Diane Arbus*, 161; most of the Warhol–de Antonio material, photocopies of which are tucked into de Antonio's journals, was later published in Andy Warhol and Pat Hackett, *POPism: The Warhol '60s* (New York: Harcourt Brace Jovanovich, 1980).

45. De Antonio, Journals, vol. 7:140.

46. Ibid., 152.

47. De Antonio, "[Karl] Marx and Warhol," unpublished typescript article.

48. The quotation appears in De Antonio, Journals, vol. 7:167; see also Sam Szurek, "An Interview with Emile de Antonio," *Downtown* (New York), September 16, 1987, 32–35.

49. De Antonio, Journals, vol. 7:167. See chapter 6 on *Painters Painting*; de Antonio conducted a rare interview with Stella in "A Passion for Painting," *Geo*, March 1982, 13–15.

50. Guiles, *Loner at the Ball*, 115; Emile de Antonio, "Pontus Hultén and Some '60's Memories in New York," in Moderna Museet, *New York Collection for Stockholm* (Stockholm: Moderna Museet, 1973).

51. De Antonio and Tuchman, *Painters Painting*, 16.

52. De Antonio, Journals, vol. 9:6; vol. 6:174; Guiles, *Loner at the Ball*, 121; Madeline de Antonio, undated typescript outline for never-published biography of Emile de Antonio, 7.

53. De Antonio to Anna-Lena [Wibom?].

54. Calvin Tompkins, "Profiles: Moving Out," *New Yorker*, February 29, 1964, 85; the recording of the concert was released as *The Twenty-five-Year Retrospective Concert of the Music of John Cage* (George Avakian, 1959).

55. De Antonio, Journals, vol. 6:9.

56. De Antonio to Geoffrey Bridson, program editor for the BBC in London, August 17, 1966; for a description of this concert, see David Revill, *The Roaring Silence: John Cage, A Life* (New York: Arcade, 1992), 184–85, 190–92.

57. De Antonio is quoted in the Warhol and Hackett manuscript for *POPism*, which appears in de Antonio, Journals, vol. 7:148.

58. De Antonio, "Notes on Film for a Film," typescript, probably from 1988; de Antonio, Journals, vol. 9:6.

59. De Antonio, Journals, vol. 4:43; vol. 5:26.

60. Ibid., vol. 6:3; see also Guiles, *Loner at the Ball*, 119.

61. Richard Routledge to de Antonio, April 17, 1962.

62. De Antonio, Journals, vol. 9:82.

63. De Antonio to Madeline de Antonio, July 10, 1956.

64. De Antonio to Adrienne [de Antonio], December 3, 1974.

65. De Antonio, notes for an autobiographical film. Colin Westerbeck, Jr., "Outtakes of a Radical Filmmaker," typescript of an article that appeared in *Sight and Sound*, Summer 1970, 140–43; FBI file 105-45304.

66. De Antonio to Madeline de Antonio, July 10, 1956.

67. De Antonio, Journals, vol. 7:149.

68. Ibid., vol. 10:8.

69. Mitch Tuchman, "Emile de Antonio: 'All Filmmakers Are Confidence Men,'" *Village Voice*, May 17, 1976, 140.

70. Susan Linfield, "De Antonio's Fireside Chat: Part 2," *New York City Independent*, July–August 1982, 22.

71. On the importance of this film, see J. Hoberman, "The Forest and the Trees," in David E. James, ed., *To Free the Cinema: Jonas Mekas and the New York Underground* (Princeton, N.J.: Princeton University Press, 1992), 100–101; see also David E. James, *Allegories of Cinema: American Film in the Sixties* (Princeton, N.J.: Princeton University Press, 1989), 94.

72. De Antonio, Journals, vol. 6:121.

73. Contract between Anita Ellis and de Antonio, March 10, 1961.

74. P. Adams Sitney, *Film Culture Reader* (New York: Praeger, 1970), 79–83.

75. De Antonio, "Pontus Hultén"; the aims of the group are aptly described in James, *Allegories of Cinema*, 87.

76. Warhol and Hackett, *POPism*, 48.

77. Jonas Mekas, "Independence for Independents," *American Film*, September 1978, 38; de Antonio, Journals, vol. 6:121.

78. Hoberman, "Forest and the Trees," 112.

79. De Antonio to Henry Rosenberg, January 17, 1961.

80. Pauline Kael to de Antonio, October 9, 1961; Madeline de Antonio, undated outline for de Antonio biography.

81. De Antonio, Journals, vol. 5:66.

82. Ibid., vol. 10:82.

Chapter 2. *Point of Order!*

1. Emile de Antonio and Daniel Talbot, Letter to the Editor, *Esquire*, April 1968, 14, 188.

2. This history of the production of *Point of Order* is drawn from the following documents: Joseph M. Gottfried (accountant) to Point Films, Inc., February 7, 1964; de Antonio to Frances FitzGerald, December 7, 1964; Madeline de Antonio, undated typescript outline for never-published biography of Emile de Antonio, 10, 14, 33–38; Daniel Talbot, "On Historic Hearings from TV to the Screen," *New York Times*, January 12, 1964; Eugene Archer, "*Point of Order*, a Surprise Hit, Belatedly Gets a Distributor," *New York Times*, February 11, 1964; press kit for *Point of Order* [1964]; de Antonio to Hubert Bals and Wendy Lidell, n.d. (probably 1985). The film's title was alternately described by de Antonio, as well as reviewers, as *Point of Order!* and *Point of Order*, though the latter appears both in the film and in later references.

3. Before the advent of videotape, kinescopes were used to record television programs on film.

4. The total budget was $164,697.99, according to Gottfried's letter to Point Films.

5. Richard H. Rovere, *Senator Joe McCarthy* (New York: Harcourt, Brace, 1959).

6. Daniel Talbot, ed., *Film: An Anthology* (New York: Simon and Schuster, 1959).

7. Tanya Neufeld, "An Interview with Emile de Antonio," *Artforum*, March 1973, 79–83.

8. De Antonio was probably unaware of another example of this technique: *Das Passagen-Werk*, Walter Benjamin's unfinished study of the Parisian arcades, which was published in 1982. Confident that a coherent narrative would emerge from fragments and quotations alone, the German philosopher predicted that "I need say nothing." See Walter Benjamin, "N (Theories of Knowledge; Theories of Progress)," *Philosophical Forum* 15, nos. 1–2 (Fall–Winter 1983–1984): 5–6; Benjamin, *Das Passagen-Werk*, ed. Rolf Tiedemann (Frankfurt: Suhrkamp, 1982).

9. See chapter 8 on de Antonio's connection to Daniel Berrigan; de Antonio assisted with the U.S. premiere of the Kipphardt film in 1968– see Steven Bach to de Antonio, May 15, 1968; de Antonio to Nick Hart Williams, December 4, 1972. On documentary theater see Robert Cohen, *Understanding Peter Weiss* (Columbia: University of South Carolina Press, 1993), 84; Peter Weiss, *The Investigation*, trans. Jon Swan and Ulu Grosbard (New York: Atheneum, 1966); Heinar Kipphardt, *In the Matter of J. Robert Oppenheimer: A Play Freely Adapted, on the Basis of Documents*, trans. Ruth Speirs (London: Methuen, 1983); Daniel Berrigan, *The Catonsville Verdict* (Boston: Beacon, 1970).

10. Emile de Antonio, "The Point of View in *Point of Order*," *Film Comment*, Winter 1964, 35–37.

11. Emile de Antonio and Mitch Tuchman, compilers, *Painters Painting: A Candid History of the Modern Art Scene, 1940–1970* (New York: Abbeville, 1984), 16.

12. William Seitz, *The Art of Assemblage*, exhibition catalogue (New York: Museum of Modern Art, 1961), 6; see also Irving Sandler, *New York School: The Painters and Sculptors of the Fifties* (New York: Harper and Row, 1978), 143–47.

13. More experimental applications of this compilation or collage approach include Dusan Makavejev's *Love Affair: Or the Case of the Missing Switchboard Operator* (1967), and Fernado Solanas's *The Hour of the Furnaces* (1966–1968), a Marxist "ideological essay" that even has stopping points marked "Space for Speakers," a concession to audience participation that went far beyond de Antonio's efforts. See Margot Kernan, "Radical Image: Revolutionary Film," *Arts in Society*, Fall 1973, 242–49; on Bruce Baillie see David E. James, *Allegories of Cinema: American Film in the Sixties* (Princeton, N.J.: Princeton University Press, 1989), 159–64; on de Antonio's desire to reach wide audiences, see Marc N. Weiss, "Conversations with Emile de Antonio," *University Review* (New York City), March 1974, 17–19.

14. I am grateful to Dan Streible, who provided invaluable comments on the manuscript of this book, for pointing out why de Antonio might have handled the editing in this fashion.

15. Robert Penn Warren, *All the King's Men* (1946; reprint, New York: Time, 1963), xii.

16. For a straightforward synopsis of the hearings, see Michael Straight, *Trial by Television* (Boston: Beacon, 1954). A transcript of the

selections that appeared in *Point of Order* was published in book form as Emile de Antonio and Daniel Talbot, *Point of Order! A Documentary of the Army-McCarthy Hearings, Produced by Emile de Antonio and Daniel Talbot* (New York: Norton, 1964).

17. Although the credits inform us that the film was born "from an idea by Dan Talbot" and delivered by "editorial director" Emile de Antonio, I am attributing authorship to de Antonio, who was adamant that he alone had imposed both the point and the order in *Point of Order*. Later versions of the film would offer a more accurate list of credits: "*Point of Order*: a film by Emile de Antonio; Emile de Antonio and Daniel Talbot, producers; Elliot Pratt and Henry Rosenberg, executive producers; Robert Duncan, editor; Emile de Antonio, director" (de Antonio to Bals and Lidell).

18. De Antonio to Mike Mauer, January 11, 1978.

19. Martin Walsh discusses Jean-Luc Godard, Dusan Makavejev, and Jean Marie Straub as Brechtian filmmakers in *The Brechtian Aspect of Radical Cinema* (London: BFI, 1981); see also Thomas Elsaesser, "From Anti-Illusionism to Hyperrealism: Bertolt Brecht and Contemporary Film," in Pia Kleber and Colin Visser, eds., *Reinterpreting Brecht: His Influence on Contemporary Drama and Film* (Cambridge, U.K.: Cambridge University Press, 1990), 170–85. On Brecht's ideology in general, see Sergey Tretiakov, "Bert Brecht," *International Literature* (Moscow), May 1937, 60–70, which was reprinted in Peter Demetz, ed., *Brecht: A Collection of Critical Essays* (Englewood Cliffs, N.J.: Prentice Hall, 1962), 16–29; Martin Esslin, *Brecht: The Man and His Work* (Garden City, N.Y.: Anchor, 1961), 124; Eugene Lunn, *Marxism and Modernism: An Historical Study of Lukacs, Brecht, Benjamin, and Adorno* (Berkeley: University of California Press, 1982), 119–27, 250; Peter Brooker, "Key Words in Brecht's Theory and Practice," in Peter Thomson and Glendyr Sacks, eds., *The Cambridge Companion to Brecht* (Cambridge, U.K.: Cambridge University Press, 1994), 185–200. The mention of the "Brechtian aesthetic" appears in Mitch Tuchman, "Freedom of Information," *Film Comment*, July–August 1990, 66.

20. De Antonio, Journals, vol. 4:n.p.; vol. 5:19.

21. Jean Baudrillard, "The Masses: The Implosion of the Social in the Media," *Jean Baudrillard: Selected Writings*, ed. Mark Poster (Palo Alto, Calif.: Stanford University Press, 1988), 206–19.

22. De Antonio, "Notes for Lecture," May 5, 1987.

23. On Brecht's techniques as applied to cinema, see Walsh, *Brechtian Aspect of Radical Cinema*, 130–31; Robert Stam, Robert Burgoyne, and Sandy Flitterman-Lewis, *New Vocabularies in Film Semiotics: Structuralism, Poststructuralism, and Beyond* (New York: Routledge, 1992), 198–99; and "Brecht and a Revolutionary Cinema," a special issue of *Screen* 15, no. 4 (Summer 1974).

24. Kay Johnson and Monika Jensen, "An Interview with Emile de Antonio," *Arts in Society*, Summer–Fall 1973, 209–19.

25. The quotation from *Life of Galileo* appears in Bertolt Brecht, *Plays: Three* (London: Methuen, 1987), 98. I have relied on Herbert Marcuse's definition of liberal ideology from *Negations: Essays in Critical Theory*, trans. Jeremy J. Shapiro (Boston: Beacon, 1968), 11.

26. James Wechsler, "A Love-Letter to Miss Liberty," *New York Post*, January 13, 1964.

27. A note of clarification about the release date of *Point of Order*, which appears as either 1963 or 1964 in various articles about de Antonio. I am using the earlier date for this reason: although the film was not released commercially until January 1964, it received public screenings in the fall of 1963, and the first reviews appeared that November. My research turned up no reason for the delay, if in fact it was delayed.

28. Madeline de Antonio, outline for de Antonio biography, 32.

29. Macdonald's review appears in *Esquire*, November 1963; Sontag is quoted in a press release for de Antonio's penultimate film, *In the King of Prussia* (1983); Gill's review ran in the *New Yorker*, January 18, 1964; Crist spoke on the *Today* program on NBC in New York on January 20, 1964. Cohn is quoted in Madeline de Antonio, undated outline for de Antonio biography, 38; she drew from an unpublished introduction that Cohn wrote for a book, also never published, that Emile de Antonio was writing about McCarthyism in the mid-1970s. Other positive reviews include Bosley Crowther, *New York Times*, January 15, 1964, and January 19, 1964; *Time*, January 17, 1964; *Variety*, September 18, 1963; *Newsweek*, January 20, 1964; *New Republic*, January 25, 1964; *Cue*, January 18, 1964; *Film Comment*, Winter 1964; *New York Daily News*, January 15, 1964; *New York Post*, January 13, 1964, and January 15, 1964; *New York Herald Tribune*, January 15, 1964; *New York World-Telegram and Sun*, January 15, 1964; *London Life*, November 18, 1966. The only negative or mixed reviews I located were *New York Daily News*, January 15, 1964, and the *National Review*, April 21, 1964,

which quotes the *World Telegram* review. Cohn's repeated threats of litigation for defamation are mentioned in a letter from Cohn's attorney, Stephen Hochhauser, to Point Films, June 14, 1963, and a letter from Sam Antar of ABC to de Antonio, March 22, 1968. Cohn's complaint about the "cropped film" appears in Roy Cohn, *McCarthy* (New York: New American Library, 1968), 212.

30. *New York Times*, February 11, 1964; Robert C. Ladendorf, "Resistance to Vision: The Effects of Censorship and Other Restraints on Emile de Antonio's Political Documentaries" (master's thesis, University of Wisconsin–Madison, 1977), 93.

31. De Antonio, Journals, vol. 9:40. See also de Antonio to [Kay Johnson?], n.d., and Warren Steibel to de Antonio, January 31, 1968.

32. The network executive is quoted in the typescript of Ellen Oumano's interview with de Antonio regarding his relationship with Paul Newman; the quote does not appear in the published form of her book, *Film Forum: Thirty-five Top Filmmakers Discuss Their Craft* (New York: St. Martin's, 1985). De Antonio also made a shortened 16mm version of the film for classroom use entitled *Charge and Countercharge* (Cinema Guild, 1968). The film has also been marketed in the home video market under the strange title *McCarthy, Death of a Witch Hunter: A Film of the Era of Senator Joseph R. McCarthy* (MPI Home Video, 1986).

33. When the ever-litigious Roy Cohn learned of the impending broadcast on ABC, he warned the network in a letter dated March 20, 1968, that the film could warrant legal action on the ground that it was a "deceptive presentation." ABC executive Sam Antar conveyed this news to de Antonio in his March 1968 letter, reminding the filmmaker that "If Mr. Cohn should make any claim or bring any action against us involving the broadcast, we shall, of course, look to you to defend and indemnify us pursuant to our agreement dated December 4, 1967."

34. *Variety*, September 18, 1963; Neufeld, "Interview."

35. On the all-too-often neglected differences between direct cinema and cinéma vérité, see Richard Barsam, *Nonfiction Film: A Critical History*, rev. ed. (Bloomington: University of Indiana Press, 1992), 300–303.

36. Perhaps with a hint of rivalry, de Antonio always saved the worst of his scorn for Wiseman. Writing in his journal in the 1970s, de Antonio claimed that *Point of Order* "was a new kind of film[,] not

syrup like Wiseman who is backed by the Ford Foundation and PBS and hence has never really rocked the boat" (vol. 9:30). Cinema verité has generally exhibited a self-reflexivity that direct cinema practitioners avoid; unfortunately, de Antonio and many others have used the two terms interchangeably. On their important differences see Brian Winston, "The Documentary Film as Scientific Inscription," in Michael Renov, ed., *Theorizing Documentary* (New York: Routledge, 1993), 51, in which he contrasts "fly-on-the-wall" detachment of direct cinema with "camera-as-provocateur" stance of cinéma vérité.

37. Gideon Bachmann, "The Frontiers of Realist Cinema," *Film Culture*, nos. 22–23 (Summer 1961): 16; Stephen Mamber, *Cinéma Vérité in America* (Cambridge, Mass.: MIT Press, 1974), 197; both quotes appear in Winston's excellent and relevant chapter, "Documentary Film as Scientific Inscription."

38. Barbara Zheutlin, "The Politics of Documentary: A Symposium," in Alan Rosenthal, ed., *New Challenges for Documentary* (Berkeley: University of California Press, 1988), 230.

39. Thomas Waugh, "Beyond Vérité: Emile de Antonio and the New Documentary of the Seventies," *Jump Cut*, no. 10–11 (Summer 1976): 35.

40. Mari Jo Buhle, Paul Buhle, and Dan Georgakas, eds., *Encyclopedia of the American Left* (New York: Garland, 1990), 529.

41. David E. James, ed., *To Free the Cinema: Jonas Mekas and the New York Underground* (Princeton, N.J.: Princeton University Press, 1992), 4.

42. Waugh, "Beyond Vérité," 35.

43. Jay Leyda, *Films Beget Films* (London: Allen and Unwin, 1964); Jack C. Ellis, *The Documentary Idea: A Critical History of English-Language Documentary Film and Video* (Englewood Cliffs, N.J.: Prentice Hall, 1989), 36.

44. Russell Campbell, *Cinema Strikes Back: Radical Filmmaking in the United States, 1930–1942* (Ann Arbor, Mich.: UMI Research Press, 1982), 21.

45. Ellis, *Documentary Idea*, 79–81.

46. On the conservative ideology of these programs, see Peter C. Rollins, "*Victory at Sea*: Cold War Epic," *Journal of American Culture*, no. 6 (1972): 463–82.

47. Erik Barnouw, *Documentary: A History of the Nonfiction Film*

(New York: Oxford University Press, 1974), 224. See also Thomas Rosteck, "Irony, Argument, and Reportage in Television Documentary: *See It Now* Versus Senator McCarthy," *Quarterly Journal of Speech* 75, no. 3 (August 1989): 277–98.

48. Barnouw, *Documentary*, 227.

49. Waugh offers another explanation for the appeal of de Antonio's work. Writing about *In the Year of the Pig*, Waugh claims that rather than the radicalism I have suggested, de Antonio tapped into a more mainstream, analytical, liberal sensibility. According to Waugh, liberals appreciated the "shrewd, deliberate, cerebral tone" of de Antonio's films, which Waugh describes as a "far cry" from more impassioned leftist films such as Joris Ivens's *The Seventeenth Parallel*. Waugh argues that by the time *In the Year of the Pig* came out in 1969, "American liberals were ready for this cold chronological collage of documents arranged with the artist's customary matter-of-factness and unmediated by any external narration." Because I suspect that de Antonio's films operated on multiple levels and that some overlap existed between liberal and radical perspectives in the sixties, I welcome Waugh's argument and believe it could help explain the appeal of *Point of Order* as well as *Pig*. See Waugh, "Beyond Vérité," 37.

50. Emile de Antonio, Review of Ellen Oumano's *Film Forum*, typescript of article that appeared in *American Film*, November 1985, p. 72.

51. Fredric Jameson, "Postmodernism and Consumer Society," in Hal Foster, ed., *The Anti-Aesthetic* (Port Townsend, Wash.: Bay Press, 1983), 127, quoted in Anne Friedberg, *Window Shopping: Cinema and the Postmodern* (Berkeley: University of California Press, 1993), 1.

52. Roy Cohn, *McCarthy* (New York: New American Library, 1968), 212–13.

53. Jean Baudrillard, "Requiem for the Media," in *For a Critique of the Political Economy of the Sign*, trans. Charles Levin (St. Louis, Mo.: Telos Press, 1981); Baudrillard, "The Masses." On the strategic function of passivity and silence in response to the media, see Baudrillard, *In the Shadow of the Silent Majorities* (New York: Semiotext(e), 1983), 105–9. On the connection of Baudrillard and documentary, see Philip Rosen, "Document and Documentary," in Renov, *Theorizing Documentary*, 58–89; Christopher Hitchens, *For the Sake of Argument: Essays and Minority Reports* (London: Verso, 1993), 220.

54. Barsam, *Nonfiction Film*, 342. In a recent article the film scholar Thomas Doherty expresses the view that this "pathbreaking compilation film" has kept alive in public memory the constitutional drama of the Army-McCarthy hearings. See Thomas Doherty, "*Point of Order!*" *History Today*, August 1998, 33–37.

Chapter 3. Genealogy of an Assassination

1. Emile de Antonio, "I was born in Scranton," typescript, 15. In 1937 Kennedy had overseen one of the most successful freshman spring dances in Harvard history; see Nigel Hamilton, *JFK: Reckless Youth* (New York: Random House, 1992), 175.

2. De Antonio, "I was born in Scranton," 14–15; Journals, vol. 4:7–8, vol. 10:88.

3. De Antonio, "I was born in Scranton," 49.

4. The photo appears in Mark Lane, *Plausible Denial: Was the CIA Involved in the Assassination of JFK?* (New York: Thunder's Mouth Press, 1991).

5. Even the Warren report conceded that "it was no longer possible to arrive at the complete story of the assassination through normal judicial procedures during the trial of the alleged assassin" (Warren Commission, *Report of the President's Commission on the Assassination of President John F. Kennedy* [New York: Associated Press, 1964], vii).

6. Barbie Zelizer, *Covering the Body: The Kennedy Assassination, the Media, and the Shaping of Collective Memory* (Chicago: University of Chicago Press, 1992), 101–20.

7. Early critics of the Warren Commission include Thomas G. Buchanan, *Who Killed Kennedy?* (New York: Putnam, 1964); Edward J. Epstein, *Inquest: The Warren Commission and the Establishment of Truth* (New York: Viking, 1966); Penn Jones, Jr., *Forgive My Grief* (Midlothian, Tex.: Midlothian Mirror, 1966); Sylvia Meagher, "Notes for a New Investigation," *Esquire*, December 1966, 211, and *Accessories After the Fact* (New York: Bobbs-Merrill, 1967); Leo Sauvage, "Oswald in Dallas: A Few Loose Ends," *New York City Reporter*, January 2, 1964, 24–26; Josiah Thompson, *Six Seconds in Dallas* (New York: Geis, 1967); Harold Weisberg, *Whitewash: The Report on the Warren Report* (Hyattstown, Md.: n.p., 1965). See also Mark Lane, *A Citizen's Dissent: Mark Lane Replies* (New York: Holt, Rinehart, and Winston, 1968).

8. Mark Lane, *Rush to Judgment* (New York: Holt, Rinehart, and Winston, 1966), 9.

9. Epstein, *Inquest*, 16.

10. Unlike Zola, however, they would not name the guilty party; Émile Zola, *J'accuse, lettre ouverte au président de la Republique, 13 Janvier 1898* (Paris: Fascquelle, [c. 1957]).

11. De Antonio, Journal, vol. 2:1; "I was born in Scranton," 15–16; de Antonio, notes on the film *Rush to Judgment*, 48, unpublished typescript in the press kit for the film.

12. Lane, *Rush to Judgment*, 5.

13. De Antonio, Journals, vol. 10:5. De Antonio goes on to write, "It was wonderful working with a camera crew," but in the next line he undermined this earnestness with an ironic gibe: "I learned what a bureaucracy can do in the arts."

14. Ibid.

15. This discussion of the film has benefited greatly from a brief unpublished article by Mitch Tuchman, who published several useful articles on de Antonio in the 1970s and 1980s (see bibliography). A copy of the unpublished article is in the de Antonio archive.

16. De Antonio to [Kay Johnson?], September 1971.

17. De Antonio to David Webster, September 27, 1965.

18. De Antonio, Journals, vol. 10:5.

19. Thomas Waugh, "Beyond Vérité: Emile de Antonio and the New Documentary of the Seventies," *Jump Cut*, no. 10–11 (1976): 36.

20. Ibid.

21. De Antonio, Journals, vol. 10:6.

22. Ibid., vol. 2:74; vol. 10:6, 12; for evidence of others who were irked by Schoenman's overprotectiveness, see Ronald W. Clark, *The Life of Bertrand Russell* (London: Cape, 1975), 619.

23. De Antonio to Kay Johnson, January 17, 1972; de Antonio, Journals, vol. 10:7; T. S. Eliot, "Mr. Apollinax," *The Complete Poems and Plays, 1909–1950* (New York: Harcourt Brace Jovanovich, 1980), 17.

24. De Antonio, Journals, vol. 10:8; De Antonio to Kay Johnson, January 17, 1972.

25. De Antonio, Journals, vol. 10:8.

26. "Recorded Interview with Bertrand Russell, 22 November 1965, Present: Ralph Schoenman, Mark Lane, Emile de Antonio,

Richard Stark," typescript, 49; de Antonio to Kay Johnson, January 17, 1972; de Antonio to Anna Rappe, n.d.

27. After Russell's death in 1970, the material was assembled into a twenty-three-minute documentary by the Swedish Broadcasting Company, which the company described as "a wonderful portrait of a wonderful man . . . where funny anecdotes mingled with serious philosophy and an interesting life story." This was done without de Antonio's consent or knowledge (Magnus Roselius to de Antonio, May 22, 1970).

28. De Antonio to Anna Rappe, n.d.; de Antonio, Journals, vol. 10:8; de Antonio to Russell, November 29, 1966; Russell to de Antonio, December 4, 1966, and January 18, 1967.

29. Neither the filmmaker nor the aborted film project is mentioned in biographies of Russell. Nor does the matter appear in the volumes of Russell's letters; Bertrand Russell, "Private Memorandum Concerning Ralph Schoenman," *Black Dwarf* (London), September 5, 1970, 9–16; Clark, *Bertrand Russell*, 634–36.

30. Lane had met the famous musician at a cocktail party, where McCartney asked to read the manuscript of *Rush to Judgment*. See Lane, *Citizen's Dissent*, 56–57.

31. Emile de Antonio and Mark Lane, "*Rush to Judgment*, A Conversation with Mark Lane and Emile de Antonio," *Film Comment*, Fall–Winter 1967, 2. The film was the cover story and focus of this double issue.

32. De Antonio, "I was born in Scranton," 17.

33. De Antonio to Claude Nedjar of NEF Diffusion, September 11, 1972; a one-page typescript of investors in the film appears in the de Antonio archive.

34. *New York Times*, August 23, 1966.

35. De Antonio, Journals, vol. 2:3.

36. Lane, *Citizen's Dissent*, 22.

37. De Antonio, Journals, vol. 2:3.

38. Bernard Weiner, "Radical Scavenging: An Interview with Emile de Antonio," *Film Quarterly*, Fall 1971, 7.

39. Lane, *Citizen's Dissent*, 53–54; de Antonio, Journals, vol. 2:2; Weiner, "Radical Scavenging," 7. The detectives were named F. N. Parks and G. A. Thomason, according to a letter dated April 2, 1967, that de Antonio sent to someone named Max.

40. Benavides was interviewed for *CBS News Inquiry: The Warren*

Commission Report, a four-hour documentary broadcast on June 25–28, 1967. According to Stephen White, Benavides did not make any stunning revelations. Instead, he merely confirmed that he saw Oswald shoot and kill Officer Tippet (*Should We Now Believe the Warren Report?* [New York: Macmillan, 1968], 198).

41. De Antonio identified this woman as Jean Hill (de Antonio to Max, April 2, 1967).

42. Ibid. The person who backed out was Dean Adams Andrews, Jr., a New Orleans attorney whose character figured prominently in Oliver Stone's *JFK* (1991).

43. De Antonio, "I was born in Scranton," 42; U.S. Government Memorandum, case number 89-43-5422, Supervisor Robert P. Gemberling to "SAC [special agent in charge], Dallas," April 6, 1966, notes that de Antonio had contacted Steven F. Wilson, office manager of the Texas School Book Depository. "Wilson requested advice as to whether he should consent to such an interview"; he did not appear in the film. For a photocopy of the memo see de Antonio, Journals, vol. 10:93.

44. De Antonio, "I was born in Scranton," 46–47; Lane claims to have accompanied de Antonio to CBS that evening (Lane, *Citizen's Dissent*, 76–77).

45. De Antonio, "I was born in Scranton," 46–47; de Antonio to David Klinger, vice president, CBS News, June 5, 1966; Klinger to de Antonio, June 17, 1966. More than a decade later Marcia Stein, a publicist for CBS News, claimed that the outtakes had been stored rather than destroyed (Mitch Tuchman, "Kennedy Death Art," *Take Over*, May 1977, 19–22).

46. Gerald R. Ford to Lane and de Antonio, August 11, 1966.

47. David W. Belin, *Final Disclosure: The Full Truth about the Assassination of President Kennedy* (New York: Scribner's, 1988), 31–32. Belin, now billing himself as "counsel to the Warren Commission," does not mention that he appeared with Arlen Specter as a commentator during the BBC premiere of *Rush to Judgment*, a scripted panel discussion that was slanted against the film. Lane presents his perspective on Belin in *Citizen's Dissent*, 61, 67–68, 210.

48. Sales figures quoted in Lane, *Rush to Judgment*, vi; the quotation from Mailer's review appeared in *Washington Post Book Week*, August 18, 1966, while Fred Graham reviewed the book in the *New York*

Times Book Review on the same day; both quotations appear on back cover of the print of *Rush to Judgment* by Thunder's Mouth Press (New York, 1992); de Antonio, Journals, vol. 2:7; Harris poll from *New York Post*, October 2, 1966.

49. To arrange distribution in France, on December 9, 1966, de Antonio composed a "Certificat d'Origine du Film" to serve as formal testimony that *Rush to Judgment* was his idea; apparently he did not share a sense authorship with his coproducer, Lane.

50. De Antonio, Journals, vol. 6:17–21.

51. Michel Foucault, *Power/Knowledge: Selected Interviews and Other Writings, 1972–1977*, ed. and trans. Colin Gordon (New York: Pantheon, 1980), 83; Pauline Marie Rosenau, *Postmodernism and the Social Sciences: Insights, Inroads, and Intrusions* (Princeton, N.J.: Princeton University Press, 1992), 67; Foucault redefines the Nietzschean concept of genealogy; see Friedrich Nietzsche, *On the Genealogy of Morals*, trans. Walter Kaufmann (New York: Random House, 1967).

52. Michel Foucault, "Nietzsche, Genealogy, History," *Language, Countermemory, Practice: Selected Essays and Interviews*, trans. Donald F. Bouchard and Sherry Simon (Ithaca, N.Y.: Cornell University Press, 1977), 139, 153.

53. For a short discussion of the film's "art brut" style, see Louis Marcorelles, "Homo Americanus," *Cinéma 67* (Paris) April 1967, 19–21; de Antonio, notes on the film *Rush to Judgment*, 49.

54. De Antonio, "I was born in Scranton," 41.

55. *New York Daily News*, June 3, 1967.

56. Hans Richter makes this point in *The Struggle for Film*, trans. Ben Brewster (New York: St. Martin's, 1986), 46.

57. Jay Ruby calls this the "uncontrolled" aesthetic in "The Image Mirrored: Reflexivity and the Documentary Film," in Alan Rosenthal, ed., *New Challenges for Documentary* (Berkeley: University of California Press, 1988), 73.

58. Bill Nichols, *Representing Reality: Issues and Concepts in Documentary* (Bloomington: University of Indiana Press, 1991), 3.

59. De Antonio, "I was born in Scranton," 45.

60. David E. James, *Allegories of Cinema: American Film in the Sixties* (Princeton, N.J.: Princeton University Press, 1989), 156–59.

61. Waugh makes this point in "Beyond Verité," 36–37.

62. De Antonio to Louis Marcorelles, March 2, 1969; Brochure, [Canadian] National Film Theatre Retrospective on de Antonio, Montreal, May–July 1974.

63. Lane, *Citizen's Dissent*, 56.

64. Perhaps the most influential recent book on the subject is Gerald Posner's *Case Closed: Lee Harvey Oswald and the Assassination of JFK* (New York: Random House, 1993), though it gives only superficial attention to Lane.

65. Glenn O'Brien, "Inter/View with Emile de Antonio," *Interview*, February 1971, 28–29.

66. See Michel Foucault, ed., *I, Pierre Riviere, Having Slaughtered My Mother, My Sister, and My Brother*, trans. Frank Jellinek (New York: Pantheon, 1975). Foucault's interest in this murder and in power in general is discussed in Edith Kurtzweil, *The Age of Structuralism: Levi-Strauss to Foucault* (New York: Columbia University Press, 1980), 193–226.

67. Michel Foucault, *Discipline and Punish: The Birth of the Prison*, trans. Alan Sheridan (New York: Vintage, 1979). Foucault's discussion of the hidden aspects (the "shadow play" and "impalpable entities") of punitive justice appears on pages 16–17.

68. Michel Foucault, *Foucault Live*, ed. Sylvere Lotringer and trans. John Johnston (New York: Semiotext(e), 1989), 98–99; Barry Smart, *Foucault, Marxism, and Critique* (London: Routledge and Kegan Paul, 1983), 81.

69. See Kurtzweil, *Structuralism*, 222–23, on Foucault's pessimism.

70. De Antonio, notes on the film *Rush to Judgment*, 49.

71. Contract between de Antonio and Geoffrey Crabb, assistant, Purchasing Section, BBC Television Enterprises, November 14, 1966.

72. Lane, *Citizen's Dissent*, 62.

73. De Antonio to Oscar Lowenstein, n.d.

74. Robert C. Ladendorf, "Resistance to Vision: The Effects of Censorship and Other Restraints on Emile de Antonio's Political Documentaries" (master's thesis, University of Wisconsin–Madison, 1977), 108.

75. Lane's highly amusing account of the BBC premiere of the film appears in *Citizen's Dissent*, 58–71.

76. Lane quotes the *Guardian* in *Citizen's Dissent*, 66–67.

77. *New York Times*, June 3, 1967; *New York Post*, June 3, 1967; *New Yorker*, June 17, 1967; *New York Daily News*, June 3, 1967.

78. Ladendorf, "Resistance," 100–103; De Antonio to Oscar Lowenstein, January 21, 1967. Charles Cooper of Contemporary Films, a smaller company than de Antonio had sought, eventually distributed the film in England.

79. "French Respond to Kennedy Plot Film Based on Mark Lane Ideas," *Variety*, March 15, 1967, 7. The film's financial problems are discussed in Ladendorf, "Resistance," 100–102.

80. Anthony Frewin, *The Assassination of John F. Kennedy: An Annotated Film, TV, and Videography, 1963–1992* (Westport, Conn.: Greenwood, 1993), 33; Mark Lane later was involved with two subsequent films based on the assassination: *Executive Action* (David Miller, 1973), and a documentary, *Two Men in Dallas* (Mark Lane, 1977).

81. Lane was an attorney for the cult leader Jim Jones. When the forced suicide occurred, the lawyer talked his way out of the compound and ran into the jungle. One of the few survivors of the disaster that killed hundreds, he then went on to lecture about the experience for a fee of $2,750 on college campuses, prompting *Esquire* and *Mother Jones* to publish articles painting him as a publicity-hungry opportunist. Lane had also sought to prove that the government had assassinated Martin Luther King, Jr. See Tim Reiterman with John Jacobs, *Raven: The Untold Story of the Reverend Jim Jones and His People* (New York: Dutton, 1982), 432, 541–42, 579.

82. De Antonio, Journals, vol. 10:102, 125.

83. De Antonio also discusses Kennedy's rise to political prominence in his autobiographical film, *Mr. Hoover and I*.

84. The first claim is made in Mark Lane's recent work, *Plausible Denial*; the second and third are debunked resoundingly in Noam Chomsky's *Rethinking Camelot: JFK, the Vietnam War, and U.S. Political Culture* (Boston: South End, 1993). Kennedy's hawkish tendencies are described in Marilyn B. Young, *The Vietnam Wars, 1945–1990* (New York: HarperCollins, 1991), 93–95, 97–102.

85. See Christopher Lasch, "The Life of Kennedy's Death," *Harper's*, October 1983, 32–40, for his analysis of the roots of the Camelot myth in the thwarted hopes of intellectuals for social change.

"Sacrificial offering" appears in Thomas Brown, *JFK: History of an Image* (Bloomington: University of Indiana Press, 1988), 104; Theodore H. White, "Camelot, Sad Camelot," *Time*, July 3, 1978, 47.

86. Chomsky, *Rethinking Camelot*, 38.

87. De Antonio and Lane, "*Rush to Judgment*, A Conversation," 2.

88. Frewin, *Assassination of John F. Kennedy*, 32. This book-length filmography includes documentaries, fiction films, home movies, and news footage.

89. Information about the CBS film comes from Frewin, *Assassination of John F. Kennedy*, 31, which uses as its source the network's book version of the series, Stephen White's *Should We Now Believe the Warren Report?* (New York: Macmillan, 1968); the jacket copy for White's book included the quotation about "further doubts." For Frewin's descriptions of the various films mentioned, see 24–33, 98–102, 106–11.

90. In addition to Frewin's filmography, see DeLloyd J. Guth and David R. Wrone, *The Assassination of John F. Kennedy: A Comprehensive Historical and Legal Bibliography, 1963–1979* (Westport, Conn.: Greenwood, 1980).

91. Zelizer, *Covering the Body*, 209, quotes the NBC poll called "Who Killed JFK?" which was commissioned for the *Today Show*, NBC News, February 7, 1992.

92. The writer was Gerald Posner, author of *Case Closed*, quoted in the *New York Times*, November 21, 1993.

93. Ron Rosenbaum, "Taking a Darker View," *Time*, January 13, 1992, 38–40.

94. Norman Mailer, "The Great American Mystery," *Washington Post*, August 28, 1966. The controversy surrounding the film was discussed in the April 1992 issue of *American Historical Review*: Marcus Raskin, "*JFK* and the Culture of Violence," 487–99; Michael Rogin, "*JFK*: The Movie," 500–505; and Robert A. Rosenstone, "*JFK*: Historical Fact/Historical Film," 506–11.

95. A number of Hollywood movies had used the assassination as a theme, including *Executive Action* (1973), based on a story by Mark Lane, *The Parallax View* (1974), and *Taxi Driver* (1976). See Zelizer, *Covering the Body*, 210; Stone's claim appears in Stephen Talbot, "'60s Something," *Mother Jones*, March–April 1991, 47.

96. "Geopolitical aesthetic" is a term from Fredric Jameson, who

wrote about conspiracy films in his essay "Totality as Conspiracy" in *The Geopolitical Aesthetic: Cinema and Space in the World System* (Bloomington: University of Indiana Press, 1993); see also J. Scott Burgeson, "Geopolitical Jazz," *San Francisco Bay Guardian Literary Supplement*, March 1993, 12–13.

97. Stone's modest claim appears on the video box of *JFK*, Warner Home Video, 1992.

98. Lane, *Rush to Judgment*, xxix–xxx. Lane distances his work from Stone's in "Fact or Fiction? The Moviegoer's Guide to the Film *JFK*," which appears in the 1992 reprint of *Rush to Judgment* put out by Thunder's Mouth Press.

99. De Antonio, "I was born in Scranton," 41.

100. In her review of *JFK* in the December 1993 issue of the *Journal of American History*, Barbie Zelizer makes a similar point about the documentary, *Who Shot President Kennedy?* (Robert Richter Productions, 1988) in regard to making us less certain of what happened in Dealey Plaza. Jacques Derrida, "Le Facteur de la Verité," *The Postcard: From Socrates to Freud and Beyond*, trans. Alan Bass (Chicago: University of Chicago Press, 1987), 467–68.

Chapter 4. Vietnam: *In the Year of the Pig*

1. Emile de Antonio to Tim [?], September 27, 1966; de Antonio to William Nee, December 30, 1969.

2. De Antonio to Rev. Emmett Hoffman, March 14, 1966; Hoffman to de Antonio, April 26, 1966; Nancy Oestreich Lurie to de Antonio, October 17, 1966; *Akwesasne Notes* (periodical published by the Mohawk, Cornwall Indian Reserve, Rooseveltown, N.Y.) to de Antonio, November 24, 1969; unnamed English department faculty member, Carleton College, to de Antonio, January 8, 1970; article on White Hawk from *Twin Citian* (Minneapolis, Minnesota), January 1970, 39. Another ambitious project on the Nuremberg trials suffered the same fate as the proposed Native American film; see de Antonio to Louis Marcorelles, March 9, 1965.

3. Form letter from de Antonio on behalf of the Defense Committee of the Catonsville Nine [March 1970].

4. United Press International report, June 28, 1972.

5. In separate books two leading scholars of the Vietnam War, Marilyn Young and Daniel Hallin, have challenged the notion that mainstream American journalists provided a substantive critique of the war during the mid- and late-1960s. Indeed, both scholars revise the standard interpretation of the mainstream media's role in the war in a way that supports de Antonio's perspective, demonstrating that critical print journalists were a minority and critical television journalists were very rare.

Important exceptions did exist. Jonathan Schell wrote two *New Yorker* pieces in the summer of 1967 in which he described the horrors of the war, but he did not draw an explicit moral lesson from the grim reality he had seen, according to Young, *The Vietnam Wars, 1945– 1990* (New York: HarperCollins, 1991), 196. The real exceptions were often far outside the mainstream press. For example, in February 1966, *Ramparts* magazine published "The Whole Thing Was a Lie!" a scathing exposé of the war by David Duncan, a highly decorated Green Beret who had served in Vietnam for eighteen months.

Both Young and Hallin suggest that the mainstream press may have become more critical as the war dragged on, but even as late as 1972 Henry Kissinger could hold a press conference in which he described problems with the peace process and not receive much of a grilling. Young writes: "Another country's press corps might have asked tougher questions, and pressed Kissinger on why negotiations, which had been completed with an agreed text and date for exchange of signatures, were now to be reopened. Instead, the American press basically accepted Kissinger's account of the history of the talks" (276).

Young does not discuss why the myth of media opposition to the war has endured, but I suspect it is because it appeals to both hawks and doves. To the former, the myth provides a convenient scapegoat to explain the U.S. defeat; to the latter, it sustains the belief that "the system worked" because a "free press" helped to bring an unjust war to a halt.

For more on this subject see Daniel Hallin, *The "Uncensored War": Vietnam and the Media* (New York: Oxford University Press, 1980), 147–48, and Young, *The Vietnam Wars*, 193–97, 277.

6. Terry de Antonio, "An In-Depth Talk with Emile de Antonio," *Shantih International Writing*, Winter–Spring 1972, 17.

7. De Antonio to Robert Friedman, September 27, 1974.

8. Bruce Cumings, *War and Television* (New York: Verso, 1992), 85; Compton is quoted in Erik Barnouw, *Tube of Plenty: The Evolution of American Television* (New York: Oxford University Press, 1975), 380.

9. For an account of the Nixon White House's pressure on the media, see Todd Gitlin, *The Whole World Is Watching: Mass Media in the Making and Unmaking of the New Left* (Berkeley: University of California Press, 1980), 277–79.

10. Media support of the official position is demonstrated in Hallin, *"Uncensored War,"* 174. For another summary of television coverage of the war see Charles Montgomery Hammond, Jr., *The Image Decade: Television Documentary, 1965–1975* (New York: Hastings House, 1981), 194–221.

11. De Antonio, Program Notes for [Canadian] National Film Theatre Retrospective, Montreal, May–July 1974; on the effects of television coverage on American viewers, see Michael Arlen, *Living Room War* (New York: Viking, 1969), 112; Joseph Morgenstern, "History Right in the Face," *Newsweek*, November 10, 1969, 108–10.

12. Hollywood was debating the issue of Vietnam indirectly in films such as *M*A*S*H** (1970) and *Patton* (1970), as Douglas Kellner and Michael Ryan show in *Camera Politica: The Politics and Ideology of Contemporary Hollywood Film* (Bloomington: University of Indiana Press, 1988), 197.

13. For a lively discussion of Hollywood's treatment of the Vietnam War, especially *The Green Berets*, see J. Hoberman, "Vietnam: The Remake," in Barbara Kruger and Phil Mariani, eds., *Remaking History* (Seattle: Bay Press, 1989), 175–98; see also Mitch Tuchman, "Celluloid Vietnam," *New Republic*, May 31, 1975, 28–30. For a good analysis of *The Green Berets*, both the best-selling book and the subsequent film, see James S. Olson and Randy Roberts, *Where the Domino Fell: America and Vietnam, 1945–1990* (New York: St. Martin's, 1991), 204–5.

14. On *Why Vietnam?* see David Culbert, ed., *Film and Propaganda in America: A Documentary History* (New York: Greenwood, 1990–1991), document 107, and David E. James, *Allegories of Cinema: American Film in the Sixties*, (Princeton, N.J.: Princeton University Press, 1989), 202; on the required viewing of this film, see Erik Barnouw, *Documentary: A History of the Nonfiction Film* (New York: Oxford University Press, 1974), 272.

15. See Fred Kaplan, *"Vietnam! Vietnam!* An Exclusive Report on

John Ford's Propaganda Documentary for the USIA," *Cinéaste*, Fall 1976, 20–24.

16. Edward W. Said, *Culture and Imperialism* (New York: Knopf, 1993), xi.

17. Russell Ferguson et al., eds., *Discourses: Conversations in Postmodern Art and Culture* (Cambridgte, Mass.: MIT Press, 1990), 91.

18. Thomas J. Slater pointed out the connection between Jones and Huston in "Teaching Vietnam: The Politics of Documentary," in Michael Anderegg, ed., *Inventing Vietnam: The War in Film and Television* (Philadelphia: Temple University Press, 1991), 269–90; on *Victory at Sea*, see Peter C. Rollins, "*Victory at Sea*: Cold War Epic," *Journal of American Culture* 6 (1972): 463–82.

19. De Antonio to George Mucha, October 2, 1967.

20. See Alan Rosenthal, ed., *The Documentary Conscience: A Casebook in Film Making* (Berkeley: University of California Press, 1980), 227.

21. For a brief introduction to nonfiction films on Vietnam, including those seized by U.S. Customs agents, see Barnouw, *Documentary*, 268–75; another useful analysis appears in James, *Allegories of Cinema*, 195–213; I have not considered more obscure experimental films, such as Bruce Baillie's *Quixote* (shot in 1964–1965; edited in 1968), which dealt in part with Vietnam (see James, *Allegories of Cinema*, 159–61).

22. The efforts of younger scholars are noted in James S. Olson, *The Vietnam War: Handbook of Literature and Research* (Westport, Conn.: Greenwood, 1993), 413.

23. De Antonio, Journals, vol. 7:17. On the development of these oppositional tendencies in sixties historiography, see Peter Novick, *That Noble Dream: The "Objectivity Question" and the American Historical Profession* (Cambridge, U.K.: Cambridge University Press, 1988), 372, 407, 416–33, 445, 448, 458. Williams came to prominence in the 1960s with such books as *The Tragedy of American Diplomacy* (Cleveland, Ohio: World, 1959), in which he interpreted U.S. foreign policy as motivated largely by market considerations.

24. De Antonio, "I was born in Scranton," typescript, 18.

25. Schell is described in Colin J. Westerbeck, Jr., "Some Outtakes from Radical Film Making: Emile de Antonio," *Sight and Sound*, Summer 1970, 143.

26. De Antonio, Journals, vol. 6:110–11.

27. De Antonio to Andy Warhol, October 30, 1967.

28. De Antonio, Journals, vol. 6:112.

29. Ibid.

30. Ibid.; see also Westerbeck, "Some Outtakes."

31. De Antonio to William Coblenz, June 26, 1968; de Antonio to Stan [?], n.d., includes the list of limited partners in the film. The list does not include Abby Rockefeller, whose financial involvement is mentioned in Westerbeck, "Some Outtakes," 143.

32. Ellen Oumano, *Film Forum: Thirty-five Top Filmmakers Discuss Their Craft* (New York: St. Martin's, 1985), 196–97; Flaherty's funding of *Louisiana Story* is discussed in Robert Barsam, *The Vision of Robert Flaherty: The Artist as Myth and Filmmaker* (Bloomington: University of Indiana Press, 1988), 99–100.

33. De Antonio, Journals, vol. 6:113; Glenn O'Brien, "Inter/View with Emile de Antonio," *Interview*, February 1971, 28–29.

34. Gary Crowdus and Dan Georgakas, "History Is the Theme of All My Films: An Interview with Emile de Antonio," in Alan Rosenthal, ed., *New Challenges for Documentary* (Berkeley: University of California Press, 1988), 165.

35. De Antonio to Jay Leyda, February 7, 1968.

36. "Radical scavenging" was a phrase de Antonio probably coined; it appears in Westerbeck, "Some Outtakes," 143.

37. Ibid.

38. De Antonio, "I was born in Scranton," 47, quoted in Robert C. Ladendorf, "Resistance to Vision: The Effects of Censorship and Other Restraints on Emile de Antonio's Political Documentaries" (master's thesis, University of Wisconsin–Madison, 1977), 69.

39. De Antonio, Journals, vol. 7:27.

40. De Antonio to Commander Edward F. Roeder, n.d. [March 1968], and June 1, 1968; Roeder to de Antonio, March 14, 1968 (all are quoted in Ladendorf, "Resistance to Vision," 70).

41. Olson, *Vietnam War*, 406; Leo Cawley, "The War about the War," in Linda Dittmar and Gene Michaud, eds., *From Hanoi to Hollywood: The Vietnam War in American Film* (New Brunswick, N.J.: Rutgers University Press, 1990), 74.

42. De Antonio and Marjorie Schell to partners of the Monday Film Production Company, February 1, 1968; Roman Karmen's film was entitled *Vietnam* (1955).

43. De Antonio to George Mucha, November 1, 1967, a copy of which appears in de Antonio, Journals, vol. 10:112; see also 111, 113. A participant in Claes Oldenburg's happenings in the early sixties, Moore was a published poet and college professor who would inspire de Antonio's cinematic foray into the New York art scene, *Painters Painting*.

44. De Antonio, Journals, vol. 10:84.

45. De Antonio, "I was born in Scranton," 7, 48; de Antonio, Journals, vol. 10:85; Ladendorf, "Resistance to Vision," 68–71;

46. De Antonio and Schell to Monday Film partners.

47. Westerbeck, "Some Outtakes."

48. Ladendorf, "Resistance to Vision," 69.

49. De Antonio loathed this film—"It's too easy to laugh at Germans and too easy to make a long film when a short when would have been better" (de Antonio to Peter Biskind, July 18, 1974); the Lord Avon episode is recounted in Ladendorf, "Resistance to Vision," 82–83, based in part on the transcript of an undated BBC newscast (available in the de Antonio archive) and on a letter from de Antonio to Ladendorf, August 26, 1976.

50. De Antonio to Jay Leyda, June 1, 1968.

51. De Antonio to [Kay Johnson?], October 14, 1976; Crowdus and Georgakas, "History Is the Theme."

52. Crowdus and Georgakas, "History Is the Theme," 168.

53. De Antonio is quoted in Hobart College newspaper, an undated clip probably from May 1969.

54. Headlines from two issues of the *San Francisco Express*, February 22, 1968, and May 30, 1968, cited in Todd Gitlin, *The Sixties: Years of Hope, Days of Rage* (New York: Bantam, 1987), 288.

55. De Antonio, Journals, vol. 6:69.

56. The broker's involvement is described in Westerbeck, "Some Outtakes," 143.

57. Sperry, Weinberg, and Kallman, de Antonio's law firm, to Leo Dratfield, Pathé-Contemporary Films, August 7, 1970.

58. Jane Kronholtz to "campus leaders and editors," October 11, 1968.

59. De Antonio to Jill Hoffman, September 22, 1974; de Antonio to Jane Fonda, October 22, 1974. Regarding the Greeks' use of motorcycles or bicycles to shuttle reels of film between theaters, Dan Streible, who

read this book in manuscript form, pointed out that this was "an old practice that says more about de Antonio's lack of understanding about how the film business worked than about how successful the film was in Greece."

60. De Antonio to John Percy, June 20, 1970.

61. Finances tabulated by Ladendorf, "Resistance to Vision," 99.

62. Bernard Weiner, "Radical Scavenging: An Interview with Emile de Antonio," *Film Quarterly*, Fall 1971, 5.

63. Ibid.; the photograph appears in an advertisement for Cine Cienega Art Theatre in Los Angeles in an unidentified newspaper clipping included in the de Antonio archive; de Antonio to Nathan Chianta of Avco Embassy, April 13, 1971, quoted in Ladendorf, "Resistance to Vision," 103, 156.

64. *Chicago Daily News*, September 25, 1969.

65. Ladendorf, "Resistance to Vision," 98–99; de Antonio to Charles Nesson, April 30, 1976.

66. De Antonio to Robert Ladendorf, March 8, 1977, quoted in Ladendorf, "Resistance to Vision," 103, 156.

67. Weiner, "Radical Scavenging," 5; de Antonio to Noam Chomsky, February 16, 1970.

68. *Boston Globe*, March 5, 1969; *New York Times*, November 11, 1969; *Harvard Crimson*, undated clipping, probably from February or March 1969; *New Yorker*, November 15, 1969; *Newsweek*, November 10, 1969; Dwight Macdonald, "A Note on a Relevant Documentary," reprinted in a brochure for the film's distributor, Contemporary Films; *National Review*, December 2, 1969. Other reviews, all laudatory, included *Christian Science Monitor*, February 27, 1969; *Commonweal*, May 9, 1969; *New York City Guardian*, May 10, 1969; *New Statesman* (London), December 6, 1968; *Chicago Daily News*, September 25, 1969. The *Washington Post* is quoted in publicity material that de Antonio released for the film; I have been unable to find the original review.

69. Michael Lee Lanning, *Vietnam at the Movies* (New York: Fawcett Columbine, 1994), 251.

70. De Antonio, "Auteur," typescript, 4.

71. De Antonio to Noam Chomsky, December 25, 1968.

72. Westerbeck, "Some Outtakes."

73. De Antonio and Schell to Monday Film partners.

74. De Antonio, Journals, vol. 7:17.

75. Ibid., vol. 4:29.

76. Reported in a letter from de Antonio and Schell to Monday Film Production Co. investors, November 3, 1969, and in de Antonio, Journals, vol. 4:30–31.

77. Turong Chinh, *The August Revolution* (Hanoi: Foreign Languages Publishing House, 1965); Ho Chi Minh, *A Heroic People* (Hanoi: Foreign Languages Publishing House, 1965).

78. De Antonio to Nguyen Thanh Le, June 30, 1969.

79. Ibid.; de Antonio to Le, September 10, 1969. De Antonio mentions that Newsreel may have executed the project in some fashion. See de Antonio, Journals, vol. 5:13–14.

80. De Antonio to Nguyen Thanh Le, September 10, 1969.

81. De Antonio, Journals, vol. 4:30.

82. De Antonio to Philip Burton, July 16, 1971.

83. Thich Quang Duc was the Buddhist monk whose self-immolation in July 1963 was captured in a photograph that appeared in newspapers around the world.

84. Crowdus and Georgakas, "History Is the Theme," 167.

85. De Antonio to Bernard Weiner, November 23, 1974; at a de Antonio retrospective at the Eighth Street Playhouse in Manhattan in October 1974, *In the Year of the Pig* was paired alternately as a double-feature with both *The Green Berets* and *Paths of Glory* (Stanley Kubrick, 1957) (*New York Post*, October 23, 1974).

86. *Commonweal*, May 9, 1969, 250.

87. De Antonio mentions the response of the Columbia audience in Crowdus and Georgakas, "History Is the Theme," 168.

88. De Antonio, "Interview," *Film Threat*, December 1987, 27.

89. Barbara Correll, "Rem(a)inders of G(l)ory: Monuments and Bodies in *Glory* and *In the Year of the Pig*," *Cultural Critique* 19 (Fall 1991): 143, 145.

90. Ibid., 170–71 n. 3.

91. Brooke Jacobson and Jill Godmilow, "Far from Finished: Deconstructing the Documentary," in Mark O'Brien and Craig Little, eds., *Reimaging America: The Arts of Social Change* (Philadelphia: New Society, 1990), 173–82. On the political ramifications of deconstruction, see Pauline Marie Rosenau, *Postmodernism and the Social Sciences: Insights, Inroads, and Intrusions* (Princeton, N.J.: Princeton University Press, 1992), 161.

92. Cumings, *War and Television*, 82.

93. De Antonio is quoted in Crowdus and Georgakas, "History Is the Theme," 168.

94. *Harvard Crimson*, undated clipping, probably from February or March 1969; Theodor Adorno, *Minima Moralia: Reflections from a Damaged Life*, trans. E. F. N. Jephcott (1951; trans. London: New Left, 1974), 55.

95. *New Statesman*, December 6, 1968.

96. The importance of sound to nonfiction film is not a topic that has been fully explored. One of the few relevant essays is Jeffrey K. Ruoff, "Conventions of Sound in Documentary," in Rick Altman, ed., *Sound Theory, Sound Practice* (New York: Routledge, 1992), 217–34.

97. Pauline Kael, "Blood and Snow," *New Yorker*, November 15, 1969.

98. Steve Addiss and Steven Smolian to de Antonio, August 31, 1968.

99. This information comes from observations by John Atlee, associate producer, collected in a "Review Analysis," December 4, 1968, in the de Antonio archive.

100. Ibid.

101. De Antonio, "Auteur," 4.

102. Studs Terkel to de Antonio, n.d. [1969].

103. De Antonio to Anna-Lena Wibom, June 8, 1971.

104. The Smiths, *Meat Is Murder*, Rough Trade, 1985.

105. Bill Nichols, *Representing Reality: Issues and Concepts in Documentary* (Bloomington: University of Indiana Press, 1991), 48.

106. The Rostow court order is described in *New York Times*, January 4, 1975.

107. Both films are reviewed in Emile de Antonio, "Visions of Vietnam," *University Review*, December 1974; de Antonio to Bernard Weiner, December 15, 1974.

108. De Antonio, Journals, vol. 10:85.

109. De Antonio to Dick Ellison, June 6, 1977.

110. John Coleman, "Reading the News," *New Statesman*, December 6, 1968.

111. As I mentioned in the introduction, Frost's poem appeared originally under the title "And All We Call American," *Atlantic Monthly*, June 1951, but was published as "America Is Hard to See" in Robert

Frost, *In the Clearing* (New York: Holt, Rinehart, and Winston, 1962), 20–23.

112. McCarthy's interest in the title is mentioned in de Antonio to Noam Chomsky, February 16, 1970, and in de Antonio to Jay Leyda, March 30, 1970.

113. De Antonio's comments on this film appear in his Journals, vol. 5:63; de Antonio to Wibom, June 8, 1971; de Antonio to Hercules [Bellville], August 17, 1969; for more comments on this film, see Terry de Antonio, "An In-Depth Talk," 19.

114. The $75,000 film received $5,000 from Anne L. Peretz; part of the budget included a $5,000 fee and 40 percent of the profits for McCarthy as a "consultant"; some information on the finances of this project can be found in Ladendorf, "Resistance to Vision," 44–45.

115. De Antonio to Jim and Alice Hoge, August 5, 1969.

116. Stevenson is quoted in Anonymous [no author given], *U.S. Senator Eugene J. McCarthy* (Minneapolis, Minn.: Gilbert Publishing, 1964), 2.

117. Joan Mellen, "America Is Hard to See," *Cinéaste*, Spring 1971, 28.

118. Ibid.; Deac Rossell, "From Joe to Eugene: To Hell and Back," *Boston After Dark*, June 2, 1970, 3.

119. De Antonio to Anna-Lena [Rappe?], August 7, 1972.

120. The description of Gibbon comes from Friedrich Meinecke, *Historicism: The Rise of a New Historical Outlook*, trans. J. E. Anderson (London: Routledge and Kegan Paul, 1972), 192.

121. Though Gibbon wrote often in England, the last three volumes of *Decline and Fall of the Roman Empire*, as well as some of his other writing, were composed in Lausanne, Switzerland. De Antonio's admiration for him was immense. See de Antonio, Journals, vol. 7:144–45.

122. Kael, "Blood and Snow," 177.

123. De Antonio, Journals, vol. 7:146.

124. De Antonio to Louis Marcorelles, February 4, 1969.

125. De Antonio to Weiner, December 15, 1974.

126. De Antonio, Journals, vol. 7:144.

127. Ibid.

128. George Santayana, *Character and Opinion in the United States* (New York: Scribner's, 1920), 187–88; Santayana "means very

much indeed to people like ourselves who[se] backgrounds are similar to his, even if our talents are infinitely smaller" (de Antonio to Ursula de Antonio, September 23, 1949).

129. De Antonio, Journals, vol. 10:82.

130. Ibid.; Alec Morgan, "But This Is Where I Belong" (interview with de Antonio), *Filmnews*, March 1981, 7–9.

131. See, for example, Gibbon's reaction to the French Revolution in Dero A. Saunder's introduction to Edward Gibbon, *The Decline and Fall of the Roman Empire* (New York: Penguin, 1980), 20.

Chapter 5. The Incursion into Richard Milhous Nixon

1. Emile de Antonio, Journals, vol. 4:71–73; vol. 5:6, 10, 20; vol. 10:146–47; Irene Stepash, "Emile de Antonio: For the Record," *East Village Eye*, November 1979, 13; *Rutland (Vermont) Herald*, November 20, 1977.

2. See Troy R. Johnson, *The Occupation of Alcatraz Island: Indian Self-Determination and the Rise of Indian Activism* (Urbana: University of Illinois Press, 1996).

3. De Antonio to Jerry Voorhis, June 29, 1970.

4. De Antonio, Journals, vol. 4:73; vol. 7:108.

5. *Liberation News Service*, April 15, 1972, 13.

6. Talbot managed to do just that several years later (de Antonio, Journals, vol. 10:146). De Antonio later realized that the Checkers speech was not copyrighted; with characteristic aplomb he sent his stolen copy to Washington, seeking to place the copyright in his name, but was turned down. Nonetheless, his distributor, Dan Talbot of New Yorker films, marketed the thirty-minute speech, unedited, with the rest of de Antonio's films, from which they derived a small amount of royalties.

7. Jerry Parker, "The Incursion into Richard M. Nixon," *Newsday*, December 14, 1971, 5.

8. De Antonio, Journals, vol. 10:146; Emile de Antonio and Albert Maher, "Chasing Checkers by Richard M. Nixon," *New York Free Press*, September 26–October 2, 1968; de Antonio to Kay [?], archivist, State Historical Society of Wisconsin, n.d.

9. *Rutland (Vermont) Herald*, November 20, 1977.

10. Parker, "Incursion into Richard M. Nixon."

11. De Antonio and Maher, "Chasing Checkers."

12. Parker, "Incursion into Richard M. Nixon"; Barbara Garson, *Macbird!* (New York: Grove, 1967).

13. Alan Lelchuk, "On Satirizing Presidents: An Interview with Philip Roth," *Atlantic*, December 1971, 81–88.

14. Gore Vidal, *An Evening with Richard Nixon, by Gore Vidal (and others)* (New York: Random House, 1972); Eric Lax, *Woody Allen: A Biography* (New York: Knopf, 1991), 118–20; Philip Roth, *Our Gang* (New York: Random House, 1971). Guston is quoted in Parker, "Incursion into Richard M. Nixon," p. 3.

15. George Orwell, "Politics and the English Language," in Denys Val Baker, ed., *Modern British Writing* (New York: Vanguard, 1947), 206.

16. Mitch Tuchman, "Introductory Notes—Emile de Antonio," unpublished typescript, de Antonio archive.

17. *Boston Globe*, February 25, 1971.

18. Lelchuk, "On Satirizing Presidents," 81.

19. Parker, "Incursion into Richard M. Nixon."

20. De Antonio to Accounting Dept., Camera [indistinct], March 4, 1970.

21. De Antonio to Richard Saxon, June 2, 1970.

22. De Antonio to Stewart R. Mott, August 5, 1970.

23. De Antonio to Frank Noonan, October 28, 1971.

24. De Antonio to Martin Peretz, November 25, 1970, and December 8, 1970.

25. "People," *Time*, September 23, 1974, 59; de Antonio to Laura Rockefeller Case, July 1, 1971.

26. De Antonio to Richard Cataldo, February 22, 1972; promissory note between Whittier Film Corp. and Laura Rockefeller Case for $11,000 loan; de Antonio to attorney David A. Strawbridge, December 8, 1971, with a note to Laura Rockefeller Case; Strawbridge to de Antonio, May 4, 1972.

27. De Antonio to Judge Morton G. Wray, October 8, 1970; de Antonio to Steve [?], June 1, 1970.

28. De Antonio to George C. Wallace, September 9, 1970; de Antonio to Robert M. Bowick, November 6, 1970.

29. Stephen E. Ambrose, *Nixon: The Education of a Politician, 1913–1962* (New York: Simon and Schuster, 1987), 209–19.

30. De Antonio to Ring Lardner, Jr., August 10, 1970; Lardner to

de Antonio, August 20, 1970; de Antonio to Arnold A. Hutschnecker, January 30, 1971; Eli S. Chesen, *President Nixon's Psychiatric Profile: A Psychodynamic-Genetic Interpretation* (New York: Wyden, 1973).

31. Ambrose, *Nixon: Education*, 70; Fawn Brodie, *Richard Nixon: The Shaping of His Character* (New York: Norton, 1981), 289.

32. Garry Wills, "Nixon's Dog," *Esquire*, August 1969, 40–52; 91–95.

33. De Antonio believed the Checkers speech to be the key to Nixon's career–in part because he now had "just about the only print that got away from our President" (de Antonio to Editor, Houghton Mifflin, June 17, 1970); Garry Wills, *Nixon Agonistes: The Crisis of the Self-Made Man* (Boston: Houghton Mifflin, 1970).

34. De Antonio to Garry Wills, June 17, 1970; de Antonio to Editor, Houghton Mifflin, June 17, 1970; two letters from Wills to de Antonio, n.d.; the Reverend John F. Cronin to de Antonio, December 30, 1970.

35. De Antonio to Madeline de Antonio, June 17, September 8, and November 12, 1970.

36. Vincent Canby, "Film: Satirical Documentary on Nixon," *New York Times*, September 24, 1971.

37. De Antonio to Voorhis, June 29 and July 23, 1970; Voorhis to de Antonio, June 12, 1970.

38. Typescript of de Antonio's interview with Maurice Rapf's screenwriting class at Dartmouth College, October 31, 1977, 29; autographed transcript of McGinniss interview by de Antonio, 1971, n.d., 1.

39. Jack D. Haley to de Antonio, July 13, 1970; de Antonio to Ted Koppel, October 29, 1970; de Antonio to William Evans, February 8, 1971; Herbert Block, *Herblock Special Report* (New York: Norton, 1974), 63; Jean Bonieskie to de Antonio, July 15, 1970; de Antonio to Joseph Pulitzer, Jr., July 24, 1970; Raymond Shapiro [?] to de Antonio, May 9, 1972.

40. Emile de Antonio, "Visions of Vietnam," *University Review* (New York City), December 1974.

41. Robert C. Ladendorf, "Resistance to Vision: The Effects of Censorship and Other Restraints on Emile de Antonio's Political Documentaries" (master's thesis, University of Wisconsin–Madison, 1977), 94.

42. De Antonio to Peter [?], May 6, 1974.

43. *Chicago Sun-Times*, October 4, 1971.

44. *Washington (D.C.) Evening Star*, June 18, 1971.

45. *Boston Globe*, August 3, 1971.

46. De Antonio to Marilynn Casselman, June 28, 1971.

47. Molière, *Tartuffe, and Other Plays by Molière* (New York: Penguin, 1967), 253.

48. Leticia Kent, "Eat, Drink, and Make 'Millhouse,' " *New York Times*, October 17, 1971.

49. De Antonio, Journals, vol. 7:172.

50. See Stephen Schlesinger and Stephen Kinzer, *Bitter Fruit: The Untold Story of the American Coup in Guatemala* (Garden City, N.Y.: Doubleday, 1982), 65–77, 221–22.

51. The connection between Nixon's speech and the Knute Rockne film had been made earlier by Gore Vidal in "The Late Show" in the *New York Review of Books*, September 12, 1968, 8. My summary of the film's humorous episodes was influenced by the most perceptive review of the film: Bernard Weiner's "Millhouse: A White Comedy," *Sight and Sound: International Film Quarterly*, Spring 1972, 113.

52. Bill Nichols, *Representing Reality: Issues and Concepts in Documentary* (Bloomington: University of Indiana Press, 1991), 45.

53. William F. Buckley, Jr., "Leave Your Wits at the Entrance," *New York Times*, October 31, 1971.

54. Berel Lang and Forrest Williams, eds., *Marx and Art: Writings in Aesthetics and Criticism* (New York: McKay, 1972), 7.

55. Darvo Suvin, "The Mirror and the Dynamo," in Lee Baxandall, ed., *Radical Perspectives in the Arts* (Middlesex, U.K.: Pelican, 1972), 68–88.

56. A transcript of *Millhouse* was published as an insert in the Folkways LP soundtrack for the film.

57. De Antonio to Michelle [?], May 8, 1971.

58. Ladendorf, "Resistance to Vision," 95.

59. Ibid., 96.

60. De Antonio, Journals, vol. 10:69; Jean W. Ross, interview with de Antonio (March 8, 1985), *Contemporary Authors*, vol. 117 (Detroit: Gale Press, 1986), 97–99.

61. Myron L. Tweed to de Antonio, September 19, 1972.

62. Claire Harrison Associates, Inc., "Itinerary for de Antonio," October 6–7, 1971.

63. Glenn O'Brien, "Inter/View with Emile de Antonio," *Interview*, February 1971, 29; Richard D. Kuratli to New Yorker Films, December

3, 1971; Gary Arnold, " 'Millhouse': Equal Time for Milhous?" [source unknown], n.d. Nowhere does de Antonio make clear which Los Angeles papers refused to print the Levine drawing.

64. Canby, "Film"; Martin F. Nolan, "The Many Lives and Laughs of 'Millhouse,'" *Boston Globe*, August 3, 1971; Jay Cocks, "Minor Surgery," *Time*, October 18, 1971, 87.

65. John Coleman, "Run of the Milhaus [*sic*]," *New Statesman*, October 27, 1972; Canadian Film Archives, National Film Theater of Canada, Bulletin #15, April 1972; Clyde Gilmour, "Movie Destroys Nixon's New Image," *Toronto Star*, March 11, 1972; Noel Taylor, "Film Anti-Nixon Show," *Ottawa Citizen*, May 1, 1972.

66. Doc Bacon, "Venom for Our Leaders," *San Francisco Examiner*, October 24, 1971.

67. Stephen Koch, "Nixonart," *New York World*, August 1, 1972, 76; Canadian Film Archives, Bulletin #15.

68. Roger Ebert, " 'Millhouse' Suits the Old Nixon Strategy," *Chicago Sun-Times*, October 22, 1971.

69. James A. Wechsler, "On Whom Is the Joke?" *New York Post*, September 29, 1971, 31.

70. *Village Voice*, September 30, 1971.

71. Parker, "Incursion into Richard M. Nixon," 5.

72. The Democratic National Committee's interest in *Millhouse* is described in Gary Crowdus and Dan Georgakas, "History Is the Theme of All My Films: An Interview with Emile de Antonio," in Alan Rosenthal, ed., *New Challenges for Documentary* (Berkeley: University of California Press, 1988), 173.

73. Donna San Antonio to de Antonio, n.d. [1972]; Maria Jolas to de Antonio, January 31, 1972; de Antonio to Jolas, February 2, 1972.

74. De Antonio to the Oxford University Union, November 7, 1978.

75. J. Anthony Lukas, *Nightmare: The Underside of the Nixon Years* (New York: Viking, 1973), 13; William A. Dobrovis et al., eds., *The Offenses of Richard Milhous Nixon: A Guide for the People of the United States* (New York: Times Book Co., 1973), 37; Stephen E. Ambrose, *Nixon: The Triumph of a Politician, 1962–1972* (New York: Simon and Schuster, 1989), 273. William Safire, *Before the Fall: An Inside View of the Pre-Watergate White House* (Garden City, N.Y.: Doubleday, 1975), 166.

76. Congressional Quarterly, *Watergate: Chronology of a Crisis*

(Washington, D.C.: Congressional Quarterly, 1975), 153. The memo on political enemies can be found in U.S. House of Representatives, *Statement of Information: Hearings Before the Committee on the Judiciary*, 93d Cong., 2d sess., May–June 1974, book 7, page 95.

77. Lukas, *Nightmare*, 12–13.

78. U.S. Senate, *Report of Proceedings, Hearing Held Before Select Committee on Presidential Campaign Activities*, 93d Cong., 1st sess., S. Res. 60–General Investigation, March 23, 1974.

79. Len Colodny and Robert Gettlin, *Silent Coup: The Removal of a President* (New York: St. Martin's, 1991), 96.

80. Tony Ulasewicz, *The President's Private Eye* (Westport, Conn.: Macsam, 1990), 245, 270.

81. John W. Dean III, *Blind Ambition: The White House Years* (New York: Simon and Schuster, 1976), 40.

82. *Washington Post*, June 18, 1971. The various White House memoranda related to *Millhouse* were published in U.S. House, *Statement of Information*, book 8, pages 18, 183–94.

83. Caulfield's assessment appears in a memo he wrote to John Dean dated August 10, 1971, and his comment about de Antonio and O'Brien appears in a memo he wrote to Dean dated August 25, 1971; both may be found in Senate, *Report of Proceedings*.

84. Although no causal link to Caulfield's request has been established, both de Antonio and his corporation were audited in 1972 and 1973. See de Antonio, Journals, vol. 9:49; district director, Internal Revenue Service, Dept. of the Treasury, to de Antonio, July 5, 1974. The information on Caulfield comes from memos he wrote to John Dean dated August 10, October 13, and October 15, 1971, copies of which are in the de Antonio archive.

85. Dean, *Blind Ambition*, 40.

86. Roger Bainbridge, "RCMP Revelations Called 'Predictable,'" article clipped from unidentified Canadian newspaper, n.d. [1971].

87. Bernard Weiner, "'Millhouse: A White Comedy' and a Real Political Bruiser," *San Francisco Examiner*, August 22, 1971.

88. De Antonio, Journals, vol. 6:69.

89. De Antonio was remarkably skeptical of mainstream journalists who took on the Washington establishment. "When you write [like Woodward and Bernstein] and tear away a few of the veils, getting rich in the process, you prove one thing: Horatio Alger, the American Dream."

De Antonio considered them as an especially hypocritical part of the same corrupt system that created Nixon, and with even more venom than usual, he described the press and the politicians as engaged in a "giant circle jerk" (De Antonio, "De Antonio Blasts *Prez's Men*," *Yipster Times*, May 1976, 20).

90. De Antonio to the Oxford University Union, November 7, 1978. See also Journals, vol. 10:126.

91. John Updike, *Hugging the Shore: Essays and Criticism* (New York: Vintage, 1983), 333–34; Ginsburg is quoted in David E. James, *Allegories of Cinema: American Film in the Sixties* (Princeton, N.J.: Princeton University Press, 1989), 166.

92. Lelchuk, "On Satirizing Presidents," 88.

Chapter 6. Art, Politics, and *Painters Painting*

1. *Millhouse: A White Comedy* (1971) was the sixth de Antonio film to be released because it interrupted the production of *Painters Painting* (1972), begun in 1969.

2. The only study of some aspects of de Antonio's early "political films" excludes *Painters Painting* from discussion. See Robert C. Ladendorf, "Resistance to Vision: The Effects of Censorship and Other Restraints on Emile de Antonio's Political Documentaries" (master's thesis, University of Wisconsin–Madison, 1977).

3. John Perrault, "Art," *Village Voice*, March 29, 1973, 32.

4. De Antonio to Robert Ladendorf, December 17, 1977.

5. Tanya Neufeld, "An Interview with Emile de Antonio," *Artforum*, March 1973, 81; Robert Smithson is quoted in "The Artist and Politics: A Symposium," *Artforum*, September 1970, 35–39; Marc N. Weiss, "Emile de Antonio," *Film Library Quarterly* 7, no. 2 (1974); Emile de Antonio, "The Agony of the Revolutionary Artist," *Northwest Passage* (Washington), May 24, 1971, 7.

6. Terry Moore was his fourth wife. His third marriage, to Lois Long, had lasted just a few years in the late 1950s.

7. See Christine Palamidessi, "A Talk with Emile de Antonio," *New Video Magazine*, Winter 1984, 68.

8. Geldzahler's fee is described as part of the budget for *Painters Painting* in a letter from de Antonio to Frank Stella, November 29, 1969.

9. De Antonio, typescript proposal for *Painters Painting*, 1.

10. Emschwiller had made both art films–*Fusion* (1967), *Image, Flesh, and Voice* (1969)–and films on art such as *Art Scene U.S.A.* (1966), one of several he made for the U.S. Information Agency. He also had experience in working on television documentaries such as *The Opinion Makers* (1964). The other members of the *Painters Painting* crew were Mary Lampson, editor and sound; Marc Weiss, assistant camera operator; Tanya Neufeld, graphics; Nancy Ogden, assistant. The loan is described in letters from de Antonio to Stella, November 29, 1969, and September 5, 1972.

11. Emile de Antonio and Mitch Tuchman, compilers, *Painters Painting: A Candid History of the Modern Art Scene, 1940–1970* (New York: Abbeville, 1984), 21.

12. Ibid.

13. Ibid., 22.

14. Willem de Kooning, *Sketchbook 1: Three Americans* (New York: Time, 1960), 6–10, quoted in Maurice Tuchman, ed., *New York School: The First Generation* (Greenwich, Conn.: New York Graphics Society, 1971), 50.

15. T. S. Eliot, "Tradition and the Individual Talent," *Selected Prose of T. S. Eliot*, ed. Frank Kermode (New York: Harcourt Brace Jovanovich, 1975), 37–44.

16. Greenberg's "brilliance" appears in a letter from de Antonio to Anna-Lena [Hultén], August 7, 1972.

17. Ibid.

18. De Antonio, Journals, vol. 10:7; Palamidessi, "Talk with Emile de Antonio," 68; de Antonio and Tuchman, *Painters Painting*, 30.

19. De Antonio, Journals, vol. 4:67; vol. 5:35; vol. 7:75, 81; vol. 10:41; de Antonio, typescript proposal for *Painters Painting*, 2; de Antonio to Clyfford Still, April 9, 1970.

20. George Avakian to de Antonio, February 27 and November 11, 1970; the Cage film is mentioned in de Antonio to Lars [?], n.d. [1983]. Unfortunately, I have been unable to determine whether this short film went past the planning stage, for no record of it seems to exist. Because of this, I have elected not to include it in the filmography at the end of this book.

21. Jasper Johns to author, March 7, 1994.

22. Transcription of interviews made by de Antonio's crew in preparation for editing *Painters Painting*, 313.

23. De Antonio to Anna-Lena [Hultén], August 7, 1972.

24. E. J. Vaughn, "*Painters Painting*: An Unprecedented Art Historical Document by Emile de Antonio," unpublished manuscript in the de Antonio archive, 1973; Neufeld, "Interview with Emile de Antonio." Vaughn's manuscript was completed in September 1973. Although I am not certain about the origin of the article or whether it was written for a particular publication, I can say that it seems not to have been published; the usual indexes carry no record of such an article, which can be found in manuscript form in the de Antonio archive in Madison, Wisconsin.

25. De Antonio and Tuchman, *Painters Painting*, 119.

26. De Antonio called this artwork "the painting of the corporation" in the "I was born in Scranton," typescript, 35.

27. For Stella's claim that a picture refers only to itself, see Irving Sandler, *American Art of the 1960s* (New York: Harper and Row, 1988), 8.

28. Erika Doss, *Benton, Pollock, and the Politics of Modernism: From Regionalism to Abstract Expressionism* (Chicago: University of Chicago Press, 1990), 346.

29. Richard Kostelanetz, *Esthetics Contemporary* (Buffalo, N.Y.: Prometheus, 1989), 208.

30. *Daily Cardinal* (University of Wisconsin–Madison), March 1, 1976.

31. Newman is quoted in Paul Wood et al., eds., *Modernism in Dispute: Art Since the Forties* (New Haven, Conn.: Yale University Press, 1993), 155.

32. *New York Times*, January 7, 1973.

33. Irving Sandler, *The New York School: The Painters and Sculptors of the Fifties* (New York: Harper and Row, 1978), 19.

34. Doss, *Benton, Pollock, and the Politics of Modernism*, 341; Motherwell is quoted in Frances K. Pohl, *Ben Shahn: New Deal Artist in a Cold War Climate, 1947–1954* (Austin: University of Texas Press, 1989), 58.

35. William C. Seitz, *Art in the Age of Aquarius, 1955–1970* (Washington, D.C.: Smithsonian Institution Press, 1992), 168. Seitz offers an informative essay on the politicization of art (pp. 167–84).

36. Hilton Kramer, "Artists and the Problem of 'Relevance,' " *New York Times*, May 4, 1969.

37. See Irving Sandler, "The Artist as Political Activist," *American Art of the 1960s*, 292–302.

38. The art historian Benjamin Buchloh is quoted in Charles Harrison and Paul Wood, "Modernity and Modernism Reconsidered," in Wood et al., eds., *Modernism in Dispute*, 229; "Artist and Politics: A Symposium," *Artforum*, March 1973, 81. Younger critics tended to support this change of attitude, much to the dismay of conservative critics such as Hilton Kramer, who was not interested in assaying "the visual equivalent of Rock" music (Kramer, *The Age of the Avant-Garde* [New York: Farrar, Straus, and Giroux, 1973], 500).

39. On postmodernism and art, see Wood et al., *Modernism in Dispute*, 237–56.

40. Weiss, "Emile de Antonio," 30.

41. De Antonio, Journals, vol. 5:3.

42. Alec Morgan, "But This Is Where I Belong," *Filmnews*, March 1981, 7.

43. Bernard Weiner, "Radical Scavenging: An Interview with Emile de Antonio," *Film Quarterly*, Fall 1971, 14; de Antonio, Journals, vol. 7:98.

44. De Antonio, "Agony of the Revolutionary Artist," 7; de Antonio, "I was born in Scranton," 35.

45. De Antonio, Journals, vol. 7:63.

46. De Antonio, "Agony of the Revolutionary Artist"; de Antonio to Anna-Lena [Hultén], August 7, 1972.

47. De Antonio to Robert Ladendorf, December 17, 1977; de Antonio, Journals, vol. 5:63.

48. Auden is quoted in Arthur C. Danto, *The Philosophical Disenfranchisement of Art* (New York: Columbia University Press, 1986), 1; on the limitations of political art, see Robert Hughes, *The Shock of the New: Art and the Century of Change*, rev. ed. (London: BBC Publications, 1991), 108–11.

49. On Hegel's position see Terry Eagleton, *Marxism and Literary Criticism* (Berkeley: University of California Press, 1976), 73; in regard to Schopenhauer see Danto, *Philosophical Disenfranchisement of Art*, 10, 25; on the connection to Sartre, see Sandler, *New York School*, 27, and Dore Ashton, *The New York School: A Cultural Reckoning* (New York: Viking, 1973), 181–82; Theodor Adorno, "Commitment," in Andrew Arato and Eike Gebhardt, eds., *The Essential Frankfurt*

School Reader (New York: Continuum, 1985), 398; on Greenberg see Donald B. Kuspit, *Clement Greenberg: Art Critic* (Madison: University of Wisconsin Press, 1979), 97; see also Meyer Schapiro, "The Liberating Quality of Avant-Garde Art," *Art News*, September 1957, 32.

50. De Antonio, Journals, vol. 9:64; his reading of recent Marcuse can be inferred from a letter de Antonio wrote to Jeremy Cott, April 9, 1970; "radical subjectivity" is quoted in Pauline Johnson, *Marxist Aesthetics* (London: Routledge and Kegan Paul, 1984), 110; for clarification of Marcuse's position see Barry Katz, *Herbert Marcuse and the Art of Liberation* (London: Verso, 1982), 189–205.

51. De Antonio and Tuchman, *Painters Painting*, 34; Weiss, "Emile de Antonio," 30.

52. Janet Wolff, *Aesthetics and the Sociology of Art* (Boston: Allen and Unwin, 1983), 42–45; Edward W. Said, *Culture and Imperialism* (New York: Knopf, 1993), 41; Serge Guilbaut, *How New York Stole the Idea of Modern Art* (Chicago: University of Chicago Press, 1983). Guilbaut's claims are seriously questioned in a review by Casey Blake in *Telos*, no. 62 (Winter 1984–1985): 211–17.

53. Said, *Culture and Imperialism*, 13–14.

54. Nicolas Calas, "The Enterprise of Criticism," *Art in the Age of Risk* (New York: Dutton, 1968), 139–42, summarized in Kuspit, *Clement Greenberg*, 18.

55. De Antonio to Jeremy Cott, April 9, 1970; see Dave Laing, *The Marxist Theory of Art* (Atlantic Highlands, N.J.: Humanities Press, 1978); on de Antonio's dislike of Marxist aesthetics, see Alec Morgan, "But This Is Where I Belong"; Weiss, "Emile de Antonio," 30.

56. See Hal Foster, ed., *The Anti-Aesthetic* (Seattle: Seattle Bay Press, 1983).

57. Sally Banes, *Greenwich Village 1963: Avant-Garde Performance and the Effervescent Body* (Durham, N.C.: Duke University Press, 1993), 7.

58. Jean Baudrillard, *For a Critique of the Political Economy of the Sign*, trans. Charles Levin (St. Louis, Mo.: Telos Press, 1981); Harrison and Wood, "Modernity and Modernism Reconsidered," 237–56. On postmodernism's inability to be "affirmative" or accept the idea of "art as truth," see Stanley Aronowitz, *Dead Artists, Live Theories, and Other Cultural Problems* (New York: Routledge, 1994), 41–42.

59. Said, *Culture and Imperialism*, 57.

60. De Antonio, Journals, vol. 5:3.

61. De Antonio, Journals, vol. 7:68, 113.

62. De Antonio, Journals, vol. 9:21; vol. 5:22.

63. Castelli noted his high regard for de Antonio when I interviewed the art dealer, March 14, 1994.

64. Tuchman, rejected typescript introduction to *Painters Painting*, 3; De Antonio and Tuchman, *Painters Painting*, 26; Tom Wolfe, *The Painted Word* (New York: Farrar, Straus, and Giroux, 1975). On de Antonio's dislike of Wolfe's book, see his Journals, vol. 10:45.

65. Richard Barsam, *Nonfiction Film: A Critical History*, rev. ed. (New York: Dutton, 1973; rev. ed., Bloomington: University of Indiana Press, 1992), 345 (page citation is to revised edition).

66. I am grateful to the film historian Dan Streible for alerting me to the existence of the relevant films by Resnais and Clouzot. The short films are Lane Slate's *Jasper Johns* (1966) and *Robert Rauschenberg* (1966) (Leo Castelli also appears in the latter); Paul Falkenberg and Hans Namuth's *Jackson Pollock* (1951) and *Willem de Kooning: The Painter* (1966); Robert Snyder's *A Glimpse of de Kooning* (1961); Warren Forma's *The Americans: Three East Coast Artists at Work* (1962), in which Hoffman appears; and *Art of the Sixties*, a thirty-minute program produced for WCBS-TV in 1967 that features de Kooning, Rauschenberg, Pollock, and Newman. A useful bibliography for this rarely discussed topic is the Canadian Center for Films on Art, *Films on Art: A Source Book* (New York: Watson-Guptill, 1977). For a more analytical discussion see Barsam, *Nonfiction Film*, 295–96, 353–55.

67. Barsam, *Nonfiction Film*, 242.

68. De Antonio, Journals, vol. 4:67.

69. De Antonio and Tuchman, *Painters Painting*, 24.

70. The academic was E. J. Vaughn, an art and film historian.

71. Tuchman is quoted in program notes for a de Antonio retrospective at the Sheldon Film Theater, University of Nebraska–Lincoln, 1977.

72. De Antonio, Journals, vol. 10:28; Newman's delight is described in de Antonio to Annalee Newman, August 26, 1970; Geldzahler is quoted in the brochure advertising de Antonio's films as part of the Museum of Modern Art Circulating Film Library; Warhol is quoted in Palamidessi, "A Talk with Emile de Antonio." For mainstream reviews of the film, see *New York Times*, January 7 and March 29, 1973; *San Francisco*

Examiner, May 3, 1973. Stanley Kauffmann's review appeared in the *New Republic*, March 17, 1973.

73. Grace Glueck, "Wishes to Build Some Dreams On," *New York Times*, January 7, 1973.

74. *Village Voice*, March 29, 1973, 32.

75. De Antonio, Journals, vol. 9:9.

76. Irving Howe, *Decline of the New* (New York: Harcourt, Brace, and World, 1970), 214, quoted in Sandler, *New York School*, 285.

77. De Antonio to [Edith] Sorel, December 14, 1971.

78. "A ripoff of *Painters Painting*," he scrawled on the invitation to the opening of the Diamonstein film at the Leo Castelli Gallery on January 22, 1980.

79. De Antonio to Arnold Glimcher, April 16, 1985. The contract between de Antonio and Castelli, dated June 20, 1985, is on the letterhead of the Andrew Wylie Agency; information about de Antonio's decision to abandon the book is from my interview with Leo Castelli.

80. The *Painters Painting* book was not the first one based on a de Antonio film: the book version of *Point of Order* had preceded it by almost a decade. More recently, Doug Kellner and Ron Mann have created a CD-ROM version of *Painters Painting*. Published in 1996, it includes clips from the film, critical assessments, and other information useful for understanding the film and the art world it details. The difficulty in putting documentaries into a new format is made clear in one review of the project: "Converting the 116-minute film (available on videotape) to a QuickTime video on this disc makes the film's talking-head interviews hard to follow and reduces much of the art to writhing, geometric mush (particularly the very ungeometric Jackson Pollocks). De Antonio's interviews with Jasper Johns, Willem de Kooning, and others, which can be turned to like pages in a book, are a fun read, but, at 40 bucks, they're not enough. Suggestion to Voyager: A deluxe laserdisc would have been a better choice" (Tim Purtell, "Emile De Antonio's *Painters Painting*," *Entertainment Weekly*, August 16, 1996, 66).

81. Jasper Johns to de Antonio, November 2, 1983.

82. De Antonio's comments appear in the manuscript version of an interview he gave to Jean W. Ross on March 8, 1985, and that appeared in *Contemporary Authors*, vol. 117 (Detroit: Gale Press, 1986), 97–99. For an excellent account of the *Tilted Arc* controversy, see Casey Nelson Blake, "An Atmosphere of Effrontery: Richard Serra, *Tilted Arc*, and

the Crisis of Public Art," in Richard Wightman Fox and T. J. Jackson Lears, eds., *The Power of Culture: Critical Essays in American History* (Chicago: University of Chicago Press, 1993), 246–89.

83. De Antonio, Journals, vol. 7:73. He was referring to Amanda Fielding's *Trepanation for the National Health*, on display from October 1 to November 15, 1978, at Project Studios One, Institute for Art and Urban Resources, New York.

84. Kay Johnson and Monika Jensen, "An Interview with Emile de Antonio," transcript of conversation of November 16, 1972, at the University of Wisconsin–Madison; on Lyght, see de Antonio, Journals, vol. 12:74; vol. 5:143–44; on Basquiat, see de Antonio, "Emile de Antonio with Jean Michel Basquiat," *Interview*, July 1984, 49–50. Robert Hughes expressed little patience for Basquiat in *Culture of Complaint: The Fraying of America* (New York: Oxford University Press, 1993), 195–96.

Chapter 7. *Underground*

1. De Antonio, typescript chapter for unpublished book on *Underground*, probably from 1976, submitted to Grosset and Dunlap, 1; Weather Underground Organization, *Prairie Fire: The Politics of Revolutionary Anti-Imperialism: Political Statement of the Weather Underground* (San Francisco: Communications Co., 1974).

2. Peter Prescott, "Stormy Weather," *Newsweek*, June 30, 1975, 64; de Antonio, Journals, vol. 6:70.

3. Bob Dylan, "Subterranean Homesick Blues," on the album *Bringing It All Back Home* (1965); Weather Underground manifesto entitled "Bringing the War Home: Less Talk, More National Action," quoted in Todd Gitlin, "White Heat Underground," *Nation*, December 19, 1981, 671.

4. Ibid.

5. David Dellinger, *From Yale to Jail: The Life Story of a Moral Dissenter* (New York: Pantheon, 1993), 389; Todd Gitlin, *The Sixties: Years of Hope, Days of Rage* (New York: Bantam, 1987), 393.

6. In *Soon to Be a Major Motion Picture* (New York: Putnam's, 1980), Abbie Hoffman claimed the bomb was to be used against Columbia University (251). Another book claimed the bomb was intended for "a dance hall full of U.S. Army enlisted men and their dates at Fort

Dix"; see Peter Collier and David Horowitz, *Destructive Generation: Second Thoughts About the Sixties* (New York: Summit, 1989), 100, 277. Despite its vindictive tone Collier and Horowitz's chapter on the Weather Underground (67–119) is a necessary part of the scant literature on the group.

7. Mari Jo Buhle, Paul Buhle, and Dan Georgakas, eds., *Encyclopedia of the American Left* (New York: Garland, 1990), 61.

8. Gitlin, *Sixties*, 402. See also *San Francisco Examiner*, October 24, 1975.

9. Ted Robert Gurr, "Political Terrorism in the United States: Historical Antecedents and Contemporary Trends," in Michael Stohl, ed., *The Politics of Terrorism* (New York: Dekker, 1988), 563.

10. Jane Alpert, *Growing Up Underground* (New York: Morrow, 1981), 331.

11. Emile de Antonio, "Visions of Vietnam," *University Review*, December 1974, 21.

12. De Antonio, Journals, vol. 5:61.

13. Mark Rudd is quoted in Collier and Horowitz, *Destructive Generation*, 112; Bernardine Dohrn refers to a "lucrative offer" from CBS in de Antonio's *Underground*.

14. De Antonio, Journals, vol. 6:7; vol. 5:61.

15. De Antonio to Haskell Wexler, October 25, 1974.

16. De Antonio, Journals, vol. 5:61.

17. The revealing document is a letter to the Underground; a copy of it appears in de Antonio, Journals, vol. 5:61–66.

18. That the publication of *Prairie Fire* demonstrated the Weather Underground's shift from violence to working-class organizing is reported in a journalistic account more reliable than its title might lead one to believe: John Castellucci, *The Big Dance: The Untold Story of Kathy Boudin and the Terrorist Family That Committed the Brink's Robbery Murders* (New York: Dodd, Mead, 1986), 127.

19. De Antonio, Journals, vol. 5:62.

20. Ibid., vol. 4:45.

21. De Antonio, typescript for introduction to the soundtrack to *Underground*, 1, which was released as *Underground: Sound Track of the Film by Emile de Antonio, Haskell Wexler, Mary Lampson, and the Weather Underground Organization* (Folkways Records, 1976).

22. Gurr, "Political Terrorism," 561.

23. Ford is quoted in the *New York Times*, March 19, 1977; Young is quoted in the *New York Times*, June 10, 1977.

24. Robert G. Picard, *Media Portrayals of Terrorism* (Ames: Iowa State University Press, 1993), 117; for the circumstances surrounding the enactment of the Prevention of Terrorism Act, see David Childs, *Britain Since 1945: A Political History* (London: Methuen, 1986), 272.

25. According to a Gallup Poll of March 25–28, 1977, 64 percent of Americans believed that the "media coverage of terrorism encourages others to commit these acts" of terrorism. A similar question had not been asked between 1972 and 1976. See George H. Gallup, *The Gallup Poll: Public Opinion, 1972–1977*, vol. 2 (Wilmington, Del.: Scholarly Resources, 1978), 1053.

26. De Antonio, Journals, vol. 5:67.

27. Ibid.

28. Ibid.

29. Wexler's documentaries include *Interviews with My Lai Veterans* (1971); *Brazil: A Report on Torture* (1972); *Interview with President Salvador Allende* (1972); *Introduction to the Enemy* (1975); *Trial of the Catonsville Nine* (1979). According to Mitch Tuchman's typescript article on Wexler, which he sent with a letter to de Antonio on October 7, 1974, Wexler had also worked uncredited on some cinema verité classics by the Maysles brothers and Donn Pennebaker.

30. De Antonio, Journals, vol. 5:69. Wexler's cars are also described in the Tuchman typescript.

31. Peter Biskind and Marc N. Weiss, "The Weather Underground, Take One," *Rolling Stone*, November 6, 1975, 38.

32. David Talbot and Barbara Zheutlin, *Creative Differences: Profiles of Hollywood Dissidents* (Boston: South End, 1978), 122.

33. Biskind and Weiss, "Weather Underground," 38.

34. De Antonio, Journals, vol. 5:69.

35. Ibid., 71.

36. Mary Lampson, typescript chapter for unpublished book on *Underground*, 1, in the de Antonio archive.

37. Ibid., 6.

38. Ibid., 1.

39. Biskind and Weiss, "Weather Underground," 39.

40. See Lampson's account in Biskind and Weiss, "Weather Underground," 39.

41. De Antonio, Journals, vol. 5:73.

42. Wexler's son Jeff had also joined the project as soundman, but he backed out during the shoot, much to the annoyance of everyone involved (Bernardine Dohrn, telephone interview by author, March 15, 1994; de Antonio, Journals, vol. 5:85).

43. De Antonio, Journals, vol. 5:73.

44. Ibid., vol. 6:23; the reference to eight thousand rounds comes from Clarence M. Kelley and James Kirkpatrick Davis, *Kelly: The Story of an FBI Director* (New York: Andrew, McMeel, and Parker, 1987), 211.

45. Biskind and Weiss, "Weather Underground," 39.

46. De Antonio, Journals, vol. 5:84.

47. Ibid., 85.

48. Gitlin, *Sixties*, 386.

49. De Antonio, Journals, vol. 5:145.

50. Ibid., 6:23; 5:146; Gitlin, *Sixties*, 386.

51. Biskind and Weiss, "Weather Underground," 41; de Antonio, Journals, vol. 6:12.

52. Biskind and Weiss, "Weather Underground," 41.

53. Ibid.

54. The reference to "vehicles" comes from an *Underground* outtake transcribed in de Antonio, Journals, vol. 5:89.

55. Ibid., 5:89; Biskind and Weiss, "Weather Underground," 80.

56. Lampson, typescript chapter, 7.

57. Barry Katz, *Herbert Marcuse and the Art of Liberation* (London: Verso, 1982), 221.

58. *New York Times*, October 16, 1975.

59. Biskind and Weiss, "Weather Underground," 83.

60. Ibid., 85.

61. Ibid., 84.

62. Ibid.

63. De Antonio, Journals, vol. 6:22.

64. De Antonio, Journals, vol. 6:14.

65. Ibid., 31.

66. Miriam Lowenkron to de Antonio, November 5, 1975.

67. FBI director [Clarence Kelley] to attorney general [Edward H. Levi], May 7, 1976. For a microfilm version of the FBI file on the SDS and the Weather Underground, see reel 7, Microfilm 54002, Government Information Services Library, University of California, Berkeley.

68. De Antonio, Journals, vol. 6:22.

69. Kelley to Levi.

70. De Antonio, Journals, vol. 6:22.

71. FBI Communications Section, Teletype, May 14, 1975. Declassified January 24, 1979, after a request by de Antonio under the Freedom of Information Act.

72. FBI agent Wesley Swearington described his participation in the Los Angeles surveillance team in an interview (in Los Angeles, circa 1981) with de Antonio and journalist Warren Hinckle, former editor of *Ramparts* magazine; the typescript of this unpublished interview is in the de Antonio archive.

73. Marc Glassman, ed., "The Documents in De's Case," in *Forbidden Films: The Filmmaker and Human Rights, in Aid of Amnesty International* (Toronto: Toronto Arts Group for Human Rights, 1984), 17.

74. De Antonio, Journals, vol. 4:35.

75. A photocopy of the subpoena issued May 22, 1975, appears in de Antonio, Journals, vol. 4:40.

76. The ACLU's credo is described in William A. Donohue, *The Politics of the American Civil Liberties Union* (New Brunswick, N.J.: Transaction, 1985), 4.

77. Peter Biskind, "Does the U.S. Have the Right to Subpoena a Film in Progress?" *New York Times*, June 22, 1975.

78. Talbot and Zheutlin, *Creative Differences*, 123.

79. The petition, dated June 6, 1975, was a one-page typescript released by the ACLU of Southern California; portions are quoted in Biskind, "Does the U.S. Have the Right?"

80. Peter Collier, "I Remember Fonda," *New West*, September 24, 1979, 19–24. Hayden denied ever supporting the Weather Underground's politics in Biskind and Weiss, "Weather Underground," 88.

81. De Antonio, Journals, vol. 6:26.

82. Ibid., vol. 7:133; vol. 10:20.

83. Jane Fonda to de Antonio, October 6, 1975; Hayden does not address this episode in his memoir, *Reunion: A Memoir* (New York: Random House, 1988).

84. Bernard F. Dick, *Radical Innocence: A Critical Study of the Hollywood Ten* (Lexington: University Press of Kentucky, 1989), 4.

85. De Antonio, Journals, vol. 5:19; de Antonio to Elia Kazan, October 15, 1975; Robert Sklar, *Movie-Made America: A Cultural History of American Movies* (New York: Random House, 1975), 262–68.

86. De Antonio, Journals, vol. 4:36.

87. Biskind, "Does the U.S. Have the Right?"

88. Leonard Boudin, typescript chapter to unpublished book on *Underground*, 1–3; *Boston Globe*, July 27, 1975; on prior restraint see Jack C. Plano and Milton Greenberg, *The American Political Dictionary* (New York: Holt, Rinehart, and Winston, 1967), 63; the Pentagon Papers case is formally known as *New York Times Company v. United States*, 403 U.S. 713 (1971), described in Richard F. Hixson, *Mass Media and the Constitution: An Encyclopedia of Supreme Court Decisions* (New York: Garland, 1989), 401–4.

89. De Antonio, Journals, vol. 4:35; Frederick Wiseman made a similar case against the censorship of his film *Titicut Follies* (1967), claiming he was part of the news media and therefore covered by the First Amendment. See Barry Keith Grant, *Voyages of Discovery: The Cinema of Frederick Wiseman* (Urbana: University of Illinois Press, 1992), 27.

90. Leonard Boudin, typescript chapter, 1–3.

91. Biskind, "Does the U.S. Have the Right?"; the "blunderbuss" reference was made by Frank Donner, director of the ACLU Project on Political Surveillance, and is quoted in Biskind and Weiss, "Weather Underground," 88.

92. *New York Times*, July 5, 1975.

93. *Boston Globe*, July 27, 1975; *Los Angeles Times*, June 6, 1975.

94. Teletype from FBI director to "SAC NY" [special agent in charge, New York], March 31, 1976; FBI director to assistant attorney general, March 7, 1976; FBI director to attorney general, May 7, 1976.

95. *Boston Globe*, June 25, 1975.

96. Patrick McGilligan, "Emile de Antonio's Fight to Film the Weatherpeople," *Boston Globe*, July 27, 1975.

97. Biskind, "Does the U.S. Have the Right?"

98. *Congressional Record*, 94th Cong., 1st sess. (July 30, 1975), vol. 121, pt. 20:26155–56.

99. De Antonio to U.S. Representative Larry McDonald, November 13, 1975.

100. See U.S. Senate Subcommittee on Security and Treason of the Committee on the Judiciary, *Domestic Security (Levi) Guidelines*, hearing, 97th Cong., 2d sess., June 24–25, and August 11–12, 1982.

101. *New York Times*, August 12, 1976.

102. Peter Goldman, "When G-Men Break the Law," *Newsweek*, May 30, 1977, 28–30; see Ward Churchill and Jim Vander Wall, *The COINTELPRO Papers: Documents from the FBI's Secret Wars Against Domestic Dissent* (Boston: South End, 1990).

103. Alan Rosenthal, ed., *The Documentary Conscience: A Casebook in Film Making* (Berkeley: University of California Press, 1980), 222; the de Antonio retrospective was in July 1975 (*New York Daily News*, July 15, 1975).

104. Gary Crowdus and Dan Georgakas, "History Is the Theme of All My Films: An Interview with Emile de Antonio," in Alan Rosenthal, ed., *New Challenges for Documentary* (Berkeley: University of California Press, 1988), 172.

105. De Antonio to Chris Marker, August 5, 1975; Rosenthal, *New Challenges for Documentary*, 172.

106. Biskind and Weiss, "Weather Underground," 88.

107. De Antonio to David Lubell, March 16, 1976.

108. De Antonio to Revolution and Arts Committee, Austin, Texas, September 1, 1976; de Antonio to George Pillsbury, September 5, 1975.

109. De Antonio to Moe Asch, August 25, 1976.

110. Unfortunately, de Antonio had not been able to locate this footage of Ho Chi Minh earlier when he was assembling *In the Year of the Pig* (1969). See chapter 4.

111. De Antonio disputed the superiority of his "negative" works in the interview with Crowdus and Georgakas, " 'History Is the Theme," 171.

112. Tom Brom, a worker for American Documentary Film, is quoted in Bill Nichols, *Newsreel: Documentary Filmmaking on the American Left* (New York: Arno, 1980), 41.

113. Dan Georgakas, "Underground: Con," *Cinéaste*, February 1977, 21–23, 51.

114. On reflexivity see Jay Ruby, "The Image Mirrored: Reflexivity and the Documentary Film," in Alan Rosenthal, ed., *New Challenges for Documentary* (Berkeley: University of California Press, 1988), 64–77; Bill Nichols, *Representing Reality: Issues and Concepts in Documentary* (Bloomington: University of Indiana Press, 1991), 56–79; on "collaborative" documentary see David MacDougal, "Whose Story Is It?" *Visual Anthropology Review* 7, no. 2 (Fall 1991): 2–10.

115. After a screening of *Underground* in Madison, Wisconsin, de Antonio expressed his desire that it unite the Left, a statement that made

its way through FBI reports into a letter from the FBI director [Clarence Kelley] to attorney general [Edward H. Levi], May 7, 1976.

116. Crowdus and Georgakas, "History Is the Theme," 172.

117. Rosenthal, *Documentary Conscience*, 206.

118. Thomas Waugh, "*Underground*: Weatherpeople at Home," *Jump Cut*, no. 12–13 (Fall 1976): 11–12.

119. *New York Times*, May 10, 1976.

120. Patrick McGilligan, "Weatherpeople Live on in 'Underground,'" *Boston Globe*, June 14, 1976 (also quoted on German promotional posters for *Underground*); *Variety*, May 10, 1976; Kevin Thomas, "A Weather Underground Report," *Los Angeles Times*, May 19, 1976; John L. Wasserman, "An Extraordinary, yet Faceless Film," *San Francisco Chronicle*, May 26, 1976.

121. *Yipster Times*, May 1976; *New York City Star*, May 15–June 15, 1976.

122. See de Antonio, Journals, vol. 6:57.

123. De Antonio to "Alex and brothers and sisters of Western Union" [members of the Weather Underground], n.d. ["Monday night"].

124. *Village Voice*, April 26, 1976.

125. Michie Gleason, "*Underground*: Pro," *Cinéaste*, February 1977; John Dean III, *Blind Ambition: The White House Years* (New York: Simon and Schuster, 1976), 40. "The film the FBI didn't want you to see" is quoted on German promotional posters for *Underground*; the phrase is used in the *Boston Globe*, June 14, 1976.

126. Stanley Kauffmann, "Underground and Above," *New Republic*, May 29, 1976.

127. De Antonio to Peter [?], June 26, 1975.

128. De Antonio, Journals, vol. 6:63.

129. Jeff Jones is quoted in de Antonio, Journals, vol. 6:12.

130. Dohrn is quoted in John Brown Book Club, ed., *The Split of the Weather Underground Organization: Struggling Against White and Male Supremacy* (Seattle: John Brown Book Club, n.d. [probably 1977]), 35; Dohrn interview.

131. Alex [Jeff Jones] to Frank [Emile de Antonio], "labor day 1976."

132. Dohrn is quoted as disavowing the film in John Brown Book Club, ed., *Split*, 35; for the reasons behind this ideological maneuver, see Collier and Horowitz, *Destructive Generation*, 113–16, and Castellucci,

The Big Dance, 128–29. When I interviewed Dohrn, she said she never disavowed the film.

133. Bill Ayers, telephone interview by author, February 3, 1994; Peter Biskind, "Weather Underground Splits on Whether to Be Overground," *Seven Days*, February 28, 1977, 16–18.

134. Ellen Frankfort, *Kathy Boudin and the Dance of Death* (New York: Stein and Day, 1983), 93.

135. See Castellucci, *The Big Dance*.

136. "Nyack was the enactment of the quintessential Weatherman fantasy," wrote Collier and Horowitz, *Destructive Generation*, 69. While billing themselves as former radicals, these writers had made a sharp turn to the right during the Reagan presidency and began to exhibit a remarkable (and quite marketable) degree of vituperation toward their former comrades on the New Left.

137. Dohrn and Ayers continued to socialize with de Antonio whenever they visited New York (Dohrn interview).

138. De Antonio, Journals, vol. 6:14; vol. 10:30.

139. This is a summary of Marcuse's speech "The Movement in a New Era of Repression: An Assessment" (originally published in the *Berkeley Journal of Sociology*, 16 [1971–1972]: 1–14) in Barry Katz, *Herbert Marcuse and the Art of Liberation* (London: Verso, 1982), 206.

140. De Antonio, Journals, vol. 10:20.

141. Ibid., vol. 6:67.

142. Ibid., vol. 5:62–66.

143. Dellinger, *From Yale to Jail*, 396.

144. De Antonio, Journals, vol. 10:130.

145. Susan Linfield, "De Antonio's Day in Court," *Village Voice*, February 8, 1983.

146. De Antonio, Journals, vol. 5:134.

147. Gramsci is quoted in Peter Novick, *That Noble Dream: The "Objectivity Question" and the American Historical Profession* (Cambridge, U.K.: Cambridge University Press, 1988), 433.

148. De Antonio, Journals, vol. 6:30.

Chapter 8. Films of the Eighties

1. This account of the case is drawn from the following sources: Fred A. Wilcox, *Uncommon Martyrs: The Berrigans, the Catholic*

Left, and the Plowshares Movement (Reading, Mass.: Addison-Wesley, 1991), xi–xvii, 46, 205–7; Charles DeBenedetti, ed., *Peace Heroes in Twentieth-Century America* (Bloomington: University of Indiana Press, 1986), 227–54, which includes an excellent bibliography on the Berrigans; Liane Ellison Norman, *Hammer of Justice: Molly Rush and the Plowshares Eight* (Pittsburgh: Pittsburgh Peace Institute, 1989); Marsha Fottler, "Plowshares Eight Go on Trial in Docudrama," *Sarasota (Fla.) Herald-Tribune*, July 20, 1986.

2. Berrigan is quoted in William Van Etten Casey and Philip Nobile, eds., *The Berrigans* (New York: Praeger, 1971), 19; de Antonio is quoted in Jay Murphy, "Emile de Antonio," *Red Bass* (Tallahassee, Fla.), Fall 1983, 9.

3. Daniel Berrigan, *America Is Hard to Find* (Garden City, N.Y.: Doubleday, 1972).

4. De Antonio describes his inability to arrange financial backing for the Agee project in Philip Agee, *On the Run* (Secaucus, N.J.: Lyle Stuart, 1987), 142.

5. De Antonio categorized his investors in Susan Linfield, "De Antonio's Day in Court," *Village Voice*, February 8, 1983.

6. De Antonio is quoted in "Emile de Antonio," *Lumières* (Montreal, Quebec), 1988, 31; for an analysis of the "promises and failures" of public broadcasting in the United States, see Douglas Kellner, *Television and the Crisis of Democracy* (Boulder, Colo.: Westview, 1990), 201–7.

7. De Antonio to Robert Rauschenberg, June 24, 1981.

8. De Antonio to Plowshares Eight, Martin Sheen, and others, June 23, 1981.

9. Linfield, "De Antonio's Day in Court," 36.

10. Ibid. Bill Nichols, *Representing Reality: Issues and Concepts in Documentary* (Bloomington: University of Indiana Press, 1991), 160. For a good introduction to the subject see Seth Feldman, " 'Footnote to Fact': The Docudrama," in Barry Keith Grant, ed., *Film Genre Reader* (Austin: University of Texas Press, 1986), 344–56; and Richard Kilborn and John Izod, *An Introduction to Television Documentary: Confronting Reality* (Manchester, U.K.: Manchester University Press, 1997). Of particular interest in the Kilborn and Izod book is chapter 6, "Making a Drama Out of a Crisis: The Drama-Documentary and Related Forms," 135–61.

11. Ian Christie, *The Last Machine: Early Cinema and the Birth of the Modern World* (London: British Film Institute, 1994), 98.

12. This claim was made by Dan Streible in his comments on this manuscript. I am grateful to him, as well as Bill Nichols, who also read this book in manuscript form, for their insights regarding docudrama.

13. For an analysis of television docudramas of the 1970s that emphasizes their liberal and sometimes progressive content, see Kellner, *Television and the Crisis of Democracy*, 57.

14. See Leslie Fishbein, "The Paterson Pageant (1913): The Birth of Docudrama in the Class Struggle," *New York History* 72, no. 2 (April 1991): 197–233.

15. The point about Grierson is made in Kilborn and Izod, *Introduction to Television Documentary*, 139.

16. The director Nicholas Ray had constructed a courtroom for his reenactment of the trial of the Chicago Seven more than a decade earlier. The film, in which real-life defendants such as Abbie Hoffman had played themselves, was entitled *We Can't Go Home Again* (1973–1976) and is discussed in Ray's book, *I Was Interrupted: Nicholas Ray on Making Movies* (Berkeley: University of California Press, 1993).

17. De Antonio to Jackson Browne, September 12, 1982.

18. The production history is drawn from the following sources: publicity materials written by de Antonio for the film; de Antonio to Plowshares Eight, Sheen, and others; de Antonio to Jackson Browne; de Antonio, "Emile de Antonio Interviews Himself," *Film Quarterly*, Fall 1982, 28–32; Joel Schechter, "Plowshares Eight, Take Two," *In These Times*, May 5–11, 1982, 19–21; Stephen Dale, "De Antonio's Long Cold War," *Now* (Toronto), February 3–9, 1983, 12–14; Murphy, "Emile de Antonio"; David Segal, "De Antonio and the Plowshares Eight," *Sight and Sound*, Summer 1992; Linfield, "De Antonio's Day in Court"; Gary Crowdus and Dan Georgakas, "History Is the Theme of All My Films: An Interview with Emile de Antonio," in Alan Rosenthal, ed., *New Challenges for Documentary* (Berkeley: University of California Press, 1988), 177.

19. De Antonio to Plowshares Eight, Sheen, and others.

20. See Michael H. Seitz, "Swords into Plowshares," *Progressive*, April 1983, 54–55.

21. De Antonio to Julia Reichert and James Klein, September 25, 1974; de Antonio, 1982 "Synopsis" from publicity materials for *In the King of Prussia*.

22. Erich Remarque, *All Quiet on the Western Front* (Boston:

Little, Brown, 1929); Nevil Shute, *On the Beach* (New York: Morrow, 1957); Jonathan Schell, *The Fate of the Earth* (New York: Knopf, 1982).

23. De Antonio, "Emile de Antonio Interviews Himself." According to a 1971 press release by Linda J. Myers that appears in the de Antonio archive, for quite some time he had been open to exploring the Christian Left, even considering a film project on the German theologian Dietrich Bonhoeffer, who was executed by the Nazis in 1945.

24. *Philadelphia Inquirer,* March 5, 1983.

25. De Antonio's admiration for Philip Berrigan is mentioned in Madeline de Antonio, undated typescript outline for never-published biography of de Antonio.

26. Martin Sheen to de Antonio, July 23, 1981; Martin Sheen to Judge Samuel Salus, July 20, 1981.

27. Emile de Antonio, "Martin Sheen," *American Film,* December 1982, 20–28.

28. De Antonio to correspondent identified only as "friend and comrade," October 11, 1986.

29. This rudimentary history of the film's reception is taken from the following sources: de Antonio to Charles Shapiro, December 13, 1983, and January 9, 1984; de Antonio to Barbara Stone, July 10, 1986; Janet Maslin, "Film: 'King of Prussia,' with Berrigan Brothers," *New York Times,* February 13, 1983; *Los Angeles Reader,* April 15, 1983; *Philadelphia Daily News,* March 4, 1983; *Progressive,* April 1983; *Boston Globe,* April 8, 1983; *Minneapolis City Pages,* November 3, 1983; *Variety,* November 17, 1982; *Nuclear Times* (New York City), January 1983; *Toronto Star,* February 2, 1983; *Village Voice,* February 15, 1983. The *Guardian* quote appears in publicity materials for the film; de Antonio is quoted in Amir Gollan, "Politically Relevant Film Is Flawed," *Burlington (Vt.) Daily Free Press,* April 7, 1983.

30. Patrick McCarthy, "Ten Years After: The Plowshares Eight," *Christianity and Crisis,* May 28, 1990; Arthur J. Laffin, "Chronology of Plowshares Disarmament Actions: September 1980–May 1989," in Wilcox, *Uncommon Martyrs,* 205–7. These pieces are unusual in giving credit to the film for the small role it played in raising public awareness about nuclear issues.

31. De Antonio to Barbara [Stone?], February 19, 1985.

32. De Antonio, Journals, vol. 7:85; Reagan is quoted in Anthony Summers, "Hidden Hoover," *Vanity Fair,* March 1993, 200–221.

33. His statement about revenge appears in *Mr. Hoover and I* (1989).

34. Mitch Tuchman, "Freedom of Information," *Film Comment*, July–August 1990, 66.

35. Hoover is quoted in Richard Gid Powers, *Secrecy and Power: The Life of J. Edgar Hoover* (New York: Free Press, 1987), 233.

36. Susan Green, "The Eggplant and the FBI," *Burlington (Vt.) Vanguard Press*, September, 21–28, 1989; other de Antonio quotes are from *Mr. Hoover and I.*

37. De Antonio, Journals, vol. 5:60.

38. De Antonio to Anna-Lena Wibom, May 1, 1986.

39. De Antonio to Barbara [Stone?], April 8, 1986.

40. De Antonio to William Davis, June 18, 1986; de Antonio to Bill Nichols [April 2, 1986]; de Antonio to Barbara [Stone?], April 8, 1986; de Antonio to Anna-Lena Wibom, May 1, 1986; de Antonio to Gherardo Gossi, September 2, 1986.

41. Powers, *Secrecy and Power*, 200–201.

42. I discuss Roth's novel in chapter 5.

43. Athan Theoharis, review of *The Secret File on J. Edgar Hoover* (William Cran and Stephanie Tepper, 1993), *Journal of American History*, December 1993, 1201–3; on Hoover and civil rights see Powers, *Secrecy and Power*, 323–32, 367–69, 395, 407–12.

44. De Antonio, Journals, vol. 10:109.

45. De Antonio to Gossi.

46. Richard Barsam, *The Vision of Robert Flaherty: The Artist as Myth and Filmmaker* (Bloomington: University of Indiana Press, 1988), 100.

47. P. Adams Sitney, *The Avant-Garde Film: A Reader of Theory and Criticism* (New York: New York University Press, 1978), 202.

48. Jim Lane, "Notes on Theory and the Autobiographical Documentary Film in America," *Wide Angle* 15, no. 3 (July 1993): 22. Lane is turning his UCLA dissertation on the subject into a book entitled *The Autobiographical Documentary Film in America: An Analysis of Modes of Cinematic Self-Inscription*; see also Elizabeth W. Bruss, "Eye for I: Making and Unmaking Autobiography in Film," in James Olney, ed., *Autobiography: Essays Theoretical and Critical* (Princeton, N.J.: Princeton University Press, 1980), 296–320. Finally, see Patricia Aufderheide, "Public Intimacy: The Development of First-Person Documentary," *Afterimage* 25, no. 1 (July–August 1997): 16–32.

49. See Brian Winston, "The Tradition of the Victim in Griersonian Documentary," in Alan Rosenthal, ed., *New Challenges for Documentary* (Berkeley: University of California Press, 1988), 269–87.

50. Jay Ruby, "The Ethics of Imagemaking: Or, 'They're Going to Put Me in the Movies. They're Going to Make a Big Star Out of Me,' " in Rosenthal, ed., *New Challenges*, 309.

51. Poststructuralists may doubt whether self-inscription offers any benefits that other modes of representation do not. For an excellent discussion of this issue, see Michael Renov, "The Subject in History: The New Autobiography in Film and Video," *Afterimage* 17, no. 1 (Summer 1989): 4–7.

52. Greg Gunn, "Dissidence in Film," *Burlington (Vt.) Vanguard Press*, September 21–28, 1989.

53. Henry Miller, *Tropic of Cancer* (New York: Grove, 1961), 2; Vincent Canby, "Emile de Antonio's Thoughts on Himself and the FBI," *New York Times*, April 20, 1990.

54. Canby, "Emile de Antonio's Thoughts," *Variety*, April 20, 1990. *F for Fake* is discussed intelligently in James Naremore, *The Magic World of Orson Welles* (Dallas: Southern Methodist University Press, 1989), 246–50.

55. Tuchman, "Freedom of Information." The comparison with Gray is made in Jay Scott's review in the *Toronto Globe and Mail*, September 9, 1989.

56. Reviews appeared in Canby, "Emile de Antonio's Thoughts"; Gary Giddens, "Wanted by the FBI," *Village Voice*, April 24, 1990; "Entertainment," *Toronto Star*, September 15, 1989; Lor, "*Mr. Hoover and I*," *Variety*, April 18, 1990; Joy Scott, "Desert Dreams: Exploring the American Nightmare," *Toronto Globe and Mail*, September 9, 1989.

57. Tuchman, "Freedom of Information," 66.

58. Stephen Holden, "AIDS Dominates Nonfiction Series of Film and Video," *New York Times*, April 6, 1990.

59. Renov, "Subject in History," 5.

Epilogue

1. Terry de Antonio, "An In-Depth Talk with Emile de Antonio," *Shantih International Writing*, Winter–Spring 1972, 19.

2. Noam Chomsky, "The Responsibility of Intellectuals," *New York Review of Books*, February 23, 1967, 16, quoted in Alan Wald, *The New York Intellectuals: The Rise and Decline of the Anti-Stalinist Left from the 1930s to the 1980s* (Chapel Hill: University of North Carolina Press, 1987), 366.

3. Alan Rosenthal, ed., *The Documentary Conscience: A Casebook in Film Making* (Berkeley: University of California Press, 1980), 206.

4. Vincent Canby, "Emile de Antonio's Thoughts on Himself and the FBI," *New York Times*, April 20, 1990.

5. Thomas Waugh, "Beyond Vérité: Emile de Antonio and the New Documentary of the Seventies," *Jump Cut*, no. 10–11 (Summer 1976): 39.

6. This list comes from the film theorist Bill Nichols, *Representing Reality: Issues and Concepts in Documentary* (Bloomington: University of Indiana Press, 1991), 48. One might add such films as *Atomic Cafe* (Jayne Loader, Kevin Rafferty, and Pierce Rafferty, 1982); *Union Maids* (James Klein, Miles Mogulescu, and Julia Reichert, 1976); *Hearts and Minds* (Peter Davis, 1974); *The War at Home* (Glenn Silber and Barry A. Brown, 1979); and *The Good Fight* (Noel Buckner, Mary Dore, and Sam Sills, 1984). These compilation films are mentioned in Jack C. Ellis, *The Documentary Idea: A Critical History of English-Language Documentary Film and Video* (Englewood Cliffs, N.J.: Prentice Hall, 1989), 289.

7. Litwack is quoted in Daniel J. Walkowitz, "Telling the Story: The Media, the Public, and American History," *Perspectives: American Historical Association Newsletter*, October 1993, 1, 6–9. The situation at PBS has become worse in the decade since Burns's success. As two recent monographs demonstrate, its programmers increasingly act as stern gatekeepers, creating an ever-more-hostile home for independent documentary filmmakers. See Ralph Engelman, *Public Radio and TV in America: A Political History* (Thousand Oaks, Calif.: Sage, 1996), and even more to the point, B. J. Bullert's very useful study, *Public Television and the Battle over Documentary* (New Brunswick, N.J.: Rutgers University Press, 1997).

8. Patricia Busa, "CompuSoap," *Texas Monthly*, January 1999, 22.

9. The Witness On-Line Documentary Series was available at http://www.worldmedia.fr/witness/ as of November 29, 1999.

10. The address for Webcorp's Web site, as of November 29, 1999, was http://webcorp.com/sounds, and it provides free downloads of the Nixon and McCarthy footage. Some production companies are beginning to explore ways to use Internet technology to extend the life of their documentary films. See Frank Beacham, "Voyager's Stein Warns of Coming Battle over Net," an article about the first Media and Democracy Congress, an event that drew seven hundred journalists, producers, and filmmakers to San Francisco from February 29 to March 3, 1996. Beacham's article was available at http://www.beacham.com/net_transition.html as of November 30, 1999.

11. Bertolt Brecht, "Theorie des Radios," *Gesammelte Werke*, vol. 18 (Frankfurt: Suhrkamp Verlag, 1967), 129.

12. Mitchell Stephens, *The Rise of the Image, the Fall of the Word* (New York: Oxford University Press, 1998), 18. Stephens's book has sparked controversy in media studies. For an interesting multiperspective review of his book, see Mark Crispin Miller, David Schenk, and Leslie Savan's hypertext comments on selected passages of Stephens's book in the on-line magazine *Feed*, available as of November 29, 1999, at http://www.feedmag.com/document/do106.shtml.

13. Gary Crowdus and Dan Georgakas, "History Is the Theme of All My Films: An Interview with Emile de Antonio," in Alan Rosenthal, ed., *New Challenges for Documentary* (Berkeley: University of California Press, 1988), 167.

14. Stephens, *Rise of the Image*, 5.

15. John E. O'Connor, *Image as Artifact: The Historical Analysis of Film and Television* (Malabar, Fla.: Kreiger, 1990), 14.

16. For a brief discussion of other documentaries in the 1960s and 1970s that had an influence on what she calls "the public narrative," see Patricia Aufderheide, "The Camera as Conscience: How Social Issues Inspire Moving Documentaries," *Chronicle of Higher Education* 45, no. 9 (October 23, 1998): B7.

Selected Bibliography

The following bibliography includes all published material cited, with the exception of newspaper and magazine reviews of de Antonio's films and works mentioned in passing. These are listed in the notes for the chapter.

Aaron, Daniel. "Cambridge, 1936–1939." *Partisan Review* (1984–1985, double anniversary issue): 833–37.

Adorno, Theodor. *Minima Moralia: Reflections from a Damaged Life*. Translated by E. F. N. Jephcott. 1951; trans. London: New Left, 1974.

Adorno, Theodor. "Commitment." In Andrew Arato and Eike Gebhardt, eds., *The Essential Frankfurt School Reader*. New York: Continuum, 1985.

Agee, Philip. *On the Run*. Secaucus, N.J.: Lyle Stuart, 1987.

Alpert, Jane. *Growing Up Underground*. New York: Morrow, 1981.

Ambrose, Stephen E. *Nixon: The Education of a Politician, 1913–1962*. New York: Simon and Schuster, 1987.

Ambrose, Stephen E. *Nixon: The Triumph of a Politician, 1962–1972*. New York: Simon and Schuster, 1989.

Anonymous. *U.S. Senator Eugene J. McCarthy*. Minneapolis, Minn.: Gilbert Publishing, 1964.

Archer, Eugene. "*Point of Order*, a Surprise Hit, Belatedly Gets a Distributor." *New York Times*, February 11, 1964.

Arlen, Michael. *Living Room War*. New York: Viking, 1969.

Aronowitz, Stanley. *Dead Artists, Live Theories, and Other Cultural Problems*. New York: Routledge, 1994.

Ashton, Dore. *The New York School: A Cultural Reckoning*. New York: Viking, 1973.

Aufderheide, Patricia. "Public Intimacy: The Development of First-

Person Documentary." *Afterimage* 25, no. 1 (July–August 1997): 16–32.

Aufderheide, Patricia. "The Camera as Conscience: How Social Issues Inspire Moving Documentaries." *Chronicle of Higher Education* 45, no. 9 (October 23, 1998): B7.

Bachmann, Gideon. "The Frontiers of Realist Cinema." *Film Culture*, nos. 22–23 (Summer 1961): 12–22.

Banes, Sally. *Greenwich Village 1963: Avant-Garde Performance and the Effervescent Body*. Durham, N.C.: Duke University Press, 1993.

Barnouw, Erik. *Documentary: A History of the Nonfiction Film*. New York: Oxford University Press, 1974.

Barnouw, Erik. *Tube of Plenty: The Evolution of American Television*. New York: Oxford University Press, 1975.

Barsam, Richard. *The Vision of Robert Flaherty: The Artist as Myth and Filmmaker*. Bloomington: University of Indiana Press, 1988.

Barsam, Richard. *Nonfiction Film: A Critical History*. Rev. ed. Bloomington: University of Indiana Press, 1992.

Baudrillard, Jean. *For a Critique of the Political Economy of the Sign*. Translated by Charles Levin. St. Louis, Mo.: Telos Press, 1981.

Baudrillard, Jean. *In the Shadow of the Silent Majorities*. New York: Semiotext(e), 1983.

Baudrillard, Jean. *Jean Baudrillard: Selected Writings*. Edited by Mark Poster. Palo Alto, Calif.: Stanford University Press, 1988.

Beacham, Frank. "Voyager's Stein Warns of Coming Battle over Net." Available at http://www.beacham.com/net_transition.html as of November 30, 1999.

Belin, David W. *Final Disclosure: The Full Truth about the Assassination of President Kennedy*. New York: Scribner's, 1988.

Benjamin, Walter. *Das Passagen-Werk*. Edited by Rolf Tiedemann. Frankfurt: Suhrkamp, 1982.

Benjamin, Walter. "N (Theories of Knowledge; Theories of Progress)." *Philosophical Forum* 15, nos. 1–2 (Fall–Winter 1983–1984): 5–6.

Berrigan, Daniel. *America Is Hard to Find*. Garden City, N.Y.: Doubleday, 1972.

Biskind, Peter. "Does the U.S. Have the Right to Subpoena a Film in Progress?" *New York Times*, June 22, 1975.

Biskind, Peter. "Weather Underground Splits on Whether To Be Overground." *Seven Days*, February 28, 1977, 16–18.

Biskind, Peter, and Marc N. Weiss. "The Weather Underground, Take One." *Rolling Stone*, November 6, 1975, 36–39.

Blake, Casey Nelson. "An Atmosphere of Effrontery: Richard Serra, *Tilted Arc*, and the Crisis of Public Art." In Richard Wightman Fox and T. J. Jackson Lears, eds., *The Power of Culture: Critical Essays in American History*. Chicago: University of Chicago Press, 1993.

Bonardi, Donato. *Biographical Highlights of Dott. Prof. Cav. Francesco de Antonio*. Alessandria, Italy: Gazzotti, 1915.

Bosworth, Patricia. *Diane Arbus: A Biography*. New York: Knopf, 1984.

"Brecht and a Revolutionary Cinema." Special issue of *Screen* 15, no. 4 (Summer 1974).

Brodie, Fawn. *Richard Nixon: The Shaping of His Character*. New York: Norton, 1981.

Brooker, Peter. "Key Words in Brecht's Theory and Practice." In Peter Thomson and Glendyr Sacks, eds., *The Cambridge Companion to Brecht*. Cambridge, U.K.: Cambridge University Press, 1994.

Brown, Les. *Encyclopedia of Television*. Detroit: Visible Ink, 1992.

Brown, Thomas. *JFK: History of an Image*. Bloomington: University of Indiana Press, 1988.

Bruss, Elizabeth W. "Eye for I: Making and Unmaking Autobiography in Film." In James Olney, ed., *Autobiography: Essays Theoretical and Critical*. Princeton, N.J.: Princeton University Press, 1980.

Buchanan, Thomas G. *Who Killed Kennedy?* New York: Putnam, 1964.

Buhle, Mari Jo, Paul Buhle, and Dan Georgakas, eds. *Encyclopedia of the American Left*. New York: Garland, 1990.

Bullert, B. J. *Public Television and the Battle over Documentary*. New Brunswick, N.J.: Rutgers University Press, 1997.

Burgeson, J. Scott. "Geopolitical Jazz." *San Francisco Bay Guardian Literary Supplement*, March 1993, 12–13.

Busa, Patricia. "CompuSoap." *Texas Monthly*, January 1999, 22.

Calas, Nicolas. *Art in the Age of Risk*. New York: Dutton, 1968.

Campbell, Russell. *Cinema Strikes Back: Radical Filmmaking in the United States, 1930–1942*. Ann Arbor, Mich.: UMI Research Press, 1982.

Canadian Center for Films on Art. *Films on Art: A Source Book*. New York: Watson-Guptill, 1977.

Carney, Ray. *American Dreaming: The Films of John Cassavetes and the American Experience.* Berkeley: University of California Press, 1984.

Carney, Ray. "Looking Without Seeing." *Partisan Review*, Fall 1991, 717–23.

Casey, William Van Etten, and Philip Nobile, eds. *The Berrigans.* New York: Praeger, 1971.

Castellucci, John. *The Big Dance: The Untold Story of Kathy Boudin and the Terrorist Family That Committed the Brink's Robbery Murders.* New York: Dodd, Mead, 1986.

Cawley, Leo. "The War About the War." In Linda Dittmar and Gene Michaud, eds., *From Hanoi to Hollywood: The Vietnam War in American Film.* New Brunswick, N.J.: Rutgers University Press, 1990.

Childs, David. *Britain Since 1945: A Political History.* London: Methuen, 1986.

Chomsky, Noam. "The Responsibility of Intellectuals." *New York Review of Books*, February 23, 1967, 16–26.

Chomsky, Noam. *Manufacturing Consent: The Political Economy of the Mass Media.* New York: Pantheon, 1988.

Chomsky, Noam. *Rethinking Camelot: JFK, the Vietnam War, and U.S. Political Culture.* Boston: South End, 1993.

Christie, Ian. *The Last Machine: Early Cinema and the Birth of the Modern World.* London: British Film Institute, 1994.

Churchill, Ward, and Jim Vander Wall. *The COINTELPRO Papers: Documents from the FBI's Secret Wars Against Domestic Dissent.* Boston: South End, 1990.

Clark, Ronald W. *The Life of Bertrand Russell.* London: Cape, 1975.

Cohen, Robert. *Understanding Peter Weiss.* Columbia: University of South Carolina Press, 1993.

Cohn, Roy. *McCarthy.* New York: New American Library, 1968.

Collier, Peter. "I Remember Fonda." *New West*, September 24, 1979, 19–24.

Collier, Peter, and David Horowitz. *Destructive Generation: Second Thoughts About the Sixties.* New York: Summit, 1989.

Colodny, Len, and Robert Gettlin. *Silent Coup: The Removal of a President.* New York: St. Martin's, 1991.

Congressional Quarterly. *Watergate: Chronology of a Crisis.* Washington, D.C.: Congressional Quarterly, 1975.

Congressional Record, 94th Cong., 1st sess. July 30, 1975, vol. 121, pt. 20:26155–56.

Corner, John, and Kay Richardson. "Documentary Meaning and the Discourse of Interpretation." In John Conner, ed., *Documentary and the Mass Media*. London: Arnold, 1988.

Correll, Barbara. "Rem(a)inders of G(l)ory: Monuments and Bodies in *Glory* and *In the Year of the Pig*." *Cultural Critique* 19 (Fall 1991): 141–71.

Crowdus, Gary, and Dan Georgakas. "History Is the Theme of All My Films: An Interview with Emile de Antonio." In Alan Rosenthal, ed., *New Challenges for Documentary*. Berkeley: University of California Press, 1988.

Culbert, David, ed. *Film and Propaganda in America: A Documentary History*. New York: Greenwood, 1990–1991.

Culler, Jonathan. *Structuralist Poetics: Structuralism, Linguistics, and the Study of Literature*. Ithaca, N.Y.: Cornell University Press, 1975.

Cumings, Bruce. *War and Television*. New York: Verso, 1992.

Dale, Stephen. "De Antonio's Long Cold War." *Now* (Toronto), February 3–9, 1983, 12–14.

Danto, Arthur C. *The Philosophical Disenfranchisement of Art*. New York: Columbia University Press, 1986.

Dean, John W., III. *Blind Ambition: The White House Years*. New York: Simon and Schuster, 1976.

de Antonio, Emile. "The Point of View in *Point of Order*." *Film Comment*, Winter 1964, 35–37.

de Antonio, Emile. "The Agony of the Revolutionary Artist." *Northwest Passage* (Washington), May 24, 1971, 7.

de Antonio, Emile. "Pontus Hultén and Some '60's Memories in New York." In Moderna Museet, *New York Collection for Stockholm*. Stockholm: Moderna Museet, 1973.

de Antonio, Emile. "A Passion for Painting." *Geo*, March 1982, 13–15.

de Antonio, Emile. "Emile de Antonio Interviews Himself." *Film Quarterly*, Fall 1982, 28–32.

de Antonio, Emile. "Martin Sheen." *American Film*, December 1982, 20–28.

de Antonio, Emile. "Emile de Antonio with Jean Michel Basquiat." *Interview*, July 1984, 49–50.

de Antonio, Emile. Review of Ellen Oumano's *Film Forum. American Film*, November 1985, 72–74.

de Antonio, Emile. "Interview." *Film Threat*, December 1987, 18–31.

de Antonio, Emile, and Mark Lane. "*Rush to Judgment*: A Conversation with Mark Lane and Emile de Antonio." *Film Comment*, Fall–Winter 1967, 2–18.

de Antonio, Emile, and Albert Maher. "Chasing Checkers by Richard M. Nixon." *New York Free Press*, September 26–October 2, 1968.

de Antonio, Emile, and Daniel Talbot. *Point of Order! A Documentary of the Army-McCarthy Hearings, Produced by Emile de Antonio and Daniel Talbot*. New York: Norton, 1964.

de Antonio, Emile, and Mitch Tuchman, compilers. *Painters Painting: A Candid History of the Modern Art Scene, 1940–1970*. New York: Abbeville, 1984.

de Antonio, Terry. "An In-Depth Talk with Emile de Antonio." *Shantih International Writing*, Winter–Spring 1972, 17–19.

DeBenedetti, Charles, ed. *Peace Heroes in Twentieth-Century America*. Bloomington: University of Indiana Press, 1986.

de Kooning, Willem. *Sketchbook 1: Three Americans*. New York: Time, 1960.

Dellinger, David. *From Yale to Jail: The Life Story of a Moral Dissenter*. New York: Pantheon, 1993.

Demetz, Peter, ed. *Brecht: A Collection of Critical Essays*. Englewood Cliffs, N.J.: Prentice Hall, 1962.

Derrida, Jacques. *The Post Card: From Socrates to Freud and Beyond*. Translated by Alan Bass. Chicago: University of Chicago Press, 1987.

Dick, Bernard F. *Radical Innocence: A Critical Study of the Hollywood Ten*. Lexington: University Press of Kentucky, 1989.

Dobrovis, William A., Joseph D. Gebhardt, Samuel J. Buffone, and Andra N. Oakes. *The Offenses of Richard Milhous Nixon: A Guide for the People of the United States*. New York: Times Book Co., 1973.

Doherty, Thomas. "*Point of Order!*" *History Today*, August 1998, 33–37.

Donohue, William A. *The Politics of the American Civil Liberties Union*. New Brunswick, N.J.: Transaction, 1985.

Doss, Erika. *Benton, Pollock, and the Politics of Modernism: From*

Regionalism to Abstract Expressionism. Chicago: University of Chicago Press, 1990.

Eagleton, Terry. *Marxism and Literary Criticism.* Berkeley: University of California Press, 1976.

Eliot, T. S. *Selected Prose of T. S. Eliot.* Edited by Frank Kermode. New York: Harcourt Brace Jovanovich, 1975.

Ellis, Jack C. *The Documentary Idea: A Critical History of English-Language Documentary Film and Video.* Englewood Cliffs, N.J.: Prentice Hall, 1989.

Elsaesser, Thomas. "From Anti-Illusionism to Hyperrealism: Bertolt Brecht and Contemporary Film." In Pia Kleber and Colin Visser, eds., *Reinterpreting Brecht: His Influence on Contemporary Drama and Film.* Cambridge, U.K.: Cambridge University Press, 1990.

"Emile de Antonio," *Lumières* (Montreal, Quebec), 1988, 31–32.

Engelman, Ralph. *Public Radio and TV in America: A Political History.* Thousand Oaks, Calif.: Sage, 1996.

Epstein, Edward Jay. *Inquest: The Warren Commission and the Establishment of Truth.* New York: Viking, 1966.

Esslin, Martin. *Brecht: The Man and His Work.* Garden City, N.Y.: Anchor, 1961.

Feldman, Seth. " 'Footnote to Fact': The Docudrama." In Barry Keith Grant, ed., *Film Genre Reader.* Austin: University of Texas Press, 1986.

Ferguson, Russell, William Olander, Marcia Tucker, and Karen Fiss, eds. *Discourses: Conversations in Postmodern Art and Culture.* Boston: MIT Press, 1990.

Fishbein, Leslie. "The Paterson Pageant (1913): The Birth of Docudrama in the Class Struggle." *New York History* 72, no. 2 (April 1991): 197–233.

Foster, Hal, ed. *The Anti-Aesthetic.* Seattle: Seattle Bay Press, 1983.

Fottler, Marsha. "Plowshares Eight Go on Trial in Docudrama." *Sarasota (Fla.) Herald-Tribune,* July 20, 1986.

Foucault, Michel. *The Archaeology of Knowledge.* Translated by A. M. Sheridan Smith. New York: Pantheon, 1972.

Foucault, Michel. *Language, Countermemory, Practice: Selected Essays and Interviews.* Translated by Donald F. Bouchard and Sherry Simon. Ithaca, N.Y.: Cornell University Press, 1977.

Foucault, Michel. *Discipline and Punish: The Birth of the Prison*. Translated by Alan Sheridan. New York: Vintage, 1979.

Foucault, Michel. *Power/Knowledge: Selected Interviews and Other Writings, 1972–1977*. Edited and translated by Colin Gordon. New York: Pantheon, 1980.

Foucault, Michel. *Foucault Live*. Edited by Sylvere Lotringer and translated by John Johnston. New York: Semiotext(e), 1989.

Foucault, Michel, ed. *I, Pierre Riviere, Having Slaughtered My Mother, My Sister, and My Brother*. Translated by Frank Jellinek. New York: Pantheon, 1975.

Frankfort, Ellen. *Kathy Boudin and the Dance of Death*. New York: Stein and Day, 1983.

"French Respond to Kennedy Plot Film Based on Mark Lane Ideas," *Variety*, March 15, 1967, 7.

Frewin, Anthony. *The Assassination of John F. Kennedy: An Annotated Film, TV, and Videography, 1963–1992*. Westport, Conn.: Greenwood, 1993.

Friedberg, Anne. *Window Shopping: Cinema and the Postmodern*. Berkeley: University of California Press, 1993.

Frost, Robert. *In the Clearing*. New York: Holt, Rinehart, and Winston, 1962.

Gallup, George H. *The Gallup Poll: Public Opinion, 1972–1977*. Vol. 2. Wilmington, Del.: Scholarly Resources, 1978.

Gitlin, Todd. *The Whole World Is Watching: Mass Media in the Making and Unmaking of the New Left*. Berkeley: University of California Press, 1980.

Gitlin, Todd. "White Heat Underground." *Nation*, December 19, 1981, 668–74.

Gitlin, Todd. *The Sixties: Years of Hope, Days of Rage*. New York: Bantam, 1987.

Glassman, Marc, ed. *Forbidden Films: The Filmmaker and Human Rights, in Aid of Amnesty International*. Toronto: Toronto Arts Group for Human Rights, 1984.

Glueck, Grace. "Wishes to Build Some Dreams On." *New York Times*, January 7, 1973.

Goldman, Peter. "When G-Men Break the Law." *Newsweek*, May 30, 1977, 28–30.

Gornick, Vivian. *The Romance of American Communism*. New York: Basic, 1977.

Grant, Barry Keith. *Voyages of Discovery: The Cinema of Frederick Wiseman*. Urbana: University of Illinois Press, 1992.

Green, Susan. "The Eggplant and the FBI." *Burlington (Vt.) Vanguard Press*, September 21–28, 1989.

Guilbaut, Serge. *How New York Stole the Idea of Modern Art*. Chicago: University of Chicago Press, 1983.

Guiles, Fred Lawrence. *Loner at the Ball: The Life of Andy Warhol*. New York: Bantam, 1989.

Gunn, Greg. "Dissidence in Film." *Burlington (Vt.) Vanguard Press*, September 21–28, 1989.

Gurr, Ted Robert. "Political Terrorism in the United States: Historical Antecedents and Contemporary Trends." In Michael Stohl, ed., *The Politics of Terrorism*. New York: Dekker, 1988.

Guth, DeLloyd J., and David R. Wrone. *The Assassination of John F. Kennedy: A Comprehensive Historical and Legal Bibliography, 1963–1979*. Westport, Conn.: Greenwood, 1980.

Hallin, Daniel. *The "Uncensored War": Vietnam and the Media*. New York: Oxford University Press, 1980.

Hamilton, Ian. "Spender's Lives." *New Yorker*, February 28, 1994, 72–85.

Hamilton, Nigel. *JFK: Reckless Youth*. New York: Random House, 1992.

Hammond, Charles Montgomery. *The Image Decade: Television Documentary, 1965–1975*. New York: Hastings House, 1981.

Harrison, Charles, and Paul Wood. "Modernity and Modernism Reconsidered." In Paul Wood, Francis Frascina, Jonathan Harris, and Charles Harrison, eds., *Modernism in Dispute: Art Since the Forties*. New Haven, Conn.: Yale University Press, 1993.

Hayden, Tom. *Reunion: A Memoir*. New York: Random House, 1988.

Herblock. *Herblock: Special Report*. New York: Norton, 1974.

Hitchcock, Frederick L. *History of Scranton and Its People*. Vol. 2. New York: Lewis Historical Publishing, 1914.

Hitchens, Christopher. *For the Sake of Argument: Essays and Minority Reports*. London: Verso, 1993.

Hixson, Richard F. *Mass Media and the Constitution: An Encyclopedia of Supreme Court Decisions*. New York: Garland, 1989.

Hoberman, J. "Vietnam: The Remake." In Barbara Kruger and Phil Mariani, eds., *Remaking History*. Seattle: Bay Press, 1989.

Hoberman, J. "The Forest and the Trees." In David E. James, ed., *To

Free the Cinema: Jonas Mekas and the New York Underground. Princeton, N.J.: Princeton University Press, 1992.

Hoffman, Abbie. *Soon to Be a Major Motion Picture.* New York: Putnam's, 1980.

Howe, Irving. *Decline of the New.* New York: Harcourt, Brace, and World, 1970.

Hughes, Robert. *The Shock of the New: Art and the Century of Change.* Rev. ed. London: BBC Publications, 1991.

Hughes, Robert. *Culture of Complaint: The Fraying of America.* New York: Oxford University Press, 1993.

Jacobson, Brooke, and Jill Godmilow. "Far from Finished: Deconstructing the Documentary." In Mark O'Brien and Craig Little, eds., *Reimaging America: The Arts of Social Change.* Philadelphia: New Society, 1990.

James, David E. *Allegories of Cinema: American Film in the Sixties.* Princeton, N.J.: Princeton University Press, 1989.

James, David E., ed. *To Free the Cinema: Jonas Mekas and the New York Underground.* Princeton, N.J.: Princeton University Press, 1992.

Jameson, Fredric. "Postmodernism and Consumer Society." In Hal Foster, ed., *The Anti-Aesthetic.* Port Townsend, Wash.: Bay Press, 1983.

Jameson, Fredric. *The Geopolitical Aesthetic: Cinema and Space in the World System.* Bloomington: University of Indiana Press, 1993.

John Brown Book Club, ed. *The Split of the Weather Underground Organization: Struggling Against White and Male Supremacy.* Seattle: John Brown Book Club, n.d. [probably 1977].

Johnson, Kay, and Monika Jensen. "An Interview with Emile de Antonio." *Arts in Society,* Summer–Fall 1973, 209–19.

Johnson, Pauline. *Marxist Aesthetics.* London: Routledge and Kegal Paul, 1984.

Johnson, Troy R. *The Occupation of Alcatraz Island : Indian Self-Determination and the Rise of Indian Activism.* Urbana: University of Illinois Press, 1996.

Jones, Penn, Jr. *Forgive My Grief.* Midlothian, Tex.: Midlothian Mirror, 1966.

Kaplan, Fred. "*Vietnam! Vietnam!* An Exclusive Report on John Ford's Propaganda Documentary for the USIA." *Cinéaste,* Fall 1976, 20–24.

Katz, Barry. *Herbert Marcuse and the Art of Liberation*. London: Verso, 1982.

Kelley, Clarence M., and James Kirkpatrick Davis. *Kelly: The Story of an FBI Director*. New York: Andrew, McMeel and Parker, 1987.

Kellner, Douglas. *Critical Theory, Marxism, and Modernity*. Baltimore, Md.: Johns Hopkins University Press, 1989.

Kellner, Douglas. *Jean Baudrillard: From Marxism to Postmodernism and Beyond*. Palo Alto, Calif.: Stanford University Press, 1989.

Kellner, Douglas. *Television and the Crisis of Democracy*. Boulder, Colo.: Westview, 1990.

Kellner, Douglas, and Michael Ryan. *Camera Politica: The Politics and Ideology of Contemporary Hollywood Film*. Bloomington: University of Indiana Press, 1988.

Kent, Leticia. "Eat, Drink, and Make 'Millhouse.'" *New York Times*, October 17, 1971.

Kernan, Margot. "Radical Image: Revolutionary Film." *Arts in Society*, Fall 1973, 242–49.

Kilborn, Richard, and John Izod. *An Introduction to Television Documentary: Confronting Reality*. Manchester, U.K.: Manchester University Press, 1997.

Kipphardt, Heinar. *In the Matter of J. Robert Oppenheimer: A Play Freely Adapted, on the Basis of Documents*. Translated by Ruth Speirs. London: Methuen, 1983.

Klehr, Harvey. *The Heyday of American Communism: The Depression Decade*. New York: Basic, 1984.

Koch, Stephen. "Nixonart." *New York World*, August 1, 1972, 76–78.

Kostelanetz, Richard. *Esthetics Contemporary*. Buffalo, N.Y.: Prometheus, 1989.

Kramer, Hilton. "Artists and the Problem of 'Relevance.'" *New York Times*, May 4, 1969.

Kramer, Hilton. *The Age of the Avant-Garde*. New York: Farrar, Straus, and Giroux, 1973.

Kurtzweil, Edith. *The Age of Structuralism: Levi-Strauss to Foucault*. New York: Columbia University Press, 1980.

Kuspit, Donald B. *Clement Greenberg: Art Critic*. Madison: University of Wisconsin Press, 1979.

Ladendorf, Robert C. "Resistance to Vision: The Effects of Censorship and Other Restraints on Emile de Antonio's Political Documentaries." Master's thesis, University of Wisconsin–Madison, 1977.

Laffin, Arthur J. "Chronology of Plowshares Disarmament Actions: September 1980–May 1989." In Fred A. Wilcox, *Uncommon Martyrs: The Berrigans, the Catholic Left, and the Plowshares Movement*, appendix 1. Reading, Mass.: Addison-Wesley, 1991.

Laing, Dave. *The Marxist Theory of Art*. Atlantic Highlands, N.J.: Humanities Press, 1978.

Lane, Jim. "Notes on Theory and the Autobiographical Documentary Film in America." *Wide Angle* 15, no. 3 (July 1993): 21–35.

Lane, Mark. "Lane's Defense Brief for Oswald." *National Guardian*, December 19, 1963.

Lane, Mark. *Rush to Judgment*. New York: Holt, Rinehart, and Winston, 1966.

Lane, Mark. *A Citizen's Dissent: Mark Lane Replies*. New York: Holt, Rinehart, and Winston, 1968.

Lane, Mark. *Plausible Denial: Was the CIA Involved in the Assassination of JFK?* New York: Thunder's Mouth Press, 1991.

Lang, Berel, and Forrest Williams, eds. *Marx and Art: Writings in Aesthetics and Criticism*. New York: McKay, 1972.

Lanning, Michael Lee. *Vietnam at the Movies*. New York: Fawcett Columbine, 1994.

Lasch, Christopher. "The Life of Kennedy's Death." *Harper's*, October 1983, 32–40.

Lax, Eric. *Woody Allen: A Biography*. New York: Knopf, 1991.

Lelchuk, Alan. "On Satirizing Presidents: An Interview with Philip Roth." *Atlantic*, December 1971, 81–88.

Lewis, Anthony. 1964. "Kennedy Slaying Relived in Detail in Warren Files." *New York Times*, November 24.

Leyda, Jay. *Films Beget Films*. London: Allen and Unwin, 1964.

Linfield, Susan. "De Antonio's Fireside Chat: Part 2." *New York City Independent*, July–August 1982, 21–28.

Linfield, Susan. "De Antonio's Day in Court." *Village Voice*, February 8, 1983.

Lukas, J. Anthony. *Nightmare: The Underside of the Nixon Years*. New York: Viking, 1973.

Lunn, Eugene. *Marxism and Modernism: An Historical Study of Lukacs, Brecht, Benjamin, and Adorno*. Berkeley: University of California Press, 1982.

McCarthy, Patrick. "Ten Years After: The Plowshares Eight." *Christianity and Crisis*, May 28, 1990, 168–70.

MacDougal, David. "Whose Story Is It?" *Visual Anthropology Review* 7, no. 2 (Fall 1991): 2–10.

McGilligan, Patrick. "Emile de Antonio's Fight to Film the Weatherpeople." *Boston Globe*, July 27, 1975.

Mailer, Norman. "The Great American Mystery." *Washington Post*, August 28, 1966.

Mamber, Stephen. *Cinéma Vérité in America*. Cambridge, Mass.: MIT Press, 1974.

Marcorelles, Louis. "Homo Americanus." *Cinéma 67* (Paris), April 1967, 19–21.

Marcuse, Herbert. *Negations: Essays in Critical Theory*. Translated by Jeremy J. Shapiro. Boston: Beacon, 1968.

Meagher, Sylvia. "Notes for a New Investigation." *Esquire*, December 1966, 211.

Meagher, Sylvia. *Accessories After the Fact*. New York: Bobbs-Merrill, 1967.

Meinecke, Friedrich. *Historicism: The Rise of a New Historical Outlook*. Translated by J. E. Anderson. London: Routledge and Kegan Paul, 1972.

Mekas, Jonas. "Independence for Independents." *American Film*, September 1978, 38–40.

Mellen, Joan. "America Is Hard to See." *Cinéaste*, Spring 1971, 28.

Morgan, Alec. "But This Is Where I Belong." *Filmnews*, March 1981, 7–9.

Morgenstern, Joseph. "History Right in the Face," *Newsweek*, November 10, 1969, 108–10.

Murphy, Jay. "Emile de Antonio." *Red Bass* (Tallahassee, Fla.), Fall 1983, 8–12.

Naremore, James. *The Magic World of Orson Welles*. Dallas: Southern Methodist University Press, 1989.

Neufeld, Tanya. "An Interview with Emile de Antonio." *Artforum*, March 1973, 79–83.

Nichols, Bill. *Newsreel: Documentary Filmmaking on the American Left*. New York: Arno, 1980.

Nichols, Bill. *Representing Reality: Issues and Concepts in Documentary*. Bloomington: University of Indiana Press, 1991.

Nichols, Bill. *Blurred Boundaries: Questions of Meaning in Contemporary Culture*. Bloomington: University of Indiana Press, 1994.

Nietzsche, Friedrich. *On the Genealogy of Morals*. Translated by Walter Kaufmann. New York: Random House, 1967.

Nolan, Martin F. "The Many Lives and Laughs of 'Millhouse.'" *Boston Globe*, August 3, 1971.

Norman, Liane Ellison. *Hammer of Justice: Molly Rush and the Plowshares Eight*. Pittsburgh: Pittsburgh Peace Institute, 1989.

Novick, Peter. *That Noble Dream: The "Objectivity Question" and the American Historical Profession*. Cambridge, U.K.: Cambridge University Press, 1988.

O'Brien, Glenn. "Inter/View with Emile de Antonio." *Interview*, February 1971, 28–29.

O'Connor, John E. *Image as Artifact: The Historical Analysis of Film and Television*. Malabar, Fla.: Kreiger, 1990.

Olson, James S. *The Vietnam War: Handbook of Literature and Research*. Westport, Conn.: Greenwood, 1993.

Olson, James S., and Randy Roberts. *Where the Domino Fell: America and Vietnam, 1945–1990*. New York: St. Martin's, 1991.

Oumano, Ellen. *Film Forum: Thirty-five Top Filmmakers Discuss Their Craft*. New York: St. Martin's, 1985.

Palamidessi, Christine. "A Talk with Emile de Antonio." *New Video Magazine*, Winter 1984, 17–19, 68.

Parker, Jerry. "The Incursion into Richard M. Nixon." *Newsday*, December 14, 1971, 3–9.

Picard, Robert G. *Media Portrayals of Terrorism*. Ames: Iowa State University Press, 1993.

Plano, Jack C., and Milton Greenberg. *The American Political Dictionary*. New York: Holt, Rinehart, and Winston, 1967.

Pohl, Frances K. *Ben Shahn: New Deal Artist in a Cold War Climate, 1947–1954*. Austin: University of Texas Press, 1989.

Posner, Gerald. *Case Closed: Lee Harvey Oswald and the Assassination of JFK*. New York: Random House, 1993.

Powers, Richard Gid. *Secrecy and Power: The Life of J. Edgar Hoover*. New York: Free Press, 1987.

Prescott, Peter. "Stormy Weather." *Newsweek*, June 30, 1975, 64–66.

Raskin, Marcus. "*JFK* and the Culture of Violence." *American Historical Review* 97, no. 2 (April 1992): 487–99.

Ray, Nicholas. *I Was Interrupted: Nicholas Ray on Making Movies*. Berkeley: University of California Press, 1993.

Reiterman, Tim, with John Jacobs. *Raven: The Untold Story of the Reverend Jim Jones and His People*. New York: Dutton, 1982.

Renov, Michael. "The Subject in History: The New Autobiography in Film and Video." *Afterimage* 17, no. 1 (Summer 1989): 4–7.

Revill, David. *The Roaring Silence: John Cage, A Life*. New York: Arcade, 1992.

Richter, Hans. *The Struggle for Film*. Translated by Ben Brewster. New York: St. Martin's, 1986.

Rogin, Michael. "*JFK*: The Movie." *American Historical Review*, April 1992, 500–505.

Rollins, Peter C. "*Victory at Sea*: Cold War Epic." *Journal of American Culture*, no. 6 (1972): 463–82.

Rosen, Philip. "Document and Documentary." In Michael Renov, ed., *Theorizing Documentary*. New York: Routledge, 1993.

Rosenau, Pauline Marie. *Postmodernism and the Social Sciences: Insights, Inroads, and Intrusions*. Princeton, N.J.: Princeton University Press, 1992.

Rosenbaum, Ron. "Taking a Darker View." *Time*, January 13, 1992, 38–40.

Rosenstone, Robert A. "*JFK*: Historical Fact–Historical Film." *American Historical Review* 97, no. 2 (April 1992): 506–11.

Rosenthal, Alan, ed. *The Documentary Conscience: A Casebook in Film Making*. Berkeley: University of California Press, 1980.

Rosenthal, Alan, ed. *New Challenges for Documentary*. Berkeley: University of California Press, 1988.

Ross, Jean W. Interview with Emile de Antonio (March 8, 1985). In *Contemporary Authors*. Vol. 117. Detroit: Gale Press, 1986.

Rossell, Deac. "From Joe to Eugene: To Hell and Back." *Boston After Dark*, June 2, 1970, 3.

Rosteck, Thomas. "Irony, Argument, and Reportage in Television Documentary: *See It Now* Versus Senator McCarthy." *Quarterly Journal of Speech* 75, no. 3 (August 1989): 277–98.

Roth, Philip. *Our Gang*. New York: Random House, 1971.

Ruby, Jay. "The Ethics of Imagemaking: Or, 'They're Going to Put Me in the Movies. They're Going to Make a Big Star Out of Me.' " In Alan Rosenthal, ed., *New Challenges for Documentary*. Berkeley: University of California Press, 1988.

Ruby, Jay. "The Image Mirrored: Reflexivity and the Documentary

Film." In Alan Rosenthal, ed., *New Challenges for Documentary*. Berkeley: University of California Press, 1988.

Ruoff, Jeffrey K. "Conventions of Sound in Documentary." In Rick Altman, ed., *Sound Theory, Sound Practice*. New York: Routledge, 1992.

Russell, Bertrand. "Private Memorandum Concerning Ralph Schoenman." *Black Dwarf* (London), September 5, 1970, 9–16.

Safire, William. *Before the Fall: An Inside View of the Pre-Watergate White House*. Garden City, N.Y.: Doubleday, 1975.

Said, Edward W. *Culture and Imperialism*. New York: Knopf, 1993.

Sandler, Irving. *The New York School: The Painters and Sculptors of the Fifties*. New York: Harper and Row, 1978.

Sandler, Irving. *American Art of the 1960s*. New York: Harper and Row, 1988.

Saunder, Dero A. Introduction to *The Decline and Fall of the Roman Empire*, by Edward Gibbon. New York: Penguin, 1980.

Sauvage, Leo. "Oswald in Dallas: A Few Loose Ends." *New York City Reporter*, January 2, 1964, 24–26.

Schapiro, Meyer. "The Liberating Quality of Avant-Garde Art." *Art News*, September 1957, 28–32.

Schechter, Joel. "Plowshares Eight, Take Two." *In These Times*, May 5–11, 1982, 19–21.

Schlesinger, Stephen, and Stephen Kinzer. *Bitter Fruit: The Untold Story of the American Coup in Guatemala*. Garden City, N.Y.: Doubleday, 1982.

Segal, David. "De Antonio and the Plowshares Eight." *Sight and Sound*, Summer 1992, 177–81.

Seitz, Michael H. "Swords into Plowshares." *Progressive*, April 1983, 54–55.

Seitz, William C. *The Art of Assemblage*. New York: Museum of Modern Art, 1961.

Seitz, William C. *Art in the Age of Aquarius, 1955–1970*. Washington, D.C.: Smithsonian Institution Press, 1992.

Sitney, P. Adams. *Film Culture Reader*. New York: Praeger, 1970.

Sitney, P. Adams. *The Avant-Garde Film: A Reader of Theory and Criticism*. New York: New York University Press, 1978.

Sklar, Robert. *Movie-Made America: A Cultural History of American Movies*. New York: Random House, 1975.

Slater, Thomas J. "Teaching Vietnam: The Politics of Documentary." In Michael Anderegg, ed., *Inventing Vietnam: The War in Film and Television*. Philadelphia: Temple University Press, 1991.

Smart, Barry. *Foucault, Marxism, and Critique*. London: Routledge and Kegan Paul, 1983.

Stam, Robert, Robert Burgoyne, and Sandy Flitterman-Lewis. *New Vocabularies in Film Semiotics: Structuralism, Poststructuralism, and Beyond*. New York: Routledge, 1992.

Stepash, Irene. "Emile de Antonio: For the Record." *East Village Eye*, November 1979, 13.

Stephens, Mitchell. *The Rise of the Image, the Fall of the Word*. New York: Oxford University Press, 1998.

Steven, Peter, ed. *Jump Cut: Hollywood, Politics, and Counter Cinema*. New York: Praeger, 1985.

Stott, William. *Documentary Expression and Thirties America*. New York: Oxford University Press, 1973.

Straight, Michael. *Trial by Television*. Boston: Beacon, 1954.

Summers, Anthony. "Hidden Hoover." *Vanity Fair*, March 1993, 200–221.

Suvin, Darvo. "The Mirror and the Dynamo." In Lee Baxandall, ed., *Radical Perspectives in the Arts*. Middlesex, U.K.: Pelican, 1972.

Szurek, Sam. "An Interview with Emile de Antonio." *New York Downtown*, September 16, 1987, 32–35.

Talbot, Daniel. "On Historic Hearings from TV to the Screen." *New York Times*, January 12, 1964.

Talbot, Daniel, ed. *Film: An Anthology*. New York: Simon and Schuster, 1959.

Talbot, David, and Barbara Zheutlin. *Creative Differences: Profiles of Hollywood Dissidents*. Boston: South End, 1978.

Talbot, Stephen. "'60s Something," *Mother Jones*, March–April 1991, 46–49.

"The Artist and Politics: A Symposium." *Artforum*, September 1970, 35–39.

Tompkins, Calvin. "Profiles: Moving Out." *New Yorker*, February 29, 1964, 39–105.

Thompson, Josiah. *Six Seconds in Dallas*. New York: Geis, 1967.

Tretiakov, Sergey. "Bert Brecht." *International Literature* (Moscow), May 1937, 60–70. (Reprinted in Peter Demetz, ed., *Brecht: A*

Collection of Critical Essays. Englewood Cliffs, N.J.: Prentice Hall, 1962.)

Tuchman, Maurice, ed. *New York School: The First Generation*. Greenwich, Conn.: New York Graphics Society, 1971.

Tuchman, Mitch. "Celluloid Vietnam." *New Republic*, May 31, 1975, 28–30.

Tuchman, Mitch. "Emile de Antonio: 'All Filmmakers Are Confidence Men.'" *Village Voice*, May 17, 1976.

Tuchman, Mitch. "Kennedy Death Art." *Take Over*, May 1977, 19–22.

Tuchman, Mitch. "Freedom of Information." *Film Comment*, July–August 1990, 66–68.

Tuchman, Mitch. "Introductory Notes: Emile de Antonio." Unpublished typescript, de Antonio archive.

Ulasewicz, Tony. *The President's Private Eye*. Westport, Conn.: Macsam, 1990.

U.S. House of Representatives. *Statement of Information: Hearings Before the Committee on the Judiciary*. 93d Cong., 2d sess., May–June 1974.

U.S. Senate. *Report of Proceedings, Hearing Held Before Select Committee on Presidential Campaign Activities*. 93d Cong., 1st sess. S. Res. 60–General Investigation. March 23, 1974.

U.S. Senate Subcommittee on Security and Treason of the Committee on the Judiciary, *Domestic Security (Levi) Guidelines*, hearing, 97th Cong., 2d sess., June 24–25, and August 11–12, 1982.

Updike, John. *Hugging the Shore: Essays and Criticism*. New York: Vintage, 1983.

Vaughn, E. J. *"Painters Painting*: An Unprecedented Art Historical Document by Emile de Antonio." Unpublished manuscript, 1973, de Antonio archive.

Vidal, Gore. "The Late Show." *New York Review of Books*, September 12, 1968, 5–8.

Vidal, Gore. *An Evening with Richard Nixon, by Gore Vidal (and Others)*. New York: Random House, 1972.

Wald, Alan. *The New York Intellectuals: The Rise and Decline of the Anti-Stalinist Left from the 1930s to the 1980s*. Chapel Hill: University of North Carolina Press, 1987.

Walkowitz, Daniel J. "Telling the Story: The Media, the Public, and American History." *Perspectives: American Historical Association Newsletter*, October 1993, 1, 6–9.

Walsh, Martin. *The Brechtian Aspect of Radical Cinema*. London: BFI, 1981.

Warhol, Andy, and Pat Hackett. *POPism: The Warhol '60s*. New York: Harcourt Brace Jovanovich, 1980.

Warren Commission. *Report of the President's Commission on the Assassination of President John F. Kennedy*. New York: Associated Press, 1964.

Waugh, Thomas. "Beyond Vérité: Emile de Antonio and the New Documentary of the Seventies." *Jump Cut*, no. 10–11 (Summer 1976): 33–39. (Reprinted as "Emile de Antonio and the New Documentary of the Seventies." In Bill Nichols, ed., *Movies and Methods*, Vol. 2: *An Anthology*. Berkeley: University of California Press, 1985.)

Weather Underground Organization. *Prairie Fire: The Politics of Revolutionary Anti-Imperialism: Political Statement of the Weather Underground*. San Francisco: Communications Co., 1974.

Weiner, Bernard. "Radical Scavenging: An Interview with Emile de Antonio." *Film Quarterly*, Fall 1971, 3–15.

Weisberg, Harold. *Whitewash: The Report on the Warren Report* Hyattstown, Md.: n.p., 1965.

Weiss, Marc N. "Conversations with Emile de Antonio." *University Review* (New York City), March 1974, 17–19.

Weiss, Marc N. "Emile de Antonio." *Film Library Quarterly* 7, no. 2 (1974): 29–35.

Weiss, Peter. *The Investigation*. Translated by Jon Swan and Ulu Grosbard. New York: Atheneum, 1966.

Westerbeck, Colin, Jr. "Some Outtakes from Radical Film Making: Emile de Antonio." *Sight and Sound*, Summer 1970, 140–43.

White, Stephen. *Should We Now Believe the Warren Report?* New York: Macmillan, 1968.

White, Theodore H. "Camelot, Sad Camelot." *Time*, July 3, 1978, 47.

Wilcox, Fred A. *Uncommon Martyrs: The Berrigans, the Catholic Left, and the Plowshares Movement*. Reading, Mass.: Addison-Wesley, 1991.

Winston, Brian. "The Tradition of the Victim in Griersonian Documentary." In Alan Rosenthal, ed., *New Challenges for Documentary*. Berkeley: University of California Press, 1988.

Winston, Brian. "The Documentary Film as Scientific Inscription." In Michael Renov, ed., *Theorizing Documentary*. New York: Routledge, 1993.

Wolff, Janet. *Aesthetics and the Sociology of Art*. Boston: Allen and Unwin, 1983.

Wood, Paul, Francis Frascina, Jonathan Harris, Charles Harrison, eds. *Modernism in Dispute: Art Since the Forties*. New Haven, Conn.: Yale University Press, 1993.

Wreszin, Michael. *A Rebel in Defense of Tradition: The Life and Politics of Dwight Macdonald*. New York: Basic, 1994.

Young, Marilyn B. *The Vietnam Wars, 1945–1990*. New York: Harper-Collins, 1991.

Zelizer, Barbie. *Covering the Body: The Kennedy Assassination, the Media, and the Shaping of Collective Memory*. Chicago: University of Chicago Press, 1992.

Zheutlin, Barbara. "The Politics of Documentary: A Symposium." In Alan Rosenthal, ed., *New Challenges for Documentary*. Berkeley: University of California Press, 1988.

Filmography

Point of Order (1963; b&w, 97 min.)

Producers: Emile de Antonio and Daniel Talbot
Executive producers: Elliot Pratt and Henry Rosenberg
Editor: Robert Duncan
Director: Emile de Antonio
Editorial consultants: David Baselon and Richard Rovere

That's Where the Action Is (1965; b&w, approx. 60 min.)

Director: Emile de Antonio

Rush to Judgment (1967; b&w, 110 min.)

Director: Emile de Antonio
Producers: Emile de Antonio and Mark Lane
Based on the book by Mark Lane

In the Year of the Pig (1969; b&w, 101 min.)

Director, producer: Emile de Antonio
Executive producer: Moxie Schell
Camera: John F. Newman
Editor: Lynn Zee Klingman, with Hannah Moreinis and Helen Levitt

329

Sound: Geoffrey Weinstock
Associate producers: Terry Morrone and John Atlee
Executive producer: Moxie Schell
Assistant director: Albert Maher
Assistants: Adrienne de Antonio and Vicky Gholson
Music: Steve Addiss

America Is Hard to See (1970; b&w, 101 min.)

Director: Emile de Antonio, with Allan Siegel, Mary Lampson, Richard
    Pearce, Stephen Ning, Lori Hiris

Millhouse: A White Comedy (1971; b&w, 93 min.)

Director, producer: Emile de Antonio
Camera: Ed Emschwiller, Michael Gray, Bruce Shah, and Richard
    Kletter
Editor: Mary Lampson

Painters Painting (1973; color, 116 min.)

Director, producer: Emile de Antonio
Editor and sound: Mary Lampson
Camera: Ed Emschwiller

Underground (1976; color, 88 min.)

Producer, director: Emile de Antonio
Sound, director: Mary Lampson
Camera: Haskell Wexler
Principal cast: Billy Ayers, Kathy Boudin, Bernadine Dohrn, Jeff Jones,
    Cathy Wilkerson, Emile de Antonio, Mary Lampson, Haskell
    Wexler

In the King of Prussia (1983; color, 92 min.)

Producer, writer, director: Emile de Antonio
Videographer: July Irola
Edited: Mark Pines
Music: Jackson Browne and Graham Nash
Principal cast: Martin Sheen, Daniel Berrigan, S.J., Philip Berrigan,
  Dean Hammer, Carl Kabat, Elmer Maas, Anne Montgomery, Molly
  Rush, John Schuchardt.

Mr. Hoover and I (1989, 90 min.)

Producer: Emile de Antonio
Editor: George Spyros
Cinematography: Morgan Wesson, Matthew Mindlin, William Rexer
Principal cast: Emile de Antonio, John Cage, Nancy de Antonio

To order the films of Emile de Antonio on VHS in the United
States, call MPI Media Group at 1-800-323-0442, or write Sphinx
Productions, 24 Mercer Street, Toronto, Ontario M5V 1H3

Index